U.S.
NATIONAL SECURITY

U.S.
NATIONAL SECURITY

Policymakers, Processes, and Politics

THIRD EDITION

Sam C. Sarkesian
John Allen Williams
Stephen J. Cimbala

LYNNE
RIENNER
PUBLISHERS

BOULDER
LONDON

Published in the United States of America in 2002 by
Lynne Rienner Publishers, Inc.
1800 30th Street, Boulder, Colorado 80301
www.rienner.com

and in the United Kingdom by
Lynne Rienner Publishers, Inc.
3 Henrietta Street, Covent Garden, London WC2E 8LU

Library of Congress Cataloging-in-Publication Data
Sarkesian, Sam Charles.
    U.S. national security : policymakers, processes, and politics / Sam C. Sarkesian,
John Allen Williams, and Stephen J. Cimbala.—3rd ed.
    p. cm.
    Includes bibliographical references and index.
    ISBN 1-55587-911-X (alk. paper)
    ISBN 1-55587-936-5 (pbk. : alk. paper)
    1. National security—United States—Decision making.   2. United States—Military
policy—Decision making.   I. Williams, John Allen, 1945–   II. Cimbala, Stephen J.
III. Title.
UA23.S275   2002
355'.033073—dc21

2002017884

British Cataloguing in Publication Data
A Cataloguing in Publication record for this book
is available from the British Library.

Printed and bound in the United States of America

        The paper used in this publication meets the requirements
 ∞   of the American National Standard for Permanence of
        Paper for Printed Library Materials Z39.48-1984.

    5   4   3   2   1

Contents

Part 4 Conclusions

Figures and Tables

Figures

Tables

Preface

THE CATASTROPHIC EVENTS IN THE UNITED STATES ON SEPTEMBER 11, 2001, were a turning point in U.S. national security. The terrorist attacks on that date created an unprecedented challenge to the very notion of a democratic and open society. As these words are being written, the United States is responding with a full range of national power. We do not yet know what costs will be incurred in the hunt for the perpetrators nor understand the full scope of the worldwide network that supports them. And no one can accurately predict how long it will take to achieve something resembling success in the effort to make the United States secure. One trend that is now evident, however, is a new emphasis on homeland security.

The opening lines of the preface to the second edition of this book told us that "dramatic changes have taken place in world politics and the security landscape." The focus then was on the post–Cold War period in the aftermath of the Gulf War. Assessing now the international context and issues of U.S. national security in the twenty-first century, we conclude that much of what was written more than six years ago remains relevant today. At the same time, the new era has created a strategic landscape that requires a rethinking of U.S. national security, particularly with respect to international terrorism and homeland security. Furthermore, any study of U.S. national interests must now encompass questions of values and concerns about unconventional conflicts. The involvement of the U.S. military in operations short of war (such as low-intensity conflicts and peacekeeping missions) has become commonplace. This has complicated the relationship of policy, strategy, national interests, and the use of force, and it highlights the need for expanded and effective intelligence apparatus. All of this is even more complicated by the impact of globalization, the information age, and the myriad uses of cyberspace.

This edition builds on the framework of the previous edition to reexamine the concepts of national interest, national security, and the role of the United States in matters of international war and peace. We also study the nature and characteristics of conflicts since 1995, projecting these into the twenty-first century, and we have added two new chapters: one on civil-military relations and one on nuclear weapons. (Due in part to debates about the politics and purposes of military commitments, the issue of civil-military relations has become contentious and needs to be examined in some detail. And the increase in the number of states with access to weapons of mass destruction has made nuclear proliferation an increasingly challenging national security matter, further complicated by efforts in the United States to develop a missile defense capability.) The focus of the book remains the same: the way that the U.S. national security system works and its effectiveness in responding to current and future global challenges.

We address these matters by trying to answer the following questions: How relevant are the institutions of the national security establishment in responding to the strategic landscape of the twenty-first century? How well do they function? How do those in the national security system assess the international strategic landscape? What is the U.S. grand strategy and policy in the twenty-first century? What role does public opinion have in U.S. national security policy? And particularly important, what are the U.S. national interests that must form the basis of national security policy?

Because of the more complex characteristics of the new era and the problems they pose for U.S. national security, it was decided that the efforts of more than one author would be important in completing this new edition. Thus, the three of us have combined our research and teaching experience, as well as our working experience in various parts of the national security system, to provide a balanced assessment of the strategic landscape of the twenty-first century.

In writing the book, we have had the invaluable help of colleagues and past and current students, particularly Michael P. Noonan, Robert A. Vitas, Steven Michels, Michelle Johns, and John Wood, whose comments on various parts of the manuscript were especially helpful. We stress, however, that the book represents only our own views and assessments.

PART 1

Introduction

I

National Interests
and National Security

THE STRATEGIC LANDSCAPE OF THE TWENTY-FIRST CENTURY IS
shaped by complex and often contradictory forces. Although the calendar
turned with a reservoir of peace, that was all shattered on September 11,
2001, by the threat of international terrorism. A United States at war against
terrorism and the notion of a new kind of war have become intermixed with
globalization, economic expansion, and the peaceful pursuit of U.S. values.
The world is characterized by turmoil, and changing patterns of state-to-
state relationships as well as conflicts within states caused by ethnic, religious, and nationalistic differences have become commonplace.
International terrorism, drug cartels, and threats created by information-age
technology add to the turmoil.

In this new environment, U.S. national interests and national security
priorities have become complicated, often ambiguous, and even inconsistent—not because of immediate threats of major conventional war but
rather the unpredictable, uncertain, and confusing characteristics of the
international arena. Disagreements and disputes within the national security
establishment, Congress, and the public have become muted by the unity
and strength in response to the September 11 attacks and the resulting war.[1]
Although questions have been raised about national interests, national security, and the U.S. role around the world, the terrorist threat seems to have
overshadowed everything—at least for a time. But over the long term, how
we define these issues is critical.

Two scholars identified the problem as follows:

> The term *national interest* has a compelling ring. It conveys a sense of
> urgency, importance, threat, and concreteness. . . . Unfortunately, just as
> with the concept of power, the concept of the national interest is not easily
> defined. At the core of the debate over its definition is the question of
> whether the national interest should be treated as an objective, measurable
> asset or a normative political symbol.[2]

3

In other words, is "national interest" a specific, measurable objective, a rhetorical symbol? Or is it something of both? Other than a war against terrorism, what other aspects of national security are relevant today?

These are not new issues. More than thirty years ago Henry A. Kissinger wrote, "What is it in our interest to prevent? What should we seek to accomplish?"[3] This was written before Kissinger became assistant to President Nixon for national security affairs (a position that is known widely as National Security Advisor). The same questions continue to challenge policymakers, scholars, and elected officials. The answers were elusive at the start of the post–Cold War period and remained so until September 2001.

Although the U.S. war against terrorism became the dominant theme in 2001, spelled out in the Bush Doctrine (President George W. Bush), such matters must go beyond the new kind of war. Why? Do Americans not know what is in their national interest? At first glance the answer seems relatively simple. The U.S. national interest is to promote U.S. values. To promote these values means to protect them by establishing and implementing effective national security policies.

Upon closer examination, however, these answers are inadequate, and they raise additional questions. What are U.S. values? How are they reflected in national interests? What is the relationship between national security and national interests? What is national security? How should U.S. national security policy be implemented? For the past three decades these questions have been addressed by many U.S. politicians and scholars. If they agree on anything, it is that there is no agreement.

Each generation of Americans seeks to interpret national values, national interest, and national security in terms of its own perspective and mind-set. Although there is agreement about core elements such as protection of the U.S. homeland, interpretations differ about the meaning of national security, the nature of external threats, and the best course of conduct for security policy. Combined with changes in the world environment, the dynamics of Kissinger's questions are even more fluid and elusive today. To be sure, the war against terrorism became the key focus of national interests beginning in late September 2001. But such interests encompass a wide range of elements that underpin an open system and society such as the United States.

It is to be expected that in a country with multiple power centers and shifting focal points there will be different interpretations as well as outright differences. Recognizing that these matters are rarely resolved by onetime solutions and that they are, at best, ambiguous, we explore the concepts of national security, national values, and national interest. In the process, we design a framework for studying and analyzing national security.

Regardless, the United States is in the world to stay. Whether

Americans like it or not, they cannot withdraw from external responsibilities; neither can they retreat to isolation. Regardless of the policies of any administration, the United States has links to most parts of the world, politically, economically, culturally, and psychologically. What the United States does or does not do has an impact on international politics.

National Interests

U.S. national interests are expressions of U.S. values projected into the international and domestic arenas. The purpose of interests includes the creation and perpetuation of an international environment that is most favorable to the peaceful pursuit of values. It follows that interests nurture and expand democracy and open systems. Similarly, the United States wishes to prevent the expansion of closed systems by the use of force or indirect aggression. In the twenty-first century, the domestic arena has become an important consideration in pursuing national interests because of asymmetrical threats, the information age, and international terrorism, all of which have roots in U.S. domestic society.[4] Such concerns were heightened by the September 11 terrorist attacks.

Three points serve as reference points. First, U.S. values as they apply to the external world are at the core of national interests. Second, pursuing national interests does not mean that U.S. strategy is limited to the homeland. This may require power projection into various parts of the world, especially when combating international terrorism. Third, the president is the focal point in defining and articulating U.S. national interests.

National interests can be categorized in order of priorities as follows:[5]

First Order: vital interests. Protection of the homeland and areas and issues directly affecting this interest. This may require total military mobilization and resource commitment—the nation's total effort. In homeland defense, this also may require a coordinated effort of all agencies of government, especially in defense against terrorist attacks and information warfare. The homeland focus was highlighted by the creation of a new cabinet-level position on homeland security by President George W. Bush following September 11. The purpose is to coordinate the efforts of several agencies in countering terrorism in the United States.

Second Order: critical interests. These are areas and issues that do not directly affect America's survival or pose a threat to the homeland but in the long run have a high propensity for becoming First Order priorities. Critical interests are measured primarily by the degree to which they maintain, nurture, and expand open systems. Many also argue that moral imperatives are important in shaping national interests.

Third Order: serious interests. These are issues that do not critically affect First and Second Order interests yet cast some shadow over such interests. U.S. efforts are focused on creating favorable conditions to preclude Third Order interests from developing into higher-order ones. Unfavorable Third Order interests serve as a warning to Second Order interests.

All other interests are peripheral in that they are placed on a so-called watch list. This means there is no immediate impact on any order of interests, but matters must be watched in case events transform these interests. In the meantime, peripheral interests require few, if any, U.S. resources.

Categories of priorities such as these can be used not only as a framework for systematic assessment of national interests and national security but also as a way to distinguish immediate from long-range security issues. Such a framework can provide a basis for rational and systematic debate within the national security establishment regarding the U.S. national security posture and is useful in studying national security. However, today there is rarely a clear line between categories of interests. Many changes have expanded the concept of national interests to include several moral and humanitarian dimensions, among others. As some argue, where can the line be drawn among categories of interests?

A realistic assignment of priorities can be better understood by looking at geopolitical boundaries of core, contiguous, and outer areas (see Figure 1.1). In specific terms, at the core of U.S. national interests is the survival of the homeland and political order. But survival cannot be limited to the "final" defense of the homeland. In light of today's weapons technology, weapons proliferation, and chemical/biological warfare, the concept of homeland survival means more than retreating to the borders and threatening anyone who might attack with total destruction. By then it is too late

Figure 1.1   U.S. National Security Priorities

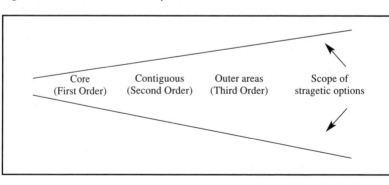

for security policy to do much good, and the attacker can be difficult to identify.

If national interest is invoked only when the homeland is directly threatened and survival is at stake, then the concept may be of little use, too late to overcome the peril. If the concept is to have any meaning for policy and strategy, then it must be something more. The interpretation and application of this broader view sparks a great deal of debate and disagreement between the executive and legislative branches of government and within the U.S. political arena. The media also become involved, more often than not with their own agendas.

However, the national security establishment and policymakers rarely have the luxury of endless debate; neither do they have unlimited time or all necessary facts in a given situation. Yet policy must be made and strategy options examined and implemented regardless of conditions, even while debates and disagreements remain intense.

The fact is that policy must be determined and implemented at some point. Before that, national interests for the particular situation must be identified and articulated. At the same time, national interests over the long range must be considered. Custom, usage, and constitutional powers give the president a basis for articulating their meaning. And though some Americans might challenge this notion today, initiatives in foreign and national security policy usually rest with the president as the commander in chief of U.S. armed forces, the chief diplomat, and the singular expositor and standard-bearer of U.S. national will.

To be sure, Congress has an important role, but the president must take the lead and is the country's only legal representative with respect to foreign relations. For better or for worse, the president articulates the national interests, and Congress responds. The same holds true with respect to the president and the variety of interest groups in the government bureaucracy and public arena.

U.S. Values and National Interests

U.S. values are based on what is esteemed and absolutely essential as the philosophical, legal, and moral basis for the continuation of the U.S. system. These attributes are deeply engrained in our political system and domestic environment; they also apply to the way in which the public perceives justice in the international system and "just cause" in the conduct of war. In other words, values are principles that give the U.S. political system and social order their innate character; they provide substance to U.S. culture and create further principles upon which to base national interests.

The Value System

Modern U.S. values derive from the Judeo-Christian heritage, the Anglo-Saxon legacy (including the Reformation, the Renaissance, the philosophies of John Locke and Jean-Jacques Rousseau, among others, and the principles rooted in the American Revolution), the Declaration of Independence, and the Constitution. Despite these many historical reference points, we identify at least six fundamental values that define the United States and its role in the international world.[6]

First, there is the right of self-determination, a dual concept in this context: it applies not only to the nation-state but also to people within that state. It is presumed that each nation-state has the right to determine its own policy and to govern in any way it chooses as long as it does not threaten neighbors. At the same time, people within that nation-state also have the right of self-determination. From the U.S. perspective, this means that through free and fair elections people in a nation-state have the right to determine how and by whom they will be ruled, with the option to replace rulers as they see fit.

However, there is another dimension: an emerging right claimed by minority groups to demand autonomy as a matter of self-determination. This duality of self-determination and state sovereignty creates serious problems in determining appropriate and legitimate action on the part of the United Nations (UN), regional organizations, and the United States. This duality also has important implications for U.S. military strategy. Moreover, this duality can lead to a dangerous confrontation between minority groups within a state demanding self-determination and the state itself, as occurred in the former Yugoslavia (i.e., between Albanians and Serbians in Kosovo, a province in Serbia). The United States and the North Atlantic Treaty Organization (NATO) intervened on behalf of the Albanian majority in Kosovo at the expense of the sovereignty of Serbia.[7] Ideally, self-determination is accomplished within a system of laws and peaceful change. The peaceful partition of the former Czechoslovakia into the Czech Republic and Slovenia offers the ideal notion of self-determination, but it is the rare exception.

Second, it follows that there is an inherent worth to any single individual in his/her relationship to others, to the political system, and to the social order. What does this mean? Put simply, every person is intrinsically a moral, legal, and political entity to which the system must respond. Each individual has the right to achieve all that he or she can, without encumbrances other than protection of fellow citizens as well as homeland protection and survival. Individual worth must therefore be reflected in economic, political, and legal systems.

Third, rulers owe their power and accountability to the people, which is the essence of democratic political legitimacy. The people are the final authority, and there is a continuing responsibility by elected and appointed officials to rule and function according to the moral and legal principles, and the right of the people to change leaders is absolute. In this respect, no consuming power can dominate government or establish its own rationale for rule. Furthermore, individual worth necessitates limited government with no absolute and permanent focal point of power. To ensure this, rule and governance must be open: decisions and policies must be undertaken in full public view, with input from a variety of formal and informal groups. The system of rule must be accessible to the people and their representatives. This is the essence of what are called "open systems."

Fourth, policies and changes in the international environment must be based on the first three values outlined above. Thus peaceful change brought about by rational discourse among nation-states is a fundamental value. Resort to war can be acceptable only if it is clearly based on homeland protection and survival or other core values, and only if all other means have failed. In this respect, diplomacy and state-to-state relationships must be based on mutually acceptable rules of the game.

Fifth, any system professing such values and trying to function according to their principles must be protected and nurtured. Nation-states whose values are compatible with U.S. values are thought to be best served by an international order based on those same values.

Sixth, U.S. values are grounded in the Judeo-Christian heritage that predated the founding of the republic in the late eighteenth century. For many Americans, this instills a sense of humanity, a sensitivity to the plight and status of individuals, and a search for divine guidance. These precepts add a dimension to what is seen to be proper and just in the minds of many Americans and are considered by many to be beyond the legal definition of government.

We do not suggest that these values are perfectly embodied in the U.S. system. There are many historical examples of value distortions and their misuse to disguise other purposes. But these values are esteemed in their own right by most Americans and are embodied in the political-social system. Furthermore, the system of rule and the character of the political system have institutionalized these values, albeit imperfectly. The expectations of most Americans and their assessment of other states are, in no small measure, based on these values.

U.S. Values: Into the Twentieth Century and Beyond

The collapse of the old order in Europe following World War I set the stage for the continental evolution of democratic as well as tyrannical Marxist-Leninist systems. Until that time, Pax Britannica provided a sense of stability and order to European affairs, as well as a security umbrella to the United States in its relationships with Europe. But for many Americans, involvement in a world conflict to save Europe seemed like a mistake. The United States withdrew into isolationism, which ended only with the start of World War II.

Even in the aftermath of World War I, Americans were accustomed to a world dominated by a European order compatible with the general nature of U.S. values and national interests. Although an imperfect order, it did not threaten the proper order of things or offend the U.S. value system. At the beginning of the twentieth century, U.S. values were expressed by progressivism, by Theodore Roosevelt's presidency, and later by Franklin Roosevelt's New Deal, focusing on individuals and the government's responsibility to them.

There was little need to translate values into the external world, as America's interest rarely extended beyond its own shores. Yet it was during this time that the United States became a great power, partly the result of acquiring territory in the Spanish American War. A decade or so later, U.S. involvement in World War I was seen as a way to make the world safe for democracy and subdue a tyrannical old-world power.

In the aftermath of World War I, most Americans were glad to see their government once again distance itself from the old world and focus on domestic matters. "It's their problem, not ours," was a common U.S. attitude with respect to Europe and the outside world. U.S. isolationism and demilitarization during the 1920s and 1930s are recognized historical facts, typified by the U.S. failure to join the League of Nations following World War I and thereby renunciating, in effect, President Woodrow Wilson's Fourteen Points for a new world order.[8] World War II changed all that, even though most Americans wanted no part of the "European War" (which started in 1939) until the surprise Japanese bombing of Pearl Harbor in 1941.

Between the two world wars (the late 1910s to the late 1930s), Americans presumed that U.S. interests were also world interests. U.S. values were viewed as morally unassailable and therefore were to be sought-after by the rest of the world. In this context, then, U.S. national security was primarily a narrow focus on the protection of the homeland, which required few armed forces and simple military strategy. Furthermore, there was little need to struggle with issues over U.S. values and how to protect them in the external world, except occasionally for the sake of international economics. We passed to others, primarily Britain and France, responsibility for keeping the democratic peace.

Regardless of the U.S. desire to return to splendid isolation following World War II, the United States was in the world to stay. Parts of Europe and Asia were smoldering from the events of war, and it soon became clear that U.S. responsibilities extended beyond the nation's borders. In addition, it was perceived that democracy and U.S. values could not be nurtured and expanded if we simply stayed at home; if democracy was the demand, then it required our presence in all parts of the world. Beyond protection of the U.S. homeland, then, what did the United States stand for? And how did it intend to achieve its goals—whatever they were?

These questions were less difficult to answer in the negative, that is, the United States was against Marxist-Leninist and other authoritarian political systems determined to subvert or overthrow the international order based on self-determination. The policy of containment reflected a U.S. policy consensus to prevent the expansion of the Soviet Union. Positive responses to such questions were seen in the U.S. role in rebuilding Europe, especially the economic recovery program known as the Marshall Plan. All of this placed the United States in a leadership role of the West, a reflection of the earlier Puritan view of Americans as a chosen people.[9] For many, the second half of the twentieth century was the American Century; such a notion would provide the moral basis for involvement in the Korean and Vietnam Wars.

But the end of the Cold War and the emergence of a new security landscape caused many Americans to focus on domestic issues. There was a turning inward, reinforced by the conviction that the fear of major wars had diminished considerably and the United States had won the Cold War. But this new landscape was muddled and obscured by the fog of peace. Indeed, some experts even argued that the United States would miss the Cold War, with its moral certainties and predictable (if difficult) responsibilities.[10]

Turning inward, Americans faced issues of diversity, gender, and race, complicated by various groups with non-Western linkages. Critics argued that the United States may never have been a true melting pot of culture, yet it benefited from the waves of immigrants who brought along their rich heritage. But that heritage, according to others, was promoted (as it is today) at the expense of Americanism. They would argue that U.S. cultural heritage and Western tradition—the bedrock of democracy—risk erosion by increasing prominence of other cultures, whose loyalties may be rooted in countries other than the United States.[11] Americanism may not be compatible with some versions of multiculturalism, in their view.

The New Era

In the new era—beyond the war against terrorism—it is difficult to agree on the principles of U.S. values as they apply to the international order. Issues of multiculturalism, diversity, race, and gender, combined with environmentalism and human rights, among other issues, have called into question the very meaning of Americanism and the U.S. value system. For example, in viewing the U.S. domestic system, the former chairman of the U.S. Joint Chiefs of Staff, Colin Powell, wrote,

> And Lord help anyone who strays from accepted ideas of political correctness. The slightest suggestion of offense toward any group . . . will be met with cries that the offender be fired or forced to undergo sensitivity training, or threats of legal action. Ironically for all the present sensitivity over correctness, we seem to have lost our shame as a society. Nothing seems to embarrass us; nothing shocks us anymore.[12]

In citing the "balkanization" of the United States, Georgie Anne Geyer argues that we must return to the idea of U.S. "citizenship." She criticizes the notion of globalization and the presumed decline of the nation-state as the focus of loyalty.[13] She concludes, "I remain convinced that the nation will rally at this important moment in a Renaissance to preserve the best of the past and to mate it with the best of the present and the future—so that we can and will be *Americans once again*."[14] However, others argue that most Americans are in the middle of the political spectrum and embrace God, family, and country. As Alan Wolfe contends, we are "One Nation, After All."[15]

As some critics point out, spokespersons for various groups in the United States often use terms like "our people" or "my people" in referring to their particular racial, ethnic, or religious group to the exclusion of others. This tends to distinguish and separate one group from Americans in general. But as President Franklin D. Roosevelt is credited with saying in 1943, "Americanism is a matter of heart and mind; Americanism is not a matter of race or ethnicity."

Nonetheless, U.S. involvement in foreign lands and cultures can cause domestic problems because one group within the United States can support a like-minded group in a foreign land regardless of U.S. policy. The greatest charge is that such a development can increase balkanization here. But as noted earlier, most Americans and policy elites gravitate toward the middle of the spectrum, preferring an inclusive instead of an exclusive definition of Americanism. Clearly, demographics and cultural issues have an impact on U.S. national security policy and strategy. When the national interest is clear and the political objectives are closely aligned with that interest, there is likely to be strong support by Americans for U.S. actions. But U.S. involvement in cultures and religions abroad can have domestic repercussions, such as the conflict in the Middle East between Israel and the Palestinians. This makes it more difficult to project U.S. values into the international arena. In sum, commitment of the U.S. military in foreign areas will not necessarily draw maximum support from the public unless it is convinced that such matters are part of America's vital interests.

National Security

The new international security landscape has clouded the concept and meaning of U.S. national security. The interpretation of national interests into meaningful national security policy has become a more difficult process. Years ago, this problem was summed up by an expert:

> No formal definition of national security as a field has been generally accepted; none may be possible. In general, it is the study of the security *problems* faced by nations, of the *policies and programs* by which these problems are addressed, and also of the governmental *processes* through which the policies and programs are decided upon and carried out.[16]

Recognizing the problems of defining and conceptualizing national security, we offer a preliminary statement: *"U.S. national security" is the confidence held by the great majority of the nation's people that it has the military capability and effective policy to prevent adversaries from using force to prevent the pursuit of national interests.*

There are at least two dimensions to that definition: physical and psychological. In the first, there is an objective measure based on the strength and military capacity of the nation to successfully challenge adversaries, including going to war if necessary. This also includes a more prominent role for intelligence, economics, and other nonmilitary measures, as well as the ability to use them as a political-military lever in dealings with other states. The psychological dimension is subjective, reflecting the opinion and attitudes of Americans on the nation's ability to remain secure relative to the external world. It includes the people's willingness to support government efforts to achieve national security goals. Underpinning this is that the majority of people have the political will and staying power to support clear policies to achieve clear national security goals.

National Security, Foreign Policy, and Domestic Policy

National security must be analyzed in the context of foreign policy, defined as the policy of a nation that encompasses all official relations with other countries. The purpose of foreign policy is multidimensional. For the United States, the purpose is to pursue national interests, prevent conditions detrimental to the United States, and maintain relations with other countries in order to create conditions favorable to our national interests. The instruments of foreign policy are primarily diplomatic and political and encompass a variety of psychological and economic measures.

National security differs from foreign policy in at least two respects: National security purposes are more narrow and focused on security and safety; and national security is primarily concerned with actual and potential adversaries and their use of force, whether overt or covert. This means there is a military emphasis, which usually is not the case in foreign policy. However, national security policy overlaps with foreign policy, sometimes blurring any distinction. But much of foreign policy requires compromise and negotiations—the dynamics of give-and-take—as well as all of the techniques and subtleties associated with traditional diplomacy. This kind of work is primarily a matter for the U.S. Department of State, with long-range implications for national security policy. These relationships are shown in Figure 1.2.

Until recently, most Americans felt that U.S. values could not be imposed on other states unless survival was at stake. However, national security is now seen by many to include the projection of U.S. values abroad (see Chapter 2). This adds to the confusion and highlights the inter-relationship among foreign, domestic, and national security policies. "America's concept of national security today is infinitely more complex than at any time in its history. The same is true for the relationship between the foreign and domestic components of national security."[17]

The difficulties of determining U.S. national interests and establishing national security priorities are compounded by the link between national security and domestic policy—a recent occurrence in U.S. history. The domestic economic impact of certain national security policies links U.S. domestic interests and policies to the international security arena. This is seen in economic sanctions, embargos on agriculture exports to adversaries or potential adversaries, diminished foreign oil sources, and the export of technologically advanced industrial products. And in a dramatic way, September 11 obscured the distinction between domestic and national security policy.

Due to the special characteristics of our democratic system and political culture, it is difficult to isolate national security issues from domestic policy. Besides the relationship and link between foreign and national security policies, domestic policy links are an important factor in establishing priorities and interests. For some scholars, this is viewed as "intermestic" politics and policies.[18]

Nonetheless, national security policy by definition involves military force. Distinctions must be made between foreign and domestic policy and national security. The primary distinction rests in the likelihood of military force, as well as use of the military as the primary instrument for implementing national security policy. Although many other matters are important in the overall notion of national interests, they are best incorporated into foreign policy and the overlap between such policy and national security.[19]

These observations are the basis for defining national security policy, expanding on the concept of national security: *National security policy is*

Figure 1.2   National Security and Foreign Policy

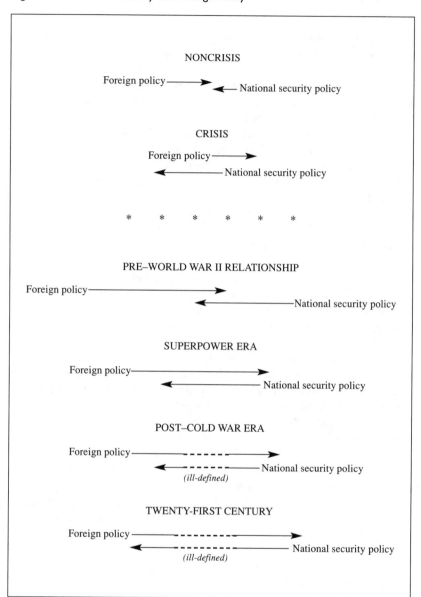

NONCRISIS

Foreign policy ——————⟶ ⟵— National security policy

CRISIS

Foreign policy ——————⟶

⟵———————— National security policy

*   *   *   *   *   *

PRE–WORLD WAR II RELATIONSHIP

Foreign policy ————————————⟶

⟵—————————National security policy

SUPERPOWER ERA

Foreign policy ———————————⟶

⟵———————— National security policy

POST–COLD WAR ERA

Foreign policy ———— – – – – – – ————⟶

⟵— – – – – – ——— National security policy
(ill-defined)

TWENTY-FIRST CENTURY

Foreign policy ——————— – – – – – – – ————⟶

⟵— – – – – – – ——— National security policy
(ill-defined)

Source: Adapted from Col. William J. Taylor Jr., "Interdependence, Specialization, and National Security: Problems for Diplomats, Soldiers, and Scholars," *Air University Review* 30, no. 5 (July–August 1979): 17–26.

Note: The gap between foreign policy and national policy indicates the relative degree of "closeness" between foreign and national security policy. The arrows indicate the relative degree of overlap. As shown, during times of crises, the gap between foreign and national security policy is minimal and virtually nonexistent. In the twenty-first century it is often difficult to clearly separate foreign policy and national security because the use of force has become closely connected with a variety of peacekeeping missions, humanitarian crises, operations of war, and operations other than war; many such missions are extensions of foreign policy or a combination of national security and foreign policy, particularly in combating international terrorism.

primarily concerned with formulating and implementing national strategy to create a favorable environment for U.S. national interests. An integral part of this is to prevent the effective use of military force and/or covert operations by adversaries or potential adversaries to obstruct or deny the ability of the United States to pursue national interests.

Thus national security means more than the capacity to conduct international wars. In light of the characteristics of the international arena and contemporary conflicts, challenges to U.S. national security might take any number of nontraditional forms, from economics to the unconventional. Yet the capacity to deter nuclear war and wage conventional conflicts remains essential for the conduct of U.S. national security policy, even in the twenty-first century. In this new era, international terrorism, weapons of mass destruction (WMD), chemical and biological warfare, and information warfare have become increasingly important dimensions of national security.

National security policy must be carefully developed and implemented according to priorities delineating survival (i.e., vital) interests from others. Too often, national security is used synonymously with any interest, suggesting that all interests are survival priorities. Taking a page from Sun-tzu, if almost everything is a matter of national security, then the concept of national security becomes virtually meaningless.[20] If national security policy and strategy followed such a pattern, the United States would be placed in a position of having to defend everything everywhere; the end result is that it would be unable to defend anything. Resources and personnel would be scattered across the globe and rarely in a position to bring sufficient force to bear, even if survival were at stake.

Short of clear threats to U.S. territory, Americans frequently disagree over priorities. Even when there is agreement on priorities, there is disagreement on resource commitment and strategy. Yet a system of priorities provides a way to identify levels of threats and helps in the design of strategies. But all this must be guided by the meaning of national security and its conceptual dimensions.

The Study of National Security

The exploration of national security and all its dimensions—including policy and priorities—leads to some basic questions. How can national security be studied? What fundamental principles provide the bases for U.S. national security policy and strategy?

There are three major approaches to the study of national security: the concentric-circle approach, elite versus participatory policymaking, and systems analysis; all concentrate on the way in which policy is made. They should be distinguished from studies that examine national security issues, such as U.S. nuclear strategy or U.S. policy in the Middle East. The three approaches should be further distinguished from studies of government institutions.

The concentric-circle approach places the president at the center of the national security policy process (see Figure 1.3). The president's staff and the national security establishment provide advice and implement national security policy. This approach shows the degree of importance of various groups as the "primary objects" of national security policy. For example, a major objective is to influence the behavior and policies of allies as well as adversaries. At the same time, Congress, the public, and the media have important roles in the national security policy process. But they are not the objects of policy, and so the more distant circles represent government structures and agencies, constituencies, and the media. The farther the institutions are from the center, the less their importance as objects of national security policy. The problem with this approach is its oversimplification of the national security policy process and its presumption of rationality.

The elite-participatory policymaking approach is based on the view that democracy's basic dilemma is that the policy process is dominated by elites (see Figure 1.4). National security policy is undertaken by elites within the national security establishment, but that elite group must in turn develop support in the broader public. On the one hand, the elite has the skill and access to information to formulate national security policy, in contrast to an uninformed public. On the other hand, for national security poli-

Figure 1.3   Concentric Circle Approach

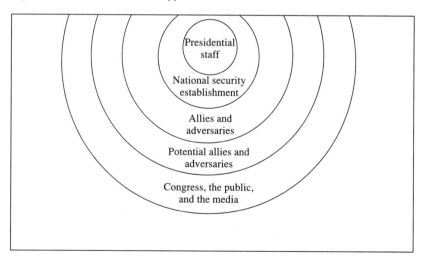

cy to be successful in the long run, there must be some degree of participation by the public and political will within the body politic. The elite model sees national security policy as being made by a small circle that includes the president, his staff, key members of Congress, high-ranking military officers, and influential members of the business community. The assumption is that this is a cohesive elite whose own interests override other concerns. The participatory model assumes the existence of a variety of elites who represent various segments of the public, interest groups, and officials. In this model, the same elites rarely control all aspects of national security policy. Coalitions are formed for particular issues, then reformed for other issues. This approach struggles to reconcile the skill and power of the elite with the demands of participatory democracy.

The systems-analysis approach emphasizes the dynamic intrarelationships among variables at all stages of the security decisionmaking process (see Figure 1.5). Many inputs go into the policy process. The policymaking machinery must reconcile competing interests and design a policy acceptable to most. In turn, the impact of policy must be measured by feedback, in terms of policy effectiveness and how it is perceived by those affected.

All three approaches, as well as variations, are useful in the study of

Figure 1.4   Elite and Participatory Models

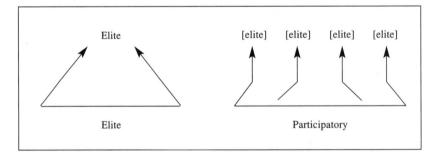

Figure 1.5   Systems-Analysis Approach

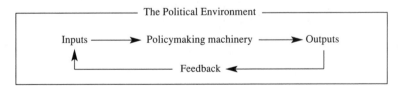

national security policy; this book incorporates something from each. We examine the formal national security establishment on the assumption that the president with government entities established by law form that establishment and are at the center of the policy process—the concentric-circle approach. We examine the National Security Council (NSC) and the Department of Defense from the concentric-circle approach and partly from the elite-participatory approach. Finally, as for the formal policy process, most attention is given to the national security network—a systems-analysis approach that considers many power clusters within the governmental structure, the political system, and the international environment that have an impact on the national security establishment and the policymaking process.

National security establishment is a normative-analytical term referring to those responsible for national security decisionmaking as well as a descriptive term that identifies a set of actors and processes that actually produce security policy outcomes. Often, however, the character and personality of the president lead to the creation of informal and parallel structures and processes for developing national security policy. This sets up a series of policy power clusters that form a national security network that drives the national security establishment and the formal policymaking process. The relationships among and within these power clusters and their actual powers are dependent upon the way the president exercises his leadership and views on how the national security establishment should function.

There are three major power clusters; their powers vary according to presidential leadership and preferences: (1) the policy triad, consisting of the secretary of state, the secretary of defense, and the National Security Advisor; (2) the Director of Central Intelligence and the chairman of the Joint Chiefs of Staff; and (3) the White House chief of staff and the counselor to the president.

These three power clusters are extremely important in shaping national security policy (see Figure 1.6). They represent critical parts of the national security establishment but operate in ways that reflect presidential leadership style and the mind-sets of those within the three power clusters. As such, they may or may not be compatible with the formal national security establishment. Put another way, the national security establishment is fluid and dynamic, and the policymaking process is not as rational and systematic as one is led to believe.

> The defense planning process . . . is beset with multiple dilemmas. Assessing the threat and acquiring the force structure to meet that threat require an efficient crystal ball—not only in the sense of defining the future in the here and now in terms of events and dangers; the process also requires accurately estimating the national mood years before the critical event.[21]

Figure 1.6   Policy Power Clusters and the National Security System

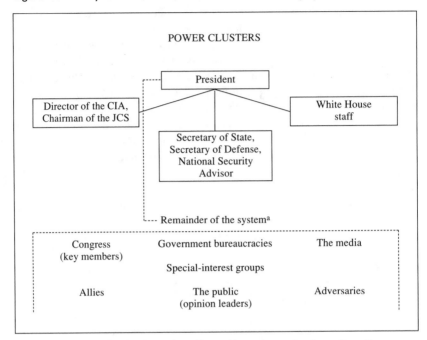

Note: a. Objects of national security policy and inputs into national security policy.

Conclusion

There is a set of boundaries, constraints, and limitations that cannot be separated from the operations of the U.S. national security establishment. The policy process cannot be viewed separately from these considerations. As a result (and aside from real threats to the homeland), there is likely to be internal disagreement and debate within the national security establishment, between the establishment and other branches and agencies of government, and between all of these and the public. The intensity of the disagreement increases in direct proportion to the size of the gap between policies and strategies, on the one hand, and well-established perspectives and the U.S. political-military posture on the other. When we add the differing views of allies and adversaries and their national security efforts—especially in the new era—it is clear that simply examining the establishment or the policy process does not do justice to the complexities and complications inherent in U.S. national security.

All of this is exacerbated by the diffusion and decentralization of power within the U.S. political system, within and among the branches of government, and also within the general population. Participatory politics and sin-gle-issue politics, the erosion of political party cohesion, changing domestic demographics, the policy role of the media, and internal power problems within government have made it almost impossible for the president to undertake any foreign policy or national security initiatives that are perceived as outside the mainstream or as requiring a new kind of military posture or preparedness. The exception may be the war on terrorism. To induce changes and to place his stamp on national security policy, the president must build a political base within the government and activate the general public, as well as convince the media of the appropriateness of new policies and strategies. This usually means that the matter must be seen as a major national security issue, with the U.S. position clearly proper and morally correct; and must involve minimum risk and a high expectation of success.

The U.S. fear of concentration of power is engrained in the constitu-tional principles of separation of powers and checks and balances; these have provided clear limits to the exercise of power of any one branch of government. Yet these restraints can also prevent effective response to chal-lenges that require concentration of power to succeed. Thus the problem is self-contradictory, and the legal niceties of U.S. constitutional practice can have little influence in the international security setting, where power and politics are often inextricable. It is in this context that the U.S. national security establishment and the process by which security policy is formu-lated and implemented meet their greatest test.

In this book our primary concern is the U.S. national security establish-ment and the security policy process. In addition, we examine the internation-al security setting, the factors that affect the substance of U.S. national securi-ty policy, and the presidential mandate (see Part Three). The chapters on the establishment and the process are written with an eye toward those issues.

Notes

1. See, e.g., "Under Seige," *U.S. News and World Report*, September 24, 2001. The entire issue reports on the September 11 attacks and the U.S. response. Needless to say, there are a variety of reports and assessments of this event in virtu-ally all elements of the media.

2. Glenn Hastedt and Kay Knickrehm, eds., *Toward the Twenty-First Century: A Reader in World Politics* (New York: Prentice-Hall, 1994), p. 142.

3. Henry A. Kissinger, *American Foreign Policy: Three Essays* (New York: W. W. Norton, 1969), p. 92.

4. See, e.g., Thomas E. Copeland, ed., *The Information Revolution and National Security* (Carlisle Barracks, PA: Strategic Studies Institute, U.S. Army War College, August 2000).

5. See The White House, *A National Security Strategy for a Global Age* (Washington, DC: U.S. Government Printing Office, December 2000).

6. For a useful study, see Eugene R. Wittkopf, ed., *The Domestic Sources of American Foreign Policy: Insights and Evidence*, 2nd ed. (New York: St. Martin's, 1994).

7. David Scheffer concludes, "I propose that we are witnessing the end of sovereignty as it has been traditionally understood in international law and in state practice. In its place we are seeing a new form of national integrity emerging." David Scheffer, "Humanitarian Intervention versus State Sovereignty," in United States Institute of Peace, *Peacemaking and Peacekeeping Implications for the United States Military* (Washington, DC: United States Institute of Peace, May 1993), p. 9.

8. See James M. McCormick, *American Foreign Policy and Process*, 3rd ed. (Itasca, IL: F. E. Peacock, 1998), pp. 28–30.

9. See, e.g., Kenneth D. Wald, *Religion and Politics in the United States*, 2nd ed. (Washington, DC: CQ Press, 1992). Also see Douglas Johnston and Cynthia Sampson, eds., *Religion: The Missing Dimension of Statecraft* (Oxford, UK: Oxford University Press, 1994).

10. See, e.g., John Mearsheimer, "Why We Will Soon Miss the Cold War," *Atlantic* (August 1990), pp. 35–50.

11. Samuel P. Huntington, *The Clash of Civilizations and the Remaking of World Order* (New York: Simon and Schuster, 1996). See also Samuel P. Huntington, "The Clash of Civilizations?" *Foreign Affairs* 72, no. 3 (Summer 1993): 22–49. For a critique of the Huntington thesis, see Shireen T. Hunter, *The Future of Islam and the West: Clash of Civilizations or Peaceful Coexistence?* (Westport, CT: Praeger, 1998).

12. Colin Powell, with Joseph E. Persico, *My American Journey* (New York: Random House, 1995), p. 610.

13. Georgie Anne Geyer, *Americans No More: The Death of Citizenship* (New York: Atlantic Monthly, 1996).

14. Ibid., p. 339.

15. Alan Wolfe, *One Nation, After All: What Americans Really Think about God, Right, The Left and Each Other* (New York: Viking, 1998). See also David Gergen, "One Nation, After All," *U.S. News and World Report*, March 16, 2000, p. 84, and James MacGregor Burns and Georgia J. Sorenson, with Robin Gerber and Scott W. Webster, *Dead Center: Clinton-Gore Leadership and the Perils of Moderation* (New York: Oxford University Press, 2000).

16. Richard Smoke, *National Security and the Nuclear Dilemma,* 2nd ed. (New York: Random House, 1987), p. 301.

17. David Jablonsky, "The State of the National Security State," in David Jablonsky, Ronald Steel, Lawrence Korb, Morton H. Halperin, and Robert Ellsworth, *U.S. National Security: Beyond the Cold War* (Carlisle Barracks, PA: Strategic Studies Institute, U.S. Army War College, July 26, 1997), pp. 39–40.

18. Charles W. Kegley Jr. and Eugene R. Wittkopf, *World Politics: Trend and Transformation*, 7th ed. (Boston: Bedford/St. Martin's, 1999), p. 46.

19. Carnes Lord, "Strategy and Organization at the National Level," in James C. Gaston, ed., *Grand Strategy and the Decisionmaking Process* (Washington, DC: National Defense University Press, 1992), pp. 141–159.

20. *Sun Tzu: The Art of War*, translated and with an introduction by Samuel B. Griffith (New York: Oxford University Press, 1971).

21. Frederick H. Hartmann and Robert L. Wendzel, *Defending America's Security* (Washington, DC: Pergamon-Brassey's, 1988), p. 146.

2

The International Landscape

THE CHANGING INTERNATIONAL LANDSCAPE AFFECTS U.S. national security policy process in several ways. First, each element of the global system is characterized by contradictory forces. These create difficulties that are often unmanageable in terms of U.S. national security. Thus there are limits to what the United States can do in any given national security issue. This has become even more difficult in the security landscape of the twenty-first century. Although September 11 united all Americans and focused attention on homeland security, many conventional threats to core security interests have diminished—and international turmoil prevails. The difficulty is to determine who and what the threats are to U.S. national interests, as well as the national security policy needed to respond effectively.

Second, the international security setting is not a neat, clearly delineated order; neither is it always driven by rational forces. Although there are commonalities, each security issue has distinct characteristics. Therefore, each U.S. national security issue can require a different set of responses. This can also require the implementation of broad policy by a variety of strategies, which at times can appear to contradict one another. Furthermore, the traditional concepts of military force can have limited utility in such a setting.

Third, international security issues can quickly develop into crisis situations demanding rapid and flexible responses. In such cases, it can be difficult for U.S. policy processes to be effective because of the character of our political system. Additionally, the national security establishment tends to be cumbersome in trying to react quickly and legitimately in crisis situations.

Fourth, U.S. national security policy can require secrecy or covert operations. Given the nature of the U.S. system, however, trying to undertake effective covert operations is challenging at best and ineffective at

23

worst. This makes it difficult for the United States to develop a coherent policy and strategy to respond to the most likely conflicts—unconventional conflicts like terrorism—that may require indirect approaches and secrecy.

Fifth, the dissolution of the Soviet Union, the reunification of Germany, the end of the Cold War, and the growing role of China, among other developments, have reshaped the international security milieu. The disappearance of the former Soviet empire, combined with the breakdown of the superpower face-off, has lead to a new world order (some might say a new world *dis*order). What is clear is that a new strategic landscape has emerged, characterized by several ethnic, religious, and nationalistic conflicts, unconventional conflicts, changing economic patterns, globalization, and the information age. Yet the Russian Federation remains a major player on the world scene, especially given its strategic nuclear stockpiles, resources, population, and influence over the newly independent republics of the former Soviet Union. Since the Soviet Union crumbled, the Russian Federation has struggled to reform its economic system and to resolve its internal political problems (currently under the administration of Vladimir Putin). China, which struggles between its history as a communist world power and its future under globalization and democratization, has been seen as an increasingly important player on the world stage.

Sixth, the problem of differences among strategic cultures has become more acute, posing a continuing challenge for U.S. national security. Strategic cultures evolving out of non-Western traditions govern the political and security orientation of many states in the world, including many in the Southern Hemisphere as well as China, India, Japan, and the Islamic world. Samuel Huntington views this as a "clash of civilizations," focusing on religion and cultural identity rather than a state-centric view of the international landscape.[1] The character of conflicts and the road to victory or defeat can differ in foreign strategic cultures, in contrast to U.S. strategic principles. Yet the United States cannot compromise its strategic culture without eroding its legitimacy and capacity as *the* world power. Maintaining and nurturing U.S. culture in the domestic and international arenas is an essential part of American identity.

Whatever conceptual application is used to assess U.S. national security, there are certain basic elements that must be included, especially in terms of the use of military force. As Paul Best has written,

> In order to be successful, any new strategy to use military forces in the post–Cold War world should be undergirded by clear, specific objectives, directed at a genuine, discernible threat, supported by high-quality military forces, assisted, as required by allies, and it must remain faithful to the prevailing strategic culture.[2]

The International Landscape

How the United States perceives and responds to the international security setting has roots in its own historical experience, including ideology, culture, and the character of the political system. At the outset, one must recognize that a great deal has changed since the start of the end of the Cold War in 1989, and even more changes came upon us all in 2001.[3] Such was also the case in 1945, the end of World War II. Each generation has witnessed enormous changes in relations between nation-states, the nature of conflicts, and the nature and character of adversaries. Indeed, change has become commonplace, and the only permanent thing in the world is change.

To study the security setting, we need to take the world as it is and understand what critical changes led to the current state of affairs. We can then try to fix some point in time to see the directions the world is moving in and the forces shaping U.S. national security issues. In designing a framework for the analysis, it is useful to do three things: (1) identify and define critical periods or events in the post–Cold War period that have a direct bearing on international and U.S. national security; (2) study what changes have taken place in the new era and what continuities there are from the post–Cold War period; and (3) identify reference points in these periods for designing a framework to study U.S. national security, recognizing that such reference points are not intended to be detailed chapters in the history of U.S. national security. Within this framework, the major features of the security setting can be outlined and guide the study of national security.

From the U.S. perspective, there are two continuities from the post–Cold War period that spilled over into the new era and beyond: the nuclear age; and the political-military shape of conflict, especially as reflected in the Vietnam War. In addition, there are four reference points that are characteristic of the current period: the shape of the new world order; the conflict environment; globalization; and communications technology. There are, of course, other important points, ranging from the character of Russia, weapons proliferation, and weapons of mass destruction to international terrorism and drug cartels. We view these from a broad strategic level and not as case studies. The continuities and reference points, however, are springboards for shaping mind-sets and worldviews within the national security establishment and for fashioning our national security posture.

Continuities into the Twenty-First Century

There are two major continuities from the post–Cold War period into the twenty-first century: the nuclear age, and the Vietnam legacy. These affect the strategic landscape of the new era and shape issues of national security policy and military force structure.

The Nuclear Age

Nuclear armaments and efforts to control them in the new era continue, and the proliferation of nuclear technology has become an increasing danger. Furthermore, this danger now encompasses WMD, which include chemical and biological weaponry. Efforts to control these weapons and their proliferation have become bogged down in matters of state and disagreements over how to implement regulatory laws and control measures. Smaller states with oil reserves and cash reserves can—and some have—recruit and employ so-called intellectual mercenaries—those with skills in developing nuclear devices, especially from the former Soviet Union. Moreover, Iran and China, for example, have bought modern weapons from Russia. Fears persist in 2002 that North Korea and Iraq are acquiring (or already have acquired) nuclear weapons. In sum, the global arms bazaar continues, with increasing efforts at acquiring sophisticated weapons and nuclear technology.

Fears of nuclear war persist, albeit at a lower level for the major powers. This was the case in continuing confrontations between India and Pakistan over Kashmir (both states had publicly joined the ranks of nuclear powers in 1998). It is also the case that nuclear proliferation has become intertwined with weapons proliferation in general, with the fear that proliferation is expanding throughout many parts of the world that heretofore were isolated from such concerns. Moreover, there are continual efforts to increase the efficiency of WMD. Complicating these problems is the fear that international terrorists can obtain nuclear weapons and chemical and biological devices. In addition, international terrorists, by linking up with drug cartels, can gain access to huge financial resources to further their causes.

The Vietnam War

Even though many have tried to put Vietnam in the past, the tragedy remains deeply embedded in the American psyche. Constant reminders of the Vietnam War appear in literature.[4] A most important reminder is the Vietnam Veterans Memorial in Washington. The sacrifices in that war and its disputed outcome remain part of military history and the military perspective. Even during the 1991 Gulf War, Vietnam surfaced. It became important to point out that the Gulf War was not like Vietnam: for instance, General H. Norman Schwarzkopf, the commander of the allied Coalition, was allowed to run the war from the battle area. Equally important, the military objectives were clear, the adversary was clear, the battle was short and pointed, and modern weaponry and sophisticated operational techniques were brought to bear to defeat Iraq. All this was in direct contrast to Vietnam. Some fears exist that combating shadowy terrorist networks worldwide will result in the Vietnamization of the war on terrorism, although such fears were put aside for the time being in light of September 11.

U.S. and NATO involvement in Bosnia-Herzegovina in 1995 and in Kosovo in 1999 reminded many Americans about the possibility that peace-keeping missions can turn into quagmires (and, in the case of the humanitarian mission to Somalia, outright catastrophe) for U.S. troops. In the Republican Party presidential primary elections in 2000, Senator John McCain and some of his supporters rekindled the Vietnam issue with periodic references to the senator's years as a POW in North Vietnam, reinforced later by his return to that country. During this time, periodic glimpses of the Vietnam experience appeared in various media outlets.[5] Thus some may argue that Vietnam is behind us, but the facts say otherwise.

A recent case in point was the revelation of former Senator Bob Kerrey's actions in Vietnam in 1969. Kerrey was the commander of a U.S. Navy SEAL team whose mission took it into a coastal village in the Mekong Delta. One member of the team claimed (but was disputed by other members) that Kerrey ordered the execution of several women and children in the village. The publicity surrounding this revelation reopened the issue of the U.S. effort in Vietnam.[6]

Yet any serious study of U.S. national security in the new era cannot dispense with the long-term impact of Vietnam on our psyche, not to mention strategic plans and the use of military force. This must also impact U.S. policy in combating international terrorism. Not everything in this realm is rooted in the Vietnam experience, but the lessons drawn from that war remain a part of the total strategic package for the future. Such lessons concern U.S. withdrawal from combat, operational doctrines, the link between conflicts and Americans and political leadership, and, of course, military professionalism. The Vietnam legacy affected U.S. military operations in Bosnia-Herzegovina and Kosovo, even though it might have been hidden in the rhetoric of the day. Vietnam also shadows the psyche of our military professionals and is engrained in the military culture; all this is likely to be reinforced in the war against terrorism.

The Twenty-First Century

Several characteristics shape U.S. national security in the twenty-first century. The following four major reference points are especially important.

The New World Order

The shape of the new world order remains elusive, yet there are signs of an emerging disorder. The end of the superpower era has given rise to several regional power clusters. In the Pacific region, China and Japan compete and are likely to become major economic and military powers. At the same time, India has the potential to become a major military power prompted by its concern over Chinese nuclear capability and its power projections into the Indian Ocean and the confrontation with Pakistan over Kashmir. In Southeast Asia, the United States established relatively cordial relations with Vietnam. In other parts of Asia, the United States was concerned about the China-Taiwan confrontation and problems in Indonesia and the Philippines. Furthermore, the 1993 North American Free Trade Agreement (NAFTA) has the potential of creating a North American economic bloc. The European Union (EU) became a reality, evolving from a number of earlier European initiatives. But the future shape of NATO remains unclear. Although NATO added several countries to its system in a process of enlargement, its role in peacekeeping in 2001 and beyond remains uncertain. Adding to these new dimensions is Vladimir Putin, who became president of Russia in 2000 despite (or perhaps because of) his background in Soviet intelligence (the KGB) and a seemingly clouded history. He has undertaken measures to strengthen the Russian state and its power in the international field.

These examples illustrate several shifts in power alignments. But the larger issue is the balance of power among states, changes in state leadership, unconventional conflicts, as well as the roles of the United Nations and other regional organizations. In any case, the world is headed toward a system of regional power clusters, economic blocs, and organizational shifts. This new world is characterized by islands of stability and economic growth surrounded by vast areas of turmoil and economic collapse. Yet while many see the United States as the lone superpower and world hegemon, others see a decline in U.S. capability internationally.[7]

These matters raise several questions from the U.S. perspective. What role should (or can) the United States play in shaping the international environment? What remains of the old alliances? Who are our friends and adversaries? What is the concept of national power in the new world order? How can such power be utilized to achieve national security objectives? Perhaps the most complex and difficult issue is this: What do U.S. national interests and national security mean in this new world order? These questions remain unanswered and troubling.

The Conflict Environment

The new era brings with it a complex mix of ethnic and religious conflicts, intrastate turmoil, international terrorism, drug cartels, and actions by a variety of nonstate actors. Combined with nuclear weaponry, WMDs, chemical/biological instruments, weapons modernity, weapons proliferation, and information warfare, it is small wonder that the strategic landscape has become complex, complicated, unclear, and challenging.

There is a popular view in the United States that the possibility for a major war has diminished considerably. This also seems to be the growing conviction among leaders of the major powers. Yet there are any number of lesser conflicts and unconventional conflicts, ranging from the former Yugoslavia (even after the ouster of indicted war criminal Slobodan Milosevic as president in October 2000), the Caucasus, areas in Southeast Asia and southwest Africa, Latin America, and some states of the former Soviet Union. In addition, the potential for a regional firestorm in the Middle East remains high, to say the least. The same is true with respect to India's continuing tensions with Pakistan, as well as the turmoil in Afghanistan following the defeat of many (but by no means all) terrorists and their supporters there.

These conflicts may not necessarily follow the patterns of conventional conflict such as those in the 1991 Gulf War. They are more likely to follow unconventional patterns, encompassing everything from revolution and counterrevolution to terrorism and counterterrorism. Even though the conflicts in the former Yugoslavia seemed on the surface to have followed conventional lines, the fear was that they could expand and eventually change into unconventional conflicts following guerrilla operational doctrines. Fears of triggering an unconventional conflict were part of the strategic overview of U.S. and UN operations in Somalia in 1993 and later in Bosnia-Herzegovina and Kosovo into 2001. And again in late 2001 and into 2002, U.S. and allied military forces in Afghanistan, the Philippines, and elsewhere were engaged in unconventional operations against suspected terrorist networks. However, in 2002 U.S. plans to remove Iraq's Saddam Hussein are likely to include both conventional and unconventional operations.

Another pressing problem is the linkup of drug cartel–revolutionary coalitions, as in Colombia and Peru, with international terrorists. There were hopes that this problem was resolved in Peru with the apparent defeat of the Shining Path terrorist organization, but the potential for violence remains. Such coalitions pose a serious domestic threat to foreign governments, but they also challenge U.S. national security because of the link between domestic and external issues into a complex and difficult threat; September 11 reinforced this view. These threats cannot be met by the visible use of conventional military forces; neither are they necessarily shaped by conventional doctrines.

In 1992 and into 1994, another dimension surfaced in U.S. and NATO debates about military intervention. Labeled "wars of conscience," such conflicts did not necessarily challenge or threaten U.S. national interests but included significant humanitarian concerns. U.S. involvement in

Somalia in 1993, Bosnia-Herzegovina in 1995, and Kosovo in 1999 and 2000 are prime examples of these types of conflicts. Some even suggested that U.S. involvement in Somalia, Bosnia-Herzegovina, and Kosovo was video-driven. In other words, the constant images of civilian suffering, especially of children, played on the public conscience and created the environment for committing the United States.

But the character of conflicts in the new era and the form of possible U.S. involvement are not likely to follow European-type or Gulf War–type scenarios, that is, major wars fought by large coalition forces. This raises several questions about the utility of military force, military operational doctrines, and the long-term support of the public. However, the more critical issue is this: How well prepared is the U.S. military to engage in unconventional conflicts shaped by foreign strategic cultures and intrastate conflicts, that is, ethnic, religious, and nationalistic conflicts? Equally important, will Americans support such involvement and, if so, for how long? Can the United States design effective strategies that take into account foreign strategic cultures and various nonconventional considerations? At the same time, so-called stability operations (the latest label for peacekeeping missions) usually require police-type duties and constabulary mind-sets; many military professionals argue that such matters are contrary to war-fighting missions and mind-sets.

Globalization (Interdependence)

The new world order has focused attention on several issues that cross national boundaries. These include the environment, humanitarian issues, the drug trade, and, perhaps most important, economic and financial power as instruments of national policy in the era of globalization. Many of these issues are relevant to national security. Environmental issues, for example, are seen as threats to the survival of the state and to the well-being of people. Similarly, some argue that unless all peoples have an acceptable quality of life free of hunger and poverty, a dangerous security environment is created for wealthier states and peoples. But the most visible dimension of interdependence is economic. Historically, economic strength has been part of national security, but it was overshadowed by the focus on military power. But in the new era, economic power has gained a prominence as a major component of national security. Some feel that the use of the economic instrument can now achieve national security objectives that are unattainable through the use of military power.

Economic power rests primarily on domestic economic strength, which increases productivity and competitive capability in the external world. This forges a close link between national security and domestic economic, financial, and political issues. The ability to bring economic power to bear against other states, whether carried out or not, shapes security and foreign policies. But small states with important resources, such as oil, can have a major impact on larger states who need that oil. Thus smaller, oil-rich states in the Middle East are important players in the national security field by virtue of their resources.

The economic dimension is a key part of the global village (a relatively new concept referring to an interdependent international community). No modern state can exist in an economic vacuum; domestic economics are closely linked to the international economic arena. States are linked through financial markets, as was demonstrated in 1998 when the Asian economic crisis had a worldwide impact. There are close ties between the domestic economic and financial systems of major states and the international economy. The increasing economic gap between developed industrial states and several developing states in the Southern Hemisphere is of particular importance. From another perspective, economic development is crucial to the well-being of any state. The continuation of any leadership in power is in no small measure contingent upon its ability to further the economic well-being of its people.

Leaders of the national security establishment must consider several factors that create the global village. The most prominent are economic power and information technology. These need to be incorporated into the national security equation more so than in the past. The more difficult problem is to design appropriate strategies for responding to interdependent issues, information technology, and the use of economic power to achieve national security objectives. Complicating the matter is that economic power cannot be viewed in isolation. It must be systematically integrated with other national security instruments and in strategic planning. Put simply, U.S. strategic thinking must go beyond the use of military power, include a variety of instruments, consider different options (including economic strategies), and may even demand the creation of new instruments.

Communications Technology

The revolution in communications technology has added to global interdependence and complicated foreign policy and national security. Moreover, it has made information available almost instantaneously throughout the globe and on a person-to-person basis and to nongovernmental actors. Empowered individuals and groups now stalk the sovereign state. Furthermore, information warfare (so-called cyberwar) has become an almost commonplace term in the international system. The technological revolution in communications promises to continue unabated.

What does this mean for national security? The ability of governments to communicate across national boundaries almost at will reshapes diplomacy and can provide a wealth of information on any particular state or groups of people. Equally important, the ability to use satellite communications makes it increasingly difficult to control the media and to censor news reports. The media are now important international actors with independent resources and political clout beyond accountability to governments.

In addition, communications technology affects the ability to conduct wars. The sophisticated communications net assembled by the Coalition against Iraq in the 1991 Gulf War was an important factor in controlling Coalition forces and in conducting the successful military operation in Kuwait. This was especially true in the use of Coalition airpower, air-to-ground missiles, and surface-to-air missiles. Favorable exploitation of communications technology was also important in the multinational peace operations in Bosnia-Herzegovina in 1995 and Kosovo in 1999. Command centers in Washington have a better grasp of military operations through the use of the communications network than even commanders in the field. And the ability of news media to use satellite communications—independent of government control—provides instantaneous reports on battlefield operations throughout the globe.

At another level, the dramatic growth in the Internet, personal computers, fax machines, and camcorders facilitates person-to-person communications across national boundaries. Total government control of such communications is an increasingly difficult task. This supports the views of some that the world has become internationalized, diminishing the notion of a state-centric world.

The implications are clear enough: access to information and the ability to cheaply transmit information links states as well as people. Moreover, authoritarian systems have lost their monopoly on communications. Many groups can access information and use information technology free from government controls. The ability of governments to shape the news and give it a particular spin is more difficult given the direct access to a variety of news sources made available by the communications explosion. Take but one example: in 2001, Al-Jazeera, the Qatar-based satellite news channel popular among Arab audiences, rocketed to overnight fame thanks to its exclusive coverage of the war in Afghanistan and its videotaped interviews with Osama bin Laden. The success of this satellite-based news outlet has affected media coverage of Arab and Middle Eastern affairs worldwide.

Those in the national security establishment must account for these advances, not only by designing national security strategy but also by implementing security policies, collecting and evaluating intelligence information, and analyzing the political-psychological dimension of security issues. In using military force, care must be taken regarding the role of the media and access to information that ultimately accompany military operations. National security has become a more complex arena with the widespread availability of sophisticated communications technology. It has also become a more visible arena as access to information by more governments and individuals increases. It is becoming more and more difficult to find a good place to hide.

National Power

The ability to successfully carry out national security policy is a direct result of the power the nation possesses and its ability to use that power effectively. But again, we face the problems of definition. The term *national power* can be viewed from at least two dimensions. It can be defined in universal terms and also with respect to power in any given situation, that is, as power potential in contrast to the effective use of force. In the first instance, national power can be measured by several indicators, ranging from the total number in the armed forces, to the ability of a nation to mobilize for war, to the nation's economic capacity. In such cases, only relatively large states with significant populations and resources can become powerful. But in any given situation, large states might not have usable and effective power; smaller states, in contrast, might possess power based on other considerations. For example, during Vietnam many argued that the United States did not have usable power to bring the war to a successful conclusion. The U.S. enemy in that war—the "minor" state of North Vietnam—had more effective power in that particular case and was able to prevail. It may be that the Soviet Union faced a similar power relationship in its decade-long war in Afghanistan, from which the Soviet Union withdrew in 1989. A similar asymmetry in usable power may also have been the case in the Russia-Chechnya conflicts in 1994–1996 and 1999–2000. The same issue is relevant in determining the effective response to international terrorism.

Put simply, national power is a complex, ambiguous concept. Nonetheless, there are several important elements (or resources) of national power that a nation must possess if it is to pursue its national interests on a global scale.

One account sees international politics primarily as a "struggle for power to protect or advance national interests and ideologies":

> National power was viewed as the general capability of a state to influence the behavior of others. Among the traditional elements of national power—geography, national resources, industrial capacity, population, military strength, national character, and political cohesion—military strength was cited as the most obvious, yet one of the most difficult to estimate accurately.[8]

It is from this concept of national power that we design a more abbreviated concept that may be useful as a road map for the national security landscape. National power is based on six major elements: military power, economic and financial power, the intelligence system, geostrategic importance, national character, and psychological congruence and cohesion between leaders and the public on national security issues.

The term *military power* is defined as a measure of the total (aggregate) physical and psychological attributes of the armed forces of a country, including the capability of its intelligence agencies. This includes such indicators as the quality and quantity of equipment, mobility, and combat effectiveness (skills, leadership, and the will to fight). Military doctrine and mind-sets are part of this power base.

Economic and financial power is defined not only as the capacity of the state to reinforce and expand its economic and financial base but also its ability to use such resources to affect the international landscape.

The *intelligence system* is a basis of national power in that it is focused on gathering intelligence within the state as well as dealings with other states and the international world. To be sure, nondemocratic systems are not necessarily bound by the principles and limits imposed on intelligence systems by democracies. Nonetheless, to secure their homelands and to deal with the external world, democracies must have a reasonably effective intelligence system (see Chapter 8).

Geostrategic importance is defined as the location of the country in terms of international economy, international security, and the national security of other states. For example, the Strait of Hormuz in the Persian Gulf is of geostrategic importance, given it is an international waterway for oil resources. In addition to this, geostrategic importance includes the availability of important resources within a country, as well as its climate and terrain. All these factors provide a measure of geostrategic importance.

National character is another important consideration. Because of the term's highly subjective nature, some discount its relevancy to national power. Nonetheless, it is important in providing insights into a nation's political processes and cohesiveness. National character is measured by such things as the homogeneity of the population, including its size and growth, population education and skills, economic system and capability, the degree of commitment to the political system, and the legitimacy and efficiency of the governing structures.

Finally, *psychological congruence* is an inextricable part of national power. This is an obviously subjective dimension and, as expected, the most difficult to measure. The fact is that all of the elements of national power may be useless if the people of a nation are unwilling to use them in pursuit of national interests. Moreover, if other states perceive that a powerful nation is hesitant to use its power, and that its people are divided over the proper course of military action, then that nation will be perceived as a paper tiger whose power is based solely on rhetoric. Even when a nation has all the other elements of power, its own people may well perceive such power to be useless and thereby actually diminish their nation's power.

Thus military power and the other elements of power are useful only if buttressed by national will, political resolve, and staying power in an effective strategy to pursue national interests. At the same time, there must be a commitment to persist over the long run—that is, staying power to see the matter through once committed. As will be discussed in Chapter 3, the United States is an open system, and U.S. national will and staying power present the most difficult problems. This is especially true when national interests and national security must tackle issues outside the homeland (i.e., some Second-Order and all Third-Order interests).

Measuring national power is even more complex than each element individually suggests. The problem becomes acute in trying to link these elements, determine their relationships, and identify their total impact on other states. Yet attention to national power does provide a sense of the relative power of the country. It also focuses attention on the need to translate national power into usable power and link it through the national security establishment and the policy process to the pursuit of national interests. Much of this has to do with strategy.

National Strategy

There is great confusion as to the use of the terms *policy* and *strategy*. Many use these terms synonymously. The fact is that there is an important difference, especially in the study of national security. The term *policy* refers to the major objectives of the state, whether in foreign policy or national security. Some writers use the term *grand strategy* as a synonym for *war policy*. The term *strategy*, however, refers to the methods and means used to achieve these purposes.

In the words of one authority,

> The term "strategy," derived from the ancient Greek, originally pertained to the art of generalship or high command. In modern times, "grand strategy" has come into use to describe the overall defense plans of a nation or coalition of nations. Since the mid-twentieth century, "national strategy" has attained wide usage, meaning the coordinated employment of the total resources of a nation to achieve its national objectives.[9]

The term *strategy* as used here refers primarily to national strategy. From time to time, references will be made to what some call *national mili-*

tary strategy, focusing on "the generation of military power and its employment in state to state relationships."[10]

At the highest level, grand strategy is the way a state intends to pursue its national security goals. From this, several other strategies are designed that are focused on specific regions or issues. Thus we have *military strategy*, *economic strategy*, *political strategy*, and *psychological strategy*. In addition, there are U.S. strategies for the Middle East and other parts of the world. No wonder there is confusion.

Writing in the nineteenth century, the renowned Prussian general and military philosopher Karl von Clausewitz concluded, "Strategy borders on politics and statesmanship or rather it becomes both itself. . . . In strategy everything is simple, but not on that account very easy."[11]

There is, of course, more to these terms. But the differences are clear: *policy* refers to goals, and *strategy* is the means to reach these goals. It follows that strategy or strategies cannot be realistically designed and implemented if policy is unclear or vacillating. In this study, the terms *policy* and *strategy* are used as defined here. Additionally, *doctrine* means a body of beliefs and teachings about national security and its implementation.

Conclusion

The study of the national security establishment and the policy process cannot be undertaken without some attention to U.S. values and culture and their close links to the concepts of national security and national interests and how they are projected into the international arena. These are reference points for the way the national security establishment operates and the way policy is made.

A former assistant secretary of defense for international security policy offers an important caution with regard to U.S. behavior in national security issues into the twenty-first century:

> The kindest thing that might be said of U.S. behaviour ten years into the post–Cold War world is that it is astrategic, responding dutifully to the *crise du jour* with little sense of priority or consistency. A less charitable characterisation would be that the United States has its priorities but they are backward, too often placing immediate intervention in minor conflicts over a "preventive-defense" strategy focused on basic, long-term threats to security.[12]

This is a fairly recent observation and is especially relevant today. This is because the new kind of war declared by President George W. Bush in the aftermath of September 11—that is, the first war of the twenty-first century—may well have shifted the United States to a preventive-defense strategy.[13]

Notes

1. Samuel P. Huntington, "The Clash of Civilizations?" *Foreign Affairs* 72, no. 3 (Summer 1993): 22–49.

2. Paul J. Best, "American Force Posture for the Twenty-First Century," in Kul B. Rai, David F. Walsh, and Paul J. Best, eds., *America in the 21st Century: Challenges and Opportunities in Domestic Politics* (Upper Saddle River, NJ: Prentice-Hall, 1998), p. 230.

3. There are many excellent textbooks and studies on the international system and international politics that offer assessments and analysis of the new world order. These include Bruce Russett and Harvey Starr, *World Politics: The Menu for Choice*, 5th ed. (New York: W. H. Freeman, 1996), Richard W. Mansbach, *The Global Puzzle: Issues and Actors in World Politics,* 3rd ed. (Boston: Houghton Mifflin, 2000), and Ronald L. Tammen et al., *Power Transitions: Strategies for the 21st Century* (New York: Chatham House, 2000).

4. See, e.g., Michael Lind, *Vietnam: The Necessary War—A Reinterpretation of America's Most Disastrous Military Conflict* (New York: Free Press, 1999).

5. For example, the front cover of the May 1, 2000, issue of *U.S. News and World Report* had a photo of a U.S. soldier and was headlined Vietnam's Forgotten Lessons; 25 Years Later, Does the Military Still Remember Why It Lost?

6. See, e.g., Julia Keller, "Vietnam Still Gives U.S. Flashbacks," *Chicago Tribune*, May 6, 2001, pp. 1, 19.

7. See, e.g., Tammen et al., *Power Transitions.*

8. Amos A. Jordan, William J. Taylor Jr., and Michael J. Mazarr, *American National Security*, 5th ed. (Baltimore: Johns Hopkins University Press, 1999), p. 26.

9. Bruce Palmer Jr., "Strategic Guidelines for the United States in the 1980s," in Bruce Palmer Jr., ed., *Grand Strategy for the 1980s* (Washington, DC: American Enterprise Institute for Public Policy Research, 1978), p. 73.

10. Klaus Knorr, "National Security Studies: Scope and Structure of the Field," in Frank N. Trager and Phillip S. Kronenberg, eds., *National Security and American Society: Theory, Process, and Policy* (Lawrence: University of Kansas Press, 1973), p. 6.

11. Anatol Rapoport, ed., *Clausewitz on War* (Baltimore: Penguin Books, 1968), p. 243.

12. Ashton B. Carter, "Adapting U.S. Defence to Future Needs," *Survival: The IISS Quarterly* (Winter 1999–2000): 101.

13. See, e.g., LTC Antulio J. Echevarria II, *The Army and Homeland: A Strategic Perspective* (Carlisle Barracks, PA: Strategic Studies Institute, U.S. Army War College, March 2001).

3

The Conflict Spectrum
and the American Way of War

IMPORTANT PREMISES ARE AT THE ROOT OF THE AMERICAN WAY of war. First, for most Americans there is a clear distinction between the instruments of peace and those of war. The instruments of war remain dormant until war erupts, at which time the instruments of peace fade into the background, allowing whatever must be done to win. This polarization is also reflected in the way Americans tend to view contemporary conflicts. Involvement is seen as an either-or situation: the United States is either at war or at peace, with very little attention given to situations that have aspects of both conditions.

Second, most Americans tend to view conflicts in the world through conventional lenses, with mind-sets shaped by the U.S. experience and by U.S. values and norms. When applied to the international world, these values and norms are often unhelpful. Issues of war and peace are seen in legalistic terms in which wars are declared and conducted according to established rules of law. For many Americans, international behavior must also abide by such rules. Seeing a new basis for U.S. interventionism, one author has written, "The new interventionism has its roots in long-standing tendencies of American foreign policy—missionary zeal, bewilderment when the world refuses to conform to American expectations and a belief that for every problem there is a quick and easy solution."[1] This applies equally well to conflicts. Yet September 11 made many aware of the new kind of war, one characterized by unconventional strategy and unconventional tactics. It is a war that does not conform to conventional mind-sets.

Third, the Vietnam experience left many Americans skeptical and ambivalent about the overseas commitment of U.S. ground combat forces, the 1991 Gulf War notwithstanding. Even though a new generation is emerging with only vague memories of Vietnam, the Vietnam Memorial in Washington and several films of varying accuracy promise to keep the Vietnam experience alive. In addition, media coverage in 2000 of the twenty-fifth anniversary of the end of the Vietnam War reopened the wound. There seems to be an undercurrent of fear—a Vietnam syndrome, if you will—whenever U.S. troops are committed to anything other than conventional war.

Fourth, U.S. involvement must be terminated as quickly as possible, with the victory reflecting clear decisions and final solutions. The fact that the public seek clear and understandable solutions to complex issues compounds the difficulties inherent in policymaking. This mind-set assumes that every problem has a solution. As Ernest van den Hagg writes:

> Many Americans still are under the impression that a benevolent deity has made sure that there is a just solution to every problem, a remedy for every wrong, which can be discovered by negotiations, based on good will and on American moral and legal ideals, self-evident enough to persuade all parties, once they are revealed by negotiators, preferably American. Reality is otherwise. Just solutions are elusive. Many problems have no solutions, not even unjust ones; at most they can be managed, prevented from getting worse or from spreading to wider areas. . . . International problems hardly ever are solved by the sedulous pursuit of legal and moral principles.[2]

The consequences drive us to search for the "doable," which in turn leads to oversimplification, whether the issue is strategic weaponry, defense budgets, humanitarian issues, or unconventional conflicts. With respect to unconventional conflicts, most simplistic solutions sidestep fundamental problems and reveal a lack of understanding regarding relationships between culture, modernity, political and economic changes, internal conflicts, and less developed systems. This predilection is reinforced by the fact that many otherwise effective responses to unconventional conflicts might not fall neatly within the framework of values and norms of open systems. The most effective response to terrorist attacks against the U.S. homeland may well require actions that fall outside the norms of democracy. This does not mean that open systems are not capable of effective response. It means that open systems have difficulty in developing policies and strategies for unconventional conflicts due to the very nature and character of those open systems.

Furthermore, there is increasing disagreement about the meaning of the American way of war. Is our traditional way of war relevant in the new era? How should the U.S. military be used in contingencies and missions short of war?

Although military capability remains an essential component of the American way of war and national security, several other components have become important: diplomacy, political power, psychological strategy, intelligence, and economics. In this environment, intelligence capability worldwide takes on an increasingly important role. But the fact is that in some situations none of these components can substitute for the appropriate and effective use of military power. This is especially important for the United States given its worldwide interests and the security objectives evolving from the new world order. This is not to suggest that military means should be the first or only option, but there may be times when national interests require the use of military force (although this must be tempered by the nature of the conflict and the appropriate use of other instruments). For many, the military has become the instrument of first choice, even in contingencies short of war. This was the case for the Clinton administration (1993–2001) when its security team met to hammer out U.S. policy in Bosnia-Herzegovina. At one point, a discussion took place between UN Ambassador Madeleine Albright and the chairman of the U.S. Joint Chiefs of Staff, General Colin Powell. As described by Powell,

> The debate exploded at one session when Madeleine Albright . . . asked me in frustration, "What's the point in having this superb military that you're always talking about if we can't use it?" I thought I would have an aneurysm. American GIs were not toy soldiers to be moved around some sort of global game board.[3]

General Powell then explained that U.S. soldiers had been used in a variety of operations other than war as well as outright war during the recent years, but in each there was a clear political goal and the military was structured and tasked to achieve those goals. Powell was clear on the point that the military should not be used until the United States had a clear political objective.[4]

Complicating the issue, the public tends to view war as a clear struggle between good and evil.[5] The military instrument in this view is an implement of war that should not be harnessed except to destroy evil. This mindset is opposite to the sense of realpolitik and balance of power that characterized the foreign relations of Europe's Great Powers from the seventeenth through the twentieth centuries. In any case, as John Spanier has written,

> Once Americans were provoked, however, and the United States had to resort to force, the employment of this force was justified in terms of universal moral principles with which the United States, as a democratic country, identified itself. Resort to the evil instrument of war could be justified only by presuming noble purposes and completely destroying the immoral enemy who threatened the integrity, if not the existence, of these principles. American power had to be "righteous" power; only its full exercise could ensure salvation or the absolution of sin.[6]

In sum, the ability of the United States to respond to situations across the conflict spectrum (discussed below) is conditioned by historical experience and the American way of war. National interests and national security policy have been shaped by the premises identified here and have influenced the way Americans see the contemporary world security environment. Yet the security issues and conflicts across the spectrum may not be relevant to U.S. perceptions, policy, and strategy. The gap between U.S. perceptions and the realities of the security environment poses a challenging and often dangerous dilemma for U.S. national security policy. This requires a rethinking of the nature of contemporary conflicts and the U.S. national security posture. This rethinking, combined with the turmoil and fog of the international security landscape, is best studied by examining the conflict spectrum.

The Conflict Spectrum

The transformation of the U.S. military to meet the challenges of the twenty-first century has become an indispensable part of its culture. These new directions are intended to ensure that the military remains capable across the conflict spectrum, spelled out by the U.S. Joint Chiefs of Staff in a publication titled *Joint Vision 2020:*

> The ultimate goal of our military force is to accomplish the objectives directed by the National Command Authorities. For the joint force of the future, this goal will be achieved through *full spectrum dominance*—the ability of U.S. forces, operating unilaterally or in combination with multinational and interagency partners, to defeat any adversary and control any situation across the full range of military operations.[7]

The concept of full spectrum dominance rests on existing as well as evolving military capabilities. Thus, according to *Joint Vision 2020*, the military expected to be capable in peacekeeping, humanitarian operations, operations other than war (OOTW), and stability operations, in addition to all the various dimensions of conventional operations and quick-reaction capabilities. All of this is to be accomplished in a strategic landscape that remains clouded in the fog of peace. In 2001, that fog dissipated somewhat as increasing attention was given to homeland security.[8] Figure 3.1 shows the conflict spectrum into the twenty-first century.

The conflict spectrum is a way of showing the nature and characteristics of international conflicts. It is a useful method for assessing U.S. capabilities and effectiveness. Contemporary conflicts are placed in various categories of intensity. In the twenty-first century, the conflict spectrum has become multidimensional, complex, and confusing. Although the fear of major war between major states has diminished, there is increasing concern about continuous intrastate conflicts as well as unconventional conflicts.

Figure 3.1   The Conflict Spectrum

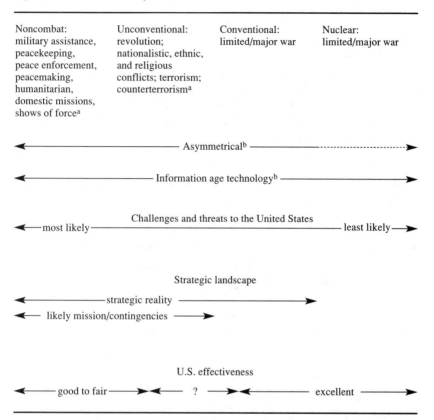

Notes: The complexity of the twenty-first-century strategic landscape and conflict characteristics is reflected in this schematic. This is even more complicated because it is possible that a variety of conflicts can occur simultaneously.

-----► indicates an unclear impact and/or end result.

a. There is rarely a clear distinction between noncombat contingencies and unconventional conflicts. The noncombat category includes a variety of humanitarian and peacekeeping operations as well as coalition strategies and military support for UN operations. Virtually all operations other than war have the potential of developing into unconventional conflicts of one type or another. Unconventional conflicts can also take place simultaneously with conventional conflicts.

b. The asymmetrical dimension and threats emanating from information-age technology cut across all the categories of conflict.

Moreover, there is some disagreement in the U.S. body politic as well as the national security system about our responses to the turmoil within other states and the international system in general.

Today and for the near term, conflicts are likely to be multidimensional, confusing, and complex. Three dimensions have become characteristic of this new international landscape. First, challenges to state sovereignty based on claims of self-determination by groups within a state are becoming international concerns. The United Nations, NATO, as well as other regional groups (such as the European Community) are increasingly apprehensive about intrastate conflicts, especially those that are likely to spill over into their areas. This has triggered intervention contrary to the traditional international norm of state sovereignty—the rule of the state over its own habitants. Some argue that state sovereignty has never been an absolute international norm. It certainly is not absolute now, as seen by NATO involvement in Kosovo.

Second, there is increasing attention to the impact of information warfare, defined as a range of activities from criminal mischief to technologically sophisticated warfare using computer networks and a variety of communication devices. This was evidently part of the U.S. strategy in challenging Slobodan Milosevic during the Kosovo conflict in 1999. It was also reported that opponents of the NATO mission in Kosovo temporarily disabled NATO's main website through e-mail bombing (including hacking and flooding of a website). In this evolving scenario, it has been argued that proficient computer users, even those living in less developed regions, can prosecute information warfare effectively against the most advanced countries. Indeed, the United States may be the most vulnerable to this kind of attack given its industrial and military dependence on information-age technology.

Third, various types of conflicts can be taking place in one area at any given time. That is, ethnic conflicts might be taking place while terrorism, extrastate intervention, or conventional invasions are occurring. Even more complicating is the fact that information warfare can take place against an adversary in the same conflict arena. This multiconflict scenario makes it difficult to not only pinpoint the specific adversary but also undertake conflict resolution. The problem of mission creep also enters into the picture, whereby the specific mission assigned to the military becomes enlarged not by choice but by one's efforts to succeed. In the process, the military involvement expands uncontrollably and can lead to unacceptable consequences.

The Range of Conflicts and Wars

In the conflict spectrum, conflicts are categorized as low intensity or high intensity, primarily for policy and strategy purposes but also in an attempt to distinguish the degree of mobilization and involvement of U.S. forces. The intensity level should in no way be construed as representative of the actual combat area; for U.S. military personnel (as well as for their adversaries), personal combat is high intensity. Too often such categorization is merely a policy posture, with little relevance to the conflict environment.

U.S. competence varies among conflict categories. At the low end of the spectrum, the United States is capable and reasonably effective in OOTW, stability operations, or whatever new missions short of war are labeled. Most of these military contingencies presume that operations are not likely to involve serious combat (or any combat at all). At the opposite end of the spectrum, the United States remains well positioned in nuclear weaponry and strategic forces to deter most adversaries. With the end of the Cold War, the likelihood of a major war or a nuclear exchange between major powers has diminished.[9] In addition, treaties between the United States and Russia to reduce strategic and tactical nuclear weapons have ushered in an era of arms control that is extending worldwide. Many such efforts are a continuation of previous attempts to control nuclear proliferation, yet some states are developing and expanding their nuclear, chemical, and/or biological capability (e.g., China, North Korea, Iraq, and Iran, the latter three being labeled an "axis of evil" by President George W. Bush in a 2002 State of the Union speech). In any event, the United States must retain a credible deterrent to counter the use of WMD. Similarly, the U.S. capability in conventional conflict was well demonstrated in the 1991 Gulf War, which was primarily based on operational principles derived from a European-oriented battle scenario. And the air war over Afghanistan in response to September 11 demonstrated a remarkable capability to use high-tech aerial weaponry to incapacitate ground-based forces deployed in difficult terrain. Still, airpower alone was not sufficient; it took ground forces under the command of the Northern Alliance to finish the task.

It is in the vast middle area on the spectrum—unconventional conflicts, the most likely conflicts for the foreseeable future—where the United States is at a distinct disadvantage. Most contemporary conflicts are included in this category, ranging from revolution and terrorism to conflicts associated with coalitions of drug cartels and revolutionary groups. The tendency is to see such conflicts in terms of commando-type operations or special operations shaped by counterterrorism contingencies, but there is much more to them than this suggests.

The label *unconventional conflicts* as used here refers to conflicts that do not follow conventional characteristics. (In contrast, the 1991 Gulf War was a conventional conflict.) Unconventional conflicts include asymmetrical conflicts, in which the U.S. adversary is employing strategy and tactics that do not correspond to U.S. force dispositions, strategy, and/or tactics. Thus the United States can challenge an adversary on the ground and air using conventional means, but that adversary might focus on unconventional strategy and tactics, terrorism, information warfare, and other means. In the case of information warfare, an adversary with information-age technology—a computer hacker, for instance—may be able to do harm to the United States, including its economy, corporations, and the U.S. government itself. At the same time, however, U.S. technology may have little ability to overcome a determined adversary due to his limited dependence on information-age technology.

It is important to examine unconventional conflicts more closely because they are likely to be based on strategic cultures that do not reflect Judeo-Christian notions or classic European-type scenarios; neither do they necessarily follow the American way of war. Moreover, competency, indeed, proficiency, in unconventional conflicts and contingencies in the middle areas of the conflict spectrum are necessary if the U.S. military is to be effective in OOTW.[10] This is not necessarily the case at present.

Unconventional Conflicts

The history of the United States—dating even to the prerevolutionary period—is filled with the exploits of elite units undertaking unconventional operations.

From Rogers' Rangers in the American Revolution, to the First Special Service Unit of World War II, to the Green Berets of the Kennedy era, to the Special Operations Command of the contemporary period, the U.S. military draws from an honored legacy of special operations and low-intensity conflict. Yet this experience was usually placed at the periphery of classic military education, professionalism, and strategy—viewed more as curiosity than curriculum—and was generally considered tangential to real issues of war and peace.

In the 1980s a new counterinsurgency era emerged and, with it, an increased interest in special units and special operations. Resources committed to special operations increased in terms of both logistics and personnel. The creation of the First Special Operations Command in 1982 was a major step in creating a permanent special operations capability within the military. In 1986 Congress provided for an assistant secretary of defense for special operations and low-intensity conflict and established a unified command for all U.S. Special Operations Forces (Army, Navy, and Air Force). By 1990 special forces personnel numbered about 12,000, organized into five active Special Forces Groups. Similar increases occurred in the U.S. Army Ranger battalions, Navy SEALS, and Air Force Special Operations Forces.[11] This organizational structure remains in place. The organization of the Special Operations Command is shown in Figure 3.2.

Although this recent effort suggests the U.S. position is strong in this area, it was tempered by policy incoherency, flawed strategy, and doctrinal

Figure 3.2   Special Operations Command

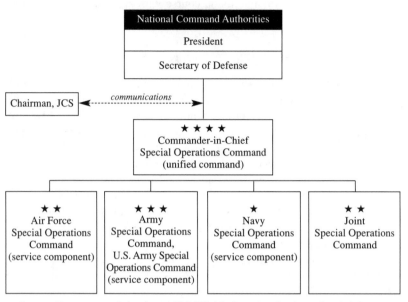

Source: Department of the Army, *FM 100-25: Doctrine for Army Special Operations Forces* (Washington, DC: U.S. Government Printing Office, 1991), pp. 4–19.

ambiguity. The prevailing view that the U.S. military was capable in unconventional conflicts seemed to apply more to special operations of a more conventional nature. In the Gulf War, for example, special operations forces were involved in long-range reconnaissance and behind-the-line operations—missions within the purview of Ranger and commando-type operations. A final judgment on U.S. capability in unconventional conflict will rest on the scope and outcome of such efforts in the war on terrorism that began in late 2001. Preliminary indications are that U.S. forces have improved in this area.

Since the early 1990s the U.S. Army Special Forces were being reshaped into an elite-type conventional force. Furthermore, the Army's efforts at "transformation" and the focus on a variety of missions short of war overlap with the role of special forces. "Threatened with irrelevance by changes that allow conventional forces to conduct missions that were once its exclusive preserve, the Green Berets are refocusing on unconventional warfare."[12] This is the theme of a one-year study by the Army special forces as reported in *Army Times* in July 2001. "The changing strategic environment makes unconventional warfare a vital mission for the early 21st century," according to those involved in the study.[13] The report noted, however, that "the shift will require changes in training, and could put Special Forces leaders on a collision course with superiors at U.S. Special Operations Command."

Conceptual Coherence

The most important aspect of developing an effective U.S. political-military posture for unconventional conflicts is conceptual clarity and coherence. During the 1960s counterinsurgency era, a variety of terms came into use to provide some analytical precision to the newfound form of warfare: *insurgency, counterinsurgency, special warfare, guerrilla warfare, wars of national liberation, people's wars,* and *internal conflicts.* The 1980s saw the revival of many of these terms and added some new ones, such as *special operations, low-intensity conflict, small wars, low-level wars, operations short of war,* and *secret armies.* With the incidence of international terrorism, *terror* and *counterterror* have become part of the special operations lexicon. In the 1990s and beyond, a variety of terms have been added, including *stability operations, peacekeeping, peacemaking, peace enforcement, humanitarian missions,* and *operations other than war.* Lost are older notions of guerrilla war, insurgency, and revolution; now the tendency is to characterize many such conflicts as *ethnic, religious,* or *nationalistic.*[14]

A case in point is *revolution,* intended to achieve a strategic goal, with both strategic and tactical dimensions. It encompasses political-psychological, as well as social and economic, components and is aimed at the entire political-social order of the existing system. Revolution is a complex, multidimensional phenomenon with origins in the political-social system and a strategy based on a sweeping attack against the existing order. Revolutionary tactics range from terror, assassinations, hit-and-run raids, robbery, and kidnapping to the use of armed force in the conduct of conventional-type operations. The center of gravity of the conflict is not usually in the armed forces but rather the political-social milieu of the existing system. The revolutionary strategy and tactics employed are shaped accordingly:

> A revolutionary war is never confined within the bounds of military action. . . . For this reason it is endowed with a dynamic quality and a dimension in depth that orthodox wars, whatever their scale, lack. This is particularly true of revolutionary guerrilla war, which is not susceptible to the type of superficial military treatment frequently advocated by antediluvian doctrinaires.[15]

Some groups will use revolutionary strategy and tactics to achieve particular political goals short of taking over the state. This is seen in ethnic, and religious, and hypernationalistic conflicts, like that in Kosovo in 1999–2000.

Terror and Counterterror

Confusion also reigns over concepts and doctrines relating to terror and counterterror, especially when they are linked with revolution and counterrevolution.

And in this new era, the notion of *cyberterrorism* has become a new phenomenon. Signs already suggest that terrorist groups will try to gain strength and extend their reach by organizing into transnational networks and developing swarming strategies and tactics for destroying targets, entirely apart from whether they can hack into a target's computer system.[16]

In the broader scheme there are at least four categorizations of terror: terror-qua-terror, revolutionary terrorism, state-supported terrorism, and state-sponsored terrorism.[17] All of these can have international dimensions and also be linked to other groups such as drug cartels. *Terror-qua-terror* is violence for the sake of violence, combining tactical means and strategic purposes, that is, the terrorist act is perceived as an end in and of itself. The aim is to strike at the system, to gain recognition for one's terrorist group, to achieve a moral victory, to fulfill a mission in life (e.g., in a religious way), or all of these. There is very little concern about anything beyond the act or state of terrorism itself. In earlier years, factions of the Baader-Meinhof Gang, the Red Brigades, and Direct Action were cases in point. U.S. examples include the Symbionese Liberation Army and the Weather Underground.[18] This is also the characteristic of so-called *new terrorism*. According to one account, "The new terrorism . . . appears pointless since it does not lead directly to any strategic goal, and it seems exotic since it is frequently couched in the visionary rhetoric of religion. It is the anti-order of the new world order of the twenty-first century."[19]

Terrorist acts have also been used by individuals or groups as statements against the government. This appears to be the case involving Timothy McVeigh and the bombing of the Murrah Federal Building in Oklahoma City in April 1995. "The bombing introduced many Americans to the disturbing underworld of domestic terrorism while shattering whatever illusions existed about terrorism as only an international or overseas threat."[20]

The September 11, 2001, attacks in New York and Washington introduced Americans to the impact and efficiency of some international terrorist groups. It also shattered some illusions regarding international terrorism. These attacks appeared to be well organized, well financed, and well executed. They created more casualties on the U.S. homeland than any other war, with the exception of the Civil War.

Revolutionary terrorism is a strategic as well as tactical instrument of the revolutionary system, that is, terrorist tactics and strategies are designed to further the revolutionary cause. The terrorist instrument is usually under the control of revolutionary leadership, and terrorist operations are conducted so as to avoid, as much as possible, alienating the very people at which the revolution is directed. Nonetheless, in light of the international scope of revolutionary strategy, terrorists can cross over into the terror-qua-terror category in the name of revolution. The Palestine Liberation Organization in former years, various groups operating in the Middle East such as Hezbollah, the Vietcong during the Vietnam War, and revolutionaries in El Salvador (i.e., the Farabundo Marti Front of National Liberation and the Popular Revolutionary Army) can generally be categorized as revolutionary terrorism. Perhaps one of the clearest examples is Sendero Luminoso (Shining Path) in Peru. In early 2000, many felt that Sendero Luminoso had been all but eliminated by the efforts of Peruvian president Alberto Fujimoro; it re-emerged in 2002. In Greece, the actions of the November 17 group in 2000 may well be a version of revolutionary terror, although the group has been active on and off for decades.

Another dimension in this category is the coalition between drug cartels and revolutionary groups, as in Colombia. (The United States has become involved in Colombia militarily as well as financially.)[21] This coalition in crime is mutually advantageous to the drug lords and the revolutionaries, at least in the short to middle term. The drug cartels pay protection money to the revolutionaries in order to protect drug operations in outlying areas. The revolutionaries provide protection in order to maintain a dependable financial source. This linkage has created internal turmoil and havoc, with the United States becoming increasingly involved. In the broader sense, revolutionaries can take a certain pleasure as well as strategic advantage in seeing Western systems, such as the United States, undermined by drug trafficking and drug use. Yet the underlying philosophical basis of revolution is contrary to the notion of long-term dependence on drug operations. From another perspective, individual revolutionaries are not immune from drug addiction.

State-supported terrorism is difficult to identify because it is often difficult to directly link terrorist activity to states. This is a result of states' ability to hide their support and involvement using a variety of techniques.[22]

State-sponsored terrorism is one in which a particular state actually organizes, trains, and finances terrorist groups. This includes identifying terror targets and providing recruits. Furthermore, sponsor states are able to engage in a form of psychological warfare by controlling information about their own system while gaining access to the media of open systems to broadcast their own messages. Some states engage in terrorism against their own citizens in order to maintain control or neutralize dissidents and resistance groups; totalitarian and authoritarian systems are especially noted for such activity (e.g., Nicaragua under Sandinista rule, Zimbabwe, and the former Soviet Union).[23] In the Middle East Iraq, Iran, Libya, and Syria have been accused of such operations.

Some observers have also identified a new dimension, *religious terrorism*, that is linked to the new terrorism. As one observer noted:

> In 1998, when Secretary of State Madeleine Albright announced a list of 30 of the world's most dangerous groups, over half were religious and included Judaism, Islam, and Buddhism. If other violent religious groups around the world were added—including the many Christian militia and other paramilitary organizations found in the United States—the number of religious terrorist groups would be considerable.[24]

The terrorist attacks on the United States in 2001 illuminated and magnified the threat of religious terrorism.

These labels are complicated by the fact that terrorism can be multidimensional, that is, a terrorist act can be a combination of all three categories discussed above. Add to this the possibility of cyberterrorism, and it becomes nearly impossible for states to design effective counterterrorism strategies.

On the international level, many countries do not hesitate to define terrorist acts such as kidnapping, hostage-taking, assassination, bombings, armed robbery, and so on as criminal in nature. However, other states, especially in the developing world, resist any definition that may have legal implications restricting the activities of groups fighting against neocolonial regimes. Moreover, some states see the use of terrorism as a low-risk, high-return policy affording an opportunity to strike the West, especially the United States. This lack of definition also reflects the general view that one man's terrorist is another man's freedom fighter. Unfortunately such a perspective ignores the characteristics of terrorist acts and the impact on their victims. Furthermore, this view is based on convoluted moral principles that elevate assassination and murder to humanistic ventures.

Unconventional Conflicts

There is a great deal of published literature on the nature and character of unconventional conflicts, ranging from Sun-tzu and Mao Tse-tung to Che Guevara and Vo Nguyen Giap.[25] The concept now includes a variety of efforts short of taking control of the state and establishing a revolutionary government. An in-depth study of revolution and counterrevolution would require serious reading of the major works. For our purposes, it is important to identify the major characteristics that have an especially significant bearing on the ability of open systems to come to grips with unconventional conflicts.

Unconventional conflicts are asymmetrical and, for those involved, they are "total" wars. The self-perception of revolution is that it is a life-and-death struggle with the existing system. Terrorists often see themselves as engaged in the ultimate struggle, bringing death to themselves, if need be, to achieve their goals. For open systems, however, involvement in unconventional conflicts is more limited. Yet the constraints and restraints of limited wars generally apply. More important, the nature of open systems limits strategy, tactical operations, and overall effort.

Unconventional conflicts tend to be protracted, as the strategies are long-range. Those who demonstrate infinite patience and persistence are more likely to be successful; the classic example is North Vietnam, which had the staying power to outlast a technologically advanced superpower. Revolutionaries thus often adopt long-term strategies based on the gradual erosion of the ability of the existing system to govern. Tactics and doctrines are designed accordingly. But revolutionaries do not necessarily choose a protracted conflict; they are forced into adopting such a strategy because of the initial power of the government they oppose. Yet some revolutionary ideologues idealize the nature of the conflict, even more than outright success. In such cases the protracted war is used to mobilize the masses, establish a revolutionary system, and create a revolutionary myth.

Unconventional conflicts are also tactically unconventional. This type of conflict is not necessarily ruled by Clausewitzian principles that place the center of gravity within the armed forces of the state; Sun-tzu's formulations are more relevant.[26] The Chinese writer emphasized deception, psychological warfare, and moral influence. Combined with hit-and-run raids, assassinations, ambushes, and surprise attacks, the tactics of unconventional conflicts are difficult for conventionally trained and postured forces to counter.

Ambiguity is another characteristic of unconventional conflicts. It is difficult in revolutionary-type conflicts to separate friend from foe and to develop clear criteria for determining success. As the United States learned in Vietnam, the amount of real estate taken, weapons recovered, body count (enemy casualties), and secure areas might not be good indicators of who is winning and losing. Furthermore, the rhetoric of revolution and counterrevolution is difficult to untangle, obscuring a clear understanding of the purposes of the antagonists.

Unconventional conflicts are also characterized by their high political content and moral dimension. Although it is true that all wars are political, in unconventional conflicts operations and purposes are shaped and conducted according to political-psychological goals. For example, the deliberate sacrifice of armed revolutionary elements for the sake of a political-psychological victory is not an uncommon occurrence. The Tet Offensive by the Vietcong and North Vietnamese in 1968 is a case in point. Even though the enemy forces were decimated by U.S. and South Vietnamese military forces, the media distortions reported to the public back home gave the impression of a great Vietcong victory. The U.S. and South Vietnamese forces won a major military battle but totally lost the political-psychological battle. In the long run, the latter proved to be the more important of the two, as it marked the turning point in public support for the war.

In sum, the shape and dimensions of unconventional conflicts do not easily fit into prevailing U.S. notions of conflict. Moreover, the principles of warfare and battlefield conduct that are part of U.S. military professionalism do not really focus on unconventional conflicts. Although U.S. military professionals seek to increase knowledge and develop skills for success in battle by defeating the armed forces of the enemy, the center of gravity of unconventional conflicts is in the political-social milieu of the contending systems. As General Bruce Palmer noted about Vietnam:

> One of our handicaps was that few Americans understood the true nature of the war—a devilishly clever mixture of conventional warfare fought somewhat unconventionally and guerrilla warfare fought in the classical manner. Moreover, from Hanoi's point of view it was an all out, total war, while from the outlook of the United States it was quite limited.[27]

This view also described U.S. thinking about the latest conflict arena, but all that may have changed as a result of September 11.

In the twenty-first century the focus on humanitarian missions as well as a variety of peacekeeping contingencies, combined with the notion of operations other than war, broadened the concept of low-intensity conflicts and special operations (unconventional conflicts), at least within many policymaking and military circles. This merely adds to the confusion already characterizing unconventional conflict concepts.

From lessons learned in a historical view of the United States and guerrilla warfare and its relevance in the current period, Anthony James Joes concludes, "Dangers lie in the path ahead. To avert or at least prepare for them, Americans need to deepen and sharpen their understanding of what guerrilla war has meant and will mean."[28] In considering involvement of the United States in future guerrilla insurgency, "the presumption should be against committing U.S. ground forces. . . . Military victory is ephemeral."[29]

Unconventional Conflicts:
U.S. Policy and Strategic Guidelines

Open Systems and Unconventional Conflicts

Open systems direct policy in their attempt to be decent societies based on values, norms, and an ideology that stresses respect for individual rights, justice, freedom, and equality. Underpinning this is the fact that elected officials are responsible to the people and can be removed if they fail in their duties and responsibilities. And although their goals are imperfectly achieved, the fact is that open systems pursue goals and in the process develop many safeguards that protect against government interference and support individual freedom. The environment of open systems is reinforced and perpetuated by counterbalancing forces, independent sources of information, and constitutionally protected independent political actions. The collectivity is subordinate to the individual. This is in sharp contrast to closed systems and, indeed, to the nature of most revolutionary systems, of which Roberta Goren wrote: "More often than not one sort of repressive regime has taken the place of another repressive regime. Often what has been represented as a left-wing 'liberating' regime overthrowing a right-wing repressive regime is no less reactionary than its predecessor."[30]

Many Americans view revolutions either as "glorious" affairs in which a freedom-loving people rises up against tyrants (e.g., the American Revolution), or as anticolonial affairs in one form or another. Although such views carry an implicit democratic rationalization and justification for revolution, they also reveal a misunderstanding of the prevailing security environment. More commonly, elites who initiate or co-opt revolutions are intent upon establishing rule by strong central government and may fall well short of the democratic ideal. Well-meaning groups here in the United States mistakenly view such revolutions through the lens of nineteenth-century liberalism. Their misperceptions and distortions can become the basis for mobilizing segments of the public against the official U.S. political-military posture.

The very character of open systems and their value base are disadvantages in unconventional conflicts. They give adversaries advantages that they would not enjoy by engaging closed systems. Personal liberty, freedom of movement, unfettered communications—all work to the advantage of the subversive enemy intent upon using those characteristics to his advantage. Complicating this is the fact that minority groups struggling for self-determination may be trying to separate from the authoritarian rule of the state. This makes the state vulnerable to intrusion by international organizations in which the United States plays a major role. The problem facing the United States is made more difficult by the American way of war. In responding to unconventional conflicts, there is a marked U.S. tendency to overwhelm the conflict area and indigenous allies, imposing a U.S.-favored environment. Policymakers are apt to design political-military responses based on bringing overwhelming U.S. forces to bear for short-term operations designed to solve the problem in one way or another. The result becomes ad hoc, short-term initiatives using conventional U.S. strategies, tactics, and doctrines. Although such approaches can be appropriate in some situations, the key for most unconventional conflicts is to penetrate the political-social milieu so as to influence it more effectively (the famous adage is "winning hearts and minds"). This means that success usually goes to the side with the best people on the ground, not necessarily to those with the largest battalions or the most sophisticated and massive firepower (such as overwhelming airpower). In the long run, solutions—if indeed there are solutions—probably require staying power over an extended period.

More than forty years ago, a noted scholar had this to say about revolution:

> Revolution, in distinction to war, will stay with us into the foreseeable future . . . those will probably win who understand revolution, while those who still put their faith in power politics in the traditional sense of the term and, therefore, in war as the last resort of all foreign policy, may well discover in a not too distant future that they have become masters in a rather useless and obsolete trade.[31]

The American Way of War and Unconventional Conflicts

Throughout history the American way of war has been based on a moral dimension; going to war had a purpose—achieving some higher good. This usually demanded a clear identification of the enemy and his alleged evil purposes. The American way of war also makes a clear distinction between war and peace. In peacetime, nonmilitary systems prevail; in war, the military prevails. Thus the presumption was a clear separation between institutions for peace and those for war. But in the contemporary international environment the lines between war and peace are not as distinct. This throws into disarray prevailing U.S. notions, and it creates a basic dilemma for the U.S. military. A condition of no war–no peace denies the U.S. military the clear political-psychological sustenance from the body politic to engage in unconventional conflicts. At the same time, the U.S. military must continue to maintain a credible posture for nuclear deterrence and major conventional conflicts, including all that implies for relationships with other states. Open systems also require that their officials and military personnel conduct themselves within the general bounds of democratic propriety. This includes behavior on the battlefield.

Overall strategy and tactical operations must also fit within democratic values and norms, that is, if policy and strategy are to maintain their credibility. Operations based on hostage-taking, terrorism, and assassinations to erode support for a revolutionary system or penetrate and neutralize terrorist groups will generally be condemned by open systems. The scope and intensity of intelligence activities, both domestic and foreign, are affected by these considerations. This is extremely important given the role of intelligence in unconventional conflicts.

In responding to unconventional conflicts, U.S. forces will usually operate on foreign soil and in conjunction with foreign governments, especially in the less developed world. Supporting an existing system that counters revolutionary challenges is a difficult proposition at best, and a fundamental problem arises from the fact that U.S. personnel socialized into the norms and values of open systems invariably have difficulty relating to and understanding those of foreign cultures. It is difficult to empathize with cultures whose view of individual worth and human rights is at variance with ours. Indeed, it is conceivable that revolutionary rhetoric such as freedom and equality can strike a more responsive chord than does the ideology of the existing system. The lack of understanding of cultures makes it difficult to understand friends as well as enemies. The same problems arise when the United States supports groups within a foreign state who seek self-determination, such as the Albanians in Kosovo in 1999–2000.

Finally, the end of the Cold War and the dissolution of the Soviet Union and its allies changed the equation as to unconventional conflicts. No longer driven by East-West ideological confrontations, such conflicts are likely to reflect indigenous issues, such as ethnic confrontation, religious freedom, and minority-group autonomy. Conflicts can occur because elites or controlling groups try to gain power and impose a set of political rules and procedures emanating from their version of society (e.g., Bosnia between 1992 and 1995). Yet unconventional conflicts arising from the Cold War period may continue in one form or another, as in the Middle East, Southeast Asia, parts of Africa, and Latin America, where some conflicts are the result of drug cartel–revolutionary conspiracy. Although unconventional conflicts generally evolve from the political, social, and economic turmoil in less developed states, wherever a power vacuum exists—or where the United States is at a distinct disadvantage—regional powers, ethnic and religious groups, nationalistic revivals within states, and indigenous revolutionary groups will attempt to fill that vacuum.[32]

Thus the very nature of open systems makes it difficult to respond to unconventional conflicts, including OOTW, conflicts short of war, stability operations, and the like.

Policy, Strategy, and Military Operations

Virtually any commitment of U.S. military forces abroad has the potential to turn into an unconventional conflict. It is important, therefore, that U.S. policymakers and the military be prepared for such conflicts, even if the mission is peacekeeping. The conflict spectrum (see Figure 3.1) provides a view of the conflict realities; they have clear political-military implications, especially for unconventional conflicts.[33] Responses can demand a political-military posture that is contrary to the American way of war as well as conventional principles and doctrine. This requires training that goes beyond purely military skills. As President John Kennedy stated in response to wars of national liberation,

> Pure military skill is not enough. A full spectrum of military, para-military, and civil action must be blended to produce success. . . . To win this struggle, our officers and men must understand and combine the political, economic and civil actions with skilled military efforts in the execution of this mission.[34]

Although Kennedy was addressing the armed forces in 1962, his words are appropriate today. The same theme was proclaimed by President George W. Bush in the aftermath of September 11, and he created a cabinet-level position in the Office of Homeland Security. In a television address to the nation on June 5, 2002, President Bush called on Congress to establish a Department of Homeland Security to replace the Office of Homeland Security. If enacted into law, it will create the third-largest department in the national government and will be the largest extension reorganization of the government since the Truman presidency.

An effective force structure for responding to unconventional conflicts cannot be wedded to conventional hierarchy or command systems. It requires planning, organization, and operations aimed at the political-social milieu of revolutionary-counterrevolutionary systems. It demands individuals with the requisite military skills who also understand and are sensitive to the cultural forces and nationalistic desires of foreign systems—especially those in the less developed world. They must be self-reliant individuals capable of operating for long periods in small groups isolated from the U.S. environment. Most of all it requires patience, persistence, political-psychological sophistication, and the ability to blend in with the indigenous political-military system.

In this respect, success in revolutionary and counterrevolutionary conflicts is not necessarily contingent upon sophisticated weaponry, large numbers of troops, and massive airpower. Rather, success depends on the quality and dedication of efficient soldiers on the ground who can blend in and function as skilled political mobilizers and teachers.

Conclusion

In the final analysis, what does all of this mean for U.S. national security policy and strategy?

First, in order to respond effectively to unconventional conflicts, policy must be based on U.S. national interests. Although this seems obvious, it is not so clear with respect to unconventional conflicts and the less developed world. In this context, national interests and policy should include support of like-minded systems. This does not mean that support should only be extended to democratic or quasidemocratic systems. There are not many of those systems in the third world, although some are moving in that direction. The fact is that true democratic systems need little help from the United States, and limiting U.S. interests to that type of system is tantamount to withdrawing from the less developed world. However, this does not mean that the United States should become involved in every corner of the third world. In fact, U.S. involvement and visible support could tarnish and undermine foreign nationalistic leaders, and in some areas U.S. involvement would achieve little or would make matters worse.

When compelling U.S. national security interests are at stake, and where long term interests can be seriously affected, U.S. involvement should include support of states and groups who are like-minded or are the lesser of evils; this can include support of revolutionary systems. However, we should never substitute one tyranny for another. It is conceivable that nominally democratic systems, even certain authoritarian systems, are more susceptible to openness than revolutionary systems. The term used to describe this strategy, in which the United States is compelled to choose among undesirable options, is *suboptimizing*. Suboptimizing accepts that the logic of policy and strategy is often subsumed by actual conditions that defy rational, logical, or just solutions.

Second, it follows that strategies must include a variety of options and phases (see Figure 3.1 on the conflict spectrum) that incorporate political, economic, and psychological components as well as military ones. The case of U.S. ground combat forces must be reserved for special situations in which the existing system is about to collapse and the area is vital to U.S. security interests. If other options are effectively implemented, however, the use of U.S. combat forces could be the exception rather than the rule. Strategic options should be based on support and assistance to expand the governing capacity of the existing system, to broaden its political-psychological base, and to develop a civic culture attuned to openness. Such strategies must not Americanize the conflict or the theater itself, except in unusual circumstances requiring direct involvement of conventional U.S. combat forces.

Third, strategies should be based on civilian-military cooperation and interservice coordination. Command structures, planning, organization, and implementation must reflect these and joint efforts. This is especially true with respect to the intelligence function. Effective intelligence requires not only military but also strategic intelligence and analysis associated with intelligence capabilities. Finally, strategies must include counterterrorism and counterrevolutionary operations in support of existing systems and revolutions against repressive systems that promise to become harsher still. Whether such a strategy could be implemented would depend on the assessment of U.S. national interests.

Fourth, within the U.S. body politic, a new realism must emerge regarding war and peace and the challenge posed by unconventional conflicts. Within military and civilian policy circles and the body politic (especially the media), there must be greater appreciation for the complexity of the conflict spectrum and a recognition of the long-term threat of unconventional conflicts. Without this new realism, it is unlikely that the necessary national will, political resolve, and staying power can be developed to respond effectively.

Fifth, to dismiss unconventional conflicts as a nonthreatening phenomenon and a natural evolution of political-social turmoil is to ignore the lessons of recent history. To dismiss the susceptibility of open systems to deception, political-psychological warfare, terrorism, and totalitarian revolutionaries as unrealistic is to create a condition described by Jean-Francois Revel: "Democratic civilization is the first in history to blame itself because another power is working to destroy it."[35] This may well have changed after September 11, when Americans united to combat international terrorism. This relates to the critical issue of staying power and national will over the long haul.

Thus the basic dilemma for the U.S. military grows out of these conditions, especially the fact that U.S. norms and values do not easily match the policy and strategy required for unconventional conflicts. The American way of war virtually precludes a military postured for the kinds of tactical and doctrinal techniques inherent in unconventional conflicts. Fighting without appearing to fight, waging war through peaceful enterprise, using morally acceptable tactics and doctrine against adversaries who abandon any pretense of moral behavior—these are the tasks facing the U.S. military. They become more pressing and dangerous in the long run compared to conventional, even nuclear, war.

The capability and effectiveness of the United States to respond to unconventional conflicts is an important part of national security policy. Conflicts in the less developed world have geostrategic as well as political-military and psychological importance. Dangers include conflict escalation, regional destabilization, and the possibility of expansion of autocratic regimes. Yet groups seeking self-determination tend to look to the United

States for support in the form of resources, including political-psychologi-cal assets. In the broader national security dimension, U.S. capability and effectiveness in unconventional conflicts is part of deterrence.

Perceptions of U.S. strength can have a deterrent effect on those who seek to influence unconventional conflicts from external sources. Furthermore, the U.S. deterrence capacity is strengthened by a balanced capability across the conflict spectrum. Much attention has been focused on unconventional conflicts here because of the conviction that the United States has historically shown weakness in this area. Yet these types of con-flict are the most likely ones to break out for the foreseeable future. By continuing to prove its weakness in this area, the United States contributes, no matter how indirectly, to the perpetuation of ongoing unconventional conflicts and reduces the costs to those who engage in them.

Finally, the decision whether the United States should become involved in unconventional conflicts must be based on national security interests and priorities, many of which have already been identified. In sev-eral instances, U.S. national interests are best served by avoiding military involvement and security guarantees. In other instances, U.S. national interests are best served by political-psychological support and the more traditional means of assistance (weaponry and humanitarian aid) and intel-ligence operations. In any case, the United States must be prepared to respond effectively—and not necessarily with military force—if it is to strengthen its credibility to pursue national security policy across the con-flict spectrum.

Notes

1. Stephen John Stedman, "The New Interventionists," *Foreign Affairs* 72, no. 1 (1993): 4.

2. Ernest van den Haag, "The Busyness of American Policy," *Foreign Affairs* 64, no. 1 (Fall 1985): 114.

3. Colin Powell, with Joseph E. Persico, *My American Journey* (New York: Random House, 1995), p. 576.

4. Ibid., pp. 576–577.

5. See, e.g., Frederick H. Hartmann and Robert L. Wendzel, *Defending America's Security* (Washington, DC: Pergamon-Brassey's, 1988), pp. 26–38.

6. John Spanier, *American Foreign Policy Since World War II,* 11th ed. (Washington, DC: CQ Press, 1988), p. 11.

7. Chairman, Joint Chiefs of Staff, *Joint Vision 2020* (U.S. Government Printing Office, Washington, DC, June 2000), p. 8, emphasis added.

8. See, e.g., Ian Roxborough, *The Hart-Rudman Commission and the Homeland Defense* (Carlisle Barracks, PA: Strategic Studies Institute, U.S. Army War College, September 2001), and Dr. Earl H. Tilford Jr., Conference Brief, *Redefining Homeland Security* (Carlisle Barracks, PA: Strategic Studies Institute, U.S. Army War College, n.d.). This was a summary of a conference sponsored by

the Army War College and the Reserve Officers Association held on March 16, 2001.

9. At the same time, nuclear proliferation has raised the danger of nuclear war between secondary powers such as India and Pakistan.

10. Xavier Raufer, "Gray Areas: A New Security Threat," *Political Warfare: Intelligence, Active Measures, and Terrorism Report*, no. 20 (Spring 1992): 1, 4.

11. For an excellent analysis of special operations, see John M. Collins, *America's Small Wars: Lessons for the Future* (Washington, DC: Brassey's U.S., 1991).

12. Sean Naylor, "A Force to Be Reckoned With—Still," *Army Times*, July 30, 2001, p. 16.

13. Ibid.

14. Bernard Fall, *Street Without Joy: Insurgency in Indochina, 1946–1963*, 3rd rev. ed. (Harrisburg, PA: Stackpole, 1963), pp. 356–357. Fall pointed out years ago, "Just about anybody can start a 'little war' . . . even a New York street gang. Almost anybody can raid somebody else's territory, even American territory. . . . But all this has rarely produced the kind of revolutionary ground swell which simply swept away the existing system. . . . It is important to understand that guerrilla warfare is nothing but a tactical appendage of a far vaster political contest, that, no matter how expertly fought by competent and dedicated professionals, cannot make up for the absence of a political rationale."

15. Samuel B. Griffith, ed., *Mao Tse-tung on Guerrilla Warfare* (New York: Praeger, 1961), p. 7.

16. See Johns Arquilla, David Ronfeldt, and Michele Zanini, "Information-Age Terrorism," *Current History* (April 2000), p. 179.

17. Terrorism can be placed into various categories. See, e.g., Cindy Combs, *Terrorism in the Twenty-First Century*, 2nd ed. (Upper Saddle River, NJ: Prentice-Hall, 2000).

18. Most of these groups emerged from the political and social turmoil of the 1960s and 1970s in Europe and the United States. The Baader Meinhof Group came out of the radicalization of the German Socialist Student Alliance. This group focused on targets in Germany, whereas the Red Brigade operated throughout Europe. The Italian Red Brigade was responsible for the kidnapping and murder of former Italian Premier Aldo Moro in 1978. It was also responsible for the 1981 kidnapping of U.S. Army Brigadier General James Dozier, who was subsequently rescued by Italian antiterrorist units. Direct Action had its roots in France. The Symbionese Liberation Army emerged in the San Francisco area and was responsible for the kidnapping of heiress Patty Hearst, who subsequently disowned her family and supported the group until she was captured by authorities. The Weather Underground split off from Students for a Democratic Society and was responsible for terrorist operations against the U.S. government and businesses.

19. Mark Jurgensmeyer, "Understanding the New Terrorism," *Current History* (April 2000), p. 158.

20. Dennis B. Downey, "Domestic Terrorism: The Enemy Within," *Current History* (April 2000), p. 158.

21. See, e.g., Joseph R. Nunez, "Fighting the Hobbesian Trinity in Colombia: A New Strategy for Peace," in *Implementing Plan Colombia: Special Series* (Carlisle, PA: Strategic Studies Institute, U.S. Army War College, April 2001).

22. There are excellent works that provide information linking the Soviet Union to terrorism. See, e.g., Roberta Goren, *The Soviet Union and Terrorism* (Boston: George Allen and Unwin, 1982). See also Claire Sterling, *The Terror*

Network: The Secret War of International Terrorism (New York: William Abrahams/Owl Books, 1985), and Ray Cline and Yonah Alexander, *Terrorism as State-Supported Covert Warfare* (Fairfax, VA: Hero Books, 1986).

23. See, e.g., Arkady N. Shevchenko, *Breaking with Moscow* (New York: Alfred A. Knopf, 1985). Also see Andre Sakharov, "My KGB Ordeal," *U.S. News and World Report*, February 24, 1986, pp. 29–35; Humberto Belli, *Breaking Faith: The Sandinista Revolution and Its Impact on Freedom and Christian Faith in Nicaragua* (Garden City, MI: Puebla Institute and Crossway Books, 1985); and Shirley Christian, *Nicaragua: Revolution in the Family* (New York: Random House, 1985).

24. Jurgensmeyer, "Understanding the New Terrorism," p. 158.

25. See, e.g., *Selected Works of Mao Tse-tung*, abridged by Bruno Shaw (New York: Harper Colophon Books, 1970); *Che Guevara: Guerrilla Warfare*, translated by J. P. Morrya (New York: Vintage Books, 1969); General Vo Nguyen Giap, *People's War, People's Army* (Washington, DC: U.S. Government Printing Office, 1962); and *Sun Tzu: The Art of War*, translated by Samuel B. Griffith (New York: Oxford University Press, 1971). See also Hannah Arendt, *On Revolution* (New York: Viking, 1965), and Jack A. Goldstone, ed., *Revolutions: Theoretical, Comparative, and Historical Studies* (New York: Harcourt, Brace, Jovanovich, 1986).

26. Griffith, *Sun Tzu: The Art of War*. According to Griffith, "Sun Tzu's essays on the 'Art of War' form the earliest of known treatises on the subject, but never have been surpassed in comprehensiveness and depth of understanding" (from the Foreword).

27. General Bruce Palmer, *The 25-Year War: America's Military Role in Vietnam* (Lexington: University Press of Kentucky, 1984), p. 176.

28. Anthony James Joes, *America and Guerrilla Warfare* (Lexington: University of Kentucky Press, 2000), p. 3.

29. Ibid., p. 328.

30. Goren, *Soviet Union*, p. 5.

31. Arendt, *On Revolution*, p. 8.

32. For an analysis of conflicts in the third world, see Donald M. Snow, *Distant Thunder: Third World Conflict and the New International Order* (New York; St. Martin's, 1993). For an analysis of such conflicts in the twenty-first century, see J. Bowyer Bell, *Dragon Wars: Armed Struggle and the Conventions of Modern War* (New Brunswick, NJ: Transaction, 1999).

33. See, e.g., Sam C. Sarkesian, *Unconventional Conflicts in a New Security Era: Lessons from Malaya and Vietnam* (Westport, CT: Greenwood, 1993).

34. *Public Papers of the Presidents of the United States: Containing the Public Messages, Speeches, and Statements of the President, John F. Kennedy, 1962* (Washington, DC: U.S. Government Printing Office, 1963), p. 454.

35. Jean-Francois Revel, *How Democracies Perish* (New York: Harper and Row, 1984), p. 7.

4

The U.S. Political System

DURING THE 1830s, FRENCHMAN ALEXIS DE TOCQUEVILLE TRAV-
eled throughout the United States observing its people and their government. He had much good to say about the new democracy. But he also
noted some problems with the way the government conducted foreign
affairs: "Foreign policy," he wrote, "does not require the use of any of the
good qualities peculiar to democracy, but does demand the cultivation of
almost all of those which it lacks."[1]

De Tocqueville's observations remain applicable; indeed, in the area of
security policy today they are even more relevant. Democracies lack many
of the qualities required to cultivate and maintain an effective national
security posture; the very nature of democracies works against defense
issues and the strategies required for long-range success. The long-term
U.S. response to the September 11 terrorist attacks, the worst ever on
homeland soil, will be a test of national will, staying power, and political
resolve. As de Tocqueville noted in the case of foreign policy: "Democracy
finds it difficult to coordinate the details of a great undertaking and to fix
on some plan and carry it through with determination in spite of
obstacles."[2] This is especially true when such plans require some degree of
secrecy.

In the twenty-first century, the United States and other democracies
face threats of international terrorism, unconventional conflicts, and a variety of contingencies short of war. At the same time, surfacing ethnic rivalries, religious conflict, and hypernationalism elsewhere promise to further
complicate the new security landscape. Whereas some analysts argue that
little has changed in the international conflict environment since 1989, others contend that much has changed; the threat of a world war between
major powers has diminished, and the likelihood of global conflict seems
remote. But there are always regional and unconventional conflicts, mostly
in the less developed world.[3]

In addition, so-called asymmetrical wars now characterize the conflict environment. Given its past experience and the nature of its political system and values, the United States finds the new strategic environment to be difficult, except in terms of conventional response, strategic deterrence, and high-tech warfare, but September 11 changed many perspectives on national security. Events now require the strategy and doctrinal wherewithal to mount an effective campaign against international terrorism.

This is not to deny earlier attention to information warfare and conflicts short of war (see Chapter 3). However, most of the threats and challenges are not clear or immediate threats to the country. Except in clear cases of national interests, the nature of open systems weighs against the effective conduct of national security policy, the implementation of which rests on military missions except in clear cases of national interests.

Why is this so? Why is it that the democratic United States finds it difficult to respond to the variety of threats to its national interests except in clear cases of overt aggression? Although the international setting and the very nature of national security are part of the explanation, much of the problem rests with the nature and character of democracy and open systems.

American Democratic Principles

Much has been written about the meaning of democracy and its variations as practiced in the United States and the Western world. Serious philosophical studies have also examined the evolution of democracy as an ideology and as political doctrine. A thorough analysis of democracy and the concept of open systems would require a lengthy study of those works, but the purpose here is more modest: to touch on critical features of democracy as they pertain to national security. Initially, we need to develop some sense of the meaning of democracy, for it is in that context that national security policy is made.

The fundamental proposition here is that democracy does not adhere to a dogmatic ideological philosophy. Indeed, one of the most pervasive features of democracy is its pluralistic and pragmatic basis. Democracy is rooted in the idea of political tolerance for many views—even extreme views—as long as they include the notion of political equality, self-determination, and individual worth and do not foreclose the possibility of future peaceful political change. Although many disagree on the specific application of these concepts, there are legitimate and historical bases for assessing the nature and credibility of a political system. Finally, the legitimacy of a system and its leaders rests on the will of the people, a basic tenet to the U.S. Constitution and the functioning of the U.S. political system. Put simply, the way the system functions, expectations regarding elected officials, and the purposes of the system must reflect the notion of government responsibility and accountability to the people.

To be sure, the U.S. political system is not perfect. And while most of the public recognizes the imperfections, it also sees the merits, as did de Tocqueville: "The vices and weaknesses of democratic governments are easy to see . . . but its good qualities are revealed only in the long run. . . . The real advantage of democracy is not . . . to favor prosperity for all, but only to serve the well-being of the greatest number."[4] Democracy may not be the most efficient system or type of government (indeed, the Founders went to great effort to prevent government from being *too* efficient), but it is, in the long run, the best when compared to all others.

If we accept the view of some observers, faith in democracy has become even more confusing and fragmented by what one can call "cultural amnesia. . . . What happened before doesn't matter; the past is no longer prologue—it is irrelevant."[5] Moreover, in the new era multiculturalism and diversity politics and their politicization complicate the shaping and nurturing of democratic institutions.

We believe that regardless of what contemporary surveys and polls show, there are fundamental principles at the root of the democratic faith that have lasted for centuries and are engrained in the American psyche and, indeed, in part of the international order. September 11 may well have reinforced such beliefs.

This brief description of the nature of U.S. democracy does not do justice to the rich literature and wide-ranging philosophical studies on the subject. But our observations provide a starting point for an analysis of democracy's relationship to national security. Traditionally there are three fundamental characteristics of democracies that are relevant to the study of national security: the distribution of power, the democratic faith, and the messianic spirit.

Power Distribution

The pluralistic nature of the U.S. system institutionalizes the diffusion of political power. This builds into the political system a need for compromise while creating an environment for power struggles among the various branches of government, within the bureaucracy, and among groups in society. Power struggles can be especially severe in cases of foreign and national security policies because the issues involve vital interests and U.S. values that are at the core of differences of political opinion in the United States. Institutionalized confrontation—the product of separation of powers—is epitomized by the struggles between the president and Congress and can become especially contentious when each branch is controlled by a different political party.

This was generally the case until the election of Bill Clinton as president in 1992. With that election, the Democratic Party gained control of the Oval Office for the first time in twelve years. The Democratic Party controlled not only the presidency and Congress but also the majority of state houses and governorships. However, this did not necessarily mean that President Clinton had an easy time of it in Congress, as shown in the difficulty he had in passing a budget package in 1993 as well as problems in his own party over health care reform, the North American Free Trade Agreement (NAFTA), changes in the military budget and force restructuring, and the nomination of a secretary of defense. Clinton's problems increased in 1994, when the Republican Party gained control of Congress as well as the majority of governorships. This balance of political power continued until the election of President George W. Bush in 2000, although this changed in 2001 when a Republican senator became an Independent and handed control of the Senate to the Democrats (the House of Representatives remained with the GOP). The attempted impeachment of President Clinton in the House and subsequent battles over foreign and domestic policy were clear examples of presidential-congressional power struggles (see Chapter 5).

But even when one party controls the Oval Office and Congress, there are likely to be disagreements. The unity within Congress and its support of President Bush in the aftermath of September 11 was a response to the new threat to the U.S. homeland. But the normal state of affairs in Congress and between Congress and the president is characterized more by debate and disagreement.

Over history, efforts by Congress to reassert itself in the making and implementation of foreign and national security policy have led to many confrontations with the executive. There are many examples: the War Powers Resolution of 1973 among other things attempted to limit and constrain the intelligence community; new initiatives with respect to Cuba; the U.S.-China relationship; the U.S.-Russian relationships; and ongoing battles over the defense budget, military force restructuring, and the commitment of the U.S. military to OOTW. These issues remain unresolved, and so the likelihood of continuing presidential-congressional confrontations remains high.

These congressional efforts to control foreign and national security policy led some to label it the "Imperial Congress."

> As America begins its third century under the Constitution, presidents might wish the framers had been less concerned with checks and balances in the area of national security. In recent years Congress has challenged

presidents on all fronts, including foreign aid; arms sales; the development, procurement, and deployment of weapons systems; the negotiation and interpretation of treaties; the selection of diplomats; and the continuation of nuclear testing.[6]

However, the "imperial" label has become questionable, as members on both sides of the aisle struggle *within* Congress over the parties' agendas, and presidents can use the veto as a major bargaining tool with Congress. The major exception is the response in the aftermath of September 11, a unity that shows signs of cracking.

During the Clinton administration, battles with the Republican-controlled Congress were numerous and often rancorous. These included U.S. force deployment in Somalia in 1993 and 1994, Bosnia-Herzegovina in 1995, and Kosovo in 1999. In 2000, the last full year of the Clinton administration, executive-legislative struggles sharpened over National Missile Defense (NMD, the latest iteration of President Ronald Reagan's "Star Wars" initiative in the early 1980s), as well as U.S. relationships with the Russian Federation, China, and Cuba. They remained unresolved during the first years of the George W. Bush administration.

The stage thus remains set for continuing power struggles between the president and Congress. In the first months of his administration, George W. Bush faced struggles over his tax-cut plan (although it passed and was considered a victory for the president) and NMD. The fact that President Bush placed experienced individuals at the helm of foreign and defense policy may make a difference; Secretary of State Colin Powell, Secretary of Defense Donald Rumsfeld, and National Security Advisor Condoleezza Rice have extensive experience in previous administrations.

Regardless of the inherent struggles, the fact is that the president has the lead role in foreign policy and national security, and the greatest source of presidential power is found in politics and public opinion, not the Constitution.

> Increasingly since the 1930s, Congress has passed laws that confer on the executive branch grants of authority to achieve some general goals, leaving up to the president and his deputies to define the regulations and programs that will actually be put into effect. Moreover, the American people look to the president—always in time of crisis, but increasingly as an everyday matter—for leadership and hold him responsible for a large and growing portion of our national affairs.[7]

Nonetheless, in the long term (the united front against international terrorism notwithstanding) the president faces many difficult problems in both foreign and national security policies, a consequence of the new security landscape. Although these problems are shaped by threats short of a major war, they remain relevant to U.S. national interests. Moreover, successful national security policy could necessitate a judicious use of nonmilitary instruments and covert operations. This requires especially effective presidential leadership in developing consensus at home for the necessity of a particular policy—a difficult prospect without bipartisan support in Congress.

This institutionalized confrontation stems partly from the sharing of power. The popular notion that the U.S. government has three separate branches with distinct powers has a corollary: the branches also share power, which allows each to influence and intervene in the affairs of one or the other, giving rise to important constitutional questions and different interpretations regarding the proper exercise of power. The U.S. Supreme Court's tipping of the scales in the 2000 presidential election (a sharply divided Court ruled in favor of Republican George W. Bush and against Democrat Al Gore in a case originating in Florida) is a prime example.

Problems of control and responsibility evolving from power-sharing is increased by the decentralization of power among the various branches of government as well as within each branch. Within the executive branch, there is usually a continuing struggle between the Departments of State and Defense, as well as between the Central Intelligence Agency (CIA) and other agencies. For example, during the Clinton presidency, problems between the Justice Department and the Federal Bureau of Investigation became well publicized. The Iran-contra hearings during the Reagan administration illuminated the conflicts between the president's national security staff and various departments. Similarly, struggles occur within Congress among various power bases: committee chairs, caucus leaders, and individual members. Combined with the two-party system, such struggles create and nurture institutional power plays, and the U.S. federal system of government adds to the fragmentation. Partisan control and party machines at the state level add yet another dimension to the power equation at the national level.

Historically only the president has been considered the legal spokesman of the United States in the international arena. However, the president does not have a monopoly of power to carry out policy, especially in today's environment. The very nature of the U.S. system creates checks and balances that can frustrate any policy and strategy. The nature of power in the U.S. system generally favors those who support mainstream policies and oppose major changes to the status quo. It goes without saying that a majority of the public is probably most comfortable with mainstream politicians who focus on bread-and-butter domestic issues.

The Democratic Faith

A historical thread running through U.S. democracy is the commitment to the free market of ideas within the body politic and the various branches of government. This supports the notion of a free press and reinforces decentralization, diffusion, and power-sharing. Linked closely to pluralism and nondogmatic philosophies, the free play of ideas is supposed to lead to the truth.

An informed and educated citizenry is essential to democracy. The citizenry must have access to information in order to exercise the will of the people and to assess the performance of government. It is a basic belief that an educated citizenry can overcome any obstacles to the functioning of democracy. This Jeffersonian notion—that information and education lead to an enlightened public—also reflects a belief in the innate goodness of people and their sense of justice; enlightened people are sure to act wisely and justly.

Pragmatism is another ingredient of the democratic faith. This is the belief that the search for practical consequences based on common sense are natural results of an enlightened citizenry. Once problems are encountered, Americans, applying their God-given common sense, can find reasonable solutions. This can-do attitude pervades most segments of U.S. society.

Finally, an important part of the democratic faith is the belief that the U.S. system is the best of all choices despite its imperfections. The U.S. public prides itself on the fact that Americans are a decent people living in a decent society. The concern with the quality of life at the community level has a parallel with the concern with individual well-being. This is not to suggest that the culture is devoid of prejudice and narrow-mindedness, but a constant in U.S. society is our concern for the individual and continuing efforts to rectify past and prevailing injustices. This is reflected in the way that the government functions and is embodied in the U.S. Constitution. Accordingly, the concern with individualism and quality of life—shaped by the political system and reflected in the goals of our democratic ideology—brings out the best in individuals and serves them best.

Multiculturalism and Cultural Diversity

The modern United States has its roots in the immigrant society. Since the 1960s, changing immigration patterns have effected U.S. society. Today, many immigrants are from the Southern Hemisphere and the Far East rather than from Europe, as was the case for decades. They bring a culture that differs from Anglo-Saxon and Western traditions, yet the United States has not become the great melting-pot of historical rhetoric. Rather, it is a system in which each culture and language exists within the broader scheme of Americanism, regardless of how imperfect the effort. The motto on U.S. currency—*E pluribus unum*, or "One out of many"—expresses this sentiment.

Efforts have been made to promote cultural diversity and gender equality, especially in institutions of higher education. To be sure, cultural diversity lends a uniqueness, richness, and strength to the notion of Americanism. But for any number of Americans the fear is that multiculturalism can be taken to such extremes that the concept of Americanism is eroded and lost in the maze of cultural diversity, politicization, and polarization. There is also a fear that cultural diversity will bring cultural confrontation and the continuation of age-old animosities that spill over from foreign homelands. This is complicated by the fact that some cultural precepts are difficult to change, limiting assimilation into mainstream America.

Yet assimilation into mainstream America has been the backbone of the immigrant society. This was based not on destroying old cultures but on learning the English language and understanding the meaning of U.S. citizenship, heritage, and culture. Such an approach placed values and the system above any particular culture. It was best expressed by President Franklin Roosevelt, who in the midst of World War II was said to have stated that "Americanism is a matter of heart and mind. Americanism is not a matter of race or ethnicity." But now concern is often expressed over the label "our people," used in reference to a specific ethnic or racial group, not to Americans as a people. How all of this will play out in the next decades is unclear; how it will shape U.S. values and national security is unclear.

The Messianic Spirit

Throughout U.S. history, religion has been an important component in shaping national values and in reinforcing the messianic spirit. This is seen in the view, held by many, that the United States as the leader of the West must be a moral as well as political-military leader and that moral principles must guide the behavior of governmental officials and the military. Although some feel that religion has no place in a secular democratic system, history suggests otherwise. The messianic spirit is reinforced by the historic role religion has played in the evolution of the U.S. system.

> Viewed against the backdrop of history, the recent rise in political activism among some religious groups is not a departure from national tradition but only the renewal of a long-standing pattern in American political life. . . . Religion was present at the creation of the American political system, and was one of several elements contributing to the design of the governmental institutions and to the core beliefs that grew into national political culture.[8]

For many Americans, the logical extension of this belief from the individual to the political results in a messianic spirit—the notion that

Americans and the political system are ordained to be "the light" for other nations, lending moral weight to the notion of democratic faith.

The Impact on National Security

These considerations—power distribution, democratic faith, and the messianic spirit—create contradictory forces. On the one hand, they strengthen the U.S. ability to respond to national security challenges. On the other hand, they reveal weaknesses and disadvantages, especially if multiculturalism detracts from national unity.

The power distribution that is characteristic of the U.S. political system provides a basis for its legitimacy and precludes a centralized power base from forming in any one branch or individual. Furthermore, it allows inputs from many interest groups, people, and elected officials—the foundation of representative government. The strength created by this base of power makes the U.S. political system and government resilient, capable of responding to mistakes, problems, and failures in a fashion not easily matched by other systems.

In developing national security policy, the president faces many constituencies and must initiate a political strategy to build a consensus throughout the political system. This makes it difficult to design new policies and strategies or ones that appear to challenge the prevailing democratic faith. Furthermore, maintaining a degree of secrecy and yet operating within traditional democratic parameters requires delicate maneuvering; covert operations, for example, tend to be perceived as undemocratic. But the need to respond to unconventional conflicts and terrorism may require these very activities. This view is not universally shared, however. Former U.S. senator Daniel Patrick Moynihan argues that there is little need for secrecy in a democracy.[9] The three fundamental characteristics of democracies relevant to the study of national security are repeated for this discussion: the distribution of power, the democratic faith, and the messianic spirit.

The Distribution of Power

The way power is distributed creates a condition in which those responsible for foreign affairs and national security do not control all the structures and resources to carry out policies and strategies. The exception, of course, is when the United States faces serious threats to its existence, as on September 11. Matters of foreign affairs and national security are susceptible to political opposition within the government and public, bureaucratic foot-dragging, policy distortions, and opposition. Foreign powers may see such internal U.S. political struggles as vacillation, weakness, and divisiveness. This has become even more complicated as information-age technology opens up the system and foreign governments, nongovernmental organizations, business corporations, and individuals gain access to policy issues that formerly existed within the closed realm of the bureaucratic establishment.

In the process of trying to fulfill their responsibilities, members of Congress and officials in the executive branch can inadvertently serve the purposes of adversaries. The same is true with respect to interest groups, the media, and other segments of the public. For example, during the Nicaraguan conflict in 1984, key members of the Democratic-controlled House, including the Speaker of the House, sent a special message to "Commandante Daniel Ortega, Managua, Nicaragua," supporting his efforts against the U.S.-supported freedom fighters.[10] Later, the election of Violeta Barrios de Chamorro and the defeat of the Sandinistas in that election seemed to underscore congressional misjudgments. In addition, during the Iran-contra hearings in 1987, indications were that certain members of Congress had used their official stationery to support groups sympathetic to the Sandinista regime, in direct opposition to publicly stated U.S. policy.

In another example, a noted expert documents the fact that a 1978 report issued by the House Intelligence Committee regarding Soviet active measures deleted references to important aspects of a World Peace Council meeting attended by some members of Congress. The same report deleted important facts revealed by the hearings. The World Peace Council had been identified as "the major Soviet-controlled international front organization with headquarters in Helsinki."[11] Interestingly, Representative Edward P. Boland presided over the committee hearings and made a public statement denying Soviet involvement in the nuclear freeze movement. "His statement received the widest national publicity," which was not in accord with the official record; however, "even those who do read the entire record of the hearing still will be denied certain facts because the House Committee under Chairman Boland withheld them."[12] Boland also initiated the Boland Amendment prohibiting U.S. aid to the groups fighting the Sandinista government in Nicaragua, which was a bone of contention in the 1987 Iran-contra hearings. And in the George W. Bush administration, debate and controversy continued over China and Taiwan, NATO enlargement, NMD, and relations with Russia over its use of force in Chechnya. These issues provided ample opportunity for criticizing U.S. proposals and policy.

But such activities do not rest solely with Congress; presidents also attempt to maintain a degree of secrecy in matters of national security. The

Iran-contra affair (whereby the administration was trying to trade arms for hostages) was but one example. In the Nixon administration, much of the conduct of foreign and national security policy was cloaked in secrecy. In fact,

> the administration was predisposed toward a secretive policy by its distrust of the State Department and intelligence community, by the convoluted personalities of its leaders, and by its belief that certain of its goals required extreme confidentiality and centralized direction of policy in the White House.[13]

In the latter part of the Reagan administration, William Casey, Director of Central Intelligence, was renowned for his efforts to limit any information to Congress, even if it was unclassified. Casey

> had developed nonresponsiveness to oversight into an art form. The Senate Select Committee on Intelligence had even built a special amplifying system into its bug-proof hearing room in an effort to make Casey's muttering intelligible. What the senators did not realize was that, when he wanted to be understood, Casey spoke as clearly as John F. Kennedy. That kind of arrogance had gotten the agency involved in the Iran-contra mess in the first place.[14]

During the George Bush administration, some members of Congress decried the secrecy surrounding weapons deliveries, among other efforts, to Iraq shortly before that country invaded Kuwait. And a continuing chorus of criticism surfaced in 1994 as to the Clinton administration's conduct of foreign and national security policy. Although such criticism had been voiced earlier during the Clinton administration, the catalyst for this round was the spy scandal involving a career CIA officer, Aldrich Ames, who passed along classified information to the Soviet Union and later to Russia.[15]

Serious questions were also raised about President Clinton's friendship with Russian President Boris Yeltsin and U.S. foreign aid to Russia. Earlier, criticism was directed at Clinton for his vacillation on Haiti, Bosnia-Herzegovina, and North Korea. Near the end of his second term in 2000, Clinton was also criticized by some in Congress for his lukewarm support of NMD. Clinton ultimately chose to defer the decision whether to deploy NMD to the next administration.

These are some examples of the continuing struggle between Congress and the president over national security policy. In this context, it is not unusual for the president to go to extraordinary lengths to develop support for administration policy and strategy. However, proposed changes to the existing order, especially changes that promise to be innovative, involve some degree of political risk, both domestically and internationally.

Furthermore, attempts at change invite the exercise of power by others to frustrate or blunt the initiatives. This leads to the conclusion that the safest political course is to maintain existing policy and strategy and seek only incremental changes to dilute the exercise of power by those outside the Oval Office. Otherwise, a president who seeks new directions must be prepared to deal with a variety of power centers that can seriously challenge his authority. Again, international terrorism might require covert operations and a higher degree of secrecy.

There are exceptions to this generalization, of course. Nixon's détente with China was a distinct change in policy that carried national security overtones, yet it received universal acclaim. In addition, after President Carter's ill-fated attempt to impose human rights criteria upon national security and foreign policy, President Reagan won praise for changing the course of the Cold War by first denouncing the Soviet Union as an "Evil Empire," then fostering a cordial relationship with Mikhail Gorbachev, the leader of the Soviet Union. In the new era, George W. Bush's speech to a joint session of Congress in the aftermath of September 11 won high praise. He spelled out a strategic course of action that was supported by a great majority of the U.S. public.

Secret diplomacy, the purpose of which is a major change in policy and strategic direction, carries great political risks. And unless the effort has an immediate, positive impact on U.S. ability to protect vital interests—and is perceived as such by the public—then the various power clusters are likely to diminish any chance for success. Even the militarily successful operations in Grenada (1983), Panama (1989–1990), and the Persian Gulf (1990–1991) had their share of critics; less successful missions such as Somalia (1993) and Haiti (1998) came under harsher criticism, not only from Republicans in Congress but also from Democratic rank-and-file and the general public.

These are but a few examples of how congressional agendas, oversight, and power plays can highlight or restrict information according to the interests of politicians—sometimes to the detriment of publicly proclaimed U.S. policy. Congressional maneuvering, however, does not start and end with any single presidential administration.

The Democratic Faith

The democratic faith creates similar dilemmas. On the one hand, the country's commitment to individual worth, justice, and fairness strengthens the credibility of its policy and strategy; it also taps a wellspring of support from the public. On the other hand, the same commitment makes it difficult to address national security issues that require the use of force or temporary alliances with nondemocratic systems (e.g., Saudi Arabia), although these may be necessary in responding to terrorism and unconventional conflicts. Those types of conflicts invariably encompass the political-social structure and make the population at large combatants whether they like it or not. Moreover, involvement in unconventional conflicts requires interjecting U.S. political-military forces into the political-social milieu of other countries, few of which may be democratic in the Western sense. The United States often has few options other than to support the lesser of evils, but relations with regimes that violate human rights run counter to U.S. morals and foster divisiveness within our political system.

The premise that we know best—part of the democratic faith—makes it difficult for many to establish realistic perspectives on the motivation and nationalistic aspirations of other peoples. Madeleine Albright, secretary of state during the Clinton administration, was quoted as saying, "If we have to use force, it is because we are America. We are the indispensable nation. We stand tall. We see further into the future."[16]

Many Americans, perhaps adopting the American Revolution as the frame of reference for all revolutions, thus fail to realize that contemporary revolutions evolve out of considerably different circumstances. The presumption that revolutions ultimately lead to democratic systems also reflects the view that the American Revolution represents the path that others should follow.

The openness of U.S. affairs, even on the most sensitive issues, provides an opportunity for adversaries to use the media as a strategic asset to further their own cause. In the twenty-first century, the access to technology offers even greater opportunity for this information-age strategy. This includes attempting to sway public opinion and elected officials and to support sympathetic interest groups. In addition, the level of debate within the system itself can send the wrong signals to adversaries regarding our political will. If adversaries incorrectly read the U.S. policy posture, it could lead to dangerous strategic choices that could force a U.S. military response.

Still, the U.S. public's commitment to the democratic faith remains a pillar of the system, an inherent strength that provides the endurance to prevail over the long haul. Although the democratic faith may not ensure success in every venture, especially in the short term, it minimizes the impact of failure as well as the formulation of unjust policies and strategies.

The Messianic Spirit

The messianic spirit pervading U.S. political culture also has strengths and weaknesses. The concern with moral and ethical issues evolving from our Judeo-Christian heritage provides strength in dealing with national security issues because its humanistic orientation strikes a sensitive chord that is beneficial to U.S. policy and strategy. The downside is that the belief in our messianic mission causes many foreign states and peoples to perceive us as self-righteous, arrogant; we ignore other cultures in trying to rule the world. Some countries, especially those in the less developed world and, increasingly, some in Europe, see this as imperialistic, further fueling anti-U.S. sentiment. At the very least, U.S. moral and ethical views can be disturbing to hundreds of millions of people, including many populations in geostrategically important areas whose heritage is not Judeo-Christian.[17] This provides ample opportunity for U.S. adversaries to take advantage of differences between Americans and other people.

National Security in a Democracy

De Tocqueville's assessment of democracy's ability to conduct foreign policy is especially relevant to U.S. national security policy today. The U.S. political system is not well suited to timely and thorough development of policy and strategy to create the most effective national security policy; in many ways the U.S. system responds only at the last minute. This is not to say that policy and strategy have not been developed and implemented in a deliberate timely way, but that generally occurs when the security issues are clear, the adversary is identifiable, and general support exists within government and the general public. Unfortunately, many serious threats to U.S. national security do not adhere to this optimistic view; the short-term threat to vital U.S. interests is not always easy to comprehend, even though we may be threatened in the long run.

The real issue, then, is how to reconcile the demands of national security with those of democracy. There are trade-offs, to be sure, but how should one balance the protection of democracy and U.S. values, on the one hand, with the threats to national security that are not amenable to democratic processes and principles? U.S. national security policy and process are bound by all the forces and power clusters characteristic of the U.S. political system, and most Americans expect the government to conform to democratic proprieties. Yet if success is to be achieved, something must give if the goal is to further democracy. This is not to suggest that the United States should design conspiratorial policies that seriously undercut moral principles and tenets. But to assume that the United States must not engage in secret or covert operations in support of its national interests is a journey through the Looking Glass. Furthermore, to presume that such initiatives cannot be undertaken in our governmental system is a simplistic misreading of the nature and character of that system. Moreover, the simplistic argument that political ends can never justify covert means precludes a nuanced and calibrated approach to subtle and complex security dilemmas. Laws and procedures are ambiguous, and policies and strategies are shaped by power struggles within the U.S. government.[18] That is the pragmatic truth of the system. Put differently,

> if the current trends continue, the [United States] will not be the pre-eminent economic or military actor in the twenty-first-century international affairs. It will not exercise global leadership or hegemony in the West, and possibly not even unchallenged hegemony in the Americas. The programme to establish a "New World Order" will have failed, if it has not already. . . . Social polarisation may lead to increased class tensions and conflict between cultural groups and to more civil disorder. Geographical zoning may reflect social and cultural distinctions and economic differences.[19]

Although this book focuses on policy and process, our study must be pursued in the context of the U.S. political culture. Those involved in designing policy and exercising power to influence the approval process operate within that context. To examine policy and process separate from U.S. political culture is not only sterile; it is likely to distort the nature of policymaking and the character of the approval process.

With all the disadvantages open systems face in their dealings with authoritarian systems, rogue regimes, and international terrorists, in the long run democracy has the advantage. The involvement of people in the governing process, their ability to freely voice their views, and the ultimate responsibility of those in office to the people establish stability, legitimacy, and capability like no other system. Therein lies the true strength of open systems: little can prevail against the strength of people who, having examined and debated the issues, are convinced of the right policy and strategy.[20]

In Part Two, we examine the institutions, offices, and individuals involved in policymaking. Similarly, we look at nongovernmental groups, the media, and the U.S. public regarding their respective roles in national security policy and the policy approval process.

Notes

1. Alexis de Tocqueville, *Democracy in America*, ed. J. P. Mayer, trans. George Lawrence (Garden City, NY: Anchor Books, 1969), pp. 228–229.

2. Ibid.

3. See Donald M. Snow, *Distant Thunder: Third World Conflict and the New International Order* (New York: St. Martin's, 1993). Also see J. Bowyer Bell, *Dragonwars: Armed Struggle and the Conventions of Modern War* (New Brunswick, NJ: Transaction, 1999).

4. de Tocqueville, *Democracy in America*, p. 233.

5. Bob Greene, "You Must Remember This (Unless You Don't)," *Chicago Tribune*, Sunday, April 9, 2000, sec. 1, p. 2.

6. Robert L. Lineberry, George C. Edwards III, and Martin P. Wattenberg, *Government in America: People, Politics, and Policy,* brief ed. (New York: Harper Collins, 1993), p. 306.

7. James Q. Wilson, *American Government: Institutions and Policies*, 5th ed. (Lexington, MA: D. C. Heath, 1992), p. 328–329.

8. Kenneth D. Wald, *Religion and Politics in the United States*, 2nd ed. (Washington, DC: CQ Press, 1992), p. 338.

9. Daniel Patrick Moynihan, *Secrecy: The American Experience* (New Haven: Yale University Press, 1998).

10. "Ten Congressmen Send a Message to Managua," *Wall Street Journal*, April 17, 1984, p. 1.

11. John Barron, *KGB Today: The Hidden Hand* (New York: Berkley Books, 1985), p. 244.

12. Ibid.

13. Terry L. Deibel, "National Strategy and the Continuity of National Interests," in James C. Gaston, *Grand Strategy and the Decisionmaking Process* (Washington, DC: National Defense University Press, 1992), p. 48.

14. Ronald Kessler, *Inside the CIA: Revealing the Secrets of the World's Most Powerful Spy Agency* (New York: Pocket Books, 1992), p. xxv.

15. See, e.g., Sam Vincent Meddis, "CIA Officer Charged as Spy," *USA Today*, February 23, 1994, pp. 1A, 3A, and a variety of TV news reports during the same week.

16. Ray Mosley, "What Went Wrong with Pax Americana," *Chicago Tribune*, February 22, 1998, Perspectives, p. 1.

17. See, e.g., Samuel P. Huntington, *The Clash of Civilizations and the Remaking of World Order* (New York: Simon and Schuster, 1999).

18. For example, Daniel Hellinger and Dennis R. Judd in *Democracy for the Few* (Belmont, CA: Wadsworth, 1993), offer a simplistic and ideological spin to their study. People like the authors seem to presume that democratic systems such as the United States do not have the right to defend themselves with all of the power at their command. What weakens their volume considerably is its lack of a comparative basis and its themes resting on unequivocal assumptions of elite rule—assumptions discredited in much of the literature.

19. K. R. Dark, with A. L. Harris, *The New World and the New World Order: U.S. Relative Decline, Domestic Instability in the Americas, and the End of the Cold War* (New York: St. Martin's, 1996), p. 144.

20. See de Tocqueville, *Democracy in America*, p. 244. For a well-reasoned view of the challenges facing democracy, see Jean-Francois Revel, *How Democracies Perish* (New York: Harper and Row, 1984).

PART 2

The National Security Establishment

5

The President
and the Presidency

SEVERAL YEARS AFTER HE LEFT OFFICE, PRESIDENT LYNDON JOHNSON
wrote, "No one can experience with the President of the United States the
glory and agony of his office. No one can share the majestic view from his
pinnacle of power. No one can share the burden of his decisions or the
scope of his duties."[1] Not only did Johnson capture the essence of the presidency with these few words; he put his finger on the reason why it is so difficult for others to comprehend the power and responsibilities of the position. Thus in studying the president and the presidency we must exercise
caution regarding the many relevant perspectives and recognize the considerable disagreement over the power, limits, and responsibilities of the
office, as well as the characteristics of the most effective type of executive.

All these factors make it especially difficult to develop a sense of the
presidential role in national security, except in cases of serious threats to
our national interests, as on September 11. As we saw in Chapters 1–4,
security policy is complex, and when studying the president and national
security policy it must be understood that issues and problems are usually
linked to domestic issues. This makes it difficult to isolate national security
policy from other policy issues under the president's authority and control.
During the Cold War, with its enormous problems related to nuclear
weapons and superpower conflicts, national security issues took on a
dimension rarely known in the past. In the twenty-first century, the problem
of weapons of mass-destruction (WMD) remains, but the possibility of
world wars between major powers has diminished considerably. The end of
the superpower era has brought with it a tendency for the U.S. public to
focus on domestic issues, but that does not make it any easier for the president because the world remains a dangerous place: the many conflicts in
progress, including international terrorism, within the changing strategic
landscape create a host of new challenges for national security policy.

Another important factor is Congress, which has asserted itself in the foreign and national security policy process. But with the inauguration of Bill Clinton as president in 1993, the view of many members of Congress was that given the end of the Cold War domestic issues should have priority over national security. Although the Clinton administration came into power in 1993 with Congress in the hands of the Democratic Party, the 1994 congressional elections swept the Republican Party into power with control of both houses of Congress. This continued throughout the Clinton administration and created a different atmosphere in congressional-executive relationships. It also ushered in growing partisanship over domestic policy as well as foreign and national security policy. Yet it is ironic that the responsibilities of the president in national security have become more complex even while the power of the office to make and implement decisions has become increasingly difficult, mainly due to the countervailing power of Congress and the unsettled international landscape. The impact of September 11 changed all this, at least in terms of a unified counterterrorism effort.

In the 1980s, one author had this to say about presidential power, which is relevant today:

> Presidential power may be greater today than ever before . . . it is misleading, however, to infer from a president's capacity to begin a nuclear war that the chief executive has similar power in most policy-making areas. . . . Presidents who want to be effective in implementing policy changes know they face a number of constraints.[2]

Although the primary purpose in this chapter is to study the president and the presidency in terms of national security policy, this cannot be done without an understanding of the nature of the office. Below we identify some benchmarks that help define the Oval Office and its occupant, with particular reference to national security in the contemporary period.

Evolution of the Office: An Overview

Political struggles over the nature of the presidential office are part of U.S. history; indeed, the disagreements began with the Constitutional Convention and the founding of the nation. During the convention some delegates considered establishing a monarchy; others favored multiple executives; still others thought that the president should be chosen by Congress rather than the people. What resulted was a series of compromises leading to the establishment of the basic structure as we know it today. The acceptance of a single executive and its powers were, in no small way, influenced by the fact that most delegates used George Washington as the model.

Washington won admiration for his fairness, honesty, and integrity, as well as his leadership in the battlefield in the drive for U.S. independence. He seemed to stand above politics. For most delegates, Washington epitomized what a president should be and the role he should fulfill. Yet upon assuming the presidency, Washington commented that he felt not unlike a "culprit who is going to the place of his execution." Other presidents have had similar feelings upon assuming office. William Howard Taft thought it was the "loneliest place in the world"; Warren Harding referred to the White House as a "prison"; Harry Truman declared that being president was "like riding a tiger. A man has to keep riding or be swallowed."

Whereas most who have held the office have commented on its demands and problems, some aggressively tried to expand its power. George Washington, Andrew Jackson, Abraham Lincoln, Theodore Roosevelt, Woodrow Wilson, and Franklin Roosevelt used their presidential powers extensively and actively, and their incumbencies are usually identified as "strong" or "expansionist" periods of the presidency. In the modern period, Truman and Ronald Reagan have been identified by several scholars as men who actively used their office to expand the scope of presidential power—even though each represented a different political party and philosophy. This was also true with respect to the Clinton presidency. Ironically, "Bill Clinton surprisingly retained and even gained popularity the longer he was in office. Indeed, the more personal trouble Clinton got into, the more his public approval ratings went up—even after he was impeached by the U.S. House of Representatives."[3]

It is paradoxical that the presidency, even though it was fashioned by men who had a deep mistrust of executive power, has become the focal point of national politics and the center of the national policy process. The president is the only nationally elected public official, and he is usually the most recognized public leader in the country, often referred to as the "leader of the free world." Yet the president depends on many other political actors to accomplish his political goals and implement policy. Although he has the power, for example, to order a worldwide alert of U.S. armed forces and the deployment of the military, he can meet overwhelming resistance in simply trying to remove a controversial bureaucrat from office or gain the approval of a Supreme Court nominee. He can submit programs to Congress, but he cannot allocate money to them without congressional approval. Truman identified this anomaly when discussing the problems his successor in office, Dwight Eisenhower, would face upon moving into the Oval Office: "He'll sit here [tapping his desk], and he'll say, 'Do this! Do that!' And nothing will happen. Poor Ike; it won't be a bit like the army. He'll find it very frustrating."[4]

The frustration is compounded by struggles between the executive and legislative branches of government over presidential authority and initiative—a conflict especially visible in national security policy. For example, the 1987 Iran-contra hearings, although focusing on covert operations and illegal transfers of funds, were at their core a struggle over presidential power and congressional attempts to control that power. This was also seen in the confrontation between President Clinton and Congress over committing the U.S. military to Haiti, Somalia, Bosnia-Herzegovina, and Kosovo. The same problem developed regarding the use of the U.S. military to support the Colombian government against the drug cartel–revolutionary coalition. Clearly, in responding to serious threats, the president is accorded almost absolute power, but the point is that today the line is fuzzy as to what the president can and cannot do in foreign and national security policy (excepting, of course, clear threats to U.S. interests).

The extent of presidential power is not determined solely by legal grants of power, by the Constitution, or necessarily by political skill. Traditions, custom, and usage play important roles in determining the power of the Oval Office. The way in which political parties operate, the relationship of political actors to the executive office, the political climate, the functioning of the federal bureaucracy, and the nature of security threats—all impact presidential powers (see Chapter 4). A realistic study of the presidency and national security thus requires an appreciation of the complex nature of the office and the presidential power base. But any study must also be based on the realization that the success and impact of the office depend on the personality, character, and leadership style of the president.

Theodore Sorenson, special counsel to President John F. Kennedy, put it this way:

> Self-confidence and self-assertion are more important than modesty. The nation selects its President, at least in part, for his philosophy and his judgement and his conscientious conviction of what is right—and he need not hesitate to apply them. He must believe in his own objectives. He must assert his own priorities. And he must always strive to preserve the power and prestige of his office, the availability of his options, and the long-range interests of the nation.[5]

Beginning with Andrew Jackson, who sowed the seeds of the so-called modern presidency, many presidents have used a variety of methods to expand the power of the Oval Office, including direct appeals to the people and broadly interpreting the Constitution to favor presidential power. For example, Jackson rationalized his view of the presidency this way: "Each public officer who takes an oath to support the Constitution swears that he will support it as he understands it, and not as it is understood by others." The growth of the power of the presidency accelerated in the twentieth century to the point where Arthur Schlesinger labeled it the "Imperial

Presidency."[6] But as President George Bush learned in dealing with Congress over the U.S. response to China, "Congress . . . restricted the president's conduct of the executive branch by involving itself extensively in the details of domestic and foreign policy."[7] Moreover, "It should be understood that the pendulum of power swings, only to swing back somewhat later. . . . Eventually Congress has always moved to reassert its position."[8] Presidents Bill Clinton and George W. Bush faced the same problems regarding their policies on China, Cuba, and National Missile Defense, among others. Nonetheless, they expanded presidential powers by utilizing the executive order, a presidential prerogative that does not require congressional approval.

How does the president exercise power in pursuit of U.S. national interests? What power does he have, and how does he deal with constraints and limitations on that power? What leadership style is effective in developing a coherent policy posture and strategy in national security? Any serious examination of the Oval Office and national security policy must begin with some attention to models and approaches. By first studying the broad dimension of the presidency, we design some method of linking to it the specifics of national security policy.

The Study of the Presidency

Virtually all studies of the presidency incorporate the various formal roles of the president (usually referred to as "institutionalized roles").[9] The most important institutionalized roles are chief of state, chief executive, commander in chief, chief diplomat, chief legislator, and party chief. The president's national security powers derive from the duties of chief of state, commander in chief, and chief diplomat.

Scholars have designed several theoretical models to study the presidency.[10] Many focus on one or two important roles, showing how they affect the political system and political actors. For example, the view of president as manager focuses on a bureaucratic model of the office. Another approach is based on personality and character and identifies the passive or active president and their consequences for leadership and policies.[11] The president-as-great-man view assesses the officeholder according to his greatness in responding to the political challenges of the time. The president's personal perception of office, which can vary from constitutional to expansionist, offers another approach. Still another approach—one that evaluates leadership style—evolves out of leadership studies that use personality and character to examine the president's ability to develop consensus, loyalty, and commitment in his staff and the executive branch and motivate them to pursue his policies. In addition, the two-presidencies model was advanced to suggest that there is a domestic president and a foreign policy president.

Each model and approach can be relevant and useful depending on the circumstances.[12] Our study is based on two elements common to all: leadership style, and personal perception of the office. We take our cue from Sorenson's view that the president's self-confidence, self-assertion, and philosophy are critical in the functioning of the office: "Each President has his own style and his own standard for making decisions—and these may differ from day to day or from topic to topic, using one blend for foreign affairs, for example, and another for domestic. The man affects the office as the office affects the man."[13] As Sorenson points out, "White House decision-making is not a science but an art. It requires, not calculation, but judgment."[14]

Our study is based on the view that the character and personality are critical in shaping the moral authority and power of the office. Thus there are four important components to a systematic study of the president's role in national security: (1) the president's leadership style, personality, and character as critical determinants of how the Oval Office functions with respect to national security policy and process; (2) how the president views the power and limitations of the office and how he sees his role in furthering its prestige and power; (3) the president's mind-set (or worldview) regarding U.S. national interests and international security environment and how it affects the posture the administration attempts to put into place; and (4) the president's ability to bring the first three components to bear upon the national security establishment so as to synthesize and integrate its efforts to develop and implement coherent policy.

These four factors must be used to develop support among Americans, the Congress, and the federal bureaucracy. This is necessary to develop the national will, political resolve, and staying power for the implementation of national security policy and strategy. The president's effectiveness in achieving these ends rests in his ability to deal with all the complex issues we have identified and yet remain within the bounds of democratic proprieties.

Leadership Style

Although in legal and organizational terms the national security policy process appears to be rational and clear, in reality it is a political and, at times, a chaotic process, reflecting the power and interests of many domestic and foreign actors. At the vital center of this process stands the president. Depending upon his leadership style and philosophy and his effectiveness in exercising the power of the office, the president can minimize the influence of other political actors and guide the process to ensure that his own views and policies prevail.

The term *leadership style* is not easy to define. It refers to the president's way of doing business, which evolves from personality and character: it is the way in which the president exercises authority and power to create trust, loyalty, commitment, and enthusiasm within the administration and is crucial for successful policymaking and implementation. The term *personality* refers to the psychological and social behavior that lays the foundation for one's perceptions and worldview. The term *character* is defined as the way in which the "president orients himself towards life—not for the moment, but enduringly."[15] Put simply, personality and character fix the political behavior and shape the way the president views the world and his own role in it. In addition, they determine the way the president relates to subordinates, to the public, and to the nation's governing institutions.

The point to remember is that the way in which a president governs is every bit as important as the inherent power of the office-as-institution. And when we talk about the powers of the presidency, we must consider three factors: sense of purpose, political skills, and character.[16] James Q. Wilson once concluded that "the public will judge the president not only in terms of what he accomplished but also in terms of its perception of his character."[17]

The leadership style that emerges from personality and character determines whether the president will follow a *magisterial, bureaucratic, managerial,* or *corporate* method of governing—or a combination of these. In the magisterial style, the president places himself as the authoritative head of the government. The bureaucratic style is one in which the official leads as the chief bureaucrat, with all the mind-sets and perceptions that that role entails. In the managerial style, the president strives for efficiency in the administration through the close supervision advocated by managerial principles. In the corporate style, the president governs like the chairman of a large business, combining the managerial approach with commitment and loyalty. Most presidents tend to centralize their role around a particular style, although there are elements of each in the way most modern presidents lead. Regardless of the chosen leadership style, it is implemented to establish a presence, so to speak: the president sets policy directions and saturates the administration with his views on world affairs. Yet the president must do this without frustrating the expression of alternative views and options—not an easy task.

A successful president can stamp national security with his personal style and outlook. If the executive is unsuccessful, then policy is likely to be incoherent and irrelevant, and other domestic political actors are likely to increase their power. This can only lead to erosion of national will, political resolve, and staying power.

Perceptions of the Office

President Johnson perceived the power of the Oval Office this way: "The source of the President's authority is the people. He is not simply responsible to an immediate electorate, either. The President always has to think of America as a continuing community. He has to prepare for the future."[18] President Richard Nixon, reaffirming the national character of the office, stated,

> The first responsibility of leadership is to gain mastery over events, and to shape the future in the image of our hopes. He must lead. The President has a duty to decide, but the people have a right to know why. The President is the only official who represents every American, rich and poor. The Presidency is a place where priorities are set and goals determined.[19]

The perceptions of office that have historically evolved and are applicable in the contemporary period cluster around three basic types:

1. The *constitutionalist*, or Buchanan-type, presidency;
2. The *stewardship*, or Eisenhower-type, presidency (although recent scholarship indicates that Dwight Eisenhower was more activist than originally thought);
3. The *prerogative*, or Lincoln-type, presidency.

Some would add a fourth type of presidency, one designed (intentionally or not) by Bill Clinton: the *public opinion* presidency, or one that follows the whims and desires of the majority of Americans. This type of president comes into office with no commitment to a particular type of role, other than maintaining power in office. In light of President Clinton's record, it would not be surprising if such a label were used by his critics.

In the constitutional presidency, the president views the power of the office as strictly bound by the U.S. Constitution: the document must clearly sanction any presidential action. This narrow view of presidential authority limits the president to reacting to the policies of others, with little presidential initiative. President James Buchanan (1857–1861)provides the example: he felt he was simply the custodian of the Constitution and tried to remain aloof from political battles. In 1860, he even denied that he had the power to use force to prevent the secession of southern states.

The stewardship view presumes that the Oval Office is nonpolitical or, at least, nonpartisan. The president acts as an agent of the nation, supervising operations of the state machinery. Dwight Eisenhower (1953–1961) was associated with such a presidency. Standing aloof from party politics and political battles, Eisenhower felt that his veto power over legislative bills was the key to the presidential office. From this he took the position that the president should advise the nation, negate ill-advised legislation and ill-advised policies, and be the chief broker of the political system. This approach borrows some elements from the constitutional as well as prerogative approaches. Two decades following the Eisenhower presidency, however, there is evidence that Eisenhower was much more active and politically involved than previously believed.[20]

The prerogative view is that the powers of the presidency are exclusive rights resting in a special trust to the benefit of the nation. This approach is best explained by Abraham Lincoln (1861–1865), who made it clear during the Civil War that the legal limits imposed by the Constitution may have to be transcended during a crisis. He felt that the president was the sole representative of all the people and the office was the only institution capable of dealing quickly and decisively with major national problems. President Theodore Roosevelt (1901–1909), another prerogative president, later put it this way:

> I did not usurp power, but I did greatly broaden the use of executive power. In other words, I acted for the public welfare, I acted for the common well-being of all our people, whenever and in whatever manner was necessary, unless prevented by direct constitutional prohibition. . . . My belief was that it was not only his right but his duty to do anything that the needs of the nation demanded unless such action was forbidden by the Constitution or by the laws.[21]

Many scholars argue that no president today can be successful if he ignores the prerogatives of office; the changed security landscape and uncertainties of the nature of international challenges mandate such an approach.

Mind-Set and External Threats

Another key element is how the president perceives external threats, that is, the president's mind-set regarding the international security environment. Presidents come to the Oval Office with an established viewpoint. Although some have more experience in foreign and national security policy, each has a mind-set that stems from public service, political involvement, and other socialization, shaped by experience with allies and adversaries alike. However, some have experience only in the domestic arena, which may not be the best background to deal with foreign adversaries and allies. Yet this can be overcome through the appointment of experienced and knowledgeable people to the inner circle. President George W. Bush appointed such people following his election in 2000 to compensate for his limited foreign policy experience. But that perceived lack of experience vanished as the United States became involved in the new war on terrorism.

From the end of World War II (1945) to the end of the Cold War (roughly 1989), the central U.S. preoccupation was the relationship with the Soviet Union as well as the threats that Marxist-Leninist ideology posed to democracy and the West. The primary focus of the conflict spectrum was on nuclear and conventional conflicts, Vietnam notwithstanding. Each type of conflict posed a different security challenge to the United States. How the president viewed the seriousness of these conflicts, what he believed was the proper world order, and the place of the United States in that order were all critical elements in presidential performance. They remain so today.

Many observers, including those in the media, tend to oversimplify a president's mind-set by categorizing it as either "hard-line" ("hawks") or "soft-line" ("doves"). Rarely does an individual's mind-set fit neatly into one category or the other. True, each president does have a unique perspective about adversaries and is likely to appoint officials with compatible mind-sets to high places in the national security establishment. But the responsibilities of office, the political forces within the domestic system, and the continuities of national security policy prevent the president from establishing and implementing a policy that rests solely on his own preferences and initiatives. The demands of office require compromises with a variety of political forces, both domestic and foreign.

Finally, the term *mind-set* does not mean strict adherence to past perspectives or a dogmatic ideology. The responsibilities for U.S. national security and protection of the homeland weigh heavily upon any president, a burden magnified by the problems of the proliferation of WMD and an uncertain world. Thus the need to reexamine U.S. security interests and the state of U.S. military posture are critical to the national security equation. In the contemporary period, such is the case because of the uncertain world order and the changing and dangerous security landscape, as well as changing leadership in many states and changing international patterns.

The degree to which the president is able to successfully establish U.S. security policy and strategy according to his own mind-set is contingent upon how he functions in the first two elements of our framework: leadership style, and perception of the office. For example, it is unlikely that a president who sees the office from a narrow constitutional perspective will be able to develop innovative policies and tackle the range of conflicts across the spectrum. Additionally, a president who cannot inspire Americans, articulate a vision for U.S. national interests, or develop a consensus within the federal bureaucracy to support presidential policies will be unable to convince adversaries, potential adversaries, and even allies of the seriousness of U.S. interests or of U.S. staying power and political resolve.

The President and the National Security Establishment

The final component of the framework for studying the presidency is the president's need to synthesize the first three components in order to ensure that the national security establishment functions effectively. Thus the president's appointments to key positions are critical in determining the degree to which he will be able to shape the establishment to his own worldview and policy directions. Appointees must have the ability to provide the necessary linkage between the establishment and the president. The assistant to the president for national security affairs (the National Security Advisor) is a principal actor in this respect. The individual selected for this position must have the president's complete trust and must be seen by those in the National Security Council (NSC), by the national security staff, and by the secretaries of defense and state as enjoying a special relationship with the president in national security matters. The National Security Advisor is a key cog in the president's inner circle. Through the National Security Advisor, the national security staff becomes an extension of presidential power and an instrument to set the tone and style of the administration.

The major problem is to ensure that this special relationship among the president, the National Security Advisor, and the national security staff is not seen by the secretaries of defense and state and their departments as infringing on their own prerogatives or as a threat to their roles and functions. The president and his inner circle must likewise be cautious in dealing with other political actors; the 1987 Iran-contra affair revealed the problems that can arise from internal political struggles. An especially contentious internal conflict between the president and the military involved homosexuals in the military.[22] In 1994, the U.S. response to ethnic conflict in Bosnia-Herzegovina and continuing involvement in the Balkans triggered disagreements within the Clinton administration that continued into the George W. Bush administration.

In sum, the president's ability to control and supervise the national security establishment and to develop national will, political resolve, and staying power are based on his leadership style, his perceptions of the office, and his mind-set. However, even if a president sees the world in realistic terms, uses the power of the presidency aggressively, and applies effective leadership, he will not always be able to develop the wherewithal within the body politic to carry out national security policy and strategy. Without a reasonably effective synthesis of these components, the president will surely fail.

In another development, the Clinton administration gave special prominence to the role of the first lady, Hillary Rodham Clinton. Some textbooks on the U.S. government have even included the president's spouse within the formal organization of the White House.[23] Hillary Clinton's efforts to design the administration's health care plan and to shape other national policies raised serious questions regarding the appropriateness of her role, which was not based upon elective office or federal civil-service guidelines. Whether this had any impact on national security policy or on appointments to the national security establishment remains unclear. Nonetheless, to understand the totality of the presidential role and power base, one must consider the role of the first lady.

The National Security Establishment

The current structure and agencies that develop national security policy were established in the aftermath of World War II. The war experience, as well as the belated recognition that a better system of unified command and control was necessary, led to passage of the National Security Act of 1947, amended by Congress in 1949, 1958, the 1980s, and later.

The 1947 act established the NSC, the Office of Secretary of Defense, the U.S. Air Force, the Joint Chiefs of Staff (JCS), and the Central Intelligence Agency (CIA). For the first time, the president was provided with a principal staff member whose purpose was to give the president advice and assistance in matters pertaining to national security. Although the secretary of defense was to oversee the national military establishment, it was presided over by three cabinet-level officers heading three separate executive departments: the Army, the Navy, and the Air Force.

The 1949 amendments created the Department of Defense, making it an executive department and reducing the services to military departments with no cabinet-level officers except the secretary of defense. The position of JCS chairman was created to preside over the JCS, which was to remain a corporate body and principal adviser to the president and secretary of defense.

The 1958 amendments reinforced the secretary of defense by granting legal authority over all elements within the Department of Defense, thereby imposing a degree of unification on the military services (additional staff assistance was also provided). The JCS chairman was given added responsibilities over the joint staff and became a voting member of the JCS for the first time. The 1958 amendments also provided that operational commanders would report to the secretary of defense, not through the military departments and service chiefs (who would be responsible for administration and logistical support). The 1986 Goldwater-Nichols Bill provided additional changes within the Department of Defense by strengthening the position of the JCS chairman to make him the principal military aide to the

secretary, establishing the position of assistant secretary of defense for special operations and low-intensity conflict, and requiring joint service duty
for future general officers, among other things.

The National Security Act of 1947 established the basis for integrating
political, military, and intelligence functions into the national security policy process through the NSC, thereby giving the president a structure for a
systematized assessment of policy and strategic options. Although the
move toward centralization and unification has achieved a great deal, many
internal problems of power decentralization and diffusion remain.

The national security establishment as it exists today is shown in
Figure 5.1. An important structural evolution since 1947 has led to the
emerging prominence of the National Security Advisor. The National
Security Advisor is appointed by the president without approval by the
Congress, and the position has been held by Henry Kissinger and Zbigniew
Brzezinski, among many others. The Iran-contra hearings revealed more
details about the functioning of the post, thanks to the testimony of
National Security Advisor Robert McFarlane and Admiral John
Poindexter.[24] In any case, the role of National Security Advisor goes

Figure 5.1   The National Security Establishment

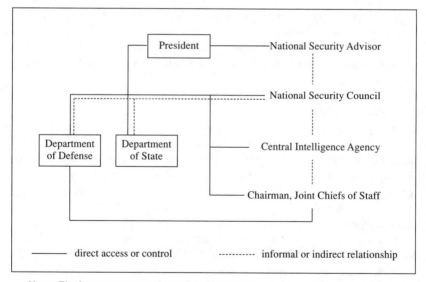

Notes: The four statutory members of the National Security Council are the president, vice
president, and secretaries of state and defense. The two statutory advisers are the director of
the CIA and the chairman of the Joint Chiefs of Staff. The national security advisor is an
important actor in the national security policy process and usually plans and coordinates the
meetings of the National Security Council.

beyond policy coordination; indeed, some observers feel the power exercised by individuals such as Kissinger and Brzezinski undermined the role of the secretary of state. The fact that the National Security Advisor can provide the president with a unique view not bound by executive-department perspectives makes his/her advice especially important. Thus the National Security Advisor's own personality and character, perceptions of the role, and personal access to the president provides that person with a power base that translates into prominence in all areas of national security. The extent of that superiority depends on the president's leadership style and his own perceptions of the position. Thus the National Security Advisor's relationship with the president is much different from that of cabinet-level officers, who must be approved by Congress and may be appointed for any number of political reasons. As Ted Sorenson has pointed out with respect to the president's personal staff, "We were appointed for our ability to fulfill the President's needs and talk the President's language. We represented no one but John Kennedy."[25]

Yet there can be disagreements within the national security establishment as well as the president's own staff. In the Clinton administration, the issue of homosexuals in the military caused serious disagreement within the national security establishment. The president, however, can foster a phenomenon labeled by one scholar as "group-think," in which the group itself takes on a certain mind-set, blocking out or ignoring alternative inputs, even from its own membership.[26] The results can lead to policy disasters and strategic failures.

The NSC, the NSC staff, and other important political actors in the national security establishment are discussed in more detail in Chapter 6.

Constraints and Limitations

The assertion that the president has the preeminent role in national security must be qualified. The first qualification is the very nature of the U.S. political system, with its emphasis on democratic proprieties and values. Any president sensitive to domestic politics and public expectations appreciates and understands that the presidency is supposed to symbolize the best of the U.S. system. Behavior and words must be in keeping with the goals and expectations of the people. The constraints this imposes on the president creates an inherent dilemma in dealing with national security.

Especially in response to unconventional conflicts, some of the most effective policies and strategies stretch democratic expectations and norms. Even though secrecy and covert operations are part and parcel of the response to unconventional conflicts, the Iran-contra hearings revealed that it is difficult for many citizens, as well as members of Congress, to accept the necessity for such operations. The view is that these operations tend to be undemocratic, an un-American way of war. Thus the president must find ways to reconcile democratic norms with acceptable and effective strategic options.

Second, the current distinctions between the national security policy process and the domestic policy process are not as clear as they once were. The turmoil of the 1960s, followed by the U.S. withdrawal from Vietnam and the Watergate affair, eroded public confidence in the presumed preeminence of the president in national security affairs. Neither was their faith restored by later events: U.S. inability to respond to Soviet power projections in Africa and the establishment of Marxist-Leninist regimes in parts of the less developed world, hostilities in the Middle East, U.S. hostages, failures with Iran, the problems with covert operations as revealed in the Iran-contra hearings, questions over U.S. policy in Central America, and so on. More questions were raised about the role of the president in national security concerning U.S.-China relations over Taiwan and U.S.-Russia relations under Russian president Boris Yeltsin (followed in 2000 by former KGB officer Vladimir Putin). The U.S. role in NATO and in a variety of operations other than war raise further questions as to presidential power and national security. There were limits to presidential power, and some called for more limits to be imposed by the U.S. Congress. This erosion of confidence, triggered by past events, was reinforced from 1993 through September 2001: U.S. involvement in Somalia, the inability to respond effectively to the crisis in Haiti, the commitment of U.S. troops to the Bosnia-Herzegovina conflict in 1995, and the continuing role of the United States in Kosovo and neighboring regions. The war against terrorism and the effort at a global response reinforced and highlighted the presidential role.

The motivations behind a certain national security policy and strategy, as well as the way in which policy is made, have been sensitive issues for Congress and many other political actors. The presumed secrecy surrounding such decisions, and the way the policy process functioned, have to a great extent lost their rationale—if for no other reason than fear of the resurgence of an imperial presidency. Writing in 1998, then-Senator Daniel Patrick Moynihan argued for more openness in government and for dismantling much of the secret system and apparatus. "*Analysis* far more than secrecy, is the key to security."[27] The events of late 2001, as well as the scope and direction of the U.S. response, muted much of this criticism for the time being.

In addition, the basis of national security has qualitatively shifted. The clear purposes that characterized the Cold War era have been replaced by the challenge of a more ambiguous security environment. This began with the ascension of Mikhail Gorbachev as head of the Soviet Union. His glasnost and perestroika initiatives paved the way for the dissolution of the Soviet empire, not to mention the Soviet Union itself. In the twenty-first century, the United States and Russia agree on many international issues, as during the 1991 Gulf War, despite some last-minute maneuvering to save Saddam Hussein's hide. This was also the case in the aftermath of September 11 and the call by President Bush for an international response to terrorism. Former enemies are becoming friends, and friends are becoming economic competitors. At the same time, developing nations, some of whom are rich with oil, are not the political-military pawns they once were. Unconventional conflicts, which now characterize much of the security environment, remain difficult security problems. Such conflicts are not easily understood given the American way of war, and the United States is not properly postured to respond quickly and effectively.

Third, any new president inherits his predecessor's budget, structures, commitments, and bureaucratic personnel, and so he does not have the freedom of action most people would assume. Part of this constraint results from the logical reluctance to dramatically change national security early on in an administration. In addition, continuity of national security policy goes beyond any one president; such continuity is necessitated by the impact of U.S. national security policy on allies and potential adversaries.

Fourth, every new president finds it difficult to deal with the national security establishment, especially the military. The character of the military profession and the general orientation of the institution, with its linkage to civilian political actors, preclude the president from becoming a free agent. Many items are the province of military experts and civilian specialists who develop a legitimacy from their expertise, and the president depends on them. But members of the military are far from apolitical; they are often drawn into the fray over national security policy, organizational issues, and social issues. Even Eisenhower, whose years of military service should have provided a firm basis for national security policy (he presided over the Allied victory in Europe during World War II), encountered intense political battles. In 1993 and 1994, President Clinton faced serious problems stemming from his avoidance of military service, his anti–Vietnam War activities, and his campaign policy of lifting the ban on open homosexuals in the military. Such views had a troubling impact within the military that dogged him until the end of his administration. An editorial in *Armed Forces Journal International* (speaking specifically to U.S. strategy and policy in committing the military into Bosnia) focused on Clinton's character and judgment:

> Although the majority of the American public has only recently come to realize that their president plays loose with the truth and has a proclivity for inducing others to follow his lead with hair-splitting semantical obfus-

cation, America's military forces have long seen evidence of those traits in their commander-in-chief. The U.S. military involvement in Bosnia provides abundant illustration of both points.[28]

Again, the response to terrorism in the aftermath of September 11 changed much of this, but the way in which those events would play out in the long term remains uncertain.

Fifth, bureaucracies in the national security policy process might resist any change that threatens their authority or budget. At times, bureaucratic loyalty overshadows policy priorities. Of central importance (especially in the military, the Departments of State and Defense, and intelligence) is the maintenance of the stature, role, and budgets of their organizations or sub-units. Put simply, their perspectives are affected by bureaucratic affiliation.[29] As Henry Kissinger observed, "The nightmare of the modern state is the hugeness of the bureaucracy, and the problem is how to get coherence and design in it."[30]

Bureaucracies' ability to frustrate a president's national security policy and strategy is reinforced if bureaucrats are able to forge alliances with actors outside the executive office. Equally important are the so-called sub-governments and power clusters that exist within many bureaucracies, which can thwart attempts to design coherent policies and strategies.

The reality of modern U.S. politics is that an opposition government of sorts exists within our federal bureaucracies. Staff members, attorneys, assistant division chiefs, and deputy administrators—a civil-service old-boys' network—stands ready to leak embarrassing information to undercut an administration. The motives are not important, yet every administration understands that it can be sandbagged by one of its own.[31]

Sixth, Congress is more assertive in national security policy through the budget process as well as its role in the policy process. For example, the House and Senate Budget Committees established by the Congressional Budget and Impoundment Act of 1974 provide Congress a structure to examine the administration's budget and prepare an alternative. In addition, Congress has expanded its staff and developed the ability to examine national security policy and strategy. Yet the global counterterrorism strategy that began developing in late 2001 may well establish new procedures and processes that actually expand presidential power.

The executive-legislative dynamic since the end of the Vietnam War has been affected by a variety of national security problems: questionable CIA involvement in Watergate, presumptions about the CIA as a rogue agency, reactions against military interventions (a hangover from the Vietnam experience), the toppling of the shah of Iran and U.S. hostage-taking, and the establishment of Marxist-Leninist regimes in parts of the less developed world. These events, among others, led many to believe that the country had lost its capacity to affect the international security environment and protect interests abroad. Many feared that a vacuum had been created in national security policy.

Congress attempted to step in, passing legislation to restrict intelligence activities, strengthen congressional oversight, and restrict the president's use of military force (the 1973 War Powers Resolution) and his authority to commit military assistance to other countries (the Clark Amendment and, later, the Boland Amendments). Congress and the country were in the mood to exert control over foreign and national security policies, regardless of the impact they had on adversaries and allies. Although the Reagan administration marked a change—restoring the executive-legislative balance during the early 1980s—the stage was set for continuing congressional involvement in national security affairs. The changes brought on by the post–Cold War period and the concentration on domestic issues and priorities reinforced the congressional role in national security affairs. In the aftermath of September 11 this relationship may well change yet again, as President George W. Bush uses some broader powers that Congress and the public appeared to have sanctioned. In the long run, national will, staying power, and political resolve will shape the scope and direction of those powers.

In any case, the need remains for flexibility and innovation—to say nothing of usable power—and thus most presidents opt for a trusted staff of advisers to conduct national security policy. For a variety of reasons, ranging from fear of media leaks to distrust of outside political actors, presidents feel more comfortable working with a select group of advisers within a structure that is under their immediate control and supervision. It is this national security establishment that is the primary structure for the president to advance and implement his national security policies.

Summary and Conclusions

Lyndon Johnson wrote that the president receives advice from many quarters, "But there is only one [person] that has been chosen by the American people to decide."[32] Decisions on national security were relatively easy to make for the president in the past. Isolationism, distance from the Old World, and military might allowed the United States relative freedom from major external threats. National security issues were relatively clear and far less difficult than domestic problems. World War II and the nuclear era changed all that. Yet there was a sense of clarity that evolved in the era of competing superpowers—a clarity that was missing until September 11.

The changes in the immediate post–World War II environment were retransformed in the 1950s in the aftermath of the Korean War. That conflict showed that beneath the nuclear umbrella the United States still requires usable conventional forces to fight limited wars and deter future ones. The evolution of regional powers, the frequency of nonnuclear conflicts, proxy wars, and the fear of direct U.S.-Soviet confrontation reshaped the international security environment, making it less vulnerable to superpower influence and more vulnerable to smaller-power actions.

Moreover, the impact of events like Vietnam and Watergate created skepticism and concern about the nature of executive power and triggered the move in Congress to reassert itself in foreign and national security policies. Furthermore, the country's reluctance to undertake foreign ventures, if they meant the use of U.S. military forces, reflected the Vietnam syndrome. It was recognized that there were limits to our ability to affect events in many parts of the world.

Although much of this remains true today, the performance of U.S. forces in the 1991 Gulf War seemed to overcome much of the fear associated with the Vietnam syndrome. Earlier, President Reagan's labeling of Vietnam as a "noble cause" began the healing process. But even in the 1990s, the Vietnam syndrome lurked beneath the surface. Indeed, in the Gulf War the commander of the coalition forces, General H. Norman Schwarzkopf, made a point of noting that U.S. operations and command and control in the Gulf War were not like in Vietnam. But U.S. involvement in Somalia in 1993 rekindled visions of Southeast Asia, as did our involvement in Bosnia-Herzegovina and Kosovo later that decade. The country's response to September 11 illustrated a focus and unity not seen since World War II.

The Reagan presidency, with its strengthening of the U.S. defense posture and its perceived confidence in dealing with international security issues, changed the pessimism of the late 1970s.

> Ronald Reagan established a pattern of leadership which his successors would be prudent to consider. He demonstrated the strength of a simple, straightforward agenda, readily explicable to the public. By concentrating his political resources on that agenda, by defining a mandate and inducing legislators of both parties to accept it, he restored the presidency as the engine that moves government.[33]

But not even Ronald Reagan could revive the earlier U.S. supremacy: "The Reagan revolution was hampered by limitations of power inherent in the presidency and the political system, by private economic decisions, and by events abroad that lay beyond its control."[34]

Following President George Bush's unifying leadership in the 1991 Gulf War, national security seemed to have taken a secondary role to other issues. Indeed, the 1992 presidential election seemed to turn on Bill Clinton's campaign mantra: "It's the economy, stupid!" In the last years of the twentieth century, a healthy U.S. economy, the demise of the Soviet Union, diminished fears of major wars, and the absence of any serious challenge to the U.S. role in the international world, among other factors, refocused the public on domestic issues. Yet the strategic landscape of the twenty-first century poses difficult and challenging problems; the September 11 terrorist attacks were the first shot in a new war.

National security issues in the twenty-first century, although reflecting continuities from the past, have unique characteristics, especially in the nature of conflicts and the relationship between economic strength and national security. This is complicated by the changing relationship between the domestic and national security agendas. The complexity of the issues and their undefined, fluid nature exacerbate the problem of presidential control and direction. In this context, internal struggles among government agencies leave the president vulnerable to agency biases and, in some instances, make him a captive of the bureaucracy. The pressures on the president are magnified by congressional involvement and its advocacy of policies and strategies that may be contrary to those of the administration. Add to this the interests and objectives of allies and adversaries and one must conclude that national security policy is fraught with peril and pitfalls. Yet national security is only one component of the president's total responsibility.

Another major component is that sovereign states can have their own ideologies and conceptions of national security that are in direct contradiction to U.S. goals. Differing strategies can challenge the Western cultural orientation of the United States.[35] Conflict in one form or another is inevitable. Thus declaratory U.S. policy, even when supported by necessary resources, does not guarantee success. There are too many imponderables and uncertainties in the external environment.

According to one assessment, the weakness of the existing state system has a negative impact on leadership:

> Leaders of states in the last years of the twentieth century are weak because the nation-state, as an institution, is weak. There has been a shift of problems from the national to the global arena. . . . The amorphous challenges that have crept up in the present era are not easily countered, or conquered, by simple direct actions. Yet the only leaders in sight with vision and conviction are possessed by some form of fanatical ideology. For most, in these circumstances, muddling through is the only, even if uninspiring, style of leadership available.[36]

In summary, the posture and power of agencies within the national security establishment, the interplay of personalities between the administration and Congress, congressional power in the policy process, the politicization of national security issues, and the changed domestic and international political and security environments have bred issues far different from those of the Cold War era. And therein lies the irony: for many people, the end of the Cold War diminished the importance of national security issues compared to domestic issues. Yet global interdependence, information-age technology, international environmental issues and ecology, the new strategic landscape, and long-term threats to U.S. quality of life have given a new impetus to the link between domestic and national security issues—a brutal reality that hit home on September 11. But it must be remembered that an increasing number of political actors (both domestic and international) affect national security and are beyond presidential control; they are constraints on the use of presidential power despite the new actions in the war on terrorism.[37]

In this environment, U.S. national objectives and interests, as well as political-military policy and strategy, are difficult to define. This applies to adversaries and allies and political actors within the United States. U.S. national security policy often does not have the luxury of clear-cut choices between good and evil. Rather, choices involve living with the lesser of evils. Serious threats are the exception to this general rule.

As Ernest van den Haag has written:

> Just solutions are elusive. Many problems have no solutions at all, not even unjust ones; at most they can be managed, prevented from getting worse or from spreading to wider areas. Other problems are best left to simmer in benign neglect until parties are disposed to settle them.[38]

The conclusion is obvious: The models, perspectives, and analyses that are key to presidential performance will always fall short of the mark because there are no simple answers. The interaction among leadership style, perceptions of the office, mind-set, and the national security establishment—in the context of the domestic and international environments—preclude neat paradigms or precise model-building. The forces that affect the president's ability to exercise power and the public's expectations are difficult to integrate. Even the most respected scholars of the presidency do not agree on the power of the office, the capacity of the president to exercise this power, and the best approach to the study of the office.[39] Thus presidential performance in national security does not neatly follow any rational model or specified approach.

Presidents who are successful in the national security area have a deep understanding of the organizational dynamics and interactions within the national security establishment. Yet this should always be tempered by sensitivity to public expectations and appreciation of the system's openness. Furthermore, the president must have a realistic perception of the international scene, adversaries, and allies. Critical to all this are the character and leadership style of the individual presiding in the Oval Office.

This brings us full circle: support and consensus are contingent upon the president's leadership style and ability to set and maintain the tone of the administration. To develop coherent policy and relevant strategy requires articulation of what the United States stands for and a national will and political resolve to use the instruments necessary to achieve national security goals. The president's mission is to reconcile the ideals of democracy with the commitment necessary to achieve these goals in the international arena. Unfortunately, this can require the use of the military and loss of life, but only the president is in a position to lead the country to accept such sacrifices and understand why they are necessary.

In the final analysis, the uniqueness of the office, the problems of U.S. national security, and the character of the public interact to create a distinctively American presidency. This is best summed up by the following observation:

> We give the President more work than a man can do, more responsibility than a man should take, more pressure than a man can bear. We abuse him often and rarely praise him. We wear him out, use him up, eat him up. And with all of this, Americans have love for the president that goes beyond loyalty or party nationality [sic]; he is ours and we exercise the right to destroy him.[40]

Notes

1. Lyndon Baines Johnson, *The Vantage Point: Perspectives of the Presidency, 1963–1969* (New York: Holt, Rinehart, and Winston, 1971), preface.

2. Harold M. Barger, *The Impossible Presidency: Illusions and Realities of Executive Power* (Glenview, IL: Scott, Foresman, 1984), p. 2.

3. James MacGregor Burns, J. W. Peltason, Thomes E. Cronin, and David B. Magleby, *Government by the People,* national version, 18th ed. (Upper Saddle River, NJ: Prentice-Hall, 2000), p. 366.

4. Margaret Truman, *Harry S. Truman* (New York: Pocket Books, 1974), p. 603.

5. Theodore Sorenson, *Decision-Making in the White House: The Olive Branch or the Arrows* (New York: Columbia University Press, 1963), p. 84.

6. Arthur Schlesinger Jr., *The Imperial Presidency* (Boston: Houghton Mifflin, 1973).

7. Sidney M. Milkis and Michael Nelson, *The American Presidency: Origins and Development, 1776–1990* (Washington, DC: CQ Press, 1990).

8. Lee Sigelman, "A Reassessment of the Two Presidencies Thesis," in Steven A. Schull, ed., *The Two Presidencies: A Quarter Century Assessment* (Chicago: Nelson-Hall, 1991), p. 60.

9. Burns et al., *Government by the People*, pp. 360–368.

10. See, e.g., Richard E. Neustadt, *Presidential Power* (New York: Wiley, 1960), p. 9; Michael Nelson, ed., *The Presidency and the Political System*

(Washington, DC: CQ Press, 1984), esp. part 1; and Clinton Rossiter, *The American Presidency*, 2nd ed. (New York: Mentor Books, 1960). See also Steven Kelman, "The Twentieth-Century Presidents," *American Democracy and the Public Good* (Fort Worth, TX: Harcourt Brace College, 1996), pp. 460–468.

11. James David Barber, *The Presidential Character: Predicting Performance in the White House* (New York: Prentice-Hall, 1977), p. 8. See also James David Barber, *Presidential Character*, 4th ed. (Englewood Cliffs, NJ: Prentice-Hall, 1992).

12. See Aaron Wildavsky, "The Two Presidencies," in Wildavsky, ed., *Perspectives on the Presidency* (Boston: Little, Brown, 1975).

13. Sorenson, *Decision-Making in the White House*, p. 5.

14. Ibid., p. 10.

15. See, e.g., James David Barber, *The Presidential Character: Predicting Performance in the White House*, 3rd ed. (Englewood Cliffs, NJ: Prentice-Hall, 1985). See also Barber, *Presidential Character*.

16. Erwin C. Hargrove and Roy Hoopes, *The Presidency: A Question of Power* (Boston: Little, Brown, 1975), p. 47.

17. James Q. Wilson, *American Government: Institutions and Policies*, 5th ed. (Lexington, MA: D. C. Heath, 1992), p. 338.

18. Johnson, *The Vantage Point*, preface.

19. Richard M. Nixon, *Six Crises* (Garden City, NY: Doubleday, 1962), p. 323.

20. Fred I. Greenstein, *The Hidden Hand Presidency: Eisenhower as Leader* (New York: Basic Books, 1982).

21. Theodore Roosevelt, *An Autobiography* (New York: Charles Scribner's Sons, 1913), p. 197.

22. See, e.g., R. D. Adair and Joseph C. Myers, "Admission of Gays in the Military," *Parameters* 23, no. 1 (Spring 1993): 10–19.

23. See Robert L. Lineberry, George C. Edwards III, and Martin P. Wattenberg, *Government in America: People, Politics, and Policy*, 6th ed. (New York: HarperCollins, 1994), p. 467.

24. For a detailed view of this matter, see Oliver L. North, with William Novak, *Under Fire: An American Story* (New York: HarperCollins, 1991).

25. Sorenson, *Decision-Making*, p. 291.

26. Irving L. Janis, *Groupthink: Psychological Studies of Policy Decisions and Fiascoes,* 2nd ed. (Boston: Houghton Mifflin, 1982).

27. Daniel Patrick Moynihan, *Secrecy: The American Experience* (New Haven: Yale University Press, 1998), p. 222.

28. John G. Roos, "Commander-in-Chief Clinton: The Military Has Already Been Marched Down the Moniker Road," *Armed Forces Journal International* (November 1998), p. 4.

29. Robert L. Gallucci, *Neither Peace nor Honor: The Politics of American Military Policy in Vietnam* (Baltimore: Johns Hopkins University Press, 1975), p. 138.

30. As quoted in Morton H. Halperin, *Bureaucratic Politics and Foreign Policy* (Washington, DC: Brookings Institution, 1974), p. 15.

31. Joseph C. Goulden, *The Superlawyers* (New York: Dell, 1973), p. 228.

32. Johnson, *The Vantage Point*, preface.

33. Louis W. Koenig, *The Chief Executive*, 5th ed. (New York: Harcourt Brace Jovanovich, 1986), p. 415.

34. Ibid., p. 2.

35. See, e.g., Adda B. Bozeman, *Strategic Intelligence and Statecraft:*

Selected Essays (Washington, DC: Brassey's U.S., 1992). See also Samuel P. Huntington, "The Clash of Civilizations?" *Foreign Affairs* 72, no. 3 (Summer 1993): 22–49.

36. International Institute for Strategic Studies, *Strategic Survey, 1994–1995* (London: Oxford University Press, 1995), pp. 15–16.

37. For insights into the irony of diffusion and concentration of power, see Wilson, *American Government*.

38. Ernest van den Haag, "The Busyness of American Foreign Policy," *Foreign Affairs* 64, no. 1 (Fall 1985): 114–115.

39. See, e.g., Thomas E. Cronin and Richard E. Neustadt, *Presidential Power: The Politics of Leadership from FDR to Carter* (New York: Wiley, 1980). Also see Edward S. Greenberg and Benjamin I. Page, *The Struggle for Democracy*, 3rd ed. (New York: Longman, 1997), pp. 402–406.

40. John Steinbeck, *America and Americans* (Boston: Little, Brown, 1980), p. 379.

6

The Policy Triad and the National Security Council

THE PRESIDENT DEPENDS UPON MANY PEOPLE TO FORMULATE and implement national security policy, coordinated at the highest level through the National Security Council. Two key presidential advisers—the secretaries of state and defense—are statutory members of the NSC along with the vice president; the assistant to the president for national security affairs (the National Security Advisor) is not. These three individuals form the so-called policy triad. The director of the CIA (the formal position is Director of Central Intelligence, or DCI) is a statutory adviser to the NSC together with the chairman of the Joint Chiefs of Staff. The CIA's functions give it a critical role in the national security establishment. But that agency's closed nature—the unavoidable legacy of intelligence-gathering and covert operations—means its relationship with the president, the Congress, and the public is quite different; it is isolated from other parts of the administration. In short, the CIA marches to its own drummer (see Chapter 9).

The NSC and its staff are primarily advisory units; even though recommendations can be made by the NSC and approved by the president, their interpretation and implementation rest mainly with the Departments of State and Defense and the CIA. Thus within the NSC the views of operational departments come into play and often clash. And as the United States Commission on National Security/21st Century concluded, "The power to determine national security policy has migrated toward the [NSC] staff. The staff now assumes policymaking and operational roles, with the result that its ability to act as an honest broker and policy coordinator has suffered."[1]

Aside from their advisory functions as statutory members of the NSC, the secretaries of state and defense also play significant roles in the national security establishment as cabinet members and department heads. Furthermore, the Departments of State and Defense have substantial links to Congress and are involved in a variety of formal relationships with other countries. Their perspectives thus reflect many influences.

Whereas these two department heads bring their own worldviews and operational methods, the National Security Advisor advances the president's perspective and performs an advisory role. This person also sets the agenda and coordinates the activities of the national security staff in support of the NSC.

It is the power and relationships of these three—the two secretaries and the National Security Advisor—relative to one another and to the president that define the direction of U.S. national security policy. The policy triad is the fulcrum around which the policy process revolves (see Figure 6.1).

The Department of State

The secretary of state is the president's primary adviser on foreign policy and the operational head of the department responsible for its conduct. The department is organized along two broad lines: functional and geographic. Country desks operate under assistant secretaries responsible for a particular region (e.g., the Nigeria country desk would fall under African affairs). The functional areas, such as intelligence and research and political-mili-

Figure 6.1   The Policy Triad

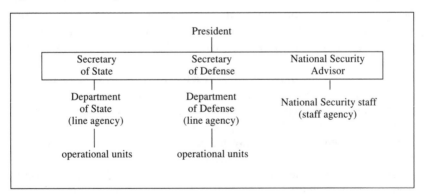

Notes: The secretaries of state and defense each wear two hats: staff adviser to the president and operational department head. Thus their perspectives on national security are usually conditioned by the capability of their departments to implement policy and strategy. The national security advisor, however, has no operational units; the national security staff is just that—a staff agency. The national security advisor and national security staff attempt to provide a presidential perspective and to stand above department issues. Perceptions, mind-sets, and responsibilities differ between the two secretaries and particularly between the two secretaries and the national security advisor.

tary affairs, cut across geographic boundaries. In 1993 and 1994, plans were implemented to change the organization to reflect the Clinton administration's foreign policy and to simplify the department's burdensome structure. This included creating the Office of the Secretary to bring together separate groups within the department and to clarify the reporting process. Efforts were also made to give more power to undersecretaries of state.[2] In addition, several embassies and consular offices were closed. Possible organizational changes by the George W. Bush administration are not yet clear.

Despite such efforts, some have concluded that during the Clinton administration the department's role in foreign and national security diminished. Indeed, the NSC's role in national security subsumed many aspects of foreign policy. "In sum, the secretary of state in the Clinton administration, like other recent administrations, will continue to be prominent, but will not dominate, policy formulation, instead policy making will increasingly be a shared responsibility."[3]

In an especially critical assessment, the United States Commission on National Security/21st Century stated,

> The Department of State is a crippled institution that is starved for resources by Congress because of its inadequacies and is thereby weakened further. The department suffers in particular from an ineffective organizational structure in which regional and functional goals compete, and in which sound management, accountability, and leadership are lacking.[4]

The organization of the State Department is shown in Figure 6.2.[5]

The end of the Cold War ushered in a changed security environment, one that continues to evolve. Yet the national security establishment created by the National Security Act of 1947 in the aftermath of World War II remained in place for the most part with only slight changes until the 1990s. At that time, the role of the secretary of state became more visible, and during Clinton's second term some felt that it was the dominant player in the policy process. At the same time, the decline of serious threats and the drawdown of the U.S. military—combined with deep cuts in the defense budget—crimped the scope and power of the secretary of defense. Thus, whereas national security issues were a driving force in U.S. policy during the Cold War, the post–Cold War shift put more attention on foreign policy. In the twenty-first century and after September 11, the focus has been on national security policy, with Secretary of Defense Donald Rumsfeld taking center stage behind only the president. But foreign policy and national security policy are increasingly intertwined. The irony is that both the secretary of state and secretary of defense have become involved in policy that interlocks foreign policy as well as national security issues.

Figure 6.2 The Department of State

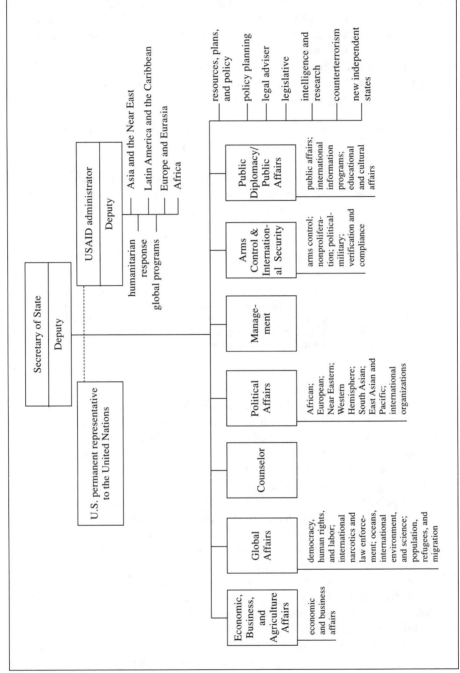

Source: U.S. Commission on National Security/21st Century, *Road Map for National Security: Imperative for Change* (January 31, 2001), p. 57.

At the same time, other players took the stage in foreign policy and national security. Arms-control initiatives and agreements with the Soviet Union and, later, Russia, as well as U.S. relations with China, Russia, and the Middle East are some of the primary concerns of the secretary of state. Yet all this has a huge impact on national security issues. As well, peace in the Middle East, primarily a foreign policy matter, has national security implications. And in the 1990s, U.S. involvement in Somalia, Haiti, and Bosnia-Herzegovina intermingled foreign and national security policies. The U.S. involvement with NATO in Kosovo beginning in 1999 also shows the close relationship between foreign and national security policies.

Other State Department activities beyond the realm of national security nevertheless influence the department's perspective on it. The secretary of state is responsible for consular services, aid to U.S. citizens overseas, diplomatic missions, and U.S. embassies—the focal point of the U.S. presence. Although ambassadors can deal directly with the president, their main contact is the secretary of state. The embassy staffs are typically given the responsibility to coordinate all official U.S. activities in the host country. This country-team concept, first formalized by President Dwight Eisenhower, was an attempt to bring consistency to U.S. activities overseas through centralized control (although U.S. military operations were not included in this concept).

The primary bureaucracy within the Department of State is deeply involved with traditional diplomatic and consular tasks, embedded in traditional notions of courtly, courteous, old-world diplomacy. The focus is negotiations and compromise. The department's organizational behavior and internal mind-sets stem from these institutional roots, imposing a template of education and socialization that produces foreign-service officers and department employees quite different from their counterparts at Defense. The result can be serious disagreements between the two secretaries. The departments at times work at cross-purposes, although accord is usually reached in clear cases of national security, such as the war on terrorism.

The State Department has been criticized as a bureaucracy committed to stability, the status quo, and self-protection of its organizational integrity and autonomy. According to some, this has produced bureaucratic inertia and burdensome procedures that allow little room for initiative and innovation. The United States Commission on National Security/21st Century had this to say about the reorganization of the Department of State:

> The President should propose to the Congress a plan to reorganize the State Department, creating five Under Secretaries with responsibility for overseeing the regions of Africa, Asia, Europe, Inter-America, and Near East/South Asia, and redefining the responsibilities of the Under Secretary

for Global Affairs. . . . The Secretary of State should give greater emphasis to strategic planning in the State Department and link it directly to the allocation of resources through the establishment of a Strategic Planning, Assistance, and Budget Office.[6]

Several studies have also shown that the department has difficulty in formulating long-range policies that link to domestic political concerns as well as foreign policy issues. As Christopher Shoemaker concluded, "This rather important deficiency stems both from the department and from historical proclivities of the Foreign Service."[7] He goes on to note that "bureaucratic power within the State Department is normally vested in the regional bureaus, which, despite their staffing by seasoned professionals, are virtually unable to come to grips with the development of long-range policy."[8] Although written in 1991, this assessment remains valid today. Yet with the inauguration of George W. Bush and the appointment of Secretary of State Colin Powell, important changes were expected.

The Department of Defense

In contrast to the 200-year tradition in the Department of State, the Department of Defense is a relatively new organization, established after World War II by the National Security Act of 1947. Major problems faced the secretary of defense in trying to centralize defense policy; changes were taking place in the late 1980s and throughout the Clinton administration (1993–2001). These changes reflected the diminished threat of war and administration efforts to reduce the military to reflect that new perception. The Department of Defense is still involved in changes in response to information-age technology and the changing international security landscape. More changes were implemented in the George W. Bush administration with Secretary of Defense Rumsfeld's own defense review and the 2001 Quadrennial Defense Review (QDR). These changes were re-revised in response to September 11; the latest organization of the Department of Defense is shown in Figure 6.3.[9]

The president's responsibility as commander in chief is usually exercised through the secretary of defense and the operational elements of the Department of Defense. Like the secretary of state in the foreign policy area, the defense secretary performs dual functions in defense policy: as primary adviser to the president on defense policy, and as head of the operational elements of the department. In the advisory capacity, the secretary focuses on the types of forces and manpower levels needed to effectively pursue the goals of U.S. national security policy. Among the secretary's concerns are the composition of forces, weapons acquisition, training, plan-

Figure 6.3 The Department of Defense

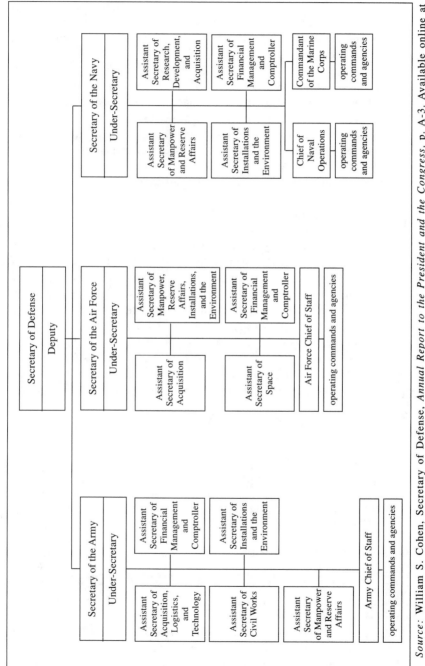

Source: William S. Cohen, Secretary of Defense, *Annual Report to the President and the Congress*, p. A-3. Available online at www.dtic.mil/execsec/adr2001.

ning, and operational implementation. The operational arms of the Department of Defense are highly visible, coercive military forces. Their symbolic—as well as substantive—role plays a great part in the perceptions of allies and adversaries regarding U.S. capability. Thus statements of the secretary of defense are important in shaping policy.

The structure of the Office of the Secretary of Defense (as distinct from the service branches) includes several functional units supervised by assistant secretaries (for example, regional affairs). In 1993, Secretary of Defense Les Aspin changed the department's structure to overlap with certain responsibilities associated with the Department of State, such as democracy and human rights. In early 1994, Secretary of Defense William Perry, who succeeded Aspin, reduced this overlap by shifting the department toward traditional roles and concerns. In addition, the service branches, as well as the Defense Intelligence Agency (DIA) and National Security Agency (NSA), operate or collect information that has a direct bearing on the function of the State Department.

Former U.S. senator William Cohen became Clinton's third secretary of defense in 1996 after Perry had refocused the department on its traditional missions and stabilized what many felt was disarray created by Aspin. Aspin's ballyhooed Bottom-Up Review—a strategy for restructuring U.S. forces and a response to contingencies in the post–Cold War era—drew much criticism. This was compounded by Aspin's effort to develop a military capable of responding to two regional conflicts simultaneously.[10] Nonetheless, the need to prepare for twin conflicts, as well as other contingencies, remained part of military strategy until the end of the Clinton presidency. New reviews by the Bush administration changed all this yet again.

In a June 1998 review of Secretary Cohen's tenure, one author wrote,

> Nearly 18 months into his initial tour of military service, U.S. Secretary of Defense William S. Cohen has become an enigma. In contrast to his 24 years of service on Capitol Hill, where he was quick to step forward and voice opinions about controversial issues, he now seems to relish the fact that the legions surrounding him provide convenient cover for avoiding the public spotlight. That's too bad.[11]

The author does credit Cohen for appointing a qualified and capable inner circle of civilian advisers yet criticizes Cohen for isolating himself from the uniformed services. In 1999 and into 2001, Cohen did attempt to link with the uniformed services and made a highly publicized trip to meet with North Vietnamese defense officials.

George W. Bush's veteran secretary of defense, Donald Rumsfeld, has brought a more cautious and selective view to the use of the military establishment. He underscores the administration's approach to defense policy and strategy. In his Senate confirmation hearings in January 2001, Rumsfeld stated,

> U.S. military forces can best be used when the military mission is clear and achievable and when there is a reasonable exit strategy. . . . When the main burden of the U.S. presence shifts to infrastructure and nation building . . . we are into missions that are not appropriate for the U.S. military.[12]

Major strategy reviews in the Bush administration are expected to redefine the requirements for military forces and their structures. The war on terrorism has placed much attention on the capability of the military to undertake nonconventional missions.

The Quadrennial Defense Review

Questions raised by many outside the Department of Defense regarding U.S. military capability led to legislation that established the Quadrennial Defense Review. This legislation directed the secretary of defense and the JCS to conduct a defense review and provide a report by 1997 and every four years thereafter. QDR 1997 reflected the status quo, retaining the focus on two major regional conflicts and conventional forces.[13] In 2000, Steven Metz wrote, "Consensus is emerging that this QDR should be strategy driven rather than budget driven like the QDR 1997."[14] That appears to be the case with QDR 2001, as Secretary Rumsfeld spelled out a new direction, shifting focus from two major regional conflicts, establishing guidance for transforming the military, budget guidelines for 2003, and so-called terms of reference for the military (these include: reassuring friends and allies of U.S. commitments; dissuading adversaries of U.S. resolve; deterring threats and countercoercion; and defeating adversaries if deterrence fails). September 11 focused attention on homeland defense, with the establishment of the cabinet-level Office of Homeland Security. Former Pennsylvania governor Tom Ridge was appointed director of homeland security, and he immediately began coordinating agencies' activities for purposes of counterterrorism. The Office of Homeland Security will be replaced by the Department of Homeland Security if Congress enacts legislation proposed by President Bush in June 2002.

The nature of the military profession, as well as the education and socialization of civilian officials and employees, shapes the institutional posture of the Department of Defense. Logically, the posture leans toward the military solution in responding to national security issues. In turn, there is an orientation within the department to ensure adequate manpower levels, resources to develop sophisticated weaponry, and satisfactory compensation and benefits for service personnel. This fits hand-in-glove with the effort to develop a skilled military that can effectively perform in war. Increasingly, these efforts have expanded to include operations other than war, unconventional conflicts, and political-military situations that in the past were primarily Department of State concerns.

The New Strategic Landscape

In the strategic landscape of the twenty-first century, the focus is on various missions—peacekeeping, peacemaking, peace enforcement, and humanitarian. Each has it own character, yet all can overlap to a degree when forces are deployed in the field. "Although the primary purpose of the armed forces is the preparation and conduct of war, the most likely future missions of the armed forces of the industrial democracies are not classic interstate war fighting but a variety of peace support missions."[15] And as one journalist wrote, "Only a few years ago, our world was a bipolar nightmare in which two superpowers threatened a fight to the finish and the soldier was seen as the bringer of destruction. No longer: The relevance of the soldier today is increasingly as a bringer of peace."[16] Yet September 11 refocused the U.S. military on contingencies and missions overseas. In addition, the tragedy rekindled a fighting spirit to engage terrorism and the states that sponsor or harbor terrorists.

Given the nature of its participation in recent conflicts, ranging from ethnic cleansing and religious struggles to nationalistic movements and a variety of unconventional conflicts, the United States is driven by moral imperatives rather than clear national security interests. Yet the primary role of the military remains success in battle to defend vital national interests. The so-called warrior mentality required of combat soldiers is not an artifact of times past; it is a necessary corollary of the professional military ethos and a prerequisite for the use of force to support diplomacy.

In the past, the institutional orientation often placed the Defense Department at odds with the State Department. If negotiation, compromise, and diplomacy characterize the latter, then displays of force, military assistance, coercive diplomacy, and military conflict characterize the former. This is not to suggest there is no mutually acceptable goal to solve problems peacefully if possible. But the "stick" component of the carrot-and-stick approach among states and groups within states is often in the hands of Defense, and its operational arm is the ultimate big stick if military confrontation is inevitable. This overriding mission dominates the rationale for the department's existence, and it strongly influences its organizational behavior (see Chapter 7, on the military establishment).

The new strategic landscape requires that the Department of Defense be more adaptable and flexible in the use of military force, that is, less concerned with actual combat and more attuned to the use of the military as a diplomatic instrument prepared to engage in multinational efforts. At the same time, unilateral use of the U.S. military as a humanitarian and peacekeeping instrument has become more frequent. One author has labeled this the "do-something syndrome."[17] All of this suggests that the department is becoming a "shadow" State Department poised to carry out political and diplomatic missions using the military as the operational instrument. This pulls the Department of State into military issues.

Then–JCS Chairman Colin Powell's views on the use of the military are worth repeating, from the following exchange with Madeleine Albright, the UN ambassador at the time:

> My constant, unwelcome message at all meetings on Bosnia was simply that we should not commit military forces until we had a clear political objective. . . . The debate exploded at one session when Madeleine Albright, our ambassador to the UN, asked me in frustration, "What's the point in having this superb military that you're always talking about if we can't use it?" I thought I would have an aneurysm. American GIs were not toy soldiers to be moved around on some sort of global game board. . . . I told Ambassador Albright that the U.S. military would carry out any mission it was handed, but my advice would always be that the tough political goals had to be set first.[18]

Until the 1990s, a large part of the U.S. military was deployed overseas on a semipermanent basis in Europe, South Korea, and Japan. Although military personnel had been reduced overall by more than 25 percent during previous years, commitments to overseas missions increased—and were overstretched, according to some. In Europe, there were some 117,000 troops; in the Persian Gulf, close to 30,000; and in East Asia, more than 100,000. In March 2001, the number of military personnel in all services committed to overseas missions was more than 257,000, a figure that will likely increase during the war on terrorism. Yet the reduction in the number of military personnel, combined with the increase in deployed forces, changed the strategic configuration of the U.S. military. In addition, military contingencies and strategic perspectives are being reshaped by the strategic landscape of the twenty-first century. Many of these changes have their roots in the late 1990s (see Chapter 7).

Because the likelihood of global war has been considerably reduced, many within the Department of Defense question the commitment of U.S. forces outside existing treaty areas. This has been the general view since the end of the Vietnam War. The Gulf War was an exception, although many within the military initially favored the extensive use of sanctions. But the Gulf War was planned and analyzed as a desert version of a

European scenario in which U.S. forces, based on traditional strategic and operational concepts, brought sophisticated weaponry to bear against a clearly identifiable and conventionally postured adversary. The caution and reluctance to engage in military operations is conditioned by the fear of involvement in situations without clear political objectives as well as outcomes that might not be resolved by military force. Equally important is the underlying concern that involvement in ambiguous operations will lead to political opposition at home and the undermining of military capability.[19] But today many are contemplating the use of military force in response to international terrorism. Although much of the action was focused on special operations and relatively casualty-free air operations, follow-on conventional forces became part of the overall strategy, and major battles involving U.S. ground forces ensued.

Because there is no sharp delineation of responsibility and power in several policy areas between the Departments of Defense and State, there is often disagreement on policy preferences. This is magnified when the departments are headed by strong personalities with their own views on the international security environment and their own policy agendas. If sufficiently strong, one secretary can dominate and impose one department's approach. In any case, traditional models of national security policy, relationships among cabinet officers, and the power and responsibility of departments rarely go by the book.

The National Security Advisor

President Eisenhower was the first to create the position of special assistant for national security affairs, later to be retitled assistant to the president for national security affairs, and now commonly known as the National Security Advisor. According to an authoritative study of U.S. foreign policy, by the mid-1970s the National Security Advisor had become a "second secretary of state."[20] The authors point out, however, that this was not the original intent. In the administrations of Harry Truman and Dwight Eisenhower, the role was simply to "arrange meetings of the [NSC] and manage the paperwork."[21] During the early years of the NSC, the secretary of state was the prominent figure in national security policy.

Several factors helped to elevate the National Security Advisor to prominence by the 1970s. President John F. Kennedy, frustrated by the bureaucratic inertia at the State Department, sought a more streamlined and responsive system for foreign policy advice and implementation. Furthermore, the relatively quiet days of the Eisenhower administration were replaced by the U.S.-Soviet confrontations over Berlin, the Bay of

Pigs, the Cuban missile crisis, and the beginning of U.S. involvement in Vietnam. President Kennedy, wanting more direct control over U.S. foreign policy strategy, appointed McGeorge Bundy as assistant to the president for national security affairs. The combination of Bundy's strong personality, expanding U.S. involvement overseas, the increased complexity of national security issues, and the difficulty in developing flexibility and responsiveness within existing departments placed the NSC and the National Security Advisor in a more prominent policy position.

The post assumed its greatest importance under Presidents Richard Nixon, Gerald Ford, and Jimmy Carter; Henry Kissinger occupied the position, followed by Brent Scowcroft and Zbigniew Brzezinski. Strong-minded, covetous of their prerogatives, and enjoying direct access to the president, Kissinger and Brzezinski expanded the power of the position and tried to impose their personal policy preferences on the national security establishment. Under Carter, there was considerable friction between Brzezinski and Secretary of State Cyrus Vance, leading to the latter's resignation.

Since then, there has been considerable debate regarding the proper role of the National Security Advisor. During the first term of Ronald Reagan, there was an attempt to restrict the role to coordinator and expediter rather than initiator and innovator. Some argued that this downgrading allowed lesser personalities to occupy the position and may have led to some of the excesses revealed in the 1987 Iran-contra hearings. The argument is that a strong personality and leader is needed to ensure the proper functioning of the national security staff.

In 1993, for the first time in twelve years, the Democratic Party controlled the Oval Office and Congress. President Clinton appointed Anthony Lake as National Security Advisor and Sandy Berger as Deputy National Security Advisor. Later Lake resigned and was replaced by Berger, who remained in that position until the end of the Clinton administration. In 2001, Condoleezza Rice was appointed National Security Advisor in the George W. Bush administration. She is the first female to hold the post and brings a vision of national security that coincides, as expected, with Secretary of State Colin Powell. This presumes a more cautious and selective approach to national security commitments, something that also reflects President Bush's perspectives. September 11 changed everything, however, leading to a global effort of determination and long-term engagement.

The fact is that the role and power of the National Security Advisor depends upon the president. Even though the NSC was established by Congress, the way in which it is used is almost entirely in the president's hands. In any case, the National Security Advisor is in a position to make a major impact on national security policy for several important reasons.

First, she is the president's personal confidante, as the post is filled without Senate consent, as required for secretaries. Second, her office is located inside the White House, so she has direct access to the president and usually sees him every working day; this fact alone creates a perception of power not accorded other officials. And third, the National Security Advisor is not tied to any agency, which grants a degree of flexibility that secretaries usually cannot match. In addition, the National Security Advisor is not encumbered by operational responsibilities, and the NSC staff is relatively small—usually about fifty—and thus more controllable than the huge bureaucracies at State and Defense. And finally, the National Security Advisor represents the president's views, in contrast to the organizational views represented by the secretaries of state and defense.

It is apparent that a strong personality can shape national security policy like no other official. Furthermore, the intermixing of foreign policy, national security, and domestic issues enhances the role. She is in a position to synthesize these policy issues and bring to bear a perspective that is closely linked to the president's perceptions of office and mind-set. This presidential confidante is appointed by him, works for him, and owes her allegiance to him.

The National Security Council

It is useful to examine the organization and function of the NSC in detail, especially with respect to the policy triad and the NSC system. Figure 6.4 illustrates the organization of the NSC, the relationship of the NSC staff, and the procedures for making recommendations and input.

The president determines how the NSC is used—even whether it should be used. Each president from Truman to George W. Bush has shaped the NSC and used it according to his leadership style and perceptions of the office. Truman, the first president to interact with the newly established NSC, made clear that he considered it to be a strictly advisory body and did not regularly attend its meetings until the Korean War. He maintained that a president could not abdicate his responsibilities in foreign and national security policy to a structure such as the NSC.

President Eisenhower possessed unmatched military experience and established a formal and systematic method for using the NSC. Besides creating the post that would eventually become known as National Security Advisor, he set up a system of committees to serve the NSC. As many scholars agree, Eisenhower's preference for complete staff work and well-defined procedures gave the NSC and its staff previously unknown prominence in national security. Following military procedures, Eisenhower wanted options exhaustively discussed within the NSC, with clear recommendations presented to him identifying the best policy.

Figure 6.4   The National Security Council

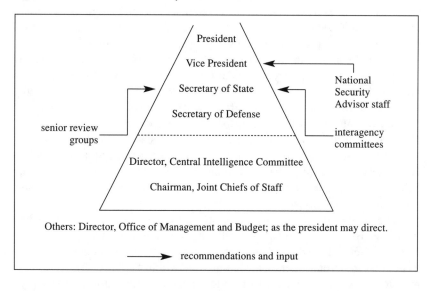

President

Vice President

Secretary of State

Secretary of Defense

senior review groups

National Security Advisor staff

interagency committees

Director, Central Intelligence Committee

Chairman, Joint Chiefs of Staff

Others: Director, Office of Management and Budget; as the president may direct.

⟶   recommendations and input

President Kennedy, however, preferred a smaller and more streamlined staff and eliminated much of Eisenhower's machinery. Kennedy's appointment of McGeorge Bundy reflected the importance he attached to integrating foreign and defense policies. His disdain of formal procedures and rigid bureaucracy made him rely more on the NSC staff and his personal staff, such as Bundy, than on the executive departments. The Bay of Pigs fiasco in April 1961 seemed to confirm Kennedy's distrust of the established bureaucracy.[22] But that event also exposed the weakness in Kennedy's approach to managing the bureaucracy. Eisenhower's more formal approach to reviewing policy proposals would have revealed the inherent absurdity of the CIA plan to invade Cuba with a small exile detachment and overthrow Castro. The diminished importance of the NSC continued under Lyndon Johnson, who also relied on a network of informal advisers.

Expansion of the NSC

The NSC did not regain its prominence until President Nixon restored much of the machinery established under Eisenhower (Nixon had served two full terms as vice president under Ike). This included a system of interdepartmental groups at the assistant secretary of state level and senior committees at the undersecretary and deputy secretary levels to examine and coordinate policies on defense, intelligence, covert operations, and other national security matters; Vietnam received special attention. This structure continued for the most part under Ford but changed under Carter, who retained the procedures but reduced the committees to two and gave more authority to the executive departments. Nonetheless, the strong personality and views of Brzezinski under Carter tended to prevail, placing the NSC staff in a powerful position vis-à-vis the executive departments.

The Reagan administration strengthened the NSC committee system and established interagency groups at the assistant secretary level to focus on defense policy, foreign policy, and intelligence. Problems surfaced, however, as Reagan's personal staff became involved and made decisions outside the purview of the established structure. Friction between the National Security Advisor and the secretaries of state and defense dogged several issues, leading to the resignation of Secretary of State Alexander Haig. Turnover was high: Richard Allen, William Clark, Robert McFarlane, John Poindexter, Frank Carlucci, and William Powell—all served as National Security Advisor under Reagan.

The George Bush administration brought in new personalities in 1989, including Brent Scowcroft. In the Bush administration, the roles of the National Security Advisor and his deputy were strengthened, as each chaired an important interagency committee within the NSC. This internal restructuring was expected to provide better coordination and sharply define policy options. In late 1991 and into 1992, Bush's national security establishment was put to the test as a range of new issues emerged that did not fit easily into the Cold War perspective. Many of these issues continued until the end of the Clinton administration and into the George W. Bush administration.

The Current Period

In 2001, President George W. Bush and his inner circle made an early impact on the NSC and staff:

> The first few weeks of President George W. Bush's tenure as Commander-in-Chief portend significant changes in the national security arena. Old hands in dealing with both the domestic and international ramifications of defense affairs—Cheney, Rumsfeld, Rice, and Powell—are contributing their collective expertise in fashioning the national security construct that will frame the political boundaries of America's military-engagement policies during the next four years . . . A top-to-bottom scrub of the National Security Council has already occurred, and about one-third of the NSC positions have been eliminated . . . The size of the professional staff at the NSC doubled under the former president, from about 50 to more than 100 full-timers.[23]

A new superstar emerged: Colin Powell, who as JCS chairman played a visible role in the 1991 Gulf War and in the transition to the Clinton administration. The more powerful political role that General Powell fulfilled was the result of the 1986 Goldwater-Nichols Act, which made the JCS chairman the principal military adviser to the president and gave him more power in dealing with senior military commanders and the military system in general. Although the exercise of this new-found power is contingent upon the personality and character of the JCS chairman, Powell's superb political savvy established a precedent in the national security process. In 2001, Powell was appointed secretary of state.

The creation of the Office of Homeland Security in September 2001 added yet another dimension to the NSC and the formulation of national security strategy. Coordination with the NSC, as well as with a host of agencies, is part of the office's responsibilities. If the Department of Homeland Security is created by Congress to replace the Office of Homeland Security, it will have the power, authority, and budget to make it one of the largest departments in the government.

The NSC Staff

The NSC staff is an arm of the NSC. As such it not only performs administrative duties but also is involved in policy-related functions. Muddling the policy process is the fact that the National Security Advisor lacks a legal basis for operational action. "The National Security Council (NSC) should be responsible for advising the President and for coordinating the multiplicity of national security activities. . . . The NSC Advisor and staff should resist the temptation to assume a central policymaking and operational role."[24] The effectiveness of the staff is limited if it becomes too large and unwieldy. Yet it must be large enough to respond to the tasks at hand. But the real source of power in the NSC staff rests in its relationship to the president. As such, it has a great degree of bureaucratic freedom and flexibility and reflects the presidential view.

After reviewing the history of the NSC staff to 1987, the Tower Commission concluded,

> What emerges from this history is an NSC staff used by each President in a way that reflected his individual preferences and working style. Over time, it has developed an important role within the Executive Branch of coordinating policy review, preparing issues for Presidential decision, and monitoring implementation. But it has remained the President's creature, molded as he sees fit, to serve as his personal staff for national security affairs. For this reason, it has generally operated out of the public view and has not been subject to direct oversight by the Congress.[25]

The Iran-contra hearings brought the role of the NSC staff into full view as Congress attempted to uncover violations of law by members of the NSC staff, specifically Lieutenant Colonel Oliver North.[26] As intelligence historian John Prados concludes, "Ultimately it is the President's responsibility to keep his house in order and banish the conflicts among unruly subordinates. Presidents have compiled a rather poor record in this regard."[27] This was no less true during the Clinton administration.

The NSC and its staff are a well-established structure with statutory authority. It has proven to be a useful and important structure when used as an advisory agency that is allowed to analyze policy and strategy options. The way the NSC and its staff function in any administration is complex and subject to personal preferences, mind-sets, and leadership styles—including those of the policy triad. To be sure, the president is central, and the NSC cannot substitute for his central role. Yet as one authority concluded:

> The decision-making process is always problematical and often controversial. The process requires the interaction of people with differing personal, political, and institutional perspectives on policy issues. By design and evolution, the system promotes rivalry among the branches of the government and within those branches as policy questions move toward resolution.[28]

Need for Change

The United States Commission on National Security/21st Century concluded:

> The dramatic changes in the world since the end of the Cold War of the last half-century have not been accompanied by any major institutional changes in the Executive Branch of the U.S. government. Serious deficiencies exist that only a significant organizational redesign can remedy. Most troublesome is the lack of an overarching strategic framework guiding U.S. national security policymaking and resource allocation. Clear goals and priorities are rarely set. Budgets are prepared and appropriated as they were during the Cold War.[29]
>
> Not only is the environment changing, but so, too, must the mechanisms by which the United States interacts with the world change. The Cold War mechanisms worked admirably to keep that competition from going hot (war). The disappearance of that threat suggests the need to adapt and fine-tune those mechanisms for a "new world order."[30]

All this must be qualified by the realities of the political process and the number of actors involved in the national security system. Examining the role of the power centers in the U.S. political system and their role in foreign and defense policies, Roger Hilsman writes:

> The president and his staff in the White House constitute the most powerful of these power centers, but the presidency is far from being all power-

ful. . . . [A] political system composed of multiple power centers gives a veto to a relatively small coalition of those power centers who oppose some new initiative.[31]

Nonetheless, the policy triad in concert with the president form a formidable power center that is at the core of national security policy and is the driving force behind the national security establishment. It becomes even more formidable when one party controls both the Oval Office and Congress. As Hilsman concludes, "Policy is made through a political process. Power is an element in politics. But power diffused can lead to evil as surely as power concentrated. Herein lies the irony."[32]

Summary and Conclusions

This overview of the primary structure for advising the president on national security provides the basis for several conclusions:

1. The president by law and of necessity has the central role in national security policy.

2. The informal policy triad is critical in shaping national security policy. The interactions among the secretaries of state and defense and the National Security Advisor strongly influence the way policy is formulated and the kind of advice given to the president.

3. All of the primary players in the NSC have their own constituencies and bases of power. Strong personalities can impose personal policy preferences on the NSC and the system, at times making it more difficult for the president to consider the full range of options.

4. Those in the policy triad and in the NSC can mobilize in a variety of ways to oppose policy options they disagree with. Adding to the problems of coordination and consensus is the fact that the secretaries of state and defense have different organizational goals and may well view problems through different lenses.

5. The NSC does not have an operational arm. If its recommendations are approved by the president, they must be implemented through the two departments—the Departments of State and Defense—and at times through the CIA. Departmental and agency perspectives and preferences come into play in this process. The way that decisions are interpreted and implemented can take on unintended directions.

6. When the interplay of power relationships within the NSC and the policy triad gives rise to multiple advocacy, the president will find it difficult not to become involved in the policy formulation process.

Strong personalities can pose a dilemma for any president, but appointing people who simply parrot the president's version of national security—the "group-think" mentality—can lead to dangerous weaknesses in national security policy. Yet the president cannot constantly interject himself into the policy formulation process to resolve differences among his top personnel. Honest disagreement can be valuable, but he should expect some fundamental meeting of the minds. Reconciling disagreements is the responsibility of the president. For this reason, presidential leadership is critical to effective national security policy formulation and execution.

Notes

1. United States Commission on National Security/21st Century, *Road Map for National Security: Imperative for Change*, final draft report (January 31, 2001), p. 47.

2. See, e.g., John M. Goshko, "State Department Reorganizes Ranks," *Washington Post*, February 6, 1994, sec. A, p. 8.

3. James M. McCormick, *American Foreign Policy and Process*, 3rd ed. (Itasca, IL: F. E. Peacock, 1998), p. 390.

4. United States Commission on National Security/21st Century, *Road Map*, p. 47.

5. Ibid., p. 57.

6. Ibid., p. 54.

7. Christopher C. Shoemaker, *The NSC Staff: Counseling the Council* (Boulder: Westview, 1991), p. 42.

8. Ibid.

9. William S. Cohen, Secretary of Defense, *Report of the Secretary of Defense to the President and Congress* (Washington, DC: Department of Defense, 2001), p. A-1.

10. John G. Roos, "First Glimpse of Bottom-Up Review Was a Nice Job of Packaging, Anyway," *Armed Forces Journal International* 132, no. 3 (October 1993): 17–18.

11. John G. Roos, "Another Bridge Too Far; It's Time for the SecDef to Fight Some Close-in Battles," *Armed Forces Journal International* (June 1998), p. 2.

12. Vince Crawley, "Bracing for Change," *Army Times*, January 22, 2001, p. 8.

13. See Steven Metz, ed. *Revising the Two MTW Force Shaping Paradigm* (Carlisle, PA: Strategic Studies Institute, U.S. Army War College, April 2001).

14. Steven Metz, *American Strategy: Issues and Alternatives for the Quadrennial Defense Review* (Carlisle, PA: Strategic Studies Institute, U.S. Army War College, September 2000), p. ix.

15. Christopher Dandeker and James Gow, "Military Culture and Strategic Peacekeeping," in Erwin A. Schmidl, ed., "Peace Operations Between War and Peace," *Small Wars and Insurgencies* 10, no. 2 (Special Issue, Autumn 1999) 58.

16. Sina Odugbemi, "Intervention; the Lure—and Limits—of Force," from *Guardian* (Lagos, Nigeria), as published in *World Press Review* 40, no. 3 (March 1993): 9–10.

17. Donald M. Snow, *Peacekeeping, Peacemaking, and Peace-Enforcement:*

The U.S. Role in the New International Order (Carlisle Barracks, PA: Strategic Studies Institute, U.S. Army War College, February 1993), p. 6.

18. Colin Powell, with Joseph E. Persico, *My American Journey* (New York: Random House, 1995), p. 576.

19. See Alan Ned Sabrosky and Robert L. Sloane, *The Recourse to War: An Appraisal of the "Weinberger Doctrine"* (Carlisle Barracks, PA: Strategic Studies Institute, U.S. Army War College, 1988).

20. John Spanier and Eric M. Uslaner, *American Foreign Policy Making and the Democratic Dilemmas*, 4th ed. (New York: Holt, Rinehart, and Winston, 1985), p. 35.

21. Ibid.

22. Although President Kennedy publicly accepted the blame for the Bay of Pigs failure, privately he placed much of the blame on the poor planning and cumbersome procedures in the military and the CIA, as well as the staff procedures of existing agencies.

23. John G. Roos, "A New Beginning," *Armed Forces Journal International* (March 2001): 2.

24. United States Commission on National Security/21st Century, *Road Map*, p. 50.

25. *President's Special Review Board* (Washington, DC: U.S. Government Printing Office, February 26, 1987), generally referred to as the "Tower Commission Report."

26. See, e.g., *Report of the Congressional Committees Investigating the Iran-Contra Affair with Supplemental, Minority and Additional Views.* 100th Cong., 1st sess., House Report No. 100–433 and Senate Report No. 100–216 (Washington, DC: U.S. Government Printing Office, 1987), esp. pp. 36–51.

27. John Prados, *Keepers of the Keys: A History of the National Security Council from Truman to Bush* (New York: John Morrow, 1991), p. 561.

28. Donald M. Snow, *National Security: Defense Policy in a Changed International Order*, 4th ed. (New York: St. Martin's, 1998), p. 100.

29. United States Commission on National Security/21st Century, *Road Map*, p. x.

30. Donald M. Snow and Eugene Brown, *Puzzle Palace and Foggy Bottom: U.S. Foreign and Defense Policy-Making in the 1990s* (New York: St. Martin's, 1994), p. 274.

31. Roger Hilsman, with Laura Gaughran and Patricia A. Weitsman, *The Politics of Policy Making in Defense and Foreign Affairs: Conceptual Models and Bureaucratic Politics* (Englewood Cliffs, NJ: Prentice-Hall, 1993), pp. 340 and 343.

32. Ibid., p. 349.

7

The Military Establishment

THE MILITARY ESTABLISHMENT IS A CRITICAL OPERATIONAL ARM of the national security system. How it is organized and its relationship to the president and other political actors are necessary considerations in the study of national security policy. Furthermore, the education, socialization, and mind-sets of military professionals are important in shaping the military establishment and in determining its ability to pursue the goals of U.S. national security policy.

Since the end of World War II, the U.S. military establishment has gone through several important changes in organizational structure and notions of military professionalism. This continued during the post–Cold War era, as it does today. The size of the military has been reduced, and it must reconcile itself to a variety of political and social forces that have affected its structure and missions. At the same time, it must adjust to an ill-defined security landscape. Aimed at making the military more responsive to prevailing threats and preparing it for future conflicts, these changes have made the conflict spectrum, as well as military organizations and professionalism, enormously complicated. Military success requires highly skilled and competent individuals at virtually all levels in the military hierarchy. This in turn has made the president and the national security establishment heavily dependent upon the military for sound advice.

The concept of national security has expanded to include military participation in humanitarian and peacekeeping missions and in combating international terrorism (see Chapter 1). As a result, military force has been used in missions and contingencies that are contrary to the views of the military establishment. All of this tends to dilute any notion that the president and Congress are captives of the military, as the use of force in the new era has become engulfed in civilian cultures and nontraditional missions. At the same time, the U.S. military is in the process of transformation—preparing for wars in the twenty-first century. This envisions changes in strategy, doctrine, and weaponry, among other factors.

The Command-and-Control Structure

The military establishment's focus of power shifted to the secretary of defense when that office was given control of the military departments; changes in 1986 further expanded his power as well as that of the JCS chairman. These changes have had an impact on the development of strategy, the formulation of national security policy, as well as presidential control over the military establishment.

Several reference points need to be reviewed with respect to the structure of the Department of Defense (see Figure 6.3). First, the secretaries of the military departments (Army, Navy, and Air Force) have no operational responsibilities; revisions to the National Security Act of 1947 downgraded their executive-department status to that of military departments (1949) and later removed them from the chain of command (1958). The primary responsibilities of the service secretaries are in administrative and logistical areas: manpower, procurement, weapons systems, service effectiveness, military welfare, and training responsibilities, among other duties. However, a strong personality in the service secretary's office can have a decided influence and political impact in shaping the posture and operational capability of the service.

Second, the role of the JCS chairman has been strengthened. Formerly, the JCS was a corporate body, and the chairman served principally as spokesman. In addition, the chairman had little control over who served on the joint staff from the services, whose commanders also rotated the chairman's functions among themselves in his absence. The chairman held a symbolic rather than a substantive position.

The 1986 Defense Reorganization Act (the Goldwater-Nichols Act) made the JCS chairman the primary military figure in the defense establishment. It gave him direct access to the president and assigned him responsibilities not only for strategic thinking but also for a range of other matters (including budget assessments and readiness evaluations), affording him a more direct relationship with the commanders in chief of specified and unified commands. He now has direct control over assignments to the joint staff. Also created by this legislation are several responsibilities assigned to the JCS vice chairman. The chairman no longer must accept joint staff members selected by the various services. In short, the chairman is now the most important member of the JCS, responsible only to the secretary of defense and the president.

Third, a new officer specialty was created by Congress.[1] This joint specialty provides for a lifetime career path for officers qualified as staff officers in joint staff positions. The objective is to have a pool of officers from all services qualified to serve on joint staffs. Although not intended to create a general staff corps on the old German army model, the program has lead to important changes within the profession and in the functioning of the joint staff. Education and experience in matters of joint staff responsibilities, as well as socialization processes, are likely to develop a staff mind-set on a long-term basis and inculcate some officers with a general staff mentality.

The chain of command and control of the operational arm of the military runs directly from the commander in chief to the secretary of defense to the JCS chairman to the commanders of the unified commands (see Figure 7.1).

Unified Commands

A unified command, as the name suggests, is a joint service operational responsibility. Until the 1986 Defense Reorganization Act, the commanders of unified commands had little control over what units were assigned to their command. This was the responsibility of the various services, whose component commanders had to depend on their own services for resources. The composition of forces was determined by each service. Thus unified commands reflected a mix of doctrines, equipment, and missions as determined by the services.

Now the commanders in chief of unified commands have been given more power in budget matters pertaining to their commands, hiring and firing authority over subordinate commanders, and direct access to the secretary of defense and JCS chairman, bypassing the respective services. The president, in turn, can give the JCS chairman primary responsibility for overseeing the activities of these commands. The 1986 Defense Reorganization Act established the JCS chairman as the spokesman for the commanders of the combatant commands, especially in operational requirements. Commanders now have the authority to act as real commanders, generally independent from control of their respective services. The changes resulting from the 1986 act have had a positive impact on jointness and in the operational direction of the various commands.

It is also the case that in the new strategic environment interservice rivalries have resurfaced as each service tries to protect its turf, not only in terms of missions but also budgets. In 2001, this remained a characteristic of the military establishment as each service attempted to prepare for twenty-first-century warfare and the new strategic landscape. Congress tried to override interservice squabbles and problems of command and control by imposing a strengthened secretary of defense and JCS chairman, as well as a strengthened command system, on the military establishment. But the problem of

Figure 7.1   The Joint Chiefs of Staff and Unified Commands

The Joint Chiefs of Staff

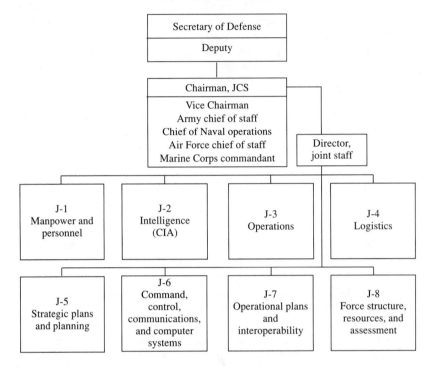

Unified Commands

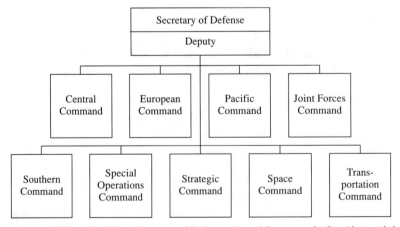

Source: William S. Cohen, Secretary of Defense, *Annual Report to the President and the Congress,* 2001, p. A-2. Available online at www.dtic.mil/execsec/adr2001.

internal rivalries remains. In the past, the number of assistant secretaries of defense reflected the variety of matters under the responsibility of the secretary of defense. Indeed, the scope of activities and the amount of resources required to maintain and expand them created a vast managerial complex—too complex, according to some—that precluded an efficient military system.

The inherent rivalries leave the Defense Department vulnerable to politicization of its operational arms and hamper development of coherent policy and feasible options. Many of these plans were thrown into organizational disarray with Secretary of Defense Les Aspin's resignation (or firing) in December 1993, compounded by the withdrawal in January 1994 of retired Admiral Bobby R. Inman from consideration after he was nominated by President Clinton for the post. Deputy Secretary of Defense William Perry was nominated and confirmed as secretary of defense in February 1994, succeeded by former U.S. senator William Cohen in 1998. With the inauguration of George W. Bush in 2001, a new national security team was put into place and, with it, a new defense system under Secretary of Defense Donald Rumsfeld. This included a system designed to operate in several unconventional environments. In 2001, this included special attention to combating international terrorism. In spring 2002, it was announced that a new command would be established in the Department of Defense to coordinate North American defense forces.

In 1993, Secretary Aspin and the Clinton administration developed plans to reduce the number of assistant secretaries. "Under Mr. Aspin's plan, the traditional civilian Pentagon functions will be handled by four branches: weapons acquisition, personnel and readiness, the office of the Pentagon comptroller, and an office of national security policy."[2] The so-called Aspin Plan was abandoned by his successor, William Perry, in favor of a more traditional structure, which was adopted by Cohen. However, Secretary Rumsfield implemented plans to transform the military into a twenty-first-century force designed to respond to threats and potential threats. This encompasses changes in the military system that focus on doctrine, training, and weaponry, and incorporate information age technology.

Congress: Guns and Butter

The role of Congress does not stop at legislation to restructure the military. Executive-legislative skirmishes over constitutional roles have already been discussed, but the division of authority over military appraisal and allocation also impact the formulation of strategy and its operational implementation. This is reflected in guns-and-butter issues: How much should be spent for defense, and how much for nondefense issues? The president may be the commander in chief, but Congress has the power of the purse. The weapons acquisition process, which obviously affects the military establishment's performance, is but one example. Congress allocates funds for research, development, and production.

All these struggles magnify the political dimension of the military establishment. Congressional hearings on strategy, resource allocation, and military performance strike at the heart of the military establishment, requiring operational commanders at all levels to become sensitive to the political nature of their responsibilities. The desire in Congress for more explicit military recommendations and more control over military commitments in contingencies short of war means it struggles with the president, the secretary of defense, the JCS chairman, individual service chiefs, and a variety of high-level operational commanders. In 1993 and 1994, these struggles were especially visible over the reduction of the military and the shrinking defense budget. This continued in 2000 and into 2001, that is, until September 11. In the aftermath, budget allocations for defense increased.

Secretary William Cohen's 2001 Annual Report details information on the budget, manpower levels, and weaponry, among other things. The report states,

> Like the three previous DoD budgets, the FY 2002 plan was developed largely based on the Department's May 1997 Quadrennial Defense Review. The QDR detailed changes needed to address new global threats and opportunities and to make the best use of constrained resources . . . Over the long-term, DoD must fund the needed post–Cold War transformation of America's defense posture and modernize U.S. forces to ensure their future combat superiority.[3]

By 2000, the president and Congress had agreed to increase defense spending, although there was disagreement over the amount. This was compounded by disagreements within the Clinton administration and between the administration and Congress over force posture and strategy. In the aftermath of September 11, the existing budget proposals and allocations became almost irrelevant as Congress allocated more money to the Bush administration for defense and combating international terrorism.

Directly and indirectly, then, Congress has increased its role and linkage to the functioning and powers of the military establishment. Indeed, it can be said that Congress has become *part of* the military establishment. As such, it brings along a variety of political considerations, from personnel issues to base-closure decisions. Its judgments influence not only budget allocations but also the concept of vital interests, the structure of the military establishment, and the development of strategic options.

Civilians employed by the Department of Defense are an important element in the relationship between the military establishment and other political actors. In 1990, there were more than 1 million civilians working for the department, not counting the more than 1 million employed in defense-related industries. During the Clinton administration, there was a reduction in the number of civilians employed and in the money devoted to defense industries. By 2000, the number of civilians working for the Department of Defense had dropped to about 700,000. Those employed in defense-related industries had also been reduced.[4] To be sure, only a small part of this civilian component has a direct impact on national security policy and the functioning of the national command authority. Nonetheless, close links with the Department of Defense provide a channel for civilian attitudes and mind-sets to penetrate the military profession. Conversely, military attitudes and mind-sets penetrate the civilian component. This interpenetration is greatest at the higher levels, as all appointments at the assistant secretary level and above are political and normally civilian; a more noticeable degree of separation exists at lower levels, where civilians are rarely present in operational units.

Thus the dual influences in the military establishment simply confirm the long-standing norm that civilian control of the U.S. military is a well-established fact in law and reality. Equally important, the military profession has accepted this as a basic premise. Over the years, civilian rule has slowly but surely permeated weapons acquisition, force composition, strategic options, and command-and-control issues. It is in such areas that the president and the military establishment face some of the most serious opposition and disagreements.

Force Restructuring and Composition

The relationship between the military and political leaders that evolved during the first years of the Clinton administration reshaped the military's command-and-control structure, force posture, and professionalism. A major part of this surfaced with Secretary of Defense Aspin's Bottom-Up Review.[5] This envisioned the restructuring and reduction of the military by the year 1999 as shown in Table 7.1.

In addition, there was a heavy reliance on reserve forces, with five-plus divisions for the Army, one aircraft carrier for the Navy, seven fighter

Table 7.1 The Restructuring of the Military, 1993–1999

	1993	1999
Army active divisions	14	10
Navy aircraft carriers	13	11
Air Force fighter wings	16	13
Marine Corps active-duty strength	182,000	174,000
Nuclear forces		
Submarines	22	18
Bombers	201	up to 184
Missiles	787	500

Source: Les Aspin, Secretary of Defense, *The Bottom Up Review: Forces for a New Era* (Washington, DC: Department of Defense, September 1, 1993).

wings in the Air Force Reserve, and 42,000 reserve personnel for the Marine Corps. There were several critics of the resulting Aspin Plan. For many, the force structure and force composition envisioned by the Bottom-Up Review was driven by budget considerations devoid of serious strategic considerations.

Then–Chief of Staff of the Army General Gordon Sullivan and Lieutenant Colonel James Dubik wrote that

> American political leaders expect the military to *contract* in both size and budget, *contribute* to domestic recovery, *participate* in global stability operations, and *retain* its capability to produce decisive victory in whatever circumstances they are employed—all at the same time. . . . International and domestic realities have resulted in the paradox of declining military resources and increasing military missions, a paradox that is stressing our armed forces. The stress is significant.[6]

All of these changes by the Clinton administration, combined with the president's efforts to lift the ban on homosexuals in the military and expand the role of women in combat, had a decided impact on the military profession, positive and negative. The negatives were reinforced by Clinton's avoidance of military service and his alleged antimilitary activities during the Vietnam War. This resulted in a gap in the relationship between the commander in chief and the military—a gap that many within the military believed had serious consequences for civil-military relations and professional status. For some, the military had become more of a social institution than a fighting institution. This was reinforced by those who challenged the use of the U.S. military in nation-building, peacekeeping, and humanitarian intervention.[7]

By the end of the Clinton administration into 2001, the military force structure was as shown in Table 7.2.[8] How all this will change as a result of the war on terrorism remains to be seen.

The Military Profession

If the command-and-control structure is an important ingredient in the formulation of national security policy, the character of the military profession—including its values, norms, and mind-sets—is equally so.[9] How military professionals perceive threats, assess the capability of the military instrument, and develop professional skills and capabilities are significant determinants of the advice they give. In addition, professional behavior has much to do with the perceptions of Congress, allies, and adversaries regarding U.S. military capability and effectiveness.

Six elements are paramount in shaping the character of military offi-

Table 7.2   Military Structure, 1990–2002

	1990	1993 Base Force	1993 BUR[a]	1997 QDR[a]	Bush Plan, 2002
Army divisions	18/10[b]	12/8	10/8	10/8	10/8
Marine Corps divisions	3/1	3/1	3/1	3/1	3/1
Aircraft carriers	15/1	12/1	11/1	11/1	12
Carrier air wings	13/2	11/2	10/1	10/1	10/1
Attack submarines	93	88	45–55	50	53
Surface combatants	203	141	n.a.	1,106/10	108/8
Battle force ships	546	430	346	n.a.	313
USAF fighter wings	24/12	14/11	13/7	12+/8	12+/7+

Source: U.S. Department of Defense, *FY 2002 Defense Budget* (Washington, DC: Department of Defense, June 2001), available online at http//www.whitehouse.gov/news/usbudget/blueprint/buddoc.html; accessed, June 28, 2001.

Notes: n.a. indicates no quantity specified in this category.

a. BUR = Bottom Up Review; QDR = Quadrennial Defense Review.

b. Dual entries show active/reserve numbers.

cers: (1) The profession has a defined area of competence based on expert knowledge; (2) there is a system of continuing education designed to maintain professional competence; (3) the profession has an obligation to society and must serve it without concern for remuneration; (4) it has a system of values that perpetuate the professional character and establish and maintain legitimate relationships with society; (5) there is an institutional framework within which the profession can function; and (6) the profession has control over the system of internal rewards and punishments and is in a position to determine the quality and quantity of those entering the profession.

One factor distinguishing the military profession from others rests in its notions of duty, honor, country. Its sole client is the state. The military professional is committed to the ultimate sacrifice—one must be prepared to give one's life for the state. But the characteristic unique to the profession lies in its primary purpose: to win wars. The military is employed as an operational arm to destroy an adversary—in more colloquial terms, "to kill and break things."

Yet the military profession is subject to constraints not found in other callings. For all practical purposes, it cannot publicly or formally engage in political partisanship to secure better wages, conditions of employment, or operational commitments. It must comply with the policy and decisions of civilian officials even if it does not agree with them. Institutional and professional loyalties as well as professional motivations preclude expressing public outrage at orders from above. The military must accept the decision to destroy the enemy with all of the power at hand once the political leadership decides it shall be done.

Professional career patterns and success depend on the ability to work within the system and follow the established path. Professional values and mind-sets, which preclude military professionals from stepping outside the system, also tend to socialize them into an institutional perspective that denotes a particular set of relationships with society. Perhaps most important, there is a system of teaching that establishes the way military professionals view themselves, their institution, society, and the outside world. To be sure, most professions tend to follow somewhat similar patterns. But nonmilitary professions have access to large segments of society and thus can move in a mainstream that has relatively undefined boundaries.

The military profession, in contrast, tends to be a more self-contained community—socially, legally, economically, and intellectually—all of which reinforces the primary professional purpose of success in battle. To be sure, the lifestyles and mind-sets engendered are what civilians find the most difficult to appreciate. This lack of understanding is at the root of the negative (and, at times, antagonistic) views that military professionals hold about self-styled military experts, especially in the media, Congress, and academia. Indeed, many military professionals tend to see such critics as ignorant of the military, which helps perpetuate the self-contained community mind-set of the military and magnifies differences between the operational arm of the military and society in general.

Since the end of the Cold War, however, there has been an increasing number of voices demanding that the military reflect society—to become, as one author has put it, a "kinder, gentler military."[10] This is reinforced by the view that the threat of major war has diminished and the military must be more society-sensitive in dealing with noncombat operations such as peacekeeping, humanitarian missions, and constabulary missions.

In the 1990s and into the twenty-first century, the military has been struggling with serious internal travails: feminization, homosexuality, sexual harassment, morale, and recruitment, among others. These internal problems make it difficult to design and commit an effective military force in support of national security policy. All of this is compounded by the argument that the military must more closely reflect society, for example, in its diversity and multiculturalism. These problems remain.[11]

In addition, the profession seemed to be troubled over the direction of political-military policy in the United States. This concern encompassed several issues, ranging from the reduction in the size of the military and the defense budget, to civil-military relations, to the shape of the profession.

The military perspective casts the external environment and the requirements for military effectiveness in a mold that differs, sometimes considerably, from the public's view and that of elected officials. Indeed, it can also differ from views within the executive branch. Evolving in no small part from the Vietnam experience, the mind-set of military professionals has become sensitive to the political dynamics created by military commitment. On the one hand, they tend toward extreme caution about military involvement in situations likely to generate domestic political opposition, a concern expressed eloquently in 1976 by Chief of Staff of the Army General Fred Weyand:

> Vietnam was a reaffirmation of the peculiar relationship between the American Army and the American people. The American Army really is a people's Army in the sense that it belongs to the American people who take a jealous and proprietary interest in its involvement. When the Army is committed the American people are committed, when the American people lose their commitment it is futile to try to keep the Army committed. In the final analysis, the American Army is not so much an arm of the Executive Branch as it is an arm of the American people. The Army, therefore, cannot be committed lightly.[12]

Note, however, that "commitment" has its own spectrum. For example, U.S. Army and Marine Corps combat troops deployed overseas have a distinctly different connotation for the public than do U.S. Navy personnel sailing aboard vessels in international waters.

Yet once committed, most military professionals expect to employ the resources at hand to prevail quickly, believing it unconscionable not to use the most effective weaponry and tactics to subdue the enemy. Furthermore, the principles of war stress that overwhelming firepower and resources should be centered on the enemy's weakest point to achieve victory. One interpretation of this is that military professionals seek overwhelming superiority, not simply adequacy. Military doctrine holds that overwhelming superiority is likely to reduce casualties and be the most economical in achieving success. The debate regarding the use of force in conflicts short of war focuses not only on the role of air power but also on combat troops engaged in any variety of humanitarian and peacekeeping missions.[13] Moreover, political fireworks accompany the use of the military in conflicts short of war. This was evident in Kosovo, where objectives became blurred and the use of military force was affected by the political views of allied NATO countries.[14] This also became a major concern in 2001–2002 after U.S. military forces were committed to the war in Afghanistan.

Homeland security is another mission that complicates the role of the military. Military professionals recognize the need for homeland security but are concerned about command and control and the coordination required between the active military, reserve forces, domestic security forces, and emergency and medical teams.[15] This has become more complicated by the creation of the Office of Homeland Security.[16] This will become even more complicated and broader in scope if President Bush's call for a Department of Homeland Security is enacted by Congress.

Finally, military professionals expect to be provided clear policy goals, strategic coherency, and operationally precise tasks. Mainstream military posture is shaped best to respond to these dimensions. Contingencies of an unconventional nature are not characterized by these types of considerations. They are likely to be policy-incoherent, strategically obscure, and operationally muddled. Security issues in the twenty-first century are largely characterized by unconventional conflicts, and this is likely to continue.

The Weinberger Doctrine

In the 1990s, professional concerns led to the resurfacing of the so-called Weinberger Doctrine, later reinforced by the Powell Doctrine. Events in Somalia in 1993 seemed to confirm the relevancy of these approaches. During the Somalia mission, the killing and wounding of U.S. soldiers in the failed attempt to capture the warlord Mohammed Farah Aideed led critics to point out that lack of clearly defined military objectives, inadequate support, and mission creep were fundamental causes of military failure.

The Weinberger Doctrine was established by the Secretary of Defense Caspar Weinberger in 1984 during the Reagan administration to spell out the conditions under which U.S. ground combat troops should be committed. The elements of this doctrine include the following:[17]

1. No overseas commitment of U.S. combat forces unless a vital national interest of the United States or important to U.S. allies is threatened.
2. If U.S. forces are committed, there should be total support—resources and manpower to complete the mission.
3. If committed, U.S. forces must be given clearly defined political

and military objectives, and the forces must be large enough to be able to achieve these objectives.

4. There must be a continual assessment between the commitment and capability of U.S. forces and the objectives, which must be adjusted, if necessary.

5. Before U.S. forces are committed, there must be reasonable assurance that Americans and their elected representatives support such commitment.

6. Commitment of U.S. forces to combat must be the last resort.

Later General Colin Powell spelled out his view on the use of force:

> Have a clear military objective and stick to it. Use all the force necessary, and do not apologize for going in big if that is what it takes. Decisive force ends wars quickly and in the long run saves lives. Whatever threats we faced in the future, I intended to make these rules the bedrock of my military counsel.[18]

The 1999 campaign in Kosovo against the Serbs and the Milosevic regime seemed to contradict the precepts of the Weinberger-Powell perspectives. The seventy-eight day air campaign led to the end of the Serbian campaign against the Albanians in Kosovo. This was done without the commitment of ground troops. Yet critics argue that the air campaign was supported by the Kosovo Liberation Army, made up of Albanians armed and supported by outside sources, and by the pressure brought to bear by the Russians. In 2002, the issue of Kosovo remained unresolved, with no solution in sight. The fact is that the massive use of military force at the center of gravity of the adversary remains a clear military principle. How this can be applied to operations other than war, stability operations, and unconventional conflicts, including international terrorism, remains contentious.

The Military and the Policy Process

The structure of the Department of Defense and the nature and character of military professionalism are the primary determinants of the military's role in the national security policy process. That role has more to do with administrative and operational considerations than with the serious formulation of strategy, in which the military is in a distinctly secondary position.

The traditional professional posture rests partly on the premise that military personnel do not become involved in politics. Hence, because the policy process is inherently political, they are expected to keep their distance; and because formulation of strategy is in turn closely linked to the political process, they find themselves outside the formulation of strategy.

In addition, the joint perspective necessary for this process is difficult for military professionals to maintain, as career success typically runs through the respective services. Even the members of the JCS, with their dual role, tend first to their service responsibilities. The same is true of joint staff officers, and although their performance on the joint staff and their relative efficiency are determined by the JCS, service perspectives and career considerations tend to erode a joint perspective. Service parochialism and professional socialization instilled over a long career are difficult to overcome by assignment to a joint staff.

Another basic problem is that the role of the military in the policy process and formulation of strategy is affected by role conflict. The technology drive in the military, reflected in sophisticated battlefield weaponry, electronic warfare, and the evolution of an intricate organizational defense structure, has tended to shape the military establishment along the lines of civilian corporate and managerial systems. Furthermore, great effort within senior service schools has been made to develop officers capable of dealing with such complex conditions. As a consequence, military managership has become an important factor in career success and military efficiency. But not everyone agrees with this approach. Many military professionals and critics argue that the real need within the military services is for leaders and warriors. According to this view, emphasis on managership erodes the ability of the military services to successfully command and lead operational units in battle. Reliance on technology shifts the focus away from the psychological-social dimensions of human behavior, thereby reducing competency in the art of leadership.[19]

Notwithstanding its coveted aloofness from politics, the military has been dragged into the fray on many fronts—weapons acquisition, budgets, and relations with Congress, among other things. Furthermore, contemporary conflicts, whether nuclear or unconventional in character, include important political considerations.[20] As some are inclined to argue, the military professional must begin functioning long before the opening salvos of war and operations other than war. Indeed, wars and conflicts in progress in the twenty-first century are characterized by inextricable political and military factors. Cases in point include the monitoring of the Iraqi military and the Kurds in northern Iraq; continuing involvement in Bosnia-Herzegovina and Kosovo; concern over political developments in Russia; and the China-Taiwan issue, among others. For military professionals to be successful, therefore, they must acquire political as well as military skills. At a minimum, military professionals must be able to deal with the political dimensions of conflict. In the twenty-first century, such considerations are no longer distinct from the operational environment.

However, the fear of many is that attention to politics not only detracts from developing military skills but also exposes the profession to politicization, which destroys professional integrity and autonomy. The only feasible posture, according to this view, is to maintain a clear separation between politics and the military profession. The traditional concept of civil-military relations and an apolitical military associated with democratic systems is based on this separatist view. Yet others argue that there is no such thing as an apolitical military—and the U.S. military is no exception. How these matters can be reconciled with the political character of conflicts and the military's role in a democracy remains a persisting dilemma for the military profession.

According to some, the military must inform the public as well as elected officials about their views regarding the military system and the use of force. The military profession cannot function as a "silent order of monks," as someone once put it.[21] "The military profession must adopt the doctrine of constructive political engagement, framing and building a judicious and artful involvement in the policy arena. A politics-savvy military profession is the basic ingredient for constructive political engagement."[22]

These characteristics of the military establishment do not allow simplistic views of its role in the national security policy process or in the formulation of strategy. On one hand, the views of the military cannot be ignored; on the other, the character of the military institution, the nature of the military profession, and the way the U.S. political system works preclude a lead role for the military. Research on the matters examined here reveals the following:

> The combination of domestic and international issues promises to weigh heavily on the military profession and its strategic and doctrinal orientation. These issues strike at the core of the professional ethos. Even more challenging is that the military profession must be prepared to respond to a variety of national security challenges with diminished resources and considerably fewer personnel, and it must do so even in the face of skepticism within the body politic regarding issues of national security. Exacerbating all of this is that few politicians and academic commentators in the new era have had any real military experience. Although military experience is not the *sine qua non* for serious examination and analysis of national security and the military profession, without that experience it is difficult to design realistic national security policies or to understand the nature and character of the military profession.[23]

How the president and the national security establishment incorporate the military establishment into the policy process—while maintaining the character of the profession and not violating the norms and expectations of a democratic system—is a problem facing every president. The challenge surely cannot be met without an understanding of the character and nature of the military establishment and its professionals. The same holds true for anyone studying national security.[24]

Notes

1. A *specialty* is a primary or secondary career pattern for which officers may qualify by virtue of performance and education, among other considerations.

2. Michael R. Gordon, "Aspin Overhauls Pentagon to Bolster Policy Role," *New York Times*, January 28, 1993, p. A17. See also William Matthews, "Aspin Puts Stamp on Pentagon Hierarchy," *Army Times*, February 8, 1993, p. 6.

3. William S. Cohen, Secretary of Defense, *Report of the Secretary of Defense to the President and the Congress*, 2001, chap. 17, p. 243.

4. Ibid., Appendix C.

5. Les Aspin, Secretary of Defense, *The Bottom Up Review: Forces for a New Era* (Washington, DC: Department of Defense, September 1, 1993).

6. General Gordon R. Sullivan and Lieutenant Colonel James M. Dubik, *Land Warfare in the 21st Century* (Carlisle Barracks, PA: Strategic Studies Institute, U.S. Army War College, February 1993).

7. See Gary T. Dempsey, with Roger W. Fontaine, *Fool's Errands: America's Recent Encounters with National Building* (Washington, DC: Cato Institute, 2001).

8. *Report of the Secretary of Defense to the President and the Congress*, 2001, p. 20.

9. For a detailed study of U.S. military professionalism, see Sam C. Sarkesian and Robert E. Connor Jr., *The U.S. Military Profession into the Twenty-First Century* (London: Frank Cass, 1999). Also see Don M. Snider and Gayle L. Watkins, "The Future of Army Professionalism: A Need for Renewal and Redefinition," *Parameters, U.S. Army War College Quarterly* 30, no. 3 (Autumn 2000): 5–20. What many consider classics on military professionalism and civil-military relations are Morris Janowitz, *The Professional Soldier: A Social and Political Portrait* (New York: Free Press, 1971), and Samuel P. Huntington, *The Soldier and the State: The Theory and Politics of Civil-Military Relations* (New York: Vintage Books, 1964).

10. Stephanie Gutmann, *The Kinder, Gentler Military: Can America's Gender-Neutral Fighting Force Still Win Wars?* (New York: Scribner, 2000).

11. Laura L. Miller and John Allen Williams, "Do Military Policies on Gender and Sexuality Undermine Combat Effectiveness?" in Peter D. Feaver and Richard H. Kohn, eds., *Soldiers and Civilians: The Civilian-Military Gap and American National Security* (Cambridge: MIT Press, 2001), pp. 386–429.

12. General Fred C. Weyand, "Vietnam Myths and Realities," *CDRS Call* (July–August 1976). General Weyand was the last commander of the Military Assistance Command Vietnam and supervised the withdrawal of U.S. military forces in 1973. This appears in Harry G. Summers, *On Strategy: The Vietnam War in Context* (Carlisle Barracks, PA: Strategic Studies Institute, U.S. Army War College, January 17, 1981), p. 7.

13. See Dempsey and Fontaine, *Fool's Errands*.

14. See, e.g., General Wesley K. Clark, U.S. Army (ret.), *Waging Modern War: Bosnia, Kosovo, and the Future of Combat* (New York: PublicAffairs, 2001).

15. See, e.g., LTC Antulio J. Echevarria II, *The Army and Homeland Security: A Strategic Perspective* (Carlisle, PA: Strategic Studies Institute, U.S. Army War College, March 2001).

16. See ibid.; and United States Commission on National Security/21st Century (the Hart-Rudman Commission), *Road Map for National Security: Imperative for Change*, final draft report (January 31, 2001).

17. This summary is based on David T. Twining, "The Weinberger Doctrine and the Use of Force in the Contemporary Era," in Alan Ned Sabrosky and Robert L. Sloane, eds., *The Recourse to War: An Appraisal of the "Weinberger Doctrine"* (Carlisle Barracks, PA: Strategic Studies Institute, U.S. Army War College, 1988), pp. 11–12. The Weinberger Doctrine appears in Department of Defense, *Report of the Secretary of Defense to the Congress for Fiscal Year 1987* (Washington, DC: U.S. Government Printing Office, February 5, 1986).

18. Colin Powell, with Joseph E. Persico, *My American Journey* (New York: Random House, 1995), p. 434.

19. Sam C. Sarkesian, "Who Serves?" *Social Science and Modern Society* 18, no. 3 (March/April 1981): 57–60, and Sam C. Sarkesian, John Allen Williams, and Fred B. Bryant, *Soldiers, Society, and National Security* (Boulder: Lynne Rienner Publishers, 1995), pp. 13–17.

20. Sarkesian and Connor, *U.S. Military Profession*, p. 169. See also Clark, *Waging Modern War*.

21. Sam C. Sarkesian, "The U.S. Military Must Find Its Voice," *Orbis: A Journal of World Affairs* 42, no. 3 (Summer 1998): 423–437.

22. Sarkesian and Connor, *U.S. Military Profession*, p. 169.

23. Sarkesian, Williams, and Bryant, *Soldiers*, p. 147.

24. There are any number of official documents dealing with issues of national security and the military, including defense budget issues. Among others, these include the following: the National Defense Panel, *Transforming Defense: National Security in the 21st Century* (Washington, DC: Report of the National Defense Panel, December 1997); Chairman, Joint Chiefs of Staff, *Joint Vision 2020* (Washington, DC: U.S. Government Printing Office, June 2000); *National Defense Budget Estimates for FY 1999* (Washington, DC: Office of the Undersecretary of Defense, March 1998); *Quadrennial Defense Review* (Washington, DC: Department of Defense, 1997); and William S. Cohen, Secretary of Defense, *Annual Report to the President and the Congress*, 2001.

8

Civil-Military Relations

THROUGHOUT THE HISTORY OF DEMOCRACIES, THE ROLE OF THE military has rested on absolute civilian control over the military.[1] This is engrained in the U.S. system, as well as in the U.S. military institution and mind-set. Although the fear of a politicized military has periodically emerged in U.S. history, the issue has become more challenging in the twenty-first century. In turn, it has become a more pressing national security issue. Although the U.S. military must be prepared to respond across the conflict spectrum, its most likely involvement will be in ethnic, religious, and nationalistic conflicts as in Bosnia and Kosovo, as well as in a variety of unconventional conflicts. In order to be effective, the military might conduct operations contrary to the American way of war, undercutting its own credibility and legitimacy in the U.S. political system.

Even though this dilemma has become a recurring and persistent problem, polls continue to show that the military is among the most admired of U.S. institutions, respected more than many other institutions such as the Congress. This was true even before the terrorist attacks on September 11, 2001, and the subsequent effective response of the U.S. military in Afghanistan. Despite the popularity of the military, however, differences in experiences and culture ensure that U.S. civil-military relations will remain troubled. This does not mean that the military is likely to disobey civilian directions or attempt to influence elections, but the degree to which the military can or should try to influence government decisions (i.e., on force structure or the use of force) remains controversial.

Hollywood films are a useful indicator of public opinion, as the media both shape the public's view of reality and react to it. This is especially true for cinema portrayals of the military, a subject of strong popular opinion. The post-Vietnam fall of the military profession, its subsequent rise, and perhaps its coming fall is well chronicled in such films as *Apocalypse Now*, *Full Metal Jacket*, *Born on the Fourth of July* (fall); *Officer and a*

Gentleman, Top Gun (rise); and *The Siege* (fall). In *The Siege*, the military rounds up Arab residents of Brooklyn in response to a series of terrorist bombings. This suggests that U.S. armed forces would be unresponsive to civilian control in an emergency—although it is more likely that a series of terrorist incidents in the United States would cause public demand for far more restrictive measures than the military would be comfortable in carrying out.

In a similar vein, Air Force Colonel Charles J. Dunlap Jr. used a hypothetical military coup in 2012 as the backdrop for writing about his concern with the direction of civil-military relations. The coup was sparked by the massive diversion of military forces to civilian uses, the monolithic unification of the armed forces, and the insularity of the military community.[2] Appearing as it did in the journal of the U.S. Army War College, it caused quite a stir.

A major question for civil-military relations is this: How can society ensure that military authorities remain in their proper sphere and yet retain the capability to respond effectively across the conflict spectrum? Is the gap between civilian and military society so serious as to pose problems for civil-military relations and civilian control and military effectiveness?[3]

Theories

Two classic discussions of civil-military relations continue to frame the debate on how the military is controlled in a democratic society: Samuel P. Huntington's *The Soldier and the State*, and Morris Janowitz's *The Professional Soldier*.[4]

For Huntington, civilian control is achieved through military professionalism. He argued that military officers exhibit three characteristics that define a profession: expertise (the management of violence), responsibility (for the defense of the state), and corporateness (institutional self-awareness and organization).[5] These properties distinguish the military from other professions, and their emphasis serves as the best basis for civilian control. The self-regulating norms of military professionalism ensure that the military will remain obedient to civilian authorities.

In Huntington's view, the nature of the military makes it a poor match with liberal civilian society. Indeed, he suggested that "the tension between the demands of military security and the values of American liberalism can, in the long run, be relieved only by the weakening of the security threat or the weakening of liberalism."[6] As a result, too close an association between the military and society weakens, rather than strengthens, civilian control. The diminished security threat (at least for the moment) brought by the end of the Cold War has eased this dilemma but has not eliminated it.

For Janowitz, the founder of the field of military sociology, civilian control is achieved through the socialization process.[7] Put another way, the military comes from society and reflects its values in important ways. The military's sympathy with the values of society makes it a more willing servant. Although military members cannot enjoy all of society's privileges, they support the democratic system that makes these privileges available to the civilian population. Even so, a distinct military culture is important: "In a private enterprise society, the military establishment could not hold its most creative talents without the binding force of service traditions, professional identifications, and honor."[8]

Thus the degree to which society should impose its values (and culture) on the military is an unresolved question. For example, the degree to which the military should focus on military effectiveness as opposed to civil liberties issues is highly controversial. The military continues to discriminate—that is, make distinctions concerning its members based on gender, sexual orientation, and physical and mental abilities—all in the name of military effectiveness. Many of these distinctions would be illegal in a civilian context but are permitted by the Congress and the courts. Reasonable people continue to differ on the degree to which these distinctions actually enhance military effectiveness.[9]

The Gap

Journalist Thomas E. Ricks has noted a widening gap between the military and society. Based on his personal observation of a U.S. Marine platoon during and after basic training, Ricks saw a contradiction between the values inculcated in the military and those increasingly prevalent in civilian society, leading to feelings of estrangement by some in the military. He suggested three reasons for this, including the end of the draft, the "politicization of the officer corps," and a more fragmented, less disciplined U.S. society.[10]

Political scientist Ole R. Holsti confirmed and extended Ricks's analysis. Among other findings, Holsti's extensive survey results over recent years documented what he called "a strong trend toward conservative Republicanism among military officers."[11] This is noteworthy in view of the previously nonpolitical nature of the military calling; indeed at one time many officers would even refuse on principle to vote. The military is voting these days, however. Voting officers in all units ensure that all who want absentee ballots receive them and have whatever help they need in meeting state requirements. In the 2000 presidential election, the votes of military personnel outside the country, legal residents of the state of Florida, may well have been the deciding factor in George W. Bush's victory.

The degree and significance of this gap are open to debate. It may be simply a curious result of different socialization processes, but it could also mark a fundamental fault line that has implications for the nature of military service, military effectiveness, and the ability of civilian society to control the military that defends it. The latter issue is of particular concern here.

There is a danger if society and the military that protects it become too disconnected from one another. Many in the military already feel estranged from civilians, whom they see as undisciplined, irresolute, and morally adrift. They view themselves as the true carriers of U.S. values and tradition, swimming against the tide of a society gone morally soft.

There are also undercurrents of contempt for some civilian leaders. Public demonstrations of disrespect remain rare, but they do occur. An early visit by President Bill Clinton to an aircraft carrier was marred by discourtesy on the part of many crew members. Contemptuous public comments about the commander in chief by an Air Force general resulted in the rapid termination of the latter's service. An op-ed piece in the *Washington Times* written by a major in the Marine Corps Reserve calling for the president's impeachment effectively ended that officer's career. Although many service members felt the piece read well, most felt it went over the line of acceptable commentary by a serving military officer—even a reservist. Wiser commanders pointedly reminded their officers of the provisions of Article 88 of the Uniform Code of Military Justice:

> CONTEMPT TOWARD OFFICIALS: Any commissioned officer who uses contemptuous words against the President, the Vice President, Congress, the Secretary of Defense, the Secretary of a military department, the Secretary of Transportation, or the Governor or legislature of any State, Territory, Commonwealth, or possession in which he is on duty or present shall be punished as a court-martial may direct.

For their part, most Americans have admiration and respect for the military but are not always eager to put their own civilian pursuits aside to join the military. Recruiting and retaining quality personnel, essential to a modern military, are continuing concerns for military leaders. For many civilians, military life is as unfathomable as life on another planet; military people are outsiders to them. This does not make them expendable—they are, after all, still Americans, and the sight of abused U.S. prisoners of war still strikes a strong nerve—but it does not mean they are part of the mainstream. Military protection is expected, but there is little understanding of the individuals who have chosen the military as a career.

This difficulty in understanding does not equate to dislike, however. There is a sense of respect for the sacrifices military people make that civilians do not, and perhaps could not, make.[12] This is a great improvement

from the Vietnam War era, when the military endured great personal sacrifice yet was tainted with the war's unpopularity and returned to a society
contemptuous of those who served. After September 11, positive feelings
toward the U.S. military as an institution and the people who serve in it
became even stronger.

Civilian and Military Cultures

Many factors drive the civilian and military cultures away from one another. Perhaps the most serious is the diminishing number of civilians—especially elites—with personal exposure to the military, either through their
own service or that of a family member. The draft ended in 1973; the only
requirement is to register with the Selective Service System, and even that
obligation applies only to males. Compulsory national service plans (usually including a civilian service option) are occasionally discussed, but there
is neither widespread political support nor military necessity for any such
system. Sociologist Charles Moskos proposed an innovative plan for fif-
teen-month enlistments to attract college students into the military, but such
a plan would likely founder as well. Yet as he noted, "If serving one's country became more common among privileged youth, future leaders in civilian society would have had a formative citizenship experience. This can
only be to the advantage of the armed forces and the nation."[13]

Bill Clinton's avoidance of service in Vietnam was a lightning-rod
issue inside the U.S. military, but it goes far beyond that. Today, compared
to years past, the president, his major advisers, Defense Department
appointees, members of Congress, senators, and their staffs are less likely
to have experienced any sort of military service. Media and economic
elites, not to mention the general public, are also less likely to have served.

This need not be fatal to military-related policy, for many civilians
have a good understanding of military matters. Yet for most people, lack of
personal military experience makes it more difficult to evaluate military-
related issues, especially those concerning the internal dynamics of the military itself.

Such personal disassociation from the military weakens the ability of
civilian society to make informed judgments about military issues, let alone
influence military decisionmaking. It is not that uninformed civilians will
necessarily distrust or dislike the military—indeed, there may be a tendency to like the military too much and to put unwarranted confidence in military solutions to international political problems. All this can have serious
implications for establishing effective national security policy and strategy.

In addition, military people perceive a double standard in light of
recent scandals. It is disheartening for military personnel, at any level, to
see the careers of contemporaries sidetracked or terminated for infractions

far less severe than those admitted to by some civilian leaders. The draconian personnel policies of Defense Department appointees and congressional staff members (especially after the 1991 Tailhook scandal, in which naval and other aviators were accused of committing sexual assaults) are widely perceived inside the military as unfair.

Integration in the Military

Because it is subservient to civilian direction, the military often finds itself ahead of society on issues of social change. Some of these policies have worked out better in the military than in civilian society, such as the generally successful attempts to achieve racial fairness.[14]

Perhaps the greatest sociological challenge for the military is the integration of women into the mainstream of military activities, including combat.[15] This is proving to be difficult, especially as pressure grows to permit women into ground combat, with questions about the military effectiveness of mixed units.[16] A recent study shows that civilian and military leaders disagree on this issue: Some 57.5 percent of civilian leaders, compared to 37.6 percent of military leaders, supported allowing women to serve in all military roles. Of course, true equality would mean not only that women could *volunteer* for combat but also that they could be *compelled* to serve in combat. Neither civilian nor military leaders are willing to go this far, however: Only 13.9 percent of the civilians and 12.7 percent of the military surveyed supported requiring women to serve in all combat jobs.[17]

Still ahead is the inevitable integration of openly gay men and lesbian women into the military, although Charles Moskos' "don't ask, don't tell" policy (adopted by the Clinton administration) has so far withstood judicial scrutiny much better than many had predicted.[18] The issue is not whether there will be gay and lesbian service members—many are on duty now and serving successfully—but how well the military cohesion so crucial in battle can withstand the stress of openly discussed homosexual orientations. This will be especially problematic to the extent that Holsti, Ricks, and others are correct about the increasing conservatism of service members. If the issue was simply civil liberties, on the one hand, and military effectiveness on the other, personnel policy decisions would be easy. In the real world, where most of us dwell, the choices are not as stark.[19]

Civilian-Military Connections

Janowitz's advice—that it is best to increase the connections between the military and civil society in order to increase mutual understanding—has serious implications for military recruiting and education. One issue is the source of military officers. An increasing percentage of officers comes from the service academies and, in the case of Reserve Officer Training Corps (ROTC) programs, from less prestigious schools. Meanwhile, Officer Candidate Schools, the least expensive option because the services do not fund candidates' college degrees, have been cut back.

The military services need a variety of sources for their officers, some of which are under their control. Successful efforts at several elite universities to remove ROTC programs from their campuses in the wake of the Vietnam War and disputes about gays in the military are sufficient testimony to this. As a result, it is less likely that the children of civilian elites who go to such universities would enter the military and perhaps continue to influence it through successful careers.

As officers advance in grade, a combination of training and education prepares them to assume higher levels of responsibility. This education needs to reinforce the lessons of proper civil-military relations, which it generally does. Especially at the war colleges, academic standards are comparable to those at civilian universities.[20] Still, there is a strong argument for sending many of the best officers to top civilian universities. The education may well be even better, and military and civilian elites can interact and grow to appreciate and understand the perspective of others.[21]

Another civil-military connection is not as well understood as it should be: the military reserve forces. These part-timers provide an invaluable connection between the active forces and society at large and will be increasingly important as budgets grow tighter and civilian technical and managerial expertise becomes more important for the military.[22]

There is a broad civil-military connection that links the active military to a variety of civil-military groups such as the Military Coalition, which includes organizations such as the Retired Officers Association, Veterans of Foreign Wars, the Air Force Association, the Navy League, the Marine Corps League, the National Guard Association, the Association of the U.S. Army, the Reserve Officers Association, and the Naval Reserve Association.

The Military and the Media

The gap between the military and society benefits no one, and efforts by both the military and civilians will be required to close it. The military needs to ensure it is training people to understand and respect civilian values, institutions, and prerogatives. This includes inculcating respect for the role of the media and even academic research bearing on military actions and the military as an institution.

In this connection, not all is well. It is too easy for the military to view criticism by outsiders as uninformed and mean-spirited and to see the free press as an enemy. Military educators are sometimes so sensitive to media criticism that they inadvertently teach students that such criticism is illegitimate. This is a bad lesson to teach future military leaders who will eventually be charged with defending a society in which a free press is of paramount importance.[23]

Of course, military points of view are not as monolithic as many would expect. Moreover, the degree to which the military should publicly express policy preferences is highly controversial. It has been forcefully argued that senior officers should voice their opinions in areas of their expertise. There has been a call for "constructive political engagement," which must steer clear of partisanship on such issues as "military democratization" (the imposition of civilian values and practices on the military institution) and the utility of military force in various contingencies.[24] Conversely, Huntington expressed many doubts about the degree to which the military can "participate in the good-politics of policy without also becoming embroiled in the bad-politics of partisanship."[25] In retrospect, the history of U.S. intervention in Vietnam (and, for that matter, in the Balkans) might have been far different had military leaders spoken out publicly.[26]

In the view of many military observers, the handling of the early stages of the 1999 Kosovo crisis helped turn a humanitarian tragedy into a catastrophe, as civilian leaders pushed for a military confrontation with Serbia yet ruled out the use of ground forces. In the minds of many, this showed how badly war can be waged by civilian policymakers who do not fully understand the uses and limits of military power. Perhaps worse, senior military leaders who knew better did not put their careers on the line by putting their doubts on the record in a timely fashion.[27] This is not a call to subvert civilian authority, but more candid advice would have better served the nation.

In assessing the role of the U.S. military in Vietnam, General Fred C. Weyand, U.S. Army chief of staff in 1976, stated, "As military professionals we must speak out, we must counsel our political leaders and alert the American public that there is no such thing as a 'splendid little war.' There is no such thing as a war fought on the cheap."[28] He went on to say that

> The American Army is really a people's Army in the sense that it belongs to the American people who take a jealous and proprietary interest in its involvement. . . . The American Army is not so much an arm of the executive branch as it is an arm of the American people. The Army, therefore, cannot be committed lightly.

Conclusion

The real danger in this country is not that military officers will defy civil authority or stage some sort of coup d'état.[29] For reasons laid out some forty years ago by Huntington and Janowitz, that is quite literally unthinkable. If military authorities *did* think in such terms, the future of U.S. democracy would be in grave doubt. As Justice Robert Jackson noted in his dissent in *Korematsu v. United States*, the Supreme Court case that upheld for a time the internment program for persons of Japanese descent in World War II:

> If the people ever let the war power fall into irresponsible and unscrupulous hands, the courts wield no power equal to its restraint. The chief restraint upon those who command the physical forces of the country, in the future as in the past, must be their responsibility to the political judgments of their contemporaries and to the moral judgments of history.[30]

To the extent that the estrangement of the military and society is real, it is not healthy. Fortunately, the remedies are straightforward. Mutual understanding between the military and society calls for increased linkages at all levels and an understanding that the military is a unique institution with standards that may not always be the same as those of the society it defends.

There is always a balance to be struck between civil rights and liberties within the military, on the one hand, and military effectiveness on the other. Even within the military, there is a difference in the degree to which forces can or should be expected to mirror society.[31] Ideologues at either end of the spectrum only make it harder to advance sensible policies.

The relationship of the military to society and the civilian-military culture gap is well stated by noted military author John Keegan:

> Soldiers are not as other men—that is the lesson that I have learned from a life cast among warriors. The lesson has taught me to view with extreme suspicion all theories and representations of war that equate it with any other activity in human affairs. War is . . . fought by men whose values and skills are not those of politicians or diplomats. They are those of a world apart, a very ancient world, which exists in parallel with the everyday world but does not belong to it. Both worlds change over time, and the warrior world adapts in steps to the civilian. It follows it, however, at a distance. The distance can never be closed, for the culture of a warrior can never be that of civilisation itself.[32]

Whatever other purposes are served by the military, it must remain a credible fighting force. If it cannot continue to fight and win our nation's wars, including the warlike operations inherent in peacekeeping operations and the new missions dictated by the war on terrorism, its reason to exist is in doubt.

Notes

1. Portions of this chapter first appeared in the September 1999 issue of *The World & I* and are reprinted with permission from *The World & I* magazine, a publication of the Washington Times Corporation.

2. Charles J. Dunlap Jr., "The Origins of the American Military Coup of 2012," *Parameters* 22, no. 4 (Winter 1992–1993): 2–20. This piece is very interesting for a lay audience to read. It was followed by his "Melancholy Reunion: A Report from the Future on the Collapse of Civil-Military Relations in the United States," *Airpower Journal* (Winter 1996): 93–109. A more detailed exposition of his argument, without the literary devices, is in his "Welcome to the Junta: The Erosion of Civilian Control of the U.S. Military," *Wake Forest Law Review* 29, no. 2 (1994): 341–392.

3. For a detailed discussion of military readiness, see Sam C. Sarkesian and Robert E. Connor Jr., *The U.S. Military Profession into the 21st Century* (London: Frank Cass, 1999).

4. Samuel P. Huntington, *The Soldier and the State: The Theory and Practice of Civil-Military Relations* (New York: Vintage Books, 1957), and Morris Janowitz, *The Professional Soldier: A Social and Political Portrait* (New York: Free Press, 1971). For a post–Cold War perspective on these arguments, see Peter D. Feaver, "The Civil-Military Problematique: Huntington, Janowitz, and the Question of Civilian Control," *Armed Forces & Society* 23, no. 2 (Winter 1996): 149–178.

5. Huntington, *The Soldier and the State*, pp. 8–18. Although the focus here is on professional military officers, the authors are indebted to Robert B. Killebrew for pointing out that this traditional emphasis is becoming outdated. Senior enlisted personnel look more and more like junior officers in their talents and responsibilities and may be no less "professional" as Huntington uses the term.

6. Huntington, *The Soldier and the State*, p. 456.

7. Janowitz founded the Inter-University Seminar on Armed Forces and Society in 1960. Subsequently led by Sam C. Sarkesian, Charles C. Moskos, and David R. Segal, it continues to serve as an interdisciplinary "invisible college" of civilian and military scholars worldwide on issues relating to the interaction of armed forces and the societies they defend. Its journal, *Armed Forces & Society*, was also founded by Morris Janowitz and is a primary scholarly outlet for studies on civil-military relations.

8. Janowitz, *The Professional Soldier*, p. 422.

9. On the issues of gender and sexual orientation and their possible effects on military effectiveness, see Laura L. Miller and John Allen Williams, "Civil Rights vs. Combat Effectiveness? Military Policies on Gender and Sexuality," in Peter D. Feaver and Richard H. Kohn, eds., *The Military Profession and American Society in Transition to the 21st Century* (Cambridge: Belfer Center for Science Informational Affairs, Harvard University–MIT Press, 2001).

10. Thomas E. Ricks, "The Widening Gap Between the Military and Society," *Atlantic Monthly* (July 1997): 66–78, and Ricks, *Making the Corps* (New York: Scribner, 1997).

11. Ole R. Holsti, "A Widening Gap Between the U.S. Military and Civilian Society: Some Evidence, 1976–1996," *International Security* 23, no. 3 (Winter 1998–1999): 5–42. Another perspective is that the gap is a good thing but should be managed. See John Hillen, "The Civilian-Military Culture Gap: Keep It, Defend It, Manage It," U.S. Naval Institute *Proceedings* 124, no. 10 (October 1998): 2–4.

12. As a Navy flag officer remarked in a personal communication, "Most civilians equate military service with sacrifice—sacrifice of personal liberties, sacrifice of personal choices, and so on—and they are very much unsure that they could do the same thing, not to mention that the thought of possibly having to would be abhorrent to them."

13. Charles C. Moskos, "Short Term Soldiers," *Washington Post*, March 8, 1999, p A19.

14. See Charles C. Moskos, with John Sibley Butler, *All That We Can Be: Black Leadership and Racial Integration the Army Way* (New York: Basic Books, 1996), for a positive interpretation of the U.S. Army's attempt to create a "race-savvy" (not race-blind) force that maximizes combat readiness.

15. See Charles C. Moskos, John Allen Williams, and David R. Segal, eds., *The Postmodern Military: Armed Forces After the Cold War* (New York: Oxford University Press, 2000), for a discussion of the many changes in relations between the military and society in twelve democratic states after the end of the Cold War.

16. Graphic reports of women soldiers who are maimed or abused as POWs would have an especially shocking effect on the U.S. public, although the loss of two female sailors during a terrorist attack on the USS *Cole* on October 12, 2000, caused no greater outcry than did the loss of fifteen men in the same incident.

17. See Miller and Williams, "Civil Rights," for detailed statistics on this issue.

18. The policy permitting gay and lesbian members to serve so long as they "don't tell" is an institutional version of the personal policy most service members have followed for years. Most can think of military associates whom they knew, or strongly suspected, to be homosexual, but it did not become an issue so long as it did not affect job performance. It did not occur to them to "ask." The continuing high number of discharges for homosexuality is attributed by the services to members "telling" so they can leave the service early.

19. Miller and Williams, "Civil Rights."

20. These are the National Defense University (Washington, DC), the Naval War College (Newport, RI), the Army War College (Carlisle Barracks, PA), and Air University (Maxwell Air Force Base, AL). Each of these institutions has an outreach program to civilians involving conferences, publications, and participation in college functions.

21. Such a case is made in Sam C. Sarkesian, John Allen Williams, and Fred B. Bryant, *Soldiers, Society, and National Security* (Boulder: Lynne Rienner Publishers, 1995).

22. As Army Chief of Staff after Vietnam, General Creighton Abrams integrated Army active and reserve forces so thoroughly that it would be impossible for the Army to fight a major war without calling up the reserves (as President Johnson refused to do in Vietnam, lest it reduce public support for the war). National Guard forces, normally under the control of state governors, are part of this equation as well.

23. See John Allen Williams, "The U.S. Naval Academy: Stewardship and Direction," U.S. Naval Institute, *Proceedings* 123, no. 5 (May 1997): 67–72.

24. Sam C. Sarkesian, "The U.S. Military Must Find Its Voice," *Orbis* 42, no. 3 (Summer 1998): 423–424.

25. Huntington, *The Soldier and the State*, pp. 459–460.

26. For an extended discussion of this issue, see H. R. McMaster, *Dereliction of Duty: Lyndon Johnson, Robert MacNamara, the Joint Chiefs of Staff, and the Lies That Led to Vietnam* (New York: Harper Collins, 1997). This book was widely read in Washington in the wake of U.S. military operations in the Balkans.

27. Unidentified leaks from the Joint Chiefs of Staff suggesting they had reservations about the military strategy do not count here. If they had such reservations, they failed to convince the proper civilian leaders in a timely fashion. It is as if senior military officials began to speak on the record only after they feared that the failure of the original strategy would be apparent to all. See Robert Burns, "Reimer Reveals His Views on Kosovo Strategy," *European Stars and Stripes*, May 27, 1999, p. 1. Whatever the details of an eventual cease-fire, the United States is likely to be militarily involved in the region indefinitely.

28. As quoted in Harry G. Summers, *On Strategy: The Vietnam War in Context* (Carlisle Barracks, PA: Strategic Studies Institute, U.S. Army War College, 1981), pp. 7, 25. These originally appeared in *CDRS Call* (July–August 1976). Summers writes, "General Weyand was the last commander of the Military Assistance Command Vietnam (MACV) and supervised the withdrawal of U.S. Military forces in 1973" (p. 7).

29. There is widespread agreement on this among those who study issues of military and society. See, e.g., Eliot A. Cohen, "Civil-Military Relations," *Orbis* 41, no. 2 (Spring 1997): 177–186.

30. *Korematsu v. United States*, 323 U.S. 214 (1944).

31. See Sarkesian, Williams, and Bryant, *Soldiers, Society, and National Security*, pp. 160–162, for a discussion of the "three-military" idea. In this conception, the support forces can reflect society closely, while it is more problematic for regular ground forces and especially the elite and special operations forces to do so.

32. John Keegan, *History of Warfare* (New York: Alfred A. Knopf, 1993), p. xvi.

9

The Intelligence Establishment

AFTER THE ATTACKS ON THE WORLD TRADE CENTER AND THE Pentagon on September 11, 2001, the importance of an effective intelligence establishment is beyond dispute. Accurate and timely intelligence, analyzed realistically and used properly, is an essential ingredient for strong national security. The key agency for intelligence collection and analysis is the Central Intelligence Agency, established by the National Security Act of 1947. Its charter reads in part:

> For the purpose of coordinating the intelligence activities of the several government departments and agencies in the interest of national security, it shall be the duty of the Agency, under the direction of the National Security Council . . . to correlate and evaluate intelligence relating to national security, and to provide for the appropriate dissemination of such intelligence within the Government using where appropriate existing agencies and facilities.[1]

Since its creation, the CIA has been vilified and praised, and some of its more public and legendary activities have raised questions about the proper role of intelligence in a democracy. The CIA has been the subject of congressional investigations since 1975, and there is continuing concern regarding its role and relationship to other instruments of government, especially in light of the war on terrorism. Unfortunately, the contemporary debate is colored by political rhetoric and reveals much misunderstanding. As one scholar has written:

> Much of the criticism of the CIA stems from the fact that its activities are secret. The public—and particularly the media—resent its being told that they can not know something. Silence is interpreted as arrogance. Moreover, when people do not know what an agency is doing, they assume it is either doing nothing and not changing with the times, or that it is doing something wrong.[2]

In any case, the requirements of national security have created dilemmas for the CIA, the president, and Congress. Although this has been true for decades, it is especially so in the new strategic environment. On the one hand, national security requires a wide range of intelligence activities, many of them necessarily secret and covert. On the other hand, some of these activities can stretch the notion of democracy and threaten individual rights and freedoms.

At the same time, questions have been raised as to what *strategic intelligence* means today. Should it include industrial espionage? How open should the CIA be now that the Cold War is over? How should the intelligence community respond to international terrorism? How we reconcile these demands yet still maintain an effective intelligence establishment is a persistent problem for the president, Congress, the CIA, and society at large. Issues with respect to covert operations are especially controversial.

Since 1947, many intelligence activities and covert operations—some successful, some not—have been attributed to the CIA. The publicized failures have caused a degree of embarrassment to the entire country, but the public is usually unaware of the successes. Many citizens are uncomfortable with secret intelligence activities, for secrecy, covert operations, clandestine activities, and certain special operations do not easily fit into the moral framework of an open system.

The fact that such problems persist was confirmed by the 1987 Iran-contra hearings (dealing with the Reagan-era scandal of diverting funds from arms sales to Iran to support antigovernment contras—who were rebels or freedom fighters depending on your point of view—in Nicaragua in possible violation of congressional restrictions), which refocused the public spotlight on the activities of some CIA operatives and threatened to expose several covert operations. Critics in Congress, the media, and the public were quick to dramatize and magnify the problems that emerged. Others placed them in perspective, noting that virtually all intelligence activities were conducted according to law and in full cooperation with Congress, Iran-contra notwithstanding. Nonetheless, the debate over the intelligence system continues, and it is not likely to be resolved anytime soon—especially in light of the perceived intelligence failure to uncover the September 11 conspiracy beforehand. This reflects problems that persist from the Cold War, as well as the new problems of the post–Cold War era.

The improprieties identified during the Iran-contra hearings, including the role CIA Director William Casey apparently played in diverting funds to the contras, were reminiscent of the outcry against the CIA a decade earlier. Congress passed a series of laws in the 1970s limiting intelligence activities and establishing more rigid congressional oversight. This was a reaction to the CIA role in Watergate and other presumed domestic activities. The Church Committee hearings in the Senate (named for the committee chairman, Democratic Senator Frank Church) and its subsequent report in 1976 detailed many congressional concerns.[3]

The Iran-contra scandal continues to trouble Congress. In an effort to preclude such operations in the future, Congress and the executive branch have attempted to reconcile secrecy and oversight. This led to the Intelligence Authorization Act of 1991.

> [The act] represents the first significant remedial intelligence oversight legislation in more than a decade. The Act provides the first statutory definition of covert action, repeals the 1974 Hughes-Ryan Amendment governing notification to Congress of covert action, requires presidential "findings" for covert action to be in writing, and prohibits the President from issuing retroactive findings.[4]

The act has been considered a "reasonable compromise between divisive political issues and competing interpretations of constitutional responsibilities."[5]

The CIA has also made some improvement in its relationship with Congress and its accountability to the public. "The DCI's Office of Legal Counsel now employs 65 attorneys to follow legal matters that relate to intelligence, compared to only 6 in the 1970s."[6] In addition, "the Office of Congressional Affairs relies on a half-dozen personnel (including more attorneys) to focus on legislative relations."[7]

Yet the issue of CIA effectiveness was raised again in February 1994 with the revelation that career CIA officer Aldrich Ames and his wife were arrested for passing classified information to the Soviet Union and later to Russia. He was also charged with aiding the exposure and subsequent execution of several Russians working for the CIA.[8] Although his activities began in 1985, they were not exposed until 1994. This was a serious matter for the CIA, and it had repercussions for U.S.-Russia relations as members of Congress from both parties raised objections to continuing U.S. foreign aid to Russia.

Constraints on intelligence activities expanded during the Jimmy Carter administration, especially with respect to covert operations. The overthrow of the shah of Iran, the abortive hostage rescue in that country, and Soviet activities in Afghanistan drew a great deal of criticism regarding the capability of the intelligence services. Criticism also surfaced as to the quality of CIA intelligence immediately prior to the Gulf War in 1991, as well as the failure to predict the attempt by Soviet hard-liners to overthrow Mikhail Gorbachev that same year (and, for that matter, to predict the collapse of the Soviet Union). Later, a great deal of criticism was directed at the inability of technology to penetrate foreign political-social networks and provide on-the-ground analyses and judgments that can be done only by agents in the field.

The most recent review of the CIA (that is, prior to the George W. Bush administration) was by the Commission on the Roles and Capabilities of the U.S. Intelligence Community, led by former defense secretary Harold Brown and former senator Warren Rudman. This commission proposed in 1998 that the amount of funds used for secret intelligence be revealed and that the size of the intelligence agencies be reduced.[9] Given the nature of intelligence operations, however, it is doubtful that there will be a full public accounting of its funding.

The new administration under President George W. Bush quickly ordered its own review of the intelligence community, led by Director of Central Intelligence (the CIA director) George Tenet. Under National Security Presidential Directive 5, Bush called for the DCI (i.e., Tenet) to form a panel of internal and external members to consider the structure and operations of the members of the intelligence community.[10] This panel was headed by Brent Scowcroft, chairman of the president's Foreign Intelligence Advisory Board and a former National Security Advisor. Early reports suggested that the panel would recommend major changes to increase the control of the DCI over all sources of intelligence, including photographic and electronic.[11] Evidence is emerging that indications of impending terrorist attacks were picked up prior to September 11, but their significance was not realized due to lack of coordination among and within U.S. intelligence agencies.

In a perceptive article written before the September 11 terrorist attacks, one scholar noted the importance of rethinking the intelligence establishment: "Despite the apparent consensus on the need for change, recent intelligence failures suggest that U.S. intelligence has yet to leave its Cold War–era methods and structure behind."[12] Better intelligence and counterintelligence are crucial for effective policy and strategy. But better intelligence and its effective use depend on an understanding of the nature and purpose of intelligence and the knowledge of the intelligence community. Any study of national security policy must include the relationship between the president and the DCI, the structure and purpose of the CIA and the intelligence community, the role of intelligence, the intelligence cycle, and the system that tries to integrate all of these into a coherent whole.

The President and the Director of Central Intelligence

The director of the Central Intelligence Agency (officially, the Director of Central Intelligence) stands at the apex of the intelligence community. The DCI holds a critical position in providing strategic intelligence to the National Security Council, where he is a statutory adviser; he is also an adviser to the president. The DCI's influence in government is determined to a great extent by his relationship with the president. The DCI is assisted in his responsibilities for running the CIA and coordinating the intelligence establishment by the Community Management Staff (for coordination and management) and the National Intelligence Council (for substantive issues and strategic thinking, whose twelve members come from the government and private sector). The late William Casey, for example, was a close friend of President Ronald Reagan. Not only did he have the president's full confidence; his elevation to cabinet rank sent a clear signal throughout the administration about his special status. His power and prestige increased accordingly. All of this allowed Casey a degree of latitude rarely enjoyed by previous directors.

Aside from the important relationship with the DCI, and through him the intelligence community, the president also receives input from two boards. The president's Foreign Intelligence Advisory Board sits within the Executive Office of the President. It has sixteen members who are appointed by the president and serve at his pleasure; many are distinguished citizens outside of government. The board has responsibility to make recommendations to improve the efficiency of U.S. intelligence efforts, so it is only fitting that its current chairman, Brent Scowcroft, heads the panel considering a new intelligence structure.[13]

The president's Intelligence Oversight Board, established in 1976, reports to the president and is a standing committee of the Foreign Intelligence Advisory Board. The responsibility of the oversight board is to examine intelligence activities on behalf of the president and to report any that would raise questions of legality or propriety.[14] It also reviews the internal guidelines of the intelligence community.

These presidential boards have a special relationship to the DCI in his capacity as director of the CIA and as leader of the intelligence community. The boards' activities require knowledge of intelligence activities, which in turn requires a degree of coordination with the DCI. The DCI speaks for the intelligence community in its relationship to these boards, and although this adds to the director's responsibilities, it also increases his prominence in the intelligence community and reinforces his role as the principal actor within the intelligence system.

The U.S. Central Intelligence Agency

The Director of Central Intelligence is an adviser, a coordinator, and a leader-manager—all in different settings and with different political and professional relationships. He serves as an adviser to the National Security

Council and coordinates all intelligence activities. But his main function is to be directly responsible for the control and operations of the CIA—the center of the intelligence system.

The CIA's organization, resources, and operations cover a range of activities and require a vast managerial effort. Actual figures are difficult to come by, but by one earlier estimate the DCI commands "roughly 20,000 employees and a classified budget estimated to fall between $1.5 billion to $2.5 billion. . . . [The DCI] is aided by a 237-member intelligence community staff that coordinates the activities and budgets of all the intelligence organizations."[15] Although "the bulk of the community's financial, human and hardware assets . . . actually reside in the Defense Department," the importance of the CIA as the lead agency in the intelligence community and the coordinator of national intelligence gives it a stature not enjoyed by other intelligence services.

The DCI is assisted by the deputy DCI, who is nominated by the president and confirmed by the Senate (see Figure 9.1, an organizational chart of the CIA).

On June 4, 2001, the CIA implemented a "Mission Focus" realignment to "strengthen the abilities and capabilities of the CIA's core mission managers: The Directorates of Operations, Intelligence, and Science and Technology."[16] These directorates are each headed by a deputy director:

Deputy Director for Operations (DDO; heads the spies): This directorate "has primary responsibility for the clandestine collection of foreign intelligence." This includes human source intelligence, sometimes referred to as "humint." Covert actions are also part of this directorate's responsibility, and domestically the DDO handles "the overt collection of foreign intelligence volunteered by individuals and organizations in the United States."[17]

Deputy Director for Intelligence (DDI; heads the analysts): "The DDI manages the production and dissemination of all-source intelligence analysis on key foreign problems. The DDI is responsible for the timeliness, accuracy, and relevance of intelligence analysis to the concerns of national security policymakers and other intelligence consumers."[18]

Deputy Director for Science and Technology (heads the engineers): This directorate is concerned with "creating and applying innovative technology to meet today's intelligence needs."[19]

These directorates are at the center of the politics and turf battles that occur within the CIA. For example, those in the Directorate of Operations consider themselves to be the cutting edge and look upon others as paper-pushers and administrators. "We got all the action. We make the world go around.

Figure 9.1   The Central Intelligence Agency

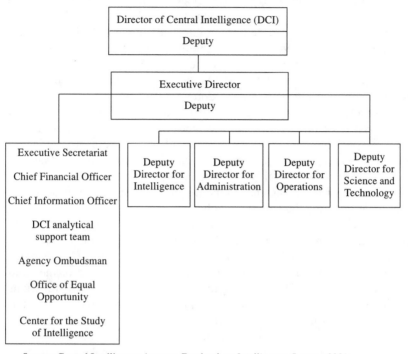

Source: Central Intelligence Agency, *Factbook on Intelligence,* January 2001.

Satellites can't tell you what people are doing."[20] The other directorates offer their own assessment of their importance to the overall intelligence effort. Even within the various directorates, separate elements tend to develop their own style and self-protective habits.

The responsibilities that used to be part of the Directorate of Administration were placed within the office of the executive director. These became the CIA's Mission Support Offices: Chief Information Officer, Chief Financial Officer, Security, Human Resources, and Global Support (facilities, logistics, publishing, etc.). Also important is the National Intelligence Council, which consists of fifteen national intelligence officers, "each expert in a particular subject area and drawn from the CIA and other agencies and from academia." The National Intelligence Council is responsible for producing national intelligence estimates, "of which about 100 are turned out per year."[21]

The responsibilities of the DCI extend beyond the CIA. As chairman of the National Foreign Intelligence Board, he influences the agenda and activities of its members. Through presidential directives, as well as those from the DCI, the board is given various tasks and responsibilities, such as interagency exchange of intelligence information and establishing procedures with foreign governments on intelligence matters. Membership on the board ranges from the directors of the National Security Agency and the director of the Defense Intelligence Agency to the secretary of energy and the commandant of the U.S. Marine Corps.

The DCI's leadership of the intelligence community involves him in the activities of intelligence agencies and organizations that also have a dual responsibility: First, they provide input for the national intelligence function; second, they have their own agency responsibilities. For example, the DIA carries responsibility as a member of the intelligence community, but it also provides intelligence to the Defense Department office that handles issues with foreign defense establishments.

Given the changing strategic landscape, as well as its current uncertainties and ambiguities in light of September 11, several voices have been raised regarding the role and purpose of the CIA. U.S. Senator Daniel Patrick Moynihan (now retired), in light of the end of the Cold War, introduced a bill dismantling the CIA and turning over its functions to the State Department.[22] Any such proposal today would likely fail miserably given the events of September 11. In 1992, David Boren, who was chairman of the Senate Intelligence Committee at the time, introduced a bill calling for a restructuring of the CIA to make it more relevant to the new strategic environment. The chairman of the House Intelligence Committee, Representative David McCurdy, introduced a similar bill.[23]

Some proposals to restructure the CIA envision the creation of a new post: Director of National Intelligence. This individual would take over the coordinating duties of the DCI and oversee all U.S. intelligence activities. The new position has been described as an intelligence czar with teeth.[24] The restructured agency would "oversee, coordinate, and synthesize the workings of the nation's several information-gathering elements to advise the President, National Security Council, and appropriate government departments on security matters."[25] The CIA would remain responsible for covert operations and human intelligence. Under this proposal, a deputy director for estimates and analysis, a deputy director for the intelligence community, and the DCI would be directly subordinate to the Director of National Intelligence. So far, President George W. Bush has maintained the general structure of the CIA while trying to respond to the myriad issues raised by budget problems and intelligence-gathering in the new strategic environment.

The Intelligence Community

The term *intelligence community* is a general reference and includes all agencies (or components of such agencies) within the executive branch that deal with intelligence on some level. It refers to the gamut of intelligence agencies and services: the CIA; intelligence agencies organized under the Department of Defense, including the DIA, the NSA, the National Imagery and Mapping Agency, the National Reconnaissance Office, and the intelligence agencies within the Army, Navy, Air Force, and Marine Corps; and the intelligence elements of the Departments of State, Energy, and Treasury and the Federal Bureau of Investigation.[26] The intelligence community comprises several components and operational levels (see Figure 9.2).

There are several important intelligence agencies within the Department of Defense. The National Reconnaissance Office (NRO) is in the category of "offices responsible for the collection of specialized national foreign intelligence." Specifically, it is responsible for all satellite reconnaissance used by the intelligence community, and its existence was only recently officially confirmed. The National Security Agency (NSA) is responsible for electronic intelligence. It intercepts and monitors radio transmissions and other electronic communications (with particular attention to the Soviet Union in the past). The NRO and NSA are especially secretive, given their advanced capabilities. The latter is under scrutiny by our European allies due to suspicions that Echelon, the NSA's assumed (but unconfirmed) communications-intercept system, is collecting economic intelligence for the benefit of U.S. corporations. The NSA denies such allegations and will not discuss the possible existence of such a system. The Defense Intelligence Agency coordinates and controls Defense intelligence sources and agencies and provides the secretary the finished intelligence product required to carry out his responsibilities. The National Imagery and Mapping Agency produces strategic and tactical maps, charts, and other data necessary to support military weapons and navigational systems and deals with open-source as well as secret data, some of it collected by the NRO. The NSA and NRO, although within the organizational framework of the Department of Defense, are focused on national-level intelligence.

The military's intelligence agencies—including Army, Navy, Air Force, and Marine Corps intelligence—exist at another level. Each has its own community that includes a variety of subagencies and sources. The service intelligence agencies focus on the battlefield intelligence necessary to support the individual services' tactical plans. This includes enemy order-of-battle information and analysis. Finally, some intelligence services are directly subordinate to unified and specified commands (see Chapter 7).

Figure 9.2   The Intelligence Community

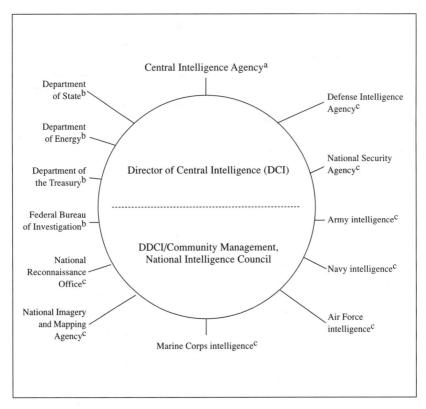

Source: Adapted from Central Intelligence Agency, *Factbook on Intelligence,* January 2001, p. 17.

Notes: a. Independent agency.

b. Departmental intelligence elements (other than Department of Defense).

c. Department of Defense elements.

Their purpose is to provide specific information on the command's area of responsibility (e.g., European Command, Southern Command, etc.). In so doing, they serve their own particular departments, services, and commands, but they also provide input into the total intelligence effort through the intelligence community.

Intelligence relationships and responsibilities are difficult to control, a problem magnified by the fact that each intelligence agency and service has its own mind-sets and loyalties. These can affect the intelligence produced, although intelligence is usually passed on to the agency requesting it (the "consumer"). Any distortions in the intelligence process are of concern given the importance of accurate intelligence for national security and the civil liberties implications of a process that has the potential to become enormously intrusive.

The DCI and other intelligence officials have relationships with the foreign intelligence services of U.S. allies (as well as those of not-so-friendly countries, especially post–September 11). Close coordination is critical to certain clandestine activities, such as counterterrorism operations; they also share intelligence information for less dramatic but mutually beneficial purposes in support of international efforts and treaties. The points of contact are the CIA (for political and psychological issues) and the Department of Defense (for military matters).

In recent years, these relationships have been under considerable stress. The intelligence services of U.S. allies were dismayed by the congressional investigations of the CIA in the 1970s, which revealed sensitive information and threatened the exposure of foreign sources. Contemporary revelations by investigative journalists, whether the reports are accurate or not, create embarrassing situations that do little to enhance the CIA's effectiveness. One result is that foreign sources become extremely cautious when dealing with U.S. intelligence groups for fear of exposure. This tends to chill relationships between the U.S. intelligence system and its friendly foreign counterparts.

The key to developing a reasonably effective intelligence system is to create an environment of trust and confidence among national agencies, Defense Department intelligence services, and their subordinate services. The responsibility rests primarily with the DCI. The structures are in place and the statutes spelling out the power and role of the CIA are on the books, but there is a great deal of room for flexibility below the national level. How all of the pieces are brought together is not only a function of managerial efficiency but also of leadership, experience, and professional competence. Equally important, the DCI and other intelligence officials need to develop close relations with foreign intelligence agencies and services. To be sure, Congress, interest groups, and journalists have a great deal of impact on images of the CIA that can tarnish and erode U.S. intelligence credibility. But this can be countered to some extent by a competent and skilled U.S. intelligence service led by a DCI whose leadership skills are up to the task.

The Intelligence Cycle

In simple terms, the term *intelligence* refers to the final product that comes from collecting and analyzing all available information on foreign nations and their operations, as well as information on group activities (such as terrorism) that are important for national security planning. To be useful, intelligence is dependent upon the intelligence services fulfilling their responsibilities in what is called "the intelligence cycle" (see Figure 9.3), described as "the process of developing raw information into finished intelligence for policymakers to use in decisionmaking and action."[27]

The intelligence cycle is normally used as the basis for studying what intelligence is and how it is related to the policy process. This is done in the context of the intelligence community and the role of the CIA, that is, the study of intelligence must be closely linked to the system processes and efficiency of the cycle.

The intelligence cycle can be viewed in five steps: (1) planning and direction, (2) collection, (3) processing, (4) all-source analysis and production, and (5) dissemination. The *planning and direction* stage involves "the management of the entire effort, from identifying the need for data to delivering an intelligence product to a consumer."[28] The process usually begins with a request from the National Security Council (or another department or agency) to collect intelligence on particular subjects. Some of these requests may be for one-time intelligence, or they may be a standing request for continuing intelligence on a particular subject, such as the development of Chinese strategic missiles.

The next stage, *collection*, "is the gathering of the raw information needed to produce finished intelligence."[29] Intelligence collection depends on a variety of operations and activities, including private sources and media accounts as well as clandestine sources. The methods used for col-

Figure 9.3   Intelligence Cycle

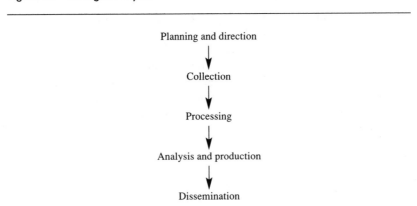

Source: Adapted from Central Intelligence Agency, *Factbook on Intelligence,* January 2001, p. 14.

lection are technical, including satellite and electronic means, as well as human.

The vast amount of collected raw intelligence must undergo *processing* to make it manageable. This step "involves converting the vast amount of information collected to a form usable by analysts through decryption, language translations, and data reduction."[30]

The *analysis and production* stage "is the conversion of basic information into finished intelligence."[31] It turns the processed intelligence into an understandable and usable form for authorized consumers. All collected intelligence is not of equal quality and so must be evaluated for reliability and credibility (i.e., as to the source of the information) as well as accuracy. The evaluation also includes the examination of other intelligence and sources that corroborate or contradict the original information.

Intelligence must be analyzed with respect to its relationship to U.S. national security, that is, its importance with respect to enemy intentions, strength, and policy. This may be one of the most difficult parts of the process, as the accuracy and reliability of the analysis depends upon the experience, sophistication, and capability of the analysts. It is especially difficult to reconcile contradictory raw intelligence to give it meaning and make it useful for policymakers. A historical note: signals intelligence might have predicted the Japanese attack on Pearl Harbor, but it was not properly analyzed until it was too late. Similarly, it is likely that hindsight will show several indications of the September 11 attacks that were missed or dismissed at the time as not important.

Production is an inherent part of analysis and refers to the shape and form of the final product. This is followed by the final step: *dissemination* of the final product to the end users.

Although this process seems to follow logically from one step to the next, in reality the steps are blurred. Furthermore, it is difficult to manage and coordinate the agencies and services involved in the cycle and therefore to provide accurate and timely information to the consumer. Because the finished product is based on the judgment of analysts, the human equation enters into the picture and, with it, the risk of mistaken judgments and human error.

In the final analysis, regardless of how good the intelligence is, how analytically precise, and how timely, the utility of the finished product depends upon the consumer. Although the use (or nonuse) of intelligence by the consumer is beyond the control of those in the intelligence system, it is an inherent part of the cycle. This creates dilemmas for the intelligence system. On the one hand, there is professional pride in producing worthy finished products and critical intelligence estimates for national security purposes. On the other hand, if they are not used or are ignored, then the system is more likely to become self-serving, enmeshed in meaningless operations, and committed more to bureaucratic efficiency than the purposes of intelligence. It is not difficult to move from this stance to policy advocacy and even operations in the belief that the intelligence generated is correct and that policymakers should act on it in a timely fashion.

Covert Operations

The most controversial aspect of the intelligence system is covert operations. The CIA has not been the only agency involved in such operations, although it is the primary one. (The deputy director of central intelligence is responsible for covert operations.) Interestingly, covert action as it is now defined was not initially identified as a role for the CIA. However, that responsibility was assumed under the provision that the CIA was to perform such functions affecting U.S. national security as the National Security Council directed.

The term *covert operations* is a convenient label used to identify a variety of clandestine activities, ranging from propaganda and psychological warfare to paramilitary operations and espionage. Indeed, published reports from post–September 11 actions in Afghanistan reveal that the CIA has a significant paramilitary capability. In the words of one authority: "Covert action is defined in the U.S. as the attempt by a government to influence events in another state or territory without revealing its involvement."[32] The concept also extends to political action and various forms of intelligence-gathering.

At the presidential level, however, the term *special activities* is used to identify a variety of covert operations. In Executive Order 12333, signed by President Ronald Reagan in 1981, special activities were defined as "propaganda, paramilitary and covert political operations. They specifically do not include the sensitive collection of foreign intelligence."[33] Thus the concept of covert operations can be assigned to virtually every part of intelligence activities as well as to some aspects of U.S. military operations. Secret and/or concealed operations and activities are the stuff of covert actions.

The purpose of covert operations is to support the foreign policy of the state engaging in them. There are two major considerations: First, the state may be involved in operations that are best served by secrecy, that is, when the public and policymakers in the target state are not aware of such operations; second, the state may be involved in operations that are public yet wishes to conceal or at least deny involvement. Paramilitary operations and political actions, for example, can be quite visible in the target state yet supported and encouraged by another state that does not want to be identi-fied for any number of reasons, such as embarrassment or fear that the suc-cess of the operation would be jeopardized. The United States was involved in such operations against Cuba in the early 1960s during the John F. Kennedy administration. There are credible reports of sabotage and multi-ple attempts to assassinate Cuban leader Fidel Castro. Other examples include U.S. involvement in Chile beginning in 1970, as well as a variety of activities revealed during the Iran-contra hearings in 1987.

As a result of the variety of covert operations in the 1980s, some of which were mismanaged, critics charged that such operations were contrary to democratic norms. In 1992, "a 20th Century Fund 'Task Force Report on Covert Action and American Democracy' blistered covert action as funda-mentally at war with democratic norms."[34] Yet most authorities agree that covert operations are an integral part of the intelligence system, often nec-essary to achieve foreign policy and national security goals. They would also agree that these are the most controversial operations undertaken by the United States, as noted above. The nature of the United States—an open system committed to law and the norms of democracy and decency—places the U.S. public in an awkward position with respect to certain secret opera-tions. Moreover, official and government representatives who must engage in them are also placed in difficult positions regarding what is proper behavior and moral conduct.

According to a former CIA intelligence officer, one of the major aspects of this "third option"—the alternative to military and diplomatic actions—is "paramilitary operations or the furnishing of *covert* military assistance to unconventional and conventional foreign forces and organiza-tions."[35] The reasoning is that the United States was faced with a variety of "insurgencies" abroad since the 1980s, which may have threatened several U.S. national interests. Thus

> the bottom line on the decision to use or ignore the third option will not be based solely on the quality of intelligence, analysis, or organizations. The decision will be made by those who have, or lack, the will to pursue poli-cy goals through techniques that have preserved our interests in diverse areas.[36]

The nature of covert operations and the dilemmas they create highlight the fundamental uneasiness that any open system has with secret intelli-gence operations and the intelligence system in general. Although recogniz-ing the importance of effective intelligence, critics feel that the require-ments of democracy—to abide by the rule of law, adhere to democratic proprieties, and protect individual freedoms and rights—provide ample rea-son to oppose at least some intelligence activities and to demand oversight and accountability. These criticisms are not confined to the United States, of course; Great Britain's MI-6 intelligence agency and Israel's Mossad have also been subjected to outside attention.

Democracy and the Intelligence Process

Many serious problems face any democracy that maintains an intelligence system. Aside from the relationship of intelligence operations to less opaque institutions in the political system, there are moral and ethical issues that compound the legal and philosophical problems inherent in such operations.

Intelligence successes (especially covert operations) are rarely revealed, but failures are often made public to the embarrassment of the United States and to the detriment of foreign and national security policies. Opponents of covert operations are quick to point out failures such as those revealed in the Iran-contra hearings. It is only a short step from this view to the support of constraints and limitations that preclude a wide range of intelligence activities, thereby reducing national security capability. In addition, revelations can become the focal point of media coverage and book-length exposés that are difficult to counter without revealing sensitive information and sources.[37]

The issue of successes and failures aside, the legality of intelligence operations creates debate. As noted earlier, in the wake of Vietnam and Watergate Congress and some interest groups attacked the CIA and the U.S. intelligence system, creating an adversarial environment. Indeed, the second half of the 1970s may have represented the nadir of the U.S. intelligence system and marked a significant decline in the U.S. capability to pursue national interests. More than anything else, the Church Committee epitomized the adversarial approach to investigations of the CIA. According to one source: "Consideration of the present mechanism of oversight and control of the U.S. intelligence agencies should begin with the final report of the [Church Committee]."[38] The report identified the problems that arise between the executive and legislative branches in their efforts to determine the scope and purpose of intelligence activities.

A series of legislative acts evolved to regulate and control the CIA and other intelligence activities. To the earlier 1974 Hughes-Ryan Amendment were added a variety of procedures—from the expansion of congressional oversight to the Boland Amendments—that were at the root of the Iran-contra hearings.[39] These acts "created permanent oversight committees in both house of Congress" with "principal budgetary authority over the intelligence agencies." In addition, statutory provisions were enacted to deal specifically "with the provision of information by the intelligence agencies to the two congressional committees"; new groups were added within the executive branch, including "the President's Intelligence Oversight Board, and . . . an Office of Intelligence Policy and Review within the Department of Justice."[40] Other new procedures included the issuance of presidential executive orders, a process of judicial review, and the strengthening of the Office of General Counsel of the intelligence agencies with respect to intelligence activities.

The underlying assumption at this time was that Congress did not know about many intelligence activities; it followed that they did not comply with existing laws. The fact is that in the majority of cases Congress was informed through its political leadership. Yet many members of Congress would prefer to distance themselves from knowledge of such activities for fear that revelations, especially of failures, would not serve their political credibility. Thus denial of knowledge can be a useful political position.[41] This was the case in the controversy that developed over the CIA mining of Nicaraguan harbors to prevent arms shipments to the insurgents in El Salvador.

One authority had harsh words over the attack on the intelligence community:

> In 1975 the community was the object of intense public scrutiny unparalleled in history. No country had ever subjected its secret organs of government to such open and extensive review. The Church Committee in the Senate, the Pike Committee in the House, and the White House's Rockefeller Commission held lengthy hearings and did voluminous research into past activities of the intelligence community. The Congressional Committees conducted their business openly and publicly, adopted an adversarial, accusatory, and investigative approach, and, perhaps, inevitably and irresistibly, dramatized its proceedings. . . . It rarely acknowledged any legitimate reasons for clandestine operations and operated under the assumptions that most clandestine or secret activities were indefensible.[42]

This statement is a sharp reminder of the persisting problems inherent in trying to reconcile intelligence needs with the norms and expectations of a democratic political system. Furthermore, it shows the divisiveness generated within the national security establishment over the role of an intelligence community in national security policy. The critical issue, however, is the proper role of an intelligence community that must adhere to the rule of law while remaining an effective instrument of U.S. national security policy. Answers to this dilemma are elusive and will continue to pose problems for the president and the National Security establishment.

Another problem is the possibility of intelligence that is fabricated to favor a particular political-military posture or policy. This so-called cooked intelligence, most recently associated with the tenures of CIA Directors

William Casey and Robert Gates, is closely related to policy advocacy: intelligence favorable to a particular stance is highlighted while contrary intelligence is ignored, downgraded, or allowed to slip through the cracks. Allegations of cooked intelligence and policy advocacy were leveled against Casey with respect to U.S. policy in Nicaragua.[43] Earlier, similar charges were made against the CIA with respect to U.S. support for the shah of Iran.

In any case, the credibility of the intelligence community rests primarily on its ability to avoid policy advocacy, retain institutional autonomy, and maintain professional competence. Any president who seeks intelligence as a basis for a preconceived policy position not only distorts the intelligence process but also erodes the credibility of the CIA and the U.S. intelligence community. Moreover, for the CIA to take any position—other than the most objective analysis of intelligence and the pursuit of the requirements in the intelligence cycle—will surely raise questions of competence and have a chilling effect on intelligence professionals whose horizons are not limited by agency protectionism or bureaucratic loyalties.

Finally, the relationships among the DCI, the president, and Congress help determine the overall effectiveness of the intelligence community. It is important to note that how the DCI carries out his responsibilities to Congress, his relationships with individual members of Congress, and his relationships with the intelligence oversight committees have much to do with the ability of the president to play an effective role in the national security policy process. The trust and confidence between the DCI and the president remain critical, and a CIA without political motivations and purposes is at the base of this relationship. The DCI must therefore be responsive to the president's national security concerns as well as those of the National Security Council while fostering objectivity within the intelligence community and maintaining good relationships with Congress—a task that requires an individual of strong character and personality, as well as competence and integrity.

All these relationships shape the public's image of the CIA and the intelligence community. For example, Senator Church's 1975 comment that the CIA is a "rogue elephant" remains a pejorative used by many critics today. Although such a comment can hardly stand close scrutiny, especially now that the country is conducting a publicly supported war against terrorism, its imagery still has an impact on public perceptions of CIA conduct. Continuing problems with and suspicions of the CIA are reflected in various publications: "There are limits to human trust and gullibility; intelligence manipulation has more often than not threatened national security and the prospects of world peace. Therefore, the question of the CIA's standing invites close attention—and it cries out for redress."[44] Another study, based on assessment of CIA records and interviews, concludes:

> The CIA is one of the most important institutions in American society, one that Americans are fortunate to have. The agency has seen the country through the most difficult times in the nation's history, providing information that has kept the country out of a major war with the Soviet Union and helped the U.S. win smaller ones, including the war in the Persian Gulf.[45]

There is another complicating factor regarding the role of the CIA in a democracy: in the post–Cold War period, some are calling for a redefinition of *intelligence*. According to one account, "The United States Congress and some intelligence experts are now increasingly prepared to use the CIA and the National Security Agency for economic intelligence-gathering."[46] It is argued that one of the most serious threats to U.S. national security is in the economic sphere. Some in the intelligence field are resisting that tack, because moving into the economic intelligence field raises several legal and ethical questions. To whom should the CIA make economic intelligence available? All of the major U.S. corporations? How ethical is it to pry economic secrets from friendly powers, even though they may be attempting to do so from us? Would such an intelligence effort require reshaping of some elements of the CIA? What effect would this have on the willingness of U.S. allies to cooperate? And no matter how *intelligence* is defined, how is the U.S. government to handle the problem of intelligence-sharing with an expanded NATO alliance that includes former enemies?

Others have argued that more effort should be placed on gathering political intelligence in the third world. Only by such efforts will the United States understand internal political realities and be able to choose more intelligently what groups and individuals to support.[47] In any case, the twenty-first century brings with it several questions, not only about the proper role of the CIA in espionage and intelligence gathering but also its role in a democracy and the issue of secrecy and covert operations.

In adapting to the new environment, the CIA has made some incremental changes in its internal procedures. For example, it has undertaken to declassify many previously classified documents; more attention is being given to international criminal networks; the CIA's structure is being reduced by about 15 percent; and more attention is being given to regional issues.

Conclusion

In summary, the dilemma of how to maintain an effective intelligence institution in an open system persists today and is likely to persist indefinitely. Those who advocate black-and-white approaches or zero-sum concepts display a lack of insight into the intelligence community and the nature of intelligence. There are no easy or simple answers. Developing an acceptable relationship, delineating proper boundaries and roles, and maintaining a dynamic and continuing assessment begins with the president and his leadership. He must be cognizant of these problems and recognize the need to maintain the moral and ethical credibility of the intelligence function. How this is translated and projected into the intelligence community rests with the leadership of the Director of Central Intelligence and is affected by the president's trust and confidence in that person. Equally important, the most effective intelligence in an open system requires an enlightened Congress and public.

The difficulties involved in maintaining an effective intelligence establishment in an open system are complex:

> To presume however, that democracies must rigidly adhere to strict application of law, even to the point of self-destruction, is the height of immorality. Equally presumptuous is the view that democracy should take no action unless a clear and present danger exists. . . . To wait until there is a clear and present danger may be too late. Even if it is not too late, waiting for the outbreak of conflict may place the open system in an extremely disadvantageous position, considerably raising the costs of effective response.[48]

Yet at the same time it is imperative that the intelligence establishment function within existing laws and regulations. With proper oversight and skilled personnel, there is no reason to believe that the CIA cannot function in this way and be effective. This might require more effort, a more flexible system of regulations and procedures, and a more understanding Congress and public. It may also mean that the opinion makers, Congress, and the media must understand that the CIA belongs to the U.S. public and serves it and the democratic system. But "the enduring irony of intelligence is its potential to destroy as well as to guard democracy."[49]

Notes

1. National Security Act of 1947, United States Statutes at Large 1947, vol. 61, pt. 1, 1948, pp. 496–505.

2. Ronald Kessler, *Inside the CIA: Revealing the Secrets of the World's Most Powerful Spy Agency* (New York: Pocket Books, 1992), p. 251.

3. For a detailed account of these matters, see Loch K. Johnson, *A Season of Inquiry: Congress and Intelligence* (Chicago: Dorsey, 1988). The volume is essential reading for those interested in the role and power of Congress in dealing with the U.S. intelligence establishment.

4. William E. Conner, *Intelligence Oversight: The Controversy Behind the FY 1991 Intelligence Authorization Act* (McLean, VA: Association of Former Intelligence Officers, 1993), p. 1.

5. Ibid., p. 39.

6. Loch K. Johnson, "Smart Intelligence," *Foreign Policy* (Winter 1992–1993): 68.

7. Ibid.

8. See, e.g., Sam Vincent Meddis, "CIA Officer Charged as Spy," *USA Today*, February 23, 1994, pp. 1, 3A. Virtually all U.S. news networks on radio and television carried the story during the week.

9. Tim Weiner, "Commission Recommends Streamlined Spy Agencies," *New York Times*, March 1, 1996, p. A17. This report is sometimes referred to as the "Brown-Aspin Report," as Defense Secretary Les Aspin was originally selected to head the commission.

10. Vernon Loeb, "U.S. Intelligence to Get Major Review," *Washington Post*, May 12, 2001, p. A3.

11. Walter Pincus, "Intelligence Shakeup Would Boost CIA: Panel Urges Transfer of NSA, Satellites, Imagery from Pentagon," *Washington Post*, November 8, 2001, p. A1.

12. Bruce Berkowitz, "Better Ways to Fix U.S. Intelligence," *Orbis* 45, no. 4 (Fall 2001): 609.

13. Central Intelligence Agency, *Fact Book on Intelligence* (Washington, DC: Central Intelligence Agency, January 2001), p. 16.

14. Ibid.

15. David C. Morrison, "From Iran to Trade to Soviet Intentions, Can Government Intelligence Officers Keep Their Judgements Free of Politics?" *Government Executive*, June 1, 1987, p. 22.

16. CIA press release, June 2001.

17. CIA *Fact Book*, pp. 9–10.

18. Ibid., p. 10.

19. Ibid.

20. Kessler, *Inside the CIA*, p. xxviii.

21. Morrison, "From Iran," p. 23.

22. See Kessler, *Inside the CIA*, p. 247. Also see "Spying Comes in from the Cold," *World Press Review*, March 1992, p. 7, a reprint of a story published in *Der Spiegel* (Hamburg).

23. David L. Boren, "The Intelligence Community: How Crucial," *Foreign Affairs* 71 (Summer 1992): 52–62. See also Sam Vincent Meddis, "New World, a New Spymaster," *USA Today*, February 6, 1992, p. 4; George Kardner Jr. and Walter Pincus, "Clearance Sought for New CIA Network," *Washington Post*, February 5, 1992, p. 1. See also notes 16 and 17, supra.

24. William Kloman, "Intelligence Reorganization Plans Feature a Czar with Teeth, a Staff of Thousands," *Armed Forces Journal International* 128, no. 10 (May 1992), p. 8.

25. Ibid.

26. CIA *Fact Book*, p. 15.

27. Ibid., p. 13.

28. Ibid.

29. Ibid.

30. Ibid.

31. Ibid., pp. 13–14.

32. Roy Godson, *Intelligence Requirements for the 1980s: Covert Action* (New Brunswick, NJ: Transaction, 1981), p. 1.

33. Standing Committee on Law and National Security, American Bar

Association, *Oversight and Accountability of the U.S. Intelligence Agencies: An Evaluation* (Washington, DC: American Bar Association, 1985), p. 19.

34. Bruce Fein, "Official Secrecy and Deception Are Not Always Bad Things," *Insight*, June 8, 1992, p. 23.

35. Theodore Shackley, *The Third Option: An American View of Counterinsurgency Operations* (New York: Reader's Digest, 1981), pp. 6–7.

36. Ibid.

37. See Gregory F. Treverton, *Covert Action: The Limits of Intervention in the Postwar World* (New York: Basic Books, 1987), p. 222: "If the United States remains in the business of covert actions, even under restrictive guidelines, it will continue to confront the paradox of secret operations in a democracy. That paradox is, if anything, sharper now because of the changes in the American body politic, particularly relations between Congress and the executive."

38. Scott D. Breckenridge, *The CIA and the U.S. Intelligence System* (Boulder: Westview, 1986), p. 230.

39. American Bar Association, *Oversight and Accountability*, p. 7.

40. Ibid. See also Johnson, "Smart Intelligence," and Breckenridge, *The CIA*.

41. American Bar Assocation, *Oversight and Accountability*, p. 1.

42. Breckenridge, *The CIA*, p. 249.

43. Stafford T. Thomas, *The U.S. Intelligence Community* (Lanham, MD: University Press of America, 1983), p. 46.

44. Rhodri Jeffreys-Jones, *The CIA and American Democracy* (New Haven: Yale University Press, 1989), p. 251.

45. Kessler, *Inside the CIA*, p. 252.

46. From *Der Spiegel* (Hamburg), as reprinted in the *World Press Review*, March 1992, p. 9. See also Stansfield Turner, "Intelligence for a New World Order," *Foreign Affairs* (Fall 1991): 151–166.

47. See Turner, "Intelligence," pp. 152–153.

48. Sam C. Sarkesian, "Open Society: Defensive Responses," in Uri Ra'anan et al., eds. *Hydra of Carnage: International Linkages of Terrorism* (Lexington, MA: Lexington Books, 1986), p. 219.

49. Johnson, "Smart Intelligence," p. 69.

PART 3

The National Security System and the Policy Process

10

The Policy Process

THE POLICY PROCESS THAT EXISTS WITHIN THE U.S. POLITICAL system is extraordinarily complex. Examining it is like trying to find the beginning of a spider web. The process might begin as a bureaucrat's idea, be triggered by a special interest group, or set off in a new direction by an adversary's surprise action. Yet the formal process appears to be reasonably straightforward when Congress goes into session and passes legislation. As a policy moves through the process, it sparks different reactions from many political actors—opposition, support, compromise. If a policy comes out of the process at all, often it bears little resemblance to the original idea.

Scholars have studied the policy process using a variety of perspectives, approaches, and theories. Yet the process remains somewhat of a mystery or a "muddling through." As one authority has observed, "Anyone bold enough to undertake a serious analysis of how policy is made in the American political system must begin with the realization that he is examining one of the most complex structures ever conceived by man."[1] In the final analysis, whether a policy is approved and implemented has more to do with political forces and the ability and attitude of leaders rather than any formal process. As such, there are many ways to affect policymaking and the process and to shape policy. "The process is complex because of its many participants and because policy-making procedures cannot be divorced from all of the independent sources that shape decision makers' responses to situations demanding action."[2]

Identifying, tracing, and evaluating U.S. policy is difficult for many reasons that evolve from the characteristics of the system (see Chapter 4). Such characteristics cause pluralistic ambiguity and obscurity out of a seemingly straightforward process. This is not the case for all policymaking, however. Policies that respond to crises or that evolve from a public consensus pass quickly thanks to the massive support. This explains the rapid approval of security and antiterrorist initiatives in the wake of

September 11. Nonetheless, some of the most important policies respond to ambiguous situations or those in which there is little agreement on the proper course.

Complexity cannot justify neglecting the study of the U.S. political system, however. The effectiveness of the national security establishment and the success of the president in furthering his national security objectives depend on his ability to manipulate the policy process.

Several approaches and models may provide some order and manageability to analyzing the policy process. Nonetheless, we need some framework as a starting point to analyze the policy process. We begin by touching on several approaches to serve as an introduction to our approach.

Approaches and Models

There are several major approaches, including varying models, to study how policy is made.[3] The differing perspectives discussed here illustrate many of the inherent problems.

Although written in the middle of the twentieth century, two approaches evolve from the distinct philosophical views of C. Wright Mills and Robert Dahl.[4] Mills argued that policy is essentially in the hands of an identifiable elite (high-level bureaucrats, business interests, and the military) that is self-centered and does not necessarily reflect the public interest. Dahl argued that even though policy is made by elites, rarely are the same groups involved with the same degree of intensity; policy therefore emerges as a result of compromise. A third approach is based on the presumption that policy is made by the people through a variety of procedures (public opinion polls, elections, constituent pressure on elected representatives, and interest group advocacy, among other things); "power to the people" takes on a meaningful dimension in this context.

Another approach is *statism*, in which the state is the primary actor with its own characteristics, objectives, and goals. Little attention is given to institutions and agencies within the state or, for that matter, to individual and group behaviors. Finally, the *bureaucratic* approach is based on the assumption that policy is driven primarily by the bureaucracies in the government, which create a network of like-minded interests. The *organizational* approach is similar in that it assumes that organizational objectives and purposes drive policy. Thus the Department of State has a particular worldview and focus in determining policy, which can differ from those of the Department of Defense and Central Intelligence Agency. Often it is difficult to make clear distinctions between the bureaucratic and organizational approaches.

Another aspect relates to differing philosophies regarding policy procedures—the mechanics rather than substance. The *idealistic* view presumes that major policy alternatives are developed at the highest levels of government. Then, through a rational process, alternatives are studied, possible courses of action identified, the best course selected, and the policy passed through. In reality, however, policy is usually made incrementally, that is, in a piecemeal fashion. Furthermore, policy initiatives occur at a variety of governmental levels or even from outside the government structure. Thus policy is often a piecemeal response to a particular situation, not part of a grand design. Furthermore, important policies can also result from citizen action, bureaucratic activity, corporate lobbying, foreign nations, or presidential initiative. This is not to deny that there are grander schemes, but even they result in piecemeal programs. In times of crisis, policymaking and the policy process follow the idealistic model more closely.

This study does not accept the elitist model; neither does it believe that people can directly control policymaking and the policy process. Although a relatively small group of persons ultimately approves and implements policy, the legitimacy and credibility of policy are usually based on a broad spectrum of the populace. The pattern is well described in the following passage:

> Few, if any, of the decisions of government are either decisive or final. Very often policy is the sum of a congeries of separate or only vaguely related actions. On other occasions it is an uneasy, even internally inconsistent, compromise among competing goals or an incompatible mixture of alternative means for achieving a single goal.[5]

The author goes on to note that policy often emerges by "halting small and usually tentative steps" full of "zigs and zags." Policy can also become the opposite of what was originally intended. And finally, it is possible that "issues continue to be debated with nothing being resolved until both the problem and the debaters disappear under the relentless pyramiding of events."[6]

Is there a more systematic approach? Policy *phases* and *political dynamics*, as well as the dynamics emerging from the *total process*, help us better grasp the big picture. Also, *politics nurture elusiveness*, placing an opaque gloss over the entire process. Addressing the role of military officers in the national security policy process, two scholars conclude:

> Because of the variety of purposes among subordinate national security professionals and especially among career military officers, the game of politics remains intense, marked always by the presence of vested interests, interorganizational conflict, intraorganizational rivalry, and the elusiveness of a "best" policy.[7]

Regardless, there are several *policy phases*, each affected by political actors and interconnected, so what occurs in one phase has an impact on the succeeding phases. These *policy phases*, each affected by political actors, lead to an *interconnected process*. Policymaking and the policy process are never-ending; established policies are constantly being revised and passed through the process.

Policy Phases

Scholars in this area often focus on the nature and character of the U.S. political system, studying and identifying the various powers, how the public agenda is set, and the results. Some scholars identify how policy is injected into the decisionmaking process, as well as the roles of agencies and groups in policy outcomes. Regardless, the approaches and perspectives have much in common regarding how policy flows through the process. Our framework for study is based on four phases: policy issue, approval, implementation, and feedback.

Policy issue refers to the shaping of a policy in response to a problem and its injection into the process. This includes the character of forces mobilized for and against. The important element is how policy is shaped and the source of the initiative—a bureaucracy, the Oval Office, interest groups, the federal court system, or Congress. This affects the environment and establishes the boundaries for struggle and compromise. The role of the media is especially important because of its ability to affect and even set the policy agenda.

Approval is the process by which policy passes through formal executive and legislative procedures. Rarely can a policy be effective without congressional approval, whether direct or indirect. Major policy implementation usually requires the commitment of financial resources, meaning congressional action. Debates in Congress, congressional hearings, interest group mobilization, and corporate lobbying are all part of the picture.

Implementation refers to how policies are carried out. The key is the bureaucracy. It plays the critical role in interpreting congressional and executive intent; it also translates intent into practical rules and regulations and applies them to the real world. Also included in this phase is how supporters and opponents affect how policy is interpreted and applied, as well as attempts to revise policy.

Feedback is the response of those affected—that is, the policy impact—and how that response is injected back into the policy process, perhaps triggering new initiatives. The role of the media is also important as a transmitter of information and in focusing public attention on agendas determined by the media elite. The policy phases and their relationships are shown in simple forms in Figure 10.1.

Figure 10.1 Policy Phases

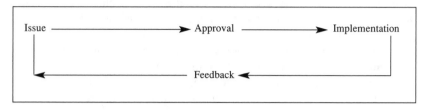

Congress and the Bureaucracy

Congress and the bureaucracy are critical political actors in the policy process. Congress has a constitutional role (see Chapter 11), broadened through oversight as well as constraints and reporting requirements it has imposed on the president and the national security establishment. Although this broader role is a relatively new development with respect to foreign and national security policy, it has always been the case with respect to domestic policy.

The bureaucracy, in contrast, finds its power in the executive branch and the president's constitutional responsibility to ensure the laws are properly administered and carried out. "In the end, the President is heavily dependent upon the ability of bureaucratic organizations for his own success."[8]

The Congressional Factor

The organization of Congress, congressional staffs, and constituent links are important elements of the policy process. Congress operates on the basis of standing committees. Those with the most seniority in the majority party chair the most important committees (Ways and Means, Appropriations, Budget, and Armed Services in the House; Armed Services, Budget, and Appropriations in the Senate). Furthermore, the party leaders are critical players (the Senate majority and minority leaders, and the Speaker of the House and the House majority and minority leaders). Together with the committee chairmen, they form an inner sanctum with its own politics and procedures. It is virtually impossible to push a policy through Congress without the direct or indirect support of the leadership.

This does not deny the importance of other members of Congress. The power base of individual members and their staffs makes each one a political entity unto himself or herself. Cooperation among members provides mutually beneficial political rewards, thereby strengthening individual power bases. But the fact is that much of the power of members of Congress resides in their staffs and constituencies. Staffs of twenty to forty spend considerable time strengthening and expanding the power base of each member. The bureaucracy and special interest groups are especially targeted. This all means that congressional staffs have a significant input on policy, and it broadens the political power of members.

The congressional focus is domestic, although that changes in times of international crisis. Most members and their staffs develop their knowledge and political power in the domestic area. Moreover, domestic politics is a direct link between policy and congressional behavior. Bread-and-butter issues determine whether a member of Congress is doing well, as well as her chances for reelection. This links the political fortunes of members to constituents, whose concerns are employment, economics, and general well-being. This is not to suggest that foreign policy and national security are unimportant, but in normal times they generally give way to domestic matters in the voting booth.

It follows that most interest groups are concerned with domestic issues, and members must be sensitive to them. The result is a link between a member of Congress, special interest groups, and bureaucrats. Once this link is forged, it provides a basis for advocacy and opposition. Such "iron triangles" create various power bases in the policy process.[9]

Both constituents and national interest groups pressure members. Sometimes a single issue, such as abortion, gun control, or the environment (so-called litmus tests), will impact the record and perceived performance of members. Several critics decry single-issue politics, arguing it distorts the legislative process. Many political action committees (PACs) are single issue–oriented.

Thus several important power clusters within Congress are critical components of the policy process. Although they have an important role in foreign and national security policy, they are especially prominent in making domestic policy.

The Bureaucratic Factor

The bureaucracy affects the way policy is carried out in the end, sometimes differently from the intent of Congress and the president. The bureaucracy also has an important impact on the kinds of policies that are injected into the higher levels of the process, whether civilian or military issues. The power of the bureaucracy rests primarily on its organizational character. The classic description is provided by Max Weber: "The decisive reason for the advance of bureaucratic organization has always been its purely technical superiority over any other form of organization. . . . Under normal conditions the power position of the fully developed bureaucracy is always overtowering."[10] Technical skills, administrative structures, and institutional loyalties are the bases for bureaucratic power.

The tendency for bureaucracies to protect their power base and responsibilities can distort policy goals. Bureaucracies often interpret policy according to organizational predispositions. In so doing they reinforce the existing state of affairs and resist major changes to the internal power structure. The dominance of the organization is reinforced by efforts to make the bureaucratic process a predictable routine. Individuality tends to become subsumed by the collective will of the organization. According to Carnes Lord,

> A realistic approach to strategy at the national level must rest on two things, a careful, distinction between the types or levels of policy-making and an appreciation of the bureaucratic faultlines that complicate and often defeat the development and implementation of national strategies.[11]

Also reinforcing the power of the bureaucracy is its influence over the emergence of policy. Power clusters within a bureaucracy, most identified with a particular organizational ideology, reflect a bureaucratic mind-set that accepts only those policy goals and procedures reinforcing the organizational posture. Policy that is generated within the organization or its subunits is vulnerable to the action and influence of gatekeepers, or the individuals with decisionmaking power over what is submitted to the higher policymaking levels. They control the flow of information, including recommendations, suggestions, and plans for policy and procedures. Items that do not fit the organizational setting and goals rarely find their way into the policy process.

In the final analysis, it is difficult to change the bureaucracy or persuade it to accept anything other than the existing state of affairs. Even once a policy is implemented, it is difficult to persuade the bureaucracy to change direction. Indeed, the tendency is for the bureaucracy to justify the policy in the most virtuous terms and perpetuate as well as expand the commitment. In other words, established policy becomes legitimized.

National Security Policy and Process

Analysis of the national security policy process can apply the four-phase pattern described earlier, but the nature of national security and related issues shape the policy process in several important respects. First, secrecy may be needed in order to respond to initiatives planned by an adversary. Second, in crisis or near-crisis situations, there is a need for speed. Third, in most cases national security policy must deal with external groups or foreign states outside the range of U.S. laws. And fourth, the instruments for carrying out national security policy are the foreign service, the military, and intelligence agencies, many of which operate overseas. In summary, national security policy issues evolve out of external sources and necessitate responses by instruments operating outside the United States. This is the context in which one must view the political actors and characteristics of the national security policy process.

The policy phases as they apply to the national security process are intermingled and collapsed into a relatively narrow time span. In addition, power clusters are usually limited to a few high-level political actors at some distance from domestic constituencies. Information is limited and often unavailable to the public, Congress, and bureaucrats outside the national security establishment. In this environment the media play an especially important, and sometimes adversarial, role.

The president usually faces the dilemmas of national security policy. On the one hand, their sensitive nature may dictate quiet diplomacy and secrecy, including undisclosed use of military, diplomatic, and intelligence instruments to affect foreign states. On the other hand, the difficulties in conducting covert operations, maintaining secrecy, and explaining troop commitments after the fact challenge notions of fairness and ethical behavior in an open system. The need to maintain the appearance of normalcy often places the president, other government officials, and bureaucrats in the position of telling half-truths or not informing the public of impending issues. Some domestic opponents of the administration and some civil libertarians are quick to find insidious intentions.

The most visible aspect is the defense budget, which is approved under established legislative procedures in Congress. Although it is a tortuous process, it does provide opportunities for public discussion of national security matters. But the fact remains that the most serious issues are handled through a process that differs from the domestic process (see Figure 10.2).[12]

Conclusion

The national security policy process is primarily, but not exclusively, the preserve of the president and the national security establishment. Although this extends to an inner circle of congressional leaders, the president has discretion in use of military force. The primary instruments and agencies are under the direct control and supervision of the executive. Congress and the public depend on the president for information and for defining national security interests. But the president does not enjoy complete freedom. Indeed, he is considerably constrained in what he can do. There are several problems associated with developing and implementing national security policy and strategy.

Figure 10.2   Differences in Policy Phases

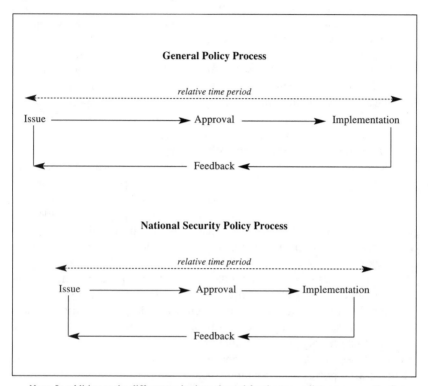

Note: In addition to the differences in time elapsed for the two policy processes, the figure portrays the relative number of political actors involved. In the national security policy process, the circle of participants is considerably narrower than in the general policy process. It must be understood, however, that in a number of national security policy issues, the process follows a pattern similar to the general policy process. Much depends on whether the issue is a "crisis," whether it requires secrecy, and, in some cases, whether the president feels it is within his existing power to execute a certain policy without reference to Congress.

First, national security policy affects domestic policy. In many cases, the best national security policy can have negative impact on domestic policy. For example, punishing an adversary through economic measures can have domestic repercussions, such as the grain embargo against the Soviet Union, which had a negative impact on U.S. wheat sales. Similarly, national security policy and strategy can trigger domestic reaction, as with U.S. involvement in Vietnam and Nicaragua. In another dimension, a determined president focused on domestic policy can be undermined if he is seen as ineffective on national security and foreign policy. Conversely, presidential effectiveness in national security and foreign policy can be eroded by ineffectiveness on the domestic front.

Second, national security failures are likely to become public and undermine the credibility of an administration. Yet many successes cannot be revealed, limiting the ability of the administration to generate support for some policies and strategies (see Chapter 9).

Third, inherent problems thwart the functioning of the national security establishment as well as policy formulation. The president must deal with the national security establishment, the bureaucratic power structure, and Congress to develop and implement his policies. In this respect, Congress is an important factor in oversight and finances, as well as its ability to affect public opinion. Moreover, PACs and other nongovernmental actors, including the media, play an important role. All of this complicates the development and implementation of an administration's national security policy.

Fourth, the environment and constituencies of national security policy differ from those of domestic policy. Foreign states and groups outside U.S. boundaries are major players. Although there is considerable interdependence between domestic and national security policy, the focus of the latter is on external actors and on deploying U.S. military forces. This is true despite new missions like humanitarian assistance, peacemaking, peacekeeping, and a variety of other peacetime engagements.[13] In domestic politics, the focus is on a domestic constituency and domestic political leaders and political actors. Thus there may be interdependence between domestic and national security policy, but there are also basic distinctions in the constituencies and in the strategies and instruments to implement policy. The character and power of international actors and the resulting politics differ in most respects from domestic politics and political actors.

Fifth, the strategic landscape is characterized by new challenges and potential threats, many with no direct link to U.S. national security and national interests. In such an environment it is difficult to design national security policy that can be understood by potential adversaries, allies, and the public.

In summary, the president is at the center of the policy process, yet national security is affected by institutional and interagency politics, individual mind-sets, domestic political and social forces, and foreign actors. Coherency in policy, cohesiveness in implementation, and credibility in commitment are presidential responsibilities. All this must evolve from a strategic vision articulated by the president and a leadership style that has a positive impact on the national security establishment.

Notes

1. John C. Donovan, *The Policy Makers* (New York: Pegasus, 1970), p. 16.

2. Charles W. Kegley Jr. and Eugene R. Wittkopf, *American Foreign Policy: Patterns and Process*, 5th ed. (New York: St. Martin's, 1996), p. 16.

3. See, e.g., Larry Berman and Bruce Allen Murphy, *Approaching Democracy*, 3rd ed. (Upper Saddle River, NJ: Prentice-Hall, 2001), pp. 544–548, and James M. McCormick, *American Foreign Policy and Process*, 3rd ed. (Itasca, IL: F. E. Peacock, 1998), pp. 271–274.

4. C. Wright Mills, *The Power Elite* (New York: Oxford University Press, 1956), and Robert A. Dahl, *Who Governs?* (New Haven: Yale University Press, 1961).

5. Roger Hilsman, with Laura Gaughran and Patricia A. Weitsman, *The Politics of Policy Making in Defense and Foreign Affairs: Conceptual Models and Bureaucratic Politics,* 3rd ed. (Englewood Cliffs, NJ: Prentice-Hall, 1993), p. 347.

6. Ibid., pp. 67, 68, and 69.

7. Richard Thomas Mattingly Jr. and Wallace Earl Walker, "The Military Professionals as Successful Politicians," *Parameters: U.S. Army War College Quarterly* 18, no. 1 (March 1988): 43.

8. Robert T. Nakamura and Frank Smallwood, *The Politics of Policy Implementation* (New York: St. Martin's, 1980), p. 171.

9. For a description of "iron triangles," see Theodore White, *The Making of the President, 1972* (New York: Bantam, 1973). See also B. Guy Peters, *American Public Policy: Promise and Performance*, 2nd ed. (Chatham, NJ: Chatham House, 1986), pp. 21–23.

10. H. H. Gerth and C. Wright Mills, eds., *From Max Weber: Essays in Sociology* (London: Routledge and Kegan Paul, 1984), pp. 214, 232.

11. Carnes Lord, "Strategy and Organization at the National Level," in James C. Gaston, ed., *Grand Strategy and the Decisonmaking Process* (Washington, DC: National Defense University Press, 1991), p. 143.

12. Examples include the policy process in the Bay of Pigs operation, the Cuban missile crisis, and the so-called secret wars in Southeast Asia. See John Prados, *President's Secret Wars: CIA and Pentagon—Covert Operations Since World War II* (New York: William Morrow, 1986).

13. Alexander M. Haig Jr., "The Question of Humanitarian Intervention," *WIRE* (Foreign Policy Research Institute) 9, no. 2 (February 2001).

11

The President and Congress

SINCE THE U.S. CONSTITUTION WAS APPROVED, THE EVOLUTION of power has placed the president in the dominant position in foreign affairs and national security. This remains the case even after passage of legislation, like the War Powers Resolution, designed to increase congressional power in these areas. Congress has an important role, but the nature of international security issues and the increasing complexity of international politics make it difficult for Congress to lead the nation or, for that matter, to check the president on policy initiatives, especially during a national crisis. In addition, presidential power has grown in response to increasingly complex U.S. economic and social systems, which have indirectly reinforced the president's power in national security policy.

In the post–Cold War era, the traditional notion of national security is being questioned, and as a consequence presidential power in national security is undergoing change. Some see a stronger congressional role; others see a stronger presidential role. Given the uncertainty, it is small wonder that the powers of the president and Congress are being reexamined. It is too early to predict the long-term effects of the war on terrorism on this balance, but we expect that the president's role will be significantly strengthened, at least in the short term.

In any case, "presidents are not kings. To understand the power that they wield we must distinguish between foreign and domestic affairs and specifically what kind of power over what kind of issue and in what circumstances and against the opposition of which other centers of power."[1] Put simply, the exercise of presidential power is a function of the president's ability to understand the nature of the political process, his constitutional power, the international climate, and the power inherent in his own leadership and skills as a politician. At the same time, Congress has increasingly reclaimed its share of responsibility.

The Presidential Power Base

Several factors complicate the policymaking process, including the nature of the presidency, public expectations, and the demands of the international security environment. These all have philosophical, ideological, and political overtones. National security goes beyond a strong military and the ability to support it financially. It includes confidence in leadership, staying power, national will, political resolve, and agreement on national security goals. In today's strategic and political climate, it also includes some agreement on the meaning of national security.

The president faces potential opposition from several quarters. Although the president and Congress cooperate in many ways on national security matters, disagreements over policy diverge from the established procedure. Special interest groups, segments of the U.S. public, and allies may also oppose the president. Add to this disagreements within the administration and the national security establishment, and one can appreciate the extent of the problem, especially in the strategic landscape of the twenty-first century.

Aside from the Constitution, the institutional characteristics of Congress and the power of individual members create conflict. Constituencies, terms of office, and mind-sets all play a role. Incumbency strengthens the hand of many members of Congress. Incumbents perpetuate their power to ensure reelection, and few are defeated. Some members of the House of Representatives have been in office for more than thirty years. This has led some to view Congress as an institution of incumbents intent on maintaining office, overriding political party issues and categorizations.

The president can use several strategies to overcome opposition in Congress. Many are inherent to the office, whereas others depend on the effectiveness of presidential leadership style and techniques.

Every president beginning with Dwight Eisenhower has used a congressional liaison staff to establish and maintain relations. It targets key members in both houses, especially potential allies. The staff keeps the president informed of congressional power clusters and the general mood and recommends tactics to develop support for presidential initiatives. Similarly, the staff keeps members informed about presidential initiatives.[2] Although the liaison staff is usually concerned with domestic issues, longer-range national security policy and defense issues are also important.

Other tactics for developing support include bargaining, threat and intimidation, and reward. For example, the attempts by Congress to invoke the War Powers Resolution over U.S. involvement in the Persian Gulf in 1987 was the focal point of much presidential maneuvering. This ultimately led to a compromise in which the president was simply expected to inform Congress of developments. The president must be cautious in following certain tactics, however, because Congress can react negatively to extreme pressure from the White House and can undermine the president's domestic and foreign agendas.

The president can decide that the best means to implement national security policy and strategy is to distance himself from Congress and provide minimum information. He can thereby maintain a degree of flexibility. The danger is that members of Congress, as well as the public, may perceive the president as isolated from major policy decisions and out of touch.

In a direct confrontation with Congress, the president can take his case to the people. In 1987, President Ronald Reagan used this tactic to develop support for financial aid to the contras opposing the Sandinista government in Nicaragua. Earlier, he took the case for Vietnam to the people, labeling U.S. involvement as a "noble cause" and honoring those who fought there. Other presidents have adopted this tactic when faced with congressional opposition to important presidential initiatives, as in 1993, when President Bill Clinton and First Lady Hillary Rodham Clinton sought to push through a health care reform package. Passage of the North American Free Trade Agreement (NAFTA) is another case in point. Here again, the president must be careful not to become overzealous. Congressional as well as public reaction to perceived inflexibility can undermine presidential initiatives; public backlash results if presidential policy fails to deliver.

In 1993 and 1994, U.S. national security strategy was not clear, and there was no clear strategic vision articulated by the Clinton administration.[3] This was seen in the apparently muddled response and misjudgments associated with U.S. involvement in Somalia, where eighteen U.S. soldiers were killed in an engagement in October 1993 (the subject of the popular film *Black Hawk Down*).[4]

The president has an advantage in dealing with Congress in the national security arena, however, because the sources of intelligence, the basis of policy and strategy skills, and the operational instruments are centered in his office. For example, the president's Cabinet, presidential advisers, national security staff, and the National Security Advisor are reinforcing powers. Even though expanded congressional staffs and their skills are important, the presidential power base—the Departments of Defense and State, the military advisery system, the Central Intelligence Agency, and the National Security Council and its staff—is dominant. Congress must rely on presidential sources for much of its information about national security.

Important exceptions include the Congressional Research Service, the committee system, and the congressional staffs, which have developed the ability to provide alternate approaches (e.g., to nuclear policy and defense budgets). However, much classified information remains the domain of the president, sometimes passed along to only a handful of members. Information leaks from Congress may cause the president to restrict congressional access to classified information, as President George W. Bush briefly considered in October 2001. Finally, nothing can substitute for face-to-face meetings between the president and other heads of state, or between the secretary of state and foreign ministers of other states, or for the knowledge that comes from liaisons with friendly intelligence agencies.

Congress: The Legislative System

The relationship between the chief executive and Congress has been described as an "invitation to struggle," as Benjamin Franklin said of democracy itself. The U.S. political system has a constitutional basis with separation of powers among the branches of government and resulting checks and balances (see Chapter 3). Although these characteristics are more pronounced in domestic politics and policy, they play an important role in national security policy. To understand the congressional role in national security, we need to review the general features of the institution and the legislative process.

The Founders expected that Congress would dominate the political process. Although the president was given important powers in foreign affairs, those at the Constitutional Convention wanted to ensure that he would not dominate the policymaking process. The president would have power to react in emergencies, but Congress would determine war policy. Furthermore, the power of Congress in the legislative process and budget matters was to provide an effective counterbalance to the president.

The scope of congressional responsibilities has increased, yet Congress is finding it more difficult to respond because of the cumbersome legislative process and the characteristics of the institution. As S. J. Deitchman concluded,

> The Congress, representing diverse and often irreconcilable interests, is gaining long-term dominance over the Executive Branch. . . . Decision making in the interest of national security will become more difficult because the conflicts inherent in having a multiplicity of national-security decisionmakers will have the effect of inhibiting, delaying, or distorting decisions that must be made in a world demanding increasing perceptiveness of international trends and more responsiveness and coherence in adapting to or attempting to influence them.[5]

Nevertheless, effective national security policy depends on congressional support and public acceptance. Because of the representative role of Congress and its power over the purse, no successful president can afford to disregard Congress, isolate himself from the legislative process, or distance himself from the leadership in Congress.

The organization and functioning of Congress rest primarily on the committee structure. In the normal course of the legislative process, a bill first goes to committees, with the chairs of committees and subcommittees exercising considerable power in determining its fate. Chairs are appointed by the majority party in each house, with seniority being critical to appointment. The internal power system of Congress does not rest solely with the committee structure, however. Congressional leadership positions, such as the Speaker of the House and the majority and minority leaders in both houses, carry power that generally exceeds that of committee chairs. Reforms in the 1970s placed final approval of leadership roles in the party caucus and eroded the disciplined party system as well as the authority of the party leadership. Combined with the committee structure and the power of individual members, these reforms have fragmented power within Congress.

Power in Congress thus derives from a mixture of sources: power over the purse, the status of the membership, relationships with colleagues, the party, and the formal leadership offices. As long as constituent support remains, members are powerful in their own right. Nonetheless, they can accomplish little by themselves; they are dependent upon colleagues to get things done. Every bill needs supporters, and this leads to constant interplay among internal forces seeking accommodation and compromise (or leading to confrontation). Thus even with internal power fragmentation, effective leadership in Congress is essential for the functioning of the legislative process.

Congress and the Executive: The Invitation to Struggle

Congress has a critical role in national security. According to Frederick Kaiser,

> National security is not a simple set of well-integrated subject matters neatly arranged along a single, consistent policy continuum. . . . It is a complex set of diverse subject matters that cross into many different policy lines; these in turn raise different issues and concerns, institutional interests, and costs that affect congressional roles.[6]

At least two important distinctions need to be made as to the president and Congress. First, the institution of the presidency rests on one individual who heads a hierarchical branch of government. The center of power is clear, and the responsibility for executing the laws of the nation is focused on the president. There is little overt fragmentation of power or responsibility. In Congress a different picture emerges. Not only is there considerable fragmentation of power within the institution; it is often difficult to place responsibility in any single member. Responsibility falls on Congress as an institution, making it possible for individual members to shift blame to the institution as a corporate body. This affords members a great deal of flexibility in taking political positions, and they can disclaim responsibility for any institutional outcome that is unacceptable to their constituencies.

Second, the president is the only nationally elected official (aside from the vice president, whose power is dependent on the president).[7] Thus only the president has a national constituency, with all that that suggests with respect to national security policy formulation. Individual members of the House of Representatives represent districts within states, many of which reflect narrow segments of the population. Furthermore, such districts can be dominated by one or two special interest groups. Senators, representing states, also reflect a small part of the total population. Even in states, the political power can rest with a handful of special interest groups.

Congress has attempted to overcome some of the disadvantages by referring to the corporate will of Congress. More often than not, this means little more than the will of a majority coalition—and if Congress is controlled by one party and the presidency by another party, the politics of the corporate will is relatively clear. The differing constituencies between the president and Congress not only reflect different power bases and interests; they create different policy mind-sets and the conditions of struggle over policy, programs, and budgets.

The War Powers Resolution of 1973 is an important reference point. During the Richard Nixon administration, the Democratic Party held majorities in both houses of Congress. Congressional concern over U.S. involvement in Vietnam and the erosion of President Nixon's power as a result of Watergate prompted Congress to pass the War Powers Resolution over presidential veto (many Republicans saw the issue as one of congressional prerogative rather than party loyalty). The resolution required the president to consult Congress prior to committing (and periodically thereafter) U.S. troops to hostile action. The War Powers Resolution provides that:

> The President in every possible instance shall consult with Congress before introducing United States Armed Forces into hostilities or into situations where imminent involvement in hostilities is clearly indicated by the circumstances, and after every such introduction shall consult regularly with the Congress until United States Armed Forces are no longer engaged in hostilities or have been removed from such situations.[8]

After sixty days U.S. forces would have to be withdrawn unless Congress declared war or passed an extension. The president has an additional thirty days to withdraw all U.S. forces if he states in writing that "unavoidable military necessity respecting the safety of United States Armed Forces requires the continued use of such armed forces in the course of bringing about a prompt removal of such forces."[9] It also provided Congress the option of passing a concurrent resolution ending U.S. involvement in hostilities. Such a resolution could not be vetoed by the president. But according to most authorities, "The War Powers Resolution cannot be regarded as a success for Congress. . . . All Presidents serving since 1973 have deemed the law an unconstitutional infringement on their powers."[10] Indeed, even when presidents consult Congress about military actions (as George Bush did before the Gulf War in 1991 and as George W. Bush did in initiating the war on terrorism in September 2001), they do not specifically invoke the War Powers Resolution, and Congress is often brought into the process long after it can affect policy.

In his relationships with Congress and in trying to establish the necessary consensus and support for national security policies, the president must deal with a variety of power clusters within the institution. In the past, given party discipline and effective leadership in Congress, the executive could focus his attention on the Speaker of the House and the majority and minority leaders in both houses; today the president must also deal with other important members, especially key committee chairs. The increase in power clusters is especially pronounced in domestic policy, but it also affects national security policy. As some authorities conclude:

> With more committees and subcommittees dealing with international issues; more staff and better information facilities at their disposal; more foreign travel by legislators and their aides; more groups, governments, and individuals trying to affect policy judgements, members of Congress, individually and collectively, have become less disposed to acquiesce in the president's initiatives. Some have even taken matters into their own hands.[11]

This was during President Reagan's second term in office. Congressman Stephen J. Solarz, for example, was directly involved in the Philippines as Ferdinand Marcos was deposed and replaced by a new government. In another example, Senator Christopher Dodd became the self-appointed spokesman for the Daniel Ortega government in Nicaragua when he visited and dealt directly with Ortega. Before the dissolution of the Soviet Union, members of Congress also visited and met with Soviet President Mikhail Gorbachev. In 1993, Senator Bob Kerrey attempted to take the lead in establishing U.S. policy on POWs/MIAs in Southeast Asia, visiting North Vietnam in a highly publicized tour to give credence to his effort.

If the president loses popular support, or if his initiatives appear vacillating and ambiguous, Congress is more likely to take the lead. For example, following the killing of eighteen U.S. Army soldiers in Somalia in late 1993, Congress set conditions for U.S. involvement there. Some observers noted the marginalization of the presidency in the matter. These are just a few examples of congressional usurpation of power in diplomatic and defense matters.

Nonetheless, the public looks to the president for leadership in national security policy. This is true also for most members of Congress, even though they debate and criticize policy. Part of this acquiescence stems from a recognition that it is difficult for Congress to lead; it is better postured to react and engage in oversight. Another factor is the tendency for Congress to be cautious in initiating national security policy for fear of being associated with failures or controversies that might affect their popularity with constituents. The safest position is to keep some distance from national security policy until it becomes clear whether it is succeeding or failing.

This allows the president some latitude in initiating national security policy, although policy failures are easily attributable to him. Equally important, the complexity of national security issues, the changed external power relationships, and the difficulty the United States faces in trying to control external situations all mean success is never assured. Failure is no longer a remote possibility. One can understand, therefore, the reluctance of members of Congress to become too closely associated, too soon, with presidential positions on national security, save for crises. In the international order of the twenty-first century, this is even more so.

In summary, no president can ignore the congressional role in national security policy. Indeed, most successful policies depend on the bipartisan involvement of congressional leadership. Congress, sensitive to its responsibilities and protective of its prerogatives, demands an equal, if different, role in national security. Because there is ambiguity as to executive power in national security policy, the case is compelling for many members to be deeply involved. Ambiguity, shared power, institutional character, and the nature of national security policy thus create the basis for confrontation between the president and Congress.

The President, Congress, and the Policy Process

The president's ability to deal with Congress and to develop the support necessary for national security policy must be viewed from two dimensions: (1) the element of national security policy being considered; and (2) how the president's sources of strength can overcome the sources of conflict.

National security policy includes a range of subpolicies, from the defense budget and military manpower levels, to executive agreements and treaties, to covert operations. There is a degree of overlap between national security and foreign policy. This overlap has become considerable in the new strategic landscape, in which national security increasingly encompasses nonmilitary matters.

The president has a great deal of latitude in committing and deploying U.S. military forces, especially in the early stages of a crisis. Nevertheless, congressional oversight and budget power restrict the president in the long term. Congress, ever sensitive to negative reaction from constituents about U.S. force commitments, will make their reaction known to the president. To be sure, in short-term commitments where success appears clear, as in the Gulf War, and even in longer-term commitments where there is a clear threat to the nation, as in the current war on terrorism, the president can enjoy popularity and support for his policies. But only he will be blamed for any failure.

An essential part of the national security policy process is reflected in debates over the defense budget and the final shape of the national budget. The annual budget process focuses attention on general issues of national security. This does not involve serious discussion and debate over strategy, but there can be exceptions (e.g., the George W. Bush administration, which initially decided not to increase defense spending).[12] Yet budget debates are usually the most visible part of national security policy formulation, although specific events (e.g., September 11, the anthrax scare, Iran-contra, the Marines barracks bombing in Lebanon, the Gulf War, Somalia, and Bosnia-Herzegovina) focus attention on specific issues that can lead to debate over national security policy. In 1993, Secretary of Defense Les Aspin's attempt to restructure the U.S. military drew criticism in Congress and other quarters and figured in defense budget debates and in national security policy in general.[13] In addition, some issues have gone beyond traditional national security notions (e.g., the Clinton administration's efforts to lift the ban on open homosexuals and to expand the role of women in the military). Such efforts can raise much criticism, with some observers linking issues to problems in national security policy.

Finally, some issues of U.S. national security may be a continual source of debate, but there is continuity in important aspects of U.S. policy, even in the new world order. The fight against terrorism, the close relationship with Western Europe, the concern over weapons proliferation, protection of freedom and nurturing of democratic systems, and control and reduction of nuclear weapons stockpiles will continue to be important priorities.

Well-established and accepted components of national security generally do not create controversial and difficult issues for the president. It is when the president wants to change direction, add a new dimension to established policy, undertake new initiatives, or fails to clarify national security policy that he faces opposition in Congress and among the public. In the past, national security included policies long understood by the U.S. public, such as the role in the North Atlantic Treaty Organization (NATO) and other security arrangements. But the end of the Cold War has thrown such relationships into disarray, even irrelevance. Questions are now being raised, for example, regarding the relevance of NATO now that the Soviet Union is no more. The George W. Bush administration clearly shares Bill Clinton's enthusiasm for expanding NATO.

In addition, recent developments have little to do with Cold War alliances. All of this has become more complicated in the twenty-first century with its uncertain world order and altered the strategic landscape. One consequence is that there can be differences among the president and Congress and the expectations of the public with respect to national security.

Presidential Leadership and Party Politics

Although developing consensus and support in Congress depends on presidential leadership, the direct involvement of the president in national security policy has an immediate bearing on his leadership style. In this respect, popular support and party politics are important factors in developing effective presidential leadership.

The relative strength of the political parties in Congress impacts the president's ability to shape national security policy through the legislative process. If the same party holds the White House and Congress, the president will likely have the advantage thanks to party loyalty. The fact that the president is also the leader of his party reinforces this. A skilled president can use this to strengthen his position on national security policy and strategy, allowing him a greater latitude for initiating changes. In a crisis, of course, party considerations tend to be less important.

Following the 2000 presidential election the Republican Party, for the first time since 1954, controlled both houses of Congress (with the Republican vice president breaking a 50-50 tie in the Senate) as well as the Oval Office. The defection of one senator (from Republican to Independent) soon gave control to the Democrats.

It does not always follow, however, that party support in Congress automatically leads to support for presidential initiatives. Policy and strategy must have a basis in the overall orientation as reflected in general posture, that is, in the mainstream political party orientation. Conversely, lack of party support does not preclude a president from developing consensus and support. As stated before, the ability of the president to use party support in Congress to his advantage is a function of his leadership skills.[14] But in general the advantage is with the president whose party holds both houses of Congress.

There is a close correlation between party support and popular support for the president. A perceived mandate from the electorate can translate into support in Congress. Even if individuals are opposed to presidential policies, they find it difficult to publicly defy a popular president. At the same time, erosion of popular support has a similar impact on congressional support, regardless of party alignments. Lyndon Johnson and Richard Nixon discovered that the hard way. President George W. Bush had extraordinary high approval ratings in the wake of September 11. But by the summer of 2002 the ratings dropped (although it remained between 60 and 70 percent approval), tempered by congressional inquiries about intelligence matters and the direction of the war on terrorism.

Sometimes the president can make a personal appeal to members of Congress. By approaching individual members, appealing to their sense of propriety, stressing the need to support the president and nation in critical national security issues, and even promising support on future issues, the president can overcome resistance to his policies. Lyndon Johnson is the acknowledged master of this tactic. A longtime member of Congress before he became president, Johnson personally knew most members and was keenly aware of congressional dynamics and politics. Making full use of this knowledge, he prevailed upon individual members to garner support for policies ranging from the Great Society to U.S. involvement in Vietnam. But when popular support of the Vietnam War eroded, a similar erosion took place in the president's popular support—causing a reduction in his congressional support.

In 1993 and 1994, President Clinton and his inner circle, though not necessarily attuned to the ways of Congress, employed similar tactics as they cajoled, prodded, and coerced various members to support presidential budget initiatives and (unsuccessfully) health care reform. The administration was more effective in its second term, convincing Congress to support permanent normal trade relations with China and the Senate to ratify an expansion of NATO to include Poland, Hungary, and the Czech Republic. In addition, the Clinton administration was not averse to compromises in developing support among the Democratic Party. Even some Democratic Party members of Congress opposed to certain presidential initiatives did eventually support him, proclaiming the need to save his presidency or the need to have this president succeed, overlooking policy-specific concerns.

If used cautiously and prudently, personal appeals can be an effective tactic. But if the president resorts to such appeals too often, they lose their effectiveness. Only when individual members of Congress feel that personal appeals are focused on special issues that have a direct bearing on presidential performance and are essential to effective policies will they tend to respond positively. In other words, the president can rapidly deplete the power associated with personal appeals.

In the final analysis, the president may need to stand up for what he believes rather than make concessions. Ultimately it is the president who is held responsible for national security policy, regardless of the actions of Congress. The president "is the only person in the government who represents the whole people."[15] Yet some presidents revel in public opposition to Congress, whether it stems from perceived do-nothingism, incompetence, corruption, or deceptive congressional practices. Some members of Congress will go to extraordinary lengths to frustrate and oppose the president as a matter of political principle.

Covert Operations and Secret Military Deployments

Covert operations are at the root of many controversial national security issues (see Chapters 6 and 7). Many times they reveal serious disagreements between the president and Congress and provide insights into the congressional role in national security issues. This was dramatically exposed during the Iran-contra hearings in 1987.[16] Even though many Republicans felt that the Democratic-controlled Congress tried to exploit the hearings in a partisan way, the matter was a valuable education on certain aspects of national security policy. The hearings revealed the character of covert operations and explained the role of Congress in the process. In addition, the logic of such operations was examined through Oliver North's dramatic testimony in support of the cause of the Nicaraguan contras, whom he portrayed as freedom fighters. The Iran-contra episode highlighted the struggles between the president and Congress over covert actions that had been ongoing since the end of the Vietnam War.[17] A review of this matter will clarify the root of these struggles.

In the late 1970s, on the heels of investigations into alleged CIA abuses and secret operations, a series of legislative bills was passed strengthening the congressional role in intelligence matters. Two of the most important features of this legislation were (1) the creation of permanent oversight committees in the House and Senate; and (2) provisions for dealing with the relationship of intelligence agencies and Congress. Although these focused specifically on intelligence agencies, information, and the relationship to Congress, they had a direct bearing on the relationship of the president with Congress on sensitive national security issues. As such, they help identify the direction and substance of the president's ability to deal successfully with Congress on national security policy and strategy.

In 1976, the Senate Select Committee on Intelligence (SSCI) was created, "composed of 15 members drawn from the Appropriations, Armed Services, Foreign Relations and Judiciary Committees, and from the Senate at large. . . . The SSCI [has] full authority to oversee the activities of U.S. intelligence agencies and to authorize their funding."[18] Two years later, the House passed similar legislation creating the House Permanent Select Committee on Intelligence (HPSCI). "The HPSCI consists of 16 members, with membership drawn from Appropriations, Armed Services, Foreign Affairs and Judiciary Committees, as well as from the House at large"[19] and has essentially the same authority as the SSCI.

The Intelligence Oversight Act of 1980 imposed several reporting requirements on the CIA director (more formally, the Director of Central Intelligence) as well as on "the heads of departments, agencies and other entities of the United States involved in intelligence activities to keep the committees 'fully and currently informed of all intelligence activities' including 'any significant anticipated intelligence activity.'"[20] The oversight provision does not require approval of intelligence activities; it is primarily consultative and informative. But a committee member can frustrate any intelligence operation by threatening to leak it to the media; in 1987, a senator acknowledged using this tactic on more than one occasion.

The act requires reporting covert operations in a timely fashion, but it is not clear what that means in this context. President Reagan agreed to make a report within forty-eight hours, and legislation evolving from the Iran-contra hearings placed specific time limits on reporting requirements.[21] Moreover, according to some scholars, Congress does have important powers in reacting to or in limiting presidential initiatives:

> It may cut off funding for foreign and defense policies. The Church Amendment to the appropriations bill for 1973 cut off U.S. government support for the Republic of Vietnam . . . and the various Boland Amendments between 1982 and 1986 (named after Representative Edward Boland, D-Mass.) sought to prevent federal funds from being provided to the Contras in Nicaragua.[22]

Congress also passed legislation to restructure Defense Department special operations and low-intensity conflict. In 1986, Senators William Cohen (R-ME) and Sam Nunn (D-GA) sponsored a bill passed by Congress that mandated an assistant secretary of defense for special operations and low intensity conflict; a U.S. Special Operations Command, along with a Low Intensity Board as part of the National Security Council; and a deputy assistant to the president for national security on low intensity conflict. These provisions triggered serious opposition within the military and the executive branch. Many feel that the assistant secretary position has not developed into an effective instrument for policymaking.

Covert operations differ from secret military operations in important aspects. In the latter (e.g., the invasions of Grenada and Panama, as well as certain actions in Afghanistan and elsewhere) the initial phase of U.S. involvement was concealed for reasons of security and safety. Secret military operations are difficult to keep under wraps for any length of time and eventually invite public debate and congressional involvement. They are often used to demonstrate U.S. policy. Covert operations, however, are special activities cloaked in secrecy that are intended to conceal U.S. government involvement, among other things.[23] Such activities range from propaganda and paramilitary operations to the use of small special operations forces for extended periods.

Leadership and Policy

This study has stressed that the success of national security policy depends on the president's leadership and his relationship with Congress. The president has the key role, the constitutional authority, and much latitude in foreign and national security policy. His ability to build support in Congress, to control and direct the national security establishment, and to gain public acceptance of his policies is a direct function of his leadership style.

No single model of leadership is sufficient (see Chapter 5). Indeed, a variety of leadership approaches can establish a basis for legislative support, just as there are various tangible means by which he can create and nurture congressional support.

Yet certain principles of leadership are essential in dealing effectively with Congress. These principles, and the way they are applied, must lead to the development of trust and confidence. This in turn evolves from the perceptions of members of Congress that the president is in control of the national security establishment, that his presence permeates that establishment, and that he clearly articulates a vision of U.S. strength and commitment. Furthermore, Congress must feel that the president's staff is knowledgeable, skilled, and supportive of his national security policy. Equally important, there must be mutual trust and confidence among the president and the national security staff, the military, and the intelligence establishment. Part of this evolves from the character, background, and experience of the commander in chief. In this respect, there is sometimes a decided gap between the president and the military.[24]

Much presidential strength is a function of personality and character. According to two prominent scholars,

> The point to remember in assessing the presidential power and the ability
> of a given president to wield it effectively—or perhaps even abuse it—is

that the style and character of the president himself is every bit as important as the inherent power of the institution. And when we talk about powers of the presidency, we must consider three factors: a president's sense of purpose; his political skills; and his character.[25]

And as James Q. Wilson concludes, "The public will judge the president not only in terms of what he accomplishes but also in terms of its perception of his character."[26] To understand the power that presidents wield, we must make some distinction between foreign and domestic affairs, specify the kind of power and the issue, identify the circumstances, and consider the opposition from other centers of power. We must also understand how well the president understands the political process itself, how deeply he feels about achieving the goals being sought, and how much political skill he brings to the job.

Trust and confidence between the executive and the legislature are strengthened by several procedures flowing out of the Oval Office. Members of Congress, especially the leadership, must feel that the president is sincere about consulting Congress and accepts the coequal status of Congress and the president. Furthermore, Congress must feel that the president is providing timely and useful information on matters of national security. This especially applies to covert operations and secret military movements, even though Congress initially is only a recipient of information and not an approving body.

Furthermore, the president must make himself reasonably accessible to members of Congress, especially to the leadership. Members become frustrated if ignored by the president and feel that such a situation damages their ability to deal with their own issues. In such an environment, confrontation and disagreement between Congress and the president are inevitable. The idea of consultation is engrained in the two institutions. Consultation can pave the way for support, provide the perception of congressional power, and become a symbolic tool for fulfilling congressional responsibility.

Even if the president does all these things, he will not be assured of success; but he will have the most favorable environment in which to pursue such goals. Leadership is the key to relationships with Congress, and leadership must begin with an understanding of the important role played by Congress as well as an appreciation for the human motivations of individual members.

Conclusion

The president cannot simply respond to popular passions of the moment; neither can he simply ingratiate himself with Congress. Such behavior can only lead to the erosion of executive credibility and project a picture of a weak leader. This can have serious negative effects on political will and can lead to the erosion of staying power in national security.

The president is ultimately responsible for the formulation and implementation of national security policy and strategy. For most elements of his policy, he is in a position to receive the support of Congress and the public. But there are elements of policy in which he may have to stand alone, taking credit for its success but assuming full responsibility for failure. How this plays out within the national security system depends on presidential leadership.

Notes

1. Roger Hilsman, with Laura Gaughran and Patricia A. Weitsman, *The Politics of Policymaking in Defense and Foreign Affairs: Conceptual Models and Bureaucratic Politics*, 3rd ed. (Englewood Cliffs, NJ: Prentice-Hall, 1993), p. 145.

2. Richard A. Watson and Norman C. Thomas, *The Politics of the Presidency*, 2nd ed. (Washington, DC: CQ Press, 1988), p. 257.

3. This was rectified somewhat later in his administration with the publishing of an annual National Security Strategy report. See, e.g., *A National Security Strategy for a Global Age* (Washington, DC: December 2000).

4. Eighteen special operations personnel (sixteen Army Rangers and two members of the elite Delta Force) were killed on October 3 and 4, 1993, in an attempt to capture Somali warlord Mohammed Farah Aideed. He was a general in the Somali army and trained in the former Soviet Union. He was also a student of Mao Tse-tung and studied the strategic pespectives of Sun-tzu. Many of these matters have to do with guerrilla warfare, but in October 1993 Aideed's background and training were hardly noted by any spokesperson in the Clinton administration or by the media.

5. S. J. Deitchman, *Beyond the Thaw: A New National Strategy* (Boulder: Westview, 1991), p. 34.

6. Frederick M. Kaiser, "Congress and National Security Policy: Evolving and Varied Roles for a Shared Responsibility," in James C. Gaston, ed., *Grand Strategy and the Decisionmaking Process* (Washington, DC: National Defense University Press, 1991), p. 217.

7. The vice president's constitutional power as president of the Senate can be important if the Senate is evenly divided, as it was for a short time after the 2000 election.

8. The War Powers Act of 1973, Public Law 93-148, sec. 3.

9. Ibid., sec. 5(b).

10. Robert L. Lineberry, George C. Edwards III, and Martin P. Wattenberg, *Government in America: People, Politics, and Policy*, 5th ed. (New York: HarperCollins, 1991), p. 486.

11. George C. Edwards and Stephen J. Wayne, *Presidential Leadership: Politics and Policy Making* (New York: St. Martin's, 1985), p. 299.

12. See Tom Ricks, "Clinton's Pentagon Budget to Stand," *Washington Post*, February 7, 2001, p. 4. Any military leader who was surprised by this failed to read the tea leaves correctly. Their visceral dislike of Clinton personally and the Clinton-

Gore military policies blinded them to the fact that the militarily hawkish Republicans were primarily *budget* hawks. If the military wanted to continue the status quo, only with more money, they should have hoped for a Gore victory.

13. Les Aspin, Secretary of Defense, "Bottom Up Review," letter dated June 25, 1993, with enclosure on "Remarks" as prepared by Les Aspin, Secretary of Defense, at the National Defense University Graduation, Fort McNair, Washington, DC, June 16, 1993. Also see Representative Les Aspin, "The New Security: A Bottom-up Approach to the Post–Cold War Era," U.S. House of Representatives, Armed Services Committee.

14. The leadership skills of President George W. Bush were severely tested in the strongly partisan atmosphere in Washington following his controversial and razor-thin victory in the 2000 election. Given historical voting trends (the president's party generally loses congressional seats in off-year elections), the Democratic Party hopes to pick up enough seats in the 2002 election to keep control of the Senate and perhaps gain control of the House of Representatives. In the aftermath of September 11 and the subsequent widespread support for President Bush, historical parallels might not apply.

15. Merle Miller, *Plain Speaking: An Oral Biography of Harry S. Truman* (New York: Berkley Medallion Books, 1974), p. 445.

16. For details on the Iran-contra affair, see *Report of the Congressional Committees Investigating the Iran-Contra Affair* (Washington, DC: U.S. Government Printing Office, 1987), and *Report of the President's Special Review Board* (Washington, DC: U.S. Government Printing Office, February 26, 1987).

17. For a useful study, see Gregory F. Treverton, *Covert Action: The Limits of Intervention in the Postwar World* (New York: Basic Books, 1987).

18. Standing Committee on Law and National Security, American Bar Association, *Oversight and Accountability of the U.S. Intelligence Agencies: An Evaluation* (Washington, DC: American Bar Association, 1985), pp. 7–8.

19. Ibid.

20. Ibid., pp. 11–12.

21. See "Text of the President's Letter on New Guidelines for Covert Operations," *New York Times*, August 8, 1987, p. 5. In this letter to Senator David Boren, chairman of the Senate Select Committee on Intelligence, President Reagan expressed his support for a number of committee recommendations on covert operations, including the following: "Except in cases of extreme emergency, all national security 'findings' should be in writing. If an oral directive is necessary, a record should be made contemporaneously and the finding reduced to writing and signed by the President as soon as possible, but in no event more than two working days thereafter. . . . I believe we cannot conduct an effective program of special activities without the cooperation and support of Congress."

22. Donald M. Snow and Eugene Brown, *Puzzle Palace and Foggy Bottom: U.S. Foreign and Defense Policy-Making in the 1990s* (New York: St. Martin's, 1994), p. 148.

23. American Bar Association, *Oversight and Accountability*, p. 19. See Chapter 7 in this book for a more detailed discussion of unconventional conflicts and covert operations.

24. David Silverberg, "Clinton and the Military: Can the Gap Be Bridged?" *Armed Forces Journal International* 129, no. 3 (October 1993): 53, 54, 57.

25. Erwin C. Hargraves and Roy Hoopes, *The Presidency: A Question of Power* (Boston: Little, Brown, 1975), p. 47.

26. James Q. Wilson, *American Government: Institutions and Policies*, 5th ed. (Lexington, MA: D. C. Heath, 1992), p. 338.

12

Empowering the People

POPULAR CONTROL OF GOVERNMENT IS A FUNDAMENTAL PRIN-
ciple of democracy. The channels to establish, nurture, and expand presidential links to the people, and from the people to the president, are the
media, political parties, and interest groups. These are usually considered
linkage institutions, linking people to government and the president. The
media transmit images, information, opinions, and the attitudes of the public to the president and vice versa. Media professionals also advance their
own agendas, even becoming active players in the policy process. Political
parties attempt to mobilize the people to win office and are the main instruments for organizing Congress and controlling the legislative agenda and
process. Interest groups reflect and shape the attitudes, opinions, and policy
positions of important segments of the public. Interest groups are a means
for individuals to have a voice and a channel for expressing their preferences.

As a general rule, the public holds broad views on policy, not informed
opinions oriented toward specific issues. Some scholars are quick to note
that public views are usually inchoate and oversimplified. But public views
can be transformed into specific policy preferences as a result of interest
groups and political parties. Interest groups (i.e., every type of organization
that tries to achieve its goals by affecting policy choices and policymakers)
can be transformed into single-issue groups, mobilizing segments of the
populace. In the course of this mobilization and policy advocacy, interest
groups provide a means to pressure policymakers and elected officials.

Public attitudes and the degree of public support are factors in influencing the relative success of a president's policies. This is especially the
case in domestic areas, but it is also true for national security policy. Public
support over the long run is necessary to the success of national security
policy and strategy. This is especially the case when the president seeks to
place U.S. armed forces in harm's way or when the public feels directly

threatened, as on September 11. Additionally, how these relationships evolve into support for or opposition to the president and national security policy is an important factor in the study of the policy process.

In this chapter we place into context the role of linkage institutions and processes in making national security policy. First, we consider the public and its relationship to national security and defense policy formulation. Second, we discuss the enormous importance of the media and other means of communication on public attitudes and policymakers. Third, we review some important fundamentals about the role of political parties as linkage institutions: some feel that they are in decline relative to other components of the policymaking process. And fourth, we examine the power and influence of interest groups in the U.S. political system generally, national security in particular.

The Public

The ability of the president to deal with Congress and develop support for his policies is contingent in large measure upon perceived and actual popular support. Much of this stems from the mandate the president receives upon election. For example, the 1980 Ronald Reagan landslide became the basis of the so-called Reagan Revolution. Reagan's landslide reelection in 1984 should have provided the basis for continuing and broadening the revolution, but in its second term the administration struggled to maintain momentum. In part, this was due to Cabinet reshuffling that placed key White House adviser James Baker in the Treasury Department, breaking up the team that so effectively advanced Reagan's agenda during his first term. The loss of the Senate to the Democratic Party in the 1986 elections also created difficulties for the Reagan program. But the president retained a high approval rating, even though many Americans did not fully support some of his policies.

Bill Clinton, winning the presidency in 1992, did so without a majority of votes, which meant that the president and his administration had to work hard to build credibility in foreign and security policy. This was reflected in several polls in the fall of 1993 in which less than a majority—and at times a bare majority—approved of his presidential performance. Public skepticism about Clinton as commander in chief was a result of ambiguous or vacillating policies in Somalia, Haiti, and Bosnia-Herzegovina, ascribed to the president's lack of military experience and possible distrust of the military profession. The controversy over homosexuals in the military added to the impression that he was clueless on matters affecting the armed services.

The relationship between the people and the president, which is complicated by the media's role in transmitting information and setting the public agenda, is thus more intricate than many might suppose. As the nation's leading political figure, the president is expected to develop and implement policies that are binding on the entire populace. People respond favorably or unfavorably to his personality and political style and to the events that occur while he is in office. They also assess the president by the way he relates to particular groups, as well as social (religious, ethnic, racial), economic (business, labor), and geographical divisions of the population.[1]

If most authorities agree that public support is an essential part of presidential effectiveness, they disagree as to the specific nature of this support and its relationship to congressional support. How support is translated into presidential effectiveness and performance is subject to dispute. On the one hand, the public gives the president high approval ratings; on the other, it shows less than majority support for specific policies. The inconsistency is more apparent than real: the public's perception of the president's reputation for success and integrity colors its judgments about individual decisions.

In addition, over time the support for specific policies and the president is affected by public fickleness; attitudes can change in the face of major policy issues or failures and because of a perception that the president has failed to live up to his promises or seems incapable of leading the nation. At times, the public may seem to act on a whim, shifting attitudes or suddenly dropping support for the president for no clear reason. Because of these intricate relationships, the president needs to be sensitive to the people and beware the fragile nature of public opinion.

This complex arena requires that the president respect the limits of public acceptance for national security policy and strategy. In times of peace and prosperity, it is difficult to energize the public and gain support for any policy and strategy that departs from the mainstream. In times of crisis and perceived national peril, the president can undertake broader initiatives for purposes of national security, defense, and intelligence. Following September 11, President George W. Bush ordered a review of U.S. counterterrorism policies. Some of the proposals, such as arming civilian airline pilots and federalizing airport security, would have been unthinkable prior to the attacks.

Presidents must be especially wary of public sensitivity to secret and covert operations. Many Americans can understand the need for and accept them (albeit reluctantly), but there are limits. Moral and ethical boundaries exist for any operation. And even though the president has flexibility in national security policy and strategy, most Americans expect an accounting of his decisions and actions, whether they are successful or not.

The Limits of Public Opinion

National security policy cannot be conducted solely according to public opinion. Public attitudes and opinions, except in crisis, are not geared toward specific national security issues. Moreover, there is some degree of secrecy involved in several contingencies, a double-edged sword: going public might justify the policy and strategy in the eyes of the people, but it would also telegraph U.S. policy and strategy to adversaries, which could lead to failure as well as place our forces in danger.

However, the president cannot neglect public opinion on national security issues. Reaction after the event is an important component of the national security equation, part of the final accounting the public expects. The history of U.S. public opinion in foreign policy demonstrates that presidents have the advantage of initiative and command of detailed and timely information. But the public, the Congress, and the media can define success or failure according to a different standard. The president and the government are sometimes preoccupied with the nuances and subtleties of small policy differences; the Congress, the media, and the public react more sharply to the impact of policy decisions.

From Nicaragua to Bosnia

The president and the national security establishment must be especially sensitive to the fact that interest groups, the media, as well as adversaries and allies play an important role in influencing the U.S. public. For example, in 1987 the Sandinista regime in Nicaragua made serious efforts to develop political networks here in the United States to convince the public of the legitimacy of the Nicaraguan system. Nicaragua hired a U.S. public relations firm to paint the best possible picture and to lobby Congress for favorable legislation. This is not necessarily an unusual or illegal tactic, as several foreign states hire local firms. During the Gulf War of 1991, the government of Kuwait hired a high-profile Washington, D.C.–based public relations firm to coordinate its public opinion campaign against Iraq in the United States. But this strategy is not always available to the president and the administration, for they cannot gain access to media in a closed system to publicize U.S. views to the foreign peoples.

In the final analysis, the public usually follows the president's lead in national security policy and overwhelmingly supports any president who takes bold and responsible action, especially during a crisis. President Reagan's orders for the raid on Libya in 1986 and the earlier invasion of Grenada were favorably received by a majority of the public. This was also the case with President George Bush's initiative in the Gulf War in 1990–1991. With the conclusion of that war, Bush's approval ratings were above 80 percent, and for a time he was considered unbeatable in the 1992 presidential race, which he lost to Bill Clinton. A decade later, President George W. Bush's approval ratings also reached 80 percent following the September 11 attacks.

But national security policy and strategy, especially if controversial, can lead to political disaster like the debacle at the Bay of Pigs in 1961, the failed attempt to rescue U.S. hostages in Iran in 1979, and Iran-contra in the mid-1980s. Even though John F. Kennedy and Ronald Reagan retained high approval ratings, the credibility of both administrations suffered at home and abroad.

Some mistakes do lead to irretrievable disaster. In the wake of the failed Iran hostage rescue in 1980, the Jimmy Carter administration was voted out of office in November. The credibility of the Clinton presidency suffered as a result of several questionable national security and foreign policy efforts in Somalia, Haiti, and Bosnia-Herzegovina during Clinton's first term, even though a historic Israel-Palestine peace accord was signed at the White House in September 1993 to the applause of many. When the public begins to lose confidence in the president's ability to respond effectively, or when it perceives that the president cannot respond positively to failure, credibility erodes, as does confidence in the president and U.S. national security policy. This public attitude impacts the national security establishment and congressional attitudes.

In contrast to Clinton's indecisiveness in Bosnia during 1993 and 1994, the administration improved its performance by brokering the Dayton peace accords of December 1995, bringing an end to an exhausting civil war and ethnic cleansing. With NATO partners, the United States established a large and highly capable military peacekeeping and peace enforcement operation (the Implementation Force, or IFOR) initially involving some 60,000 NATO troops. IFOR was succeeded a year later by the Stabilization Force (SFOR). Although scaled down from its original size, SFOR remained in place in 2002. The Clinton administration also claimed victory in NATO's U.S.-led bombing campaign against Serbia in 1999, undertaken to end the ethnic cleansing of Kosovar Albanians by Serbs. Even though the air campaign was a one-sided affair, its political effects were uncertain, and the U.S. public was ambivalent.

The Media and National Security

The role of the media in national security policy derives from their important position in an open system. A free press is a fundamental principle of the U.S. system. First Amendment freedoms often have priority, and individual freedom of speech and freedom of the press are two sides of the same coin. Indeed, most would agree that an essential ingredient of any open system is the role and freedom of the media.

This gives the media a degree of power in an open system not enjoyed by other groups and institutions. This is not a new development. In the nineteenth century, the French aristocrat and political essayist Alexis de Tocqueville observed that even with some limitations "the power of the American press is still immense. . . . When many organs of the press do come to take the same line, their influence in the long run is almost irresistible, and public opinion continually struck in the same spot, ends by giving way under the blows."[2] A modern version of this view is described by one scholar as "pack journalism."[3]

There is an inherent dilemma with respect to the role of the media and national security policy. On the one hand, some security policy must be formulated and implemented in secret. On the other hand, the media's mission is a direct challenge to that secrecy. In addition, media technology has changed so drastically; it has become an unwieldy global network of electronic, print, and visual sources of information of variable accuracy and integrity.

The quandaries posed to any administration are numerous. Some administrations have engaged in deception to avoid premature publicity of security strategy. In dealing with the Cuban missile crisis in 1962, for example, the Kennedy administration deceived the media and the public, at least initially (most eventually accepted the need for secrecy in this case). The Iran-contra hearings revealed the half-truths and deceptions of administration officials in dealing with Iran and the Nicaraguan contras.[4] Other administrations have openly tried to prevent publication of sensitive information. *The Pentagon Papers*, stolen government documents that revealed aspects of the Vietnam War, were published widely by the media, even though much of the content was classified.[5] When the government brought a lawsuit, the court ruled in favor of the media on the grounds that the First Amendment prohibited prior restraint of publications by government.

The media perform important functions, which affect their role with respect to national security matters and the presidency. The media inform the public of what is going on in government, the country, and the world; they transmit information from political leaders both in and outside government to the public and political actors. The media are also used by political leaders and government officials to signal policy intentions and test reactions. In this sense, the media play a quasi-official role, knowingly or otherwise, and provide a channel to signal foreign adversaries and allies of government policy. For example, once the Cuban missile crisis became public knowledge in October 1962, President Kennedy and Soviet Premier Nikita Khrushchev used the media as a means of negotiation: trial balloons were floated in the press, and at least one prominent U.S. media personality was used as a go-between during a sensitive time in diplomatic negotiations.

The media business is highly competitive. Whichever reporter or corporate news structure breaks the news first has an important advantage.

Furthermore, TV news anchors are rated on physical appearance and their impact on the viewing public, which appears to be more a function of symbols and gimmicks than of substantive news reporting skills. This tends to place TV news reporting in the area of entertainment rather than information. This is to be expected given the fact that TV ratings are key indicators of commercial success, which influences the way the news is selected and presented. It follows that news events and images of political leaders are shaped by a variety of factors that have more to do with sales than content.

The role and function of the media in an open system are further complicated by the emergence of investigative reporting and adversarial journalism. Investigative reporting is the aggressive pursuit of news; it is an intense uncovering of facts and is associated with a presumption of wrongdoing. Watergate blasted into the public consciousness thanks to two reporters from the *Washington Post* who uncovered a burglary of the Democratic Party offices in Washington, D.C.; it was directed by high officials in the White House, ultimately implicating President Richard Nixon.[6] The unnamed source for many facts in the story, Deep Throat, has never been identified.

Adversarial journalism assumes that the best approach is to view government officials, individuals, and groups under investigation as the enemy. In one sense, the targets are presumed guilty until proven innocent. Presidential press conferences reflect one aspect of adversarial journalism: it is not uncommon for a reporter to ask the president questions beginning with a statement that points out a blunder or lack of sincerity. Seeing themselves as adversaries, such reporters focus the spotlight on the president as well as themselves. This is also seen in editorials, in the way the news is presented, and in the images of political leaders.

Investigative journalism and adversarial journalism serve a purpose in challenging government officials and policies. Indeed, according to some observers, the media emerges as the only visible counter to the government's national security policy and strategy—the only check on government excesses. Yet journalistic excesses occur as well due to professional and commercial competition. These excesses can cause a well-conceived policy to fail and even endanger the lives of U.S. officials and agents operating in foreign countries.

In addition, when investigative and adversarial journalism are combined with hidden political agendas, there is the potential for distortion of the political process by interest groups promoting partisan agendas. The seemingly unending debate about the personal conduct of President Clinton and his possible impeachment were distorted by many people working in or with partisan media, talk radio, and the Internet. As the president's domestic situation was perceived to have weakened, his ability to conduct foreign and defense policy was impaired.

Investigative journalism is a necessary part of media coverage. The government should never be trusted to reveal its own shortcomings, especially corruption and illegality. Yet investigative journalism can become a feeding frenzy, and the willingness to rely on unattributed or dubious sources, combined with a subtle antimilitary agenda, can lead to biased reports. Even history can be reenacted within the framework of a morality play critical of the U.S. armed forces.

A complicating factor is the perceived liberal political leaning of media elites. Although it is debatable, there is evidence to suggest the existence of "a media elite with a particular political and social predisposition that places it distinctly left of center of the American political spectrum."[7] One of the most authoritative studies of the media elite concludes,

> Today's leading journalists are politically liberal and alienated from traditional norms and institutions. Most place themselves to the left of center and regularly vote the Democratic ticket. . . . They would like to strip traditional powerbrokers of their influence and empower black leaders, consumer groups, intellectuals, and . . . the media.[8]

Additionally, journalists tend to see a world that is "peopled by brutal soldiers, corrupt businessmen, and struggling underdogs."[9] From this it is not unreasonable to conclude that such perceptions seep into news reporting, editorials, and the way political leaders are projected to the public. Of particular concern is that these perceptions can set the public agenda.

> To control what people will see and hear means to control the public's view of political reality. By covering certain news events, by simply giving them space, the media signals the importance of these events to the citizenry. By not reporting other activities, the media hides portions of reality from everyone but the few people directly affected. . . . Events and problems placed on the national agenda by the media excite public interest and become objects of government action.[10]

Reporting and a Political Agenda

The role of the media in an open system, the functions they perform, and their agenda-setting establish one set of important considerations. The political predispositions of the media elite establish another set. Combining the two creates a powerful profession, one that is able to set its own agenda and shape the image of reality according to its own views. Fortunately, there are some media professionals who place fairness and objectivity above personal agendas. In addition, the public can access a variety of news sources and has the opportunity to compare news reporting. For the concerned individual, analysis and comparison of news sources and the substance of news reporting can reveal misjudgments, errors, and political bias in reporters and editorial staffs.

A classic example of patently incorrect reporting is the Tet Offensive during the Vietnam War. In 1968, during the Buddhist New Year, Vietcong and North Vietnamese forces launched an offensive across South Vietnam in the hope of triggering a people's uprising. The U.S. and South Vietnamese military reacted, with the enemy suffering a military disaster. Yet the media reported it as a disaster for the United States! This version was accepted as true by many groups and was publicized by antiwar groups and others to such an extent that it became the common view. This perception played a role in prompting President Lyndon Johnson not to stand for reelection in 1968. As Peter Braestrup concluded: "The general effect of the news media's commentary coverage of Tet in February–March 1968 was a distortion of reality—through sins of omission and commission—on a scale that helped spur major repercussions in U.S. domestic politics, if not in foreign policy."[11] There are other examples of distortions and predispositions coloring the news, but the coverage of Tet stands out for its massive impact on U.S. politics and national security policy.[12]

In the Gulf War, the media, especially cable TV, played an important role in informing an international audience and in shaping the images that impacted the political agenda and public perceptions of the war.

> Daily, live coverage briefings from the headquarters in the Gulf and from the Pentagon via television and radio, reports from the 1,500 and then echoes—and there were lots of echoes from columnists, correspondents, consultants and assorted pundits in the United States and abroad—all served to keep the American public informed.[13]

Some critics contended that the U.S. military's controlled press environment in the Kuwaiti theater of operations slanted coverage favorably toward administration policy. Yet there was serious criticism of TV reporting from Baghdad, the enemy capital, by a CNN reporter who enjoyed exclusive access.[14] Many argued that the one-sided reporting undermined coalition efforts. Some also pointed out how global TV news affected U.S. and international perceptions, much of it based on TV-driven strategy and policy. U.S. forces exploited this, staging amphibious exercises off the Saudi Arabian coast in full view of CNN cameras. Iraq's leadership was thus tricked into believing that an amphibious assault was imminent along the Kuwaiti border, and several Iraqi divisions were tied down awaiting an attack that never materialized.[15]

To say that the president must establish good working relations with the media is an understatement. But the president cannot control all of the news associated with national security policy and strategy. Neither can he control what members of the national security establishment say to the media. Confidential sources and leaks provide the media ample opportunity to gain access to classified material. Furthermore, partisan members of Congress can easily leak information to the media to thwart administration policy. To complicate matters, policy and strategy extend to the international arena, where a variety of sources and events can trigger exposure of U.S. intentions and actions.

At times the president tends to court the media; although unseemly to traditionalists, media savvy is required for holding public office. Even before the advent of television, President Franklin Roosevelt masterfully exploited the media by means of carefully orchestrated fireside chats reaching nationwide radio audiences. Like it or not, the president must assuredly give the media their due given the important role they play in an open system. It is best for the president to be confident in his national security posture, attuned to the dynamics of the national security establishment, and sensitive to the support of the public and Congress. These factors are not lost on the media. Yet it is also important that the president recognize the media's responsibility as a friendly adversary, remaining skeptical of government claims and actions until shown otherwise.

For their part, the media must be aware of the responsibility to provide objective and fair reporting, as well as the risks of reporting classified information and prematurely disclosing policies and strategies that might jeopardize U.S. national security interests. There is no clear line between the people's right to know and U.S. national security interests. Indeed, some argue that there is nothing in the legal domain that makes the media the people's representative or that the public has a right to know anything. The media must therefore police themselves. One responsibility is not to be a conduit for manipulation of public opinion by foreign adversaries, including state and nonstate actors such as terrorists; likewise they must not become the mouthpiece for domestic cranks and ideologues. Examples of manipulation of public opinion by foreign powers include atrocity accusations, demonizing the opponent, claiming divine sanction for one's global agenda, and hyperbole that inflates the stakes involved in a conflict ("the war to end all wars").[16] Examples of the unfiltered media transmission include accusations that the U.S. Navy shot down TWA flight 800 in 1996, and the even broader coverage given to reports that the Central Intelligence Agency sold crack cocaine to inner-city neighborhoods in California to raise money for the anti-Sandinista rebels in Nicaragua.[17]

The Presidential Role

The president's leadership and personality shape the environment in which the media function, at least in terms of the national security establishment. Trust and confidence in the president and the perception of direction and initiative in U.S. national security policy are key ingredients in shaping this environment. Even the best environment does not preclude political disasters and failures, but it does provide the president an opportunity to respond. The best presidents accept responsibility for failure while maintaining public confidence and trust—not an easy challenge but one that has been successfully met. The media's important role in this environment was recognized by de Tocqueville more than 150 years ago: "I admit that I do not feel toward the freedom of the press that complete and instantaneous love which one accords to things by nature supremely good. I love it more from considering the evils it prevents than on account of the good it does."[18]

All of this became more complex as cable TV developed into a major information source, especially internationally. A major characteristic of the strategic landscape is the role of global TV.[19] Many conflicts and international problems become highly publicized, virtually dominating national security and foreign policy agendas. For example, the starvation and conflict in Somalia in 1993 became an international crisis thanks to the tragic images broadcast on cable TV. Some in the United States bemoan the fact that national security and foreign policy have become video-driven in this way.

Another phenomenon is the radio talk show. Talk radio has expanded to include discussions on any variety of domestic and international issues. It provides an information source and allows listeners to express personal views over the airwaves. In 1993 and 1994, talk radio became a focus for attacks on the Clinton administration. Clinton supporters were quick to point to Rush Limbaugh's show as the chief culprit.

A global communications network is in place and continues to expand thanks to fax machines, portable phones, computers, copy machines, and satellite TV. Indeed, the information age has become a reality, and governments must rapidly respond to events as international audiences are exposed to issues almost instantaneously. With its variety of information channels and news sources, the information age has reaffirmed the case that the media shape the political agenda.[20] If policymakers are not careful, the media will drive, instead of merely influencing, the agenda for security decisions. Involvement in major conflicts can be driven by media conglomerates thirsting for news.

It is also the case that "the public's evaluation of the incumbent president rises and falls in accordance with cues provided by the media. The more prominent the coverage accorded critics of the president, the lower the level of presidential popularity will be."[21] To reduce the amount of criticism, the administration can limit information provided to the media and make determined efforts to manage the news or at least shift its focus. Spin-doctoring is a proven White House strategy. In the Clinton administration there were many attempts to mute the criticism over Somalia and Haiti: by focusing on TV events such as Hillary Clinton's visit to Chicago for health care reform; conducting a trade fair on the lawn of the White House to drum up support for the North American Free Trade Agreement; and publicizing the need for free mammograms for women.

The Clinton administration also spun the strong U.S. economy in its favor to offset public and media uncertainty about defense and security policy, including alleged Chinese penetration of U.S. nuclear weapons laboratories. Public reaction to news good and bad reminds us that "the president is *the* big story in Washington."[22] By his presence and attention to certain events, he can (re)focus the media and the public. The president and the media have a competitive and cooperative relationship in national agenda-setting. The president requires media attention to explain and defend administration policy yet must remain wary of the media's ability to place that same policy under the microscope. The media need the president, a unique focal point for U.S. national politics and a good source for boosting ratings. But the media must always remain alert to the possibility of White House spin-doctoring. This love-hate relationship was typical during Clinton's second term.

Political Parties

The role of political parties needs little review here, but we will summarize the basic essentials. Parties are a vital connection between elected officials and the public; in theory they take positions on important issues of the day. Thus parties, more than politicians, can be held accountable for the passage or failure to pass programs consistent with their views. Parties also relate to interest groups but perform a different function. Traditionally, U.S. political parties, at least those that aspire to majority party status, have attempted to be large tents that accommodate a diversity of many intraparty factions and viewpoints. When the party's agenda is captured by one faction or wing, as with liberal Democrats in the 1970s and conservative Republicans in the 1990s, presidential hopes dim. Thus parties seeking to win Congress and the White House must promote issues that appeal to the middle of the electorate.

Some points need to be emphasized with respect to national security and parties. Often it is difficult to distinguish the role that political parties play in the national security policy process and in Congress because of the impact of interest groups. But the majority party in Congress has the power to control the legislative agenda and to select the leadership positions. At the same time, the party out of power is supposed to provide a "loyal opposition"—essential to the nation's two-party system. It follows that a democratic system presumes that there is a viable two-party system at the national level and the periodic retransfer of power from one party to the other. This is also supposed to be the case for the president.

Thus in terms of national security, political parties are expected to offer viable alternatives when out of power and develop political resolve and strategic visions when in power. During the Cold War, it was generally presumed that partisan politics stopped at the water's edge—that both parties, regardless of their position, would support national security goals and, if necessary, mobilize party and public support for the president. Nonpartisanship did not always hold, of course, as partisan wrangling over national security issues characterized the Carter and Reagan presidencies.

However, in the post–Cold War period, with its ill-defined challenges and uncertain threats, the two national political parties, though offering a traditional channel to the public for winning office, have yet to fix on a particular national security policy or clearly articulate a strategic vision.[23] The parties do serve as instruments to debate and mobilize party members in focusing on the shape of the military, the defense budget, and responses to immediate national security issues. During President Clinton's two terms in office, immediate issues included humanitarian crises and civil wars in Somalia and Bosnia, the NATO air war against the former Yugoslavia, and relations with Russia, as well as the reduction of U.S. military forces. But in the long run, barring clear cases of threats to vital national interests, political parties tend to be driven by domestic issues; for President Clinton they were the economy, health care, education, welfare, and crime. The issues in the 1992 presidential campaign are a case in point.

As the presidential campaign unfolded in the first few months of 1992, debate became increasingly parochial. Voters seemed to care little about foreign policy, except when it impacted domestic issues such as unemployment and trade. The leading presidential candidates—including President George H. Bush, an avowed internationalist—pandered to this point of view. Given the self-involved mood of the country, the idea that the U.S. military might function as a global cop was simply laughable. The United States was turning inward; the only question was how far the process would go.[24]

In 1992 Ross Perot emerged to energize voters disaffected by the major parties. With many voters alienated by the Republican and Democratic standard-bearers, the multimillionaire won 19 percent of the popular vote, precluding a majority vote for either Bush or Clinton. Bush supporters were quick to point out that Perot took more votes away from their candidate. Perot's use of the media and town meetings bypassed party structures. In the razor-thin presidential election of 2000 between Republican George W. Bush and Democrat Al Gore, Gore supporters resented the Green Party candidacy of Ralph Nader, who siphoned votes from Gore. Nader probably tipped the balance in some swing states like Florida. Nader, vilified by congressional Democrats, nevertheless committed to going after as many as eighty congressional seats in 2002.

Public opinion data demonstrate that the two major parties are losing support. The numbers of voters who decline to express any partisan preference or declare themselves as independents indicate growing alienation toward the party organizations and their principal donors, whether corporate or other special interest groups. The high visibility of third parties like the Reform Party and its candidates, such as former pro wrestler Jesse Ventura, in the late 1990s reflected dissatisfaction with the partisan status quo at national and state levels. The temporary appeal of Senator John McCain in the 2000 Republican presidential primary, and of former senator Bill Bradley in the Democratic primary, suggested flagging enthusiasm for party establishments and their preferred candidates backed by prodigious amounts of so-called soft money. Nader ran for the White House in 2000 as an antiestablishment candidate, railing against both majority parties. At this time, it is hard to tell how third parties and independent candidacies will affect national security policy.

Interest Groups and Coalition Politics

Interest groups provide useful ways to mobilize the public and affect policy. Yet some groups can be more concerned with their own agendas than in serving the public good; some tend to serve their small group of leaders and do not necessarily seek out the public to mobilize votes and influence elected officials. In any case, interest groups serve an important purpose in an open system.

Interest groups have become increasingly important and powerful in the U.S. political system. Part of this is in response to the vacuum left by the decline of political parties. The rise of single-issue politics (i.e., political activism based on one narrow issue, such as abortion) has reinforced the role of some interest groups. The performance of public officials tends to be judged according to that one issue—a litmus test—regardless of their record on other matters. Additionally, single-issue activism can be co-opted by broader-based interest groups to take on a particular policy or official. An example is the 1999–2000 controversy surrounding Elián Gonzales. He and his mother fled Cuba by raft in 1999; she drowned, but he was rescued off the coast of Florida. His relatives in Miami then fought a long battle against U.S. immigration authorities and the Justice Department, going to court to prevent Elián's return to Cuba. Court decisions favorable to the Justice Department and a successful night raid to remove Elian from the control of his anti-Castro relatives were required to terminate the imbroglio.

The emergence of PACs and soft money further complicated the relationships among the president, Congress, and interest groups. PACs have become major instruments used by corporations, business, and labor groups to influence elections and remain within the federal election laws. PACs donate to election campaigns and often become the vanguard in establishing political positions for larger groups. As expected, PACs have influence in Congress, partly because direct influence in the White House is difficult; also, the nature of congressional constituencies leaves members of Congress vulnerable to the influence of PACs. Soft money, that is, money not given directly to candidates but to issue development or under other auspices, indirectly, if not directly, supports the conduct of a political campaign. Both Republicans and Democrats have charged the other side with commingling soft and hard money, which is given explicitly and directly to the candidate.

Think tanks are included in our discussion, but not because they necessarily engage in the political activity characteristic of interest groups. The reports and activities of think tanks can have political consequences and are used by interest groups to advocate their own policies. Yet certain think tanks are identified with partisan worldviews, whether liberal or conservative, such as the Brookings Institution (liberal) and the Heritage Foundation (conservative). The national security establishment as well as important political actors in the policy process can be, and have been, influenced by the research and publications produced by think tanks. In this sense, think tanks can serve, consciously or otherwise, as the basis for positions adopted by interest groups and political actors.

The fragmentation of power and the decline of central authority in Congress make it likely that the president will need to become involved in interest group politics. To develop support for legislation and promote consensus for national security policies, the president often must appeal to interest groups and form coalitions with them. Obviously, he seeks the support of groups most likely to favor his policies. For example, the president might turn to defense contractors and politicians in communities where military bases are located in order to build support for favored weapons programs and defense policies. Congress sometimes deliberately spreads defense spending for a new weapons system around as many states and communities as possible to maximize the political reward.

The underlying motivation for presidential involvement in interest

group politics is that PACs, lobbyists, and other interest groups have significant influence on Congress, which is vulnerable to persuasion by external
actors. In addition, there is a need for the president as well as Congress and
the bureaucracy to respond to the growing power of organized interests to
develop coalitions for supporting a policy and to thwart those opposed to a
policy. The growing power and influence of interest groups was one major
factor in establishing the Office of Public Liaison during the Gerald Ford
administration. This office was created to help shape friendly relationships
between the president and interest groups; its primary purpose is to mobilize support for the president.[25]

Interest groups also attempt to influence public opinion, hoping that
public pressure will reach not only Congress but also the White House. For
example, during the early 1990s in the aftermath of the Clarence Thomas
nomination fiasco and the Tailhook investigations, feminist groups and
their political allies pressured the president and the Pentagon to prevent
sexual harassment in the military. And throughout the 1990s gay-rights
groups, with a great deal of support in the Clinton White House as well as
Congress, led efforts to sensitize the military chain of command to the
problems of discrimination against, and harassment of, gays in uniform.
The same groups monitored Defense Department performance and contributed to the revisions of policies affecting women as well as gays in the
late 1990s, especially the department's antiharassment directives of 2000.
The U.S. political scene is full of such examples, covering issues from the
environment and abortion to the Strategic Defense Initiative (Star Wars)
and the defense budget.

Domestic and National Security Policies

It seems that interest groups have less of an impact in the national security
arena than in domestic politics. The intermingling of the two areas, however, blurs the distinction between interest group activity and national security policy. For example, interest groups and PACs involved in the domestic
economy invariably become involved in defense spending, more out of
domestic concern. In addition, social-issues groups have an impact on the
federal budget and defense outlays by demanding spending on welfare and
social programs and because of their belief that cuts in defense will help
their programs. Unfortunately, few such groups make a serious effort to
examine and analyze defense issues and strategy from a balanced perspective.

In some cases, the link between national security and domestic policy
is straightforward. For example, it is difficult to boycott a state that imports

U.S. goods without causing some economic hardship at home. A case in point: during the Cold War, a decision not to sell agricultural products to the Soviet Union raised protests and triggered opposition by interest groups representing U.S. farmers. Yet this was one method to respond to Soviet policies that threatened U.S. interests. Similarly, restricting imported goods to protect domestic industries can have an impact on U.S. relationships with states that are important to U.S. security policy. In February 1994, for example, President Clinton lifted the trade embargo on Vietnam that had been in place for nineteen years, primarily to stimulate the U.S. economy. POW/MIA groups and several Vietnam veterans strongly opposed such a move. Many interest group activities were seen in the intense campaign by the Clinton administration to pass NAFTA in 1993. Labor unions mounted massive opposition campaigns, whereas some business groups as well as congressional Republicans spoke out in support of NAFTA. The agreement was passed by Congress.

Although most interest group activity is focused on domestic issues, some groups can have an important, albeit indirect, role in national security issues. These include church groups, friendship societies, cultural groups, and policy advocacy groups. Interest groups with concerns about national security can make alliances across ideological lines. An example is the coalition of liberal and conservative groups that warned against overzeal in prosecuting the war against terrorism. This ad hoc coalition defended U.S. freedoms and included liberal groups such as the American Civil Liberties Union and conservative organizations such as the National Rifle Association. Others reacting to September 11 showed the diversity among U.S. interest groups; some raised humanitarian aid, others rallied patriotic support for the president and nation, and others clamored for improved security at airports and called for a house-cleaning in the U.S. intelligence community.

Other examples of interest group activity are aimed at the U.S. role in the international arena. For example, human rights groups can affect U.S. policy by publicizing human rights violations in other countries, which can lead to moral indignation at home, requiring some response. The events at Tiananmen Square in 1989 led to many demands for U.S. sanctions against China. Amnesty International, which analyzes human rights activities, serves this purpose. Also, veterans' organizations have a similar impact on the use of U.S. military forces overseas. Human rights groups helped publicize widespread ethnic cleansing and humanitarian abuses in Somalia in 1992, in Bosnia from 1992 through 1995, and in the Serbian province of Kosovo in 1999.

Foreign countries also try to influence U.S. public opinion and congressional views.

Large research and lobbying staffs are maintained by governments of the largest U.S. trading partners, such as Japan, Korea, the Philippines, and the European Community. . . . Frequently, these foreign interests hire ex-representatives or ex-senators to promote their position on Capitol Hill.[26]

Bureaucratic Interest Groups

Informal groups and networks within the federal bureaucracy play a less visible but important role in influencing national security policy and strategy. Bureaucratic groups are active in defending parts of the defense budget, especially as part of the iron triangle.

Within the administration, power clusters may prefer one policy and strategy over another. During the Reagan administration, there was a considerable amount of infighting regarding the proposed Intermediate Nuclear Forces (INF) agreement with the Soviet Union. On the one hand, some high-level military officers opposed INF, forming an implicit alliance with some members of Congress. On the other hand, at the highest levels of the State Department, there was considerable effort to reach an accord. During the Clinton administration, competing power centers doomed national health care. And pertinent to security issues, JCS Chairman Colin Powell publicly expressed disagreement with others in the administration on the issue of military intervention. And a 1992 Clinton campaign promise to permit gays to serve openly in the military was defeated by a sit-down strike among the members of the JCS shortly after Clinton assumed office in 1993. Clinton and the JCS finally settled for the compromise "don't ask, don't tell" policy.

It is interesting to note that a textbook on U.S. government states that "the Defense Department is assisted by almost 350 lobbyists on Capital Hill; it maintains some 2,850 public relations representatives in the United States and foreign countries."[27] During the Clinton administration, groups within the Department of Defense and the military services formed implicit alliances with members of Congress to expedite action on policy issues favored by the military (such as increased readiness spending) and to block unfavorable proposals (such as permitting gays to serve openly in the armed forces). The point is that any number of interest groups evolve from the bureaucracy and become involved in advocating and supporting policy or strategy.

Iron Triangles

Domestic politics is characterized by interest groups trying to influence the public, Congress, the bureaucracy, and their own constituents. Equally important, interest groups become deeply involved in political campaigns and party politics. Although members of Congress can become captive to interest groups, especially if they dominate the member's district, members use interest groups to support their own legislative agendas. Furthermore, interest groups can become influential within the federal bureaucracy. Individuals with close links to interest groups are often appointed to administrative positions. Moreover, as bureaucrats implement a given policy over the years, they tend to acquire views similar to those of interest groups active in the field.

When the interests of members of Congress, interest groups, and bureaucrats come together, a power cluster results. Such iron triangles are coalitions of interests that are nearly impossible to penetrate and influence from the outside.[28] Throughout the process, several iron triangles may be at work advocating or opposing policy; they can even form a network of triangles that can frustrate almost any policy. Iron triangles confront the theory of democracy with the actuality of elitism and inside-track policymaking.

Put simply, it is a fact of political life that the president faces power clusters and interest group activities while establishing national security policy and directing the policy process. Although far stronger in domestic policy, such influences are affecting national security policy and strategy. Thus the president needs to build a coalition of power clusters for policies that are likely to be debated in Congress or that require resources only Congress can approve. At the same time, if policies are undertaken in secrecy, the president must be sensitive to the fact that publicity, especially occasioned by failure, will require an explanation and taking responsibility. Support from various power clusters and interest groups eases the political damage and makes it less difficult to design and undertake even risky policies.

Summary and Conclusions

The impact of public opinion on security policy should not be underestimated. Although only small pools of voters pay close attention to the details of security and defense policymaking, public awareness of broad trends is stimulated by the media, political parties, and interest groups. The distortion created by media reports, partisan politics, and self-motivated interest groups undermines public understanding of public policy, including security policy. Yet competition among the media, political parties, and interest groups within a pluralistic system ensures that voters are exposed to multiple and competing perspectives.

The president has more latitude, at least at the outset of a new initiative, in defense and foreign policy compared to domestic policy. Tradition and the advantages held by executive branch agencies vis-à-vis Congress ensure that a president who gets out in front of events and who seems to lead will have high approval ratings—at least for a while. Whether strong approval ratings can be sustained depends upon skill in getting the message across to the government, Congress, and the media. In security policy, as in other aspects of the U.S. political system, there is no single government policy but an array of competing policy preferences, each supported by powerful internal constituencies. If there is a threat of war or actual hostilities, the enemy and his perceptions and goals need to be taken into account as well.

In the final analysis, the president cannot simply assume that national security policy is self-executing. The president and the national security establishment, as well as executive agencies, trigger the instruments of policy and its supporting strategies. Orders must be passed down to apply the policy, then its implementation must be undertaken. When policies do not require appropriations from Congress or are hidden from view, the president and his staff must recognize that other political actors can shape the final result.

Even with an ethically dubious or controversial policy, the president must be prepared to accept responsibility and the political damage that results. Regardless of the nature and character of national security policy and its strategic implementation, presidents will be judged by their effectiveness in national security and how it furthered democracy and society. In the end, this final assessment is critical in the overall performance and credibility of the president. Even more important, it has a direct bearing on the capability of the United States to effectively pursue its national security interests. Presidential decisionmaking about peace, war, and crisis leave indelible legacies to successors in the Oval Office.

Notes

1. Richard A. Watson and Norman C. Thomas, *The Politics of the Presidency*, 2nd ed. (Washington, DC: CQ Press, 1988), p. 153.

2. Alexis de Tocqueville, *Democracy in America*, ed. J. P. Mayer, trans. George Lawrence (Garden City, NY: Anchor Books, 1969), p. 186.

3. Doris Graber, "Media Magic: Fashioning Characters for the 1983 Mayoral Race," in Melvin G. Holli and Paul M. Green, eds., *The Making of the Mayor, Chicago, 1983* (Grand Rapids, MI: William B. Eerdmans, 1984), p. 68.

4. Bruce D. Berkowitz and Allan E. Goodman, *Best Truth: Intelligence in the Information Age* (New Haven: Yale University Press, 2000), pp. 133–135.

5. See, e.g., *The Pentagon Papers*, Senator Gravel ed. (Boston: Beacon, 1971).

6. See, e.g., *Watergate Hearings: Break-In and Cover-up: Proceedings* (New York: Viking Press, 1973).

7. Sam C. Sarkesian, "Soldiers, Scholars, and the Media," *Parameters* 17, no. 3 (September 1987): 77.

8. S. Robert Lichter, Stanley Rothman, and Linda S. Lichter, *The Media Elite* (Bethesda, MD: Adler and Adler, 1986), p. 299.

9. Ibid., p. 95.

10. Thomas E. Patterson and Robert D. McClure, *The Unseeing Eye: The Myth of Television Power in National Elections* (New York: G. P. Putnam's Sons, 1976), p. 75.

11. Peter Braestrup, *Big Story: How the American Press and Television Reported and Interpreted the Crisis of Tet 1968 in Vietnam and Washington* (Boulder: Westview, 1977), p. 184.

12. See, e.g., Editorial, "The End of the 'Jimmy' Story," in *Washington Post*, April 16, 1981, p. A18; Don Kowet, *Matter of Honor: General Westmoreland Versus CBS* (New York: Macmillan, 1984), and Edith Efron, *The News Twisters* (New York: Manor Books, 1972).

13. General Michael J. Dugan, USAF (ret.), "Perspectives from the War in the Gulf," in Peter R. Young, ed., *Defence and the Media in Time of Limited War, Small Wars and Insurgencies* 2, no. 3 (Special Issue, December 1991): 179.

14. For a particularly scathing criticism of the media, see William V. Kennedy, *The Military and The Media: Why the Press Cannot Be Trusted to Cover a War* (Westport, CT: Praeger, 1993).

15. Dorothy E. Denning, *Information Warfare and Security* (Reading, MA: Addison-Wesley, 1999), p. 6.

16. Alvin Toffler and Heidi Toffler, *War and Anti-War: Survival at the Dawn of the 21st Century* (Boston: Little, Brown, 1993), pp. 167–168.

17. Denning, *Information Warfare*, p. 115.

18. de Tocqueville, *Democracy in America*, p. 180.

19. Donald M. Snow and Eugene Brown, *Puzzle Palace and Foggy Bottom: U.S. Foreign and Defense Policy-Making in the 1990s* (New York: St. Martin's, 1994), pp. 21–22.

20. See Bruce W. Jentleson, *American Foreign Policy: The Dynamics of Choice in the 21st Century* (New York: W. W. Norton, 2000), p. 215, and Stephen Ansolabehere, Roy Behr, and Shanto Iyengar, *The Media Game: American Politics in the Television Age* (New York: Macmillan, 1993), pp. 142–144.

21. Ibid., p. 201.

22. Ibid., p. 199.

23. Daniel Goure and Jeffrey M. Ranney, *Averting the Defense Train Wreck in the New Millenium* (Washington, DC: Center for Strategic and International Studies, 1999), p. 2.

24. International Institute for Strategic Studies, *Strategic Survey, 1991–1992* (London: Brassey's UK, 1992), p. 54.

25. Ansolabehere, Behr, and Iyengar, *The Media Game*, p. 199.

26. Steffen W. Schmidt, Mack C. Shelley II, and Barbara A. Bardes, *American Government and Politics Today, 1993–1994* (Minneapolis–St. Paul: West Publishing, 1993), p. 301.

27. Ibid., p. 253.

28. Theodore White, *The Making of the President, 1972* (New York: Bantam, 1973).

13

Who's Who in
the International System

THE UNITED STATES IS UNDOUBTEDLY A POWERFUL COUNTRY.
As the twentieth century drew to a close, economic strength and military
power both placed the United States in a class by itself. Yet the United
States is powerless to affect many international issues. Potential does not
always translate into influence over policy outcomes.[1] This disparity hit
home on September 11, 2001. One reason is that the United States coexist-
ed with hundreds of other state and nonstate actors within an international
environment or system. The term *system* simply means that states and other
actors interact with one another in more or less regular and predictable
ways.

The international system, with some 190 states and many nonstate
actors, is a complex web and places the United States in relationships that
constrain U.S. goals and the means, including military, to pursue those
goals. Even though the United States is a superpower with vast resources to
implement national security policy, its power is limited in the international
arena. First, several major powers (e.g., Russia, China, and Japan) have
their own agendas and national interests, which they project into the international arena. Second, not all states share the view of the world held by
the United States. U.S. culture, for better or worse, is unique: a blend of
pragmatism, economic, and technological assertiveness, political inclusiveness, with future-oriented instead of traditional perspectives on social
development.

Third, the United States has limited resources and must be judicious
about how and when they are used to achieve national security objectives.
Fourth, regional powers pursue interests that may be contradictory to those
of the United States. Fifth, democratic proprieties require that the United
States use diplomacy, negotiations, and consensus-building as the primary
means to achieve its national security goals—which means compromise
and recognition of the national interests of other states. Sixth, the United

States shares power and responsibility with a variety of other states with common purposes and some cultural affinity, the most visible and successful of which is NATO.

Thus the United States must operate in a world environment that is not orderly, even unattuned to U.S. concepts of world order. Within the context of U.S. national security, sovereign states can be grouped into broad categories: *allies, adversaries, potential adversaries,* and *others.* Allies are best illustrated by fellow members of NATO. With the demise of the Soviet Union, NATO has no clear adversary, which is one of the most important changes from the Cold War era. Potential adversaries include states that have adopted explicit anti-U.S. policies and have the military means to pursue their goals. Some are motivated by strategic cultures exuding suspicion of, and hostility to, Western cultural heritage.[2] Some also have the potential to evolve into a U.S. adversary. "Others" include virtually the entire third world, with the exception of some states in the Middle East as well as other states that have the potential to become adversaries (Iran) or allies (Egypt), depending upon the specific security issue.

In this chapter, we discuss the international system of U.S. security policymaking, following a sequence of steps. First, we review major U.S. alliance commitments, especially those related to European security and NATO. Because NATO is exceptional in its durability and success, we also look at other U.S. commitments with the flavor, although not the texture, of an alliance such as NATO. Second, we consider past and possible future U.S. adversaries and some of the problems they might pose for U.S. defense and foreign policymaking. Third, we discuss the other actors who fall outside the category of allies or adversaries as used here but whose relationships with the United States on security matters might be important in the future.

The Current State of Alliances

Historically, the United States has been suspicious of so-called entangling alliances. Even with respect to Europe, whose cultural affinity with the United States is a historical fact, the United States has tried to keep its distance. Until World War II, Old World Europe retained its tarnished image of monarchy and radical revolutionaries. U.S. isolationism in the 1920s and 1930s was intended to keep the United States at a distance from Europe. Even after World War I the United States did not ratify the formation of the League of Nations but simply maintained its observer status during debates at the League. During this period, U.S. military forces were primarily concerned with defending U.S. boundaries rather than engaging in offensive contingencies and global power projections. There were exceptions, of course, especially at the turn of the twentieth century with respect to the Southern Hemisphere and parts of the Pacific, and Theodore Roosevelt's dispatch of the Great White Fleet across the oceans was a classic projection of U.S. military might.

In the aftermath of World War II, the era of permanent U.S. international involvement began, and the United States became one of the prime movers in the creation of the United Nations. U.S. provincialism gave way as the U.S. public became aware of U.S. involvement in a variety of Cold War confrontations, including the Berlin crisis and the Cuban missile crisis. In addition, Americans became accustomed to a variety of foreign diplomats living almost permanently on U.S. soil and traveling throughout the United States with few restrictions.

North Atlantic Treaty Organization

The most important alliance for the United States is NATO, formed in the aftermath of World War II. Designed primarily as a defensive military alliance of sixteen countries against the Soviet Union, NATO moved toward a more expansive definition of its purpose in the 1990s following the dissolution of the Soviet Union. In 1994, NATO initiated its Partnership for Peace program, intended to provide a closer relationship with several Eastern European countries and the former republics of the Soviet Union.[3] Somewhat earlier, the North Atlantic Cooperation Council (NACC) was formed. With regard to NACC, one appraisal suggested: "For the moment, like the [Conference on Security and Cooperation in Europe (CSCE), which evolved into the Organization for Security and Cooperation in Europe (OSCE)], this new organization [i.e., NACC] is more a series of conferences and consultations than formal mechanisms for collective security."[4] Another consultative vehicle was created by NATO in 1997 as a result of the NATO-Russia Founding Act, enabling Russia to be heard on security issues of interest to NATO but without giving Russia a veto over NATO decisions.

Partnership for Peace turned out to be among NATO's most important and successful innovations of the decade. Partner agreements allowed countries not yet eligible for NATO membership to establish routine military cooperation with NATO and, in some cases, helped pave the way for later admission. This was the case, for example, with Poland, the Czech Republic, and Hungary, which joined NATO in 1999. Those on the waiting list, and even those with no aspirations for permanent membership, regarded the joint military exercises and other experiences under Partnership for Peace as favorable to military stability and arms control transparency in Europe.

NATO Enlargement

NATO's expanded membership in 1999 reflected its success in redefining its Cold War mission for post–Cold War Europe. In addition to its Cold War "Article 5" mission (collective self-defense), NATO announced a willingness to take the lead in conflict prevention, conflict management and resolution, and preventing or assuaging humanitarian disasters. These broader missions were tested in Bosnia, where NATO deployed the 60,000-person IFOR beginning in December 1995 pursuant to the Dayton peace accords. IFOR was changed to SFOR one year later, and SFOR remains in Bosnia at this writing, albeit considerably downsized. Russia and other NATO nonmembers also participated in the SFOR deployments in Bosnia.

Throughout the 1990s the subject of Europe's post–Cold War security relationship with North America became an important agenda item. NATO was supportive of the establishment of a "European pillar" within the Atlantic alliance under which Europeans might become more self-reliant in regional security issues that did not call for direct U.S. participation. European members and nonmembers pursued the related but distinct European Security and Defense Identity, which has ties to the European Union (EU).[5] NATO's European-pillar concept would permit various coalitions among the European NATO members, probably under the aegis of the Western European Union (WEU), to undertake conflict prevention and conflict resolution missions with purpose-built forces (perhaps combined joint task forces). Arranging for NATO-related or NATO-congruent, but not NATO-controlled, security architectures was complicated by the problem of partially overlapping memberships among NATO, WEU, and EU. This partial overlap is summarized below.

Members of the WEU, EU, and NATO include: Belgium, France, Germany, Greece, Italy, Luxembourg, the Netherlands, Portugal, Spain, and the United Kingdom; members of the EU and NATO include: Belgium, Denmark, France, Germany, Greece, Italy, Luxembourg, the Netherlands, Portugal, Spain, and the United Kingdom; EU-only members include Austria, Denmark, Finland, Ireland, and Sweden.

An additional problem in integrating European defenses without breaking European ties to NATO is the diversity of competencies among European NATO defense forces. Equally significant is the technology gap relative to high-end conventional warfare between the United States and the other NATO members. This disparity—in long-range precision strike, stealth aircraft, and advanced C4/ISR systems (command, control, communications, computers/intelligence, surveillance, reconnaissance) was apparent to observers during Operation Allied Force, NATO's air campaign against the former Yugoslavia in 1999.[6] NATO's Defense Capabilities Initiative is intended to beef up Europe's military competencies in precision-strike, stealth, and battle space awareness and control during the next decade in order to close the technology gap.

NATO has been the most enduring, but by no means the only, U.S. security alliance commitment since the end of World War II. But given the changing international landscape, the arrangements may well become obsolete and irrelevant. In addition, economic agreements and alliances have become increasingly important. During the 1991 Gulf War, President George Bush was forced to improvise a coalition of the willing that cut across traditional Cold War alliances. President Clinton supported peace operations using U.S., NATO, and other forces in coalitions tailored for particular missions, even when NATO accepted formal responsibility for peacekeeping and peace enforcement. Such was the case with Operation Joint Endeavour in Bosnia after 1995 and in Kosovo in 1999; in both cases a significant number of participants came from outside NATO, including Russia.

The U.S.-European relationship may become strained as a result of increased integration within the EU, including the establishment of a common currency (the euro). The passage of NAFTA appeared to be one reaction to possible trade limitations on non-EU countries. In addition, there was some concern in the United States over what impact European integration would have on NATO membership and relationships.

But other collective arrangements have strengthened the U.S.-European relationship. The Conference on Security and Cooperation in Europe was formed in 1973 to provide a Europewide forum for considering human rights issues. It evolved into the Organization for Security and Cooperation in Europe and in the 1990s was Russia's preferred institutional locus for resolving European security issues. But the OSCE has only consultative machinery and lacks standing military assets of the kind that NATO can use to support peace enforcement and other activities. NATO enlargement in 1999, which included three former Warsaw Pact states, demonstrated that NATO had become, despite Russia's wishes and some doubts among NATO traditionalists, the all-purpose security guarantor for post–Cold War Europe.

In the world order that evolved in the early 1990s, the Cold War alliance system unraveled and NATO underwent changes. A new system of alliances and relationships is emerging, with the United States and Russia, for example, establishing ties not contemplated several years earlier. Additionally, the U.S.-China relationship is becoming increasingly important and is changing as China develops free-market areas and faces potential changes to its political system. Furthermore, regional groupings and regional alliances have emerged, often with little reference to the United States (e.g., the Association of Southeast Asian Nations). Economic associations and alliances have become increasingly important in light of global interdependence.

Yet the Gulf War demonstrated the effectiveness of temporary coalitions under the auspices of the United Nations in responding to overt aggression. This represents a reference point and perhaps a model for future responses to international crises. And in such cases, it is likely that prevailing alignments will not deter the formation of temporary coalitions to achieve mutually acceptable objectives. However, the victorious Gulf War Coalition and other coalitions of the willing are dependent on immediate circumstances, personal leadership, and influence among heads of state. It was doubtful that any U.S. president could have put together the Coalition that won the Gulf War; chances for a repeat in the twenty-first century were dim, even against a resurgent Iraq. However, the September 11 attacks caused the George W. Bush administration to mobilize an unexpected coalition that included NATO, Russia, and China, with support from some Arab and Islamic states, against Afghanistan for sheltering and supporting the Osama bin Laden terrorist network. Whether this coalition would hold together when the war on terrorism was extended to other states (e.g., Iraq) remained an open question, but the United States did send signals in early 2002 that it was prepared to deal with Saddam Hussein on its own.

Allies, Friends, and Temporary Alignments

National security interests demand that the United States do more than develop and maintain close relationships with its allied states that have committed through formal agreement to mutually acceptable goals. Several states, however, are reluctant to enter formal arrangements (like treaties and executive agreements) with the United States; some short-term issues may require U.S. involvement. Furthermore, circumstances may dictate indirect relationships to pursue independent but mutually supportive policies and strategies.

National interests can evolve and emerge in unanticipated ways—sometimes rising to crisis proportions. The lengthy and complicated treaty process may be inappropriate for timely and effective responses. Additionally, national security issues can arise when formal U.S. arrangements with foreign states are not feasible, leaving informal arrangements as the only solution. Since the end of World War II the United States has signed many treaties, which require a two-thirds vote in the Senate for ratification. Treaties that involve long-range U.S. commitments or other controversial matters are likely to provoke debate. Because there is no assurance that treaties will be ratified, presidents have turned to executive agreements, which allow them to commit the country to a course of action through formal agreement with foreign nation without Senate approval; this offers considerable flexibility.

However, in cases of controversy or failure, the president is vulnerable to criticism from the legislative branch and the body politic. In addition, many senators abhor the overuse of executive agreements, arguing they violate the spirit of the Constitution and bypass elected representatives. Even though executive agreements give the president a degree of freedom, he will likely have to explain his actions to the public.

There are many examples of nontreaty agreements, including the Gulf War Coalition and our earlier support of anti-Vietnam forces in Cambodia, where the United States and China were pursuing similar policies. Likewise, U.S. support of the mujahideen (Afghan resistance forces) in the 1980s during the Soviet invasion was consistent with the policies of China and Iran. The point is that national security policy can be pursued in many ways and, when necessary or expedient, through unexpected coalitions. And although Congress plays an important role, the moving force is the president operating through the national security establishment.

Some states are not adversaries, although they certainly are not allies or even friendly, including states that promote or support fundamentalist Islamic movements; third world states that are neither democratic nor established totalitarian regimes; as well as nationalist states that fear any alliance, especially with the West—a vestige of the colonial experience. It is in these relationships that unexpected alliances can evolve, causing concern and disagreement among U.S. political circles. Similarly, indirect relationships with unfriendly states may require the president to explain the U.S. role to the public. Such circumstances can create contradictory U.S. national security policy and strategy.

For example, what seemed especially difficult for many Americans to understand during the 1980s was the U.S. policy of supporting freedom fighters in Africa and Central America against established regimes, on the one hand, and the support of established regimes, as in El Salvador, against Marxist-Leninist revolutionaries on the other hand. These complex relationships show that the United States was involved in treaty obligations and commitments through such structures as NATO while it also pursued national security interests through other relationships—friends, potential adversaries, and others. As for friendly Arab states, formal treaty arrangements might not be as feasible in light of Arab nationalism and the U.S.-Israeli relationship. Nonetheless, an understanding was reached for positioning U.S. forces in the Persian Gulf and for overflying Arab airspace by President George Bush in 1990. His son, President George W. Bush, faced similar issues after September 11, 2001, in obtaining Saudi support for U.S.

military retaliation against transnational terrorists. Such friendly relationships can become well established and form an integral part of the U.S.
national security effort.

As for potential adversaries, the United States cannot simply adopt a
military posture; it must establish formal relationships and use the range of
diplomatic, political, economic, and psychological tools available to push
for change in their posture and even their government, if necessary. Some
regimes resist even the most persistent diplomatic overtures, especially if
hard-pressed by revolution or civil war (the Taliban regime in Afghanistan
in the late 1990s is a good example).

An important dimension of treaties, friends, and temporary alliances is
that each imposes an obligation and commitment on each party, which con-
strains the ability to shift policies and strategies. Put simply, the more political actors that are involved, the more likely it is that the United States will
have its options limited. Thus in any relationship established with foreign
states in pursuit of U.S. national security interests, the advantages must be
weighed carefully against the need for flexibility and maintaining options.

These characteristics of national interests and policy goals illustrate
that national security policy and strategy can appear contradictory and confusing. The general public, accustomed to straightforward distinctions
between good and evil, can find national security policy to be incoherent,
thereby generating domestic opposition, especially in Congress. This is a
consequence of the disparate character of national interests and national
security policy, the public's lack of understanding of these complex issues,
as well as an engrained partisanship among certain groups.

Finally, U.S. commitments—whether they derive from formal or informal arrangements—must be honored by each succeeding president. Thus a
new president takes office with the network of alliances and geostrategic
commitments that are already in place. Usually, it is only through major
changes in the security environment that such commitments are altered.

There is some general agreement among policymakers and scholars as
to national security policy in the coming future; the following might be
considered as the critical alliances and relationships for U.S. national security interests:

- U.S.-Russia;
- U.S.–Western Europe, which carries consequences for the U.S.-
  Russia relationship;
- The U.S.-China-Japan triangle—considered important in shaping
  the nature of the security environment in the Pacific, including the
  Asia-Pacific Economic Cooperation;
- The North America alliance, including the various permutations of
  U.S.-Canada-Mexico relationship; and

- U.S.–Middle East, evolving from the U.S.-Israeli alliance and the Israeli-Palestinian agreements signed during the Clinton administration.

These relationships are not listed in priority—indeed, they may be of equal importance. Thus balancing U.S. efforts and dealing with each, individually as well as in the aggregate, makes designing national security policy a complex and often frustrating task. Considerations range from trade to foreign policy to technology, yet each relationship will impact U.S. national security. Third world areas, not listed above, are also important.

The end of the Cold War and the apparent demise of Marxist-Leninist states have made the old system of alliances obsolete. Expanded NATO membership and reevaluation, Middle East peace initiatives, and the rush to armaments by several states in the Pacific Rim mean realignment of relationships is likely. In fact only recently, North Korea's development of nuclear weapons, as well as its bellicose rhetoric, have brought Japan and South Korea closer. In the aftermath of India's and Pakistan's nuclear testing and declared nuclear status in 1998, their relationships with one another, as well as with China, create a security arc of major importance to U.S. policy and threaten regional security and stability. These developments, as well as others in Russia and Eastern Europe, raise questions about the utility and continued relevance of formal treaties and alliances entered after World War II. Indeed, the very notion of friend, ally, and adversary has become muddled.

In sum, the new world order has created a strategic landscape that does not lend itself to Cold War alliances. In addition, there is a prevailing theme in U.S. politics that resists alliances that entangle the United States in uncertain political-military contingencies, like Somalia in 1993, or involve a combat role. Alliances during the early twenty-first century may very well have an entirely new character: flexible in composition, adaptable to short-term missions, and reversible if conditions dictate.

Adversaries and Potential Adversaries

The United States at the turn of the twenty-first century was in the unusual position of having no official enemy or adversary state, or hostile coalition of states, against which to benchmark its security threat assessments. The singularity of its military power and economic potential also induced complacency on the topic of international security among members of Congress, the media, and the public at large. Relations with Russia, the core of former Soviet military power and influence, are now friendly or at least nonhostile. Threats to U.S. security are now ad hoc, defying categorization except in broad terms: by type of action that might harm U.S. interests (e.g., terrorism) instead of by potentially hostile countries and coalitions. Not even England during the nineteenth century, the period of Pax Britannica, presided over such a one-sided international system.

U.S. military supremacy in information-based warfare, televised globally in Operation Desert Storm, guaranteed that few if any states would take on the United States and allied NATO forces on their own terms as Saddam Hussein did. But this is not a threat-free environment for U.S. military planners. As Clausewitz taught, politics causes hostile intentions between states; military forces are merely the instruments that express that hostility. And the paradox of U.S. power at this time is that it motivates envy and resentment on the part of dissatisfied state and nonstate actors. Security is highly context-dependent. And part of that context is the uncertainty of future U.S. relations with post–Cold War Russia.

The Cold War and the Soviet Union

To fully understand the changes wrought by the dissolution of the Soviet Union, it is useful to review the Cold war period and the changes that brought Boris Yeltsin to power as Russia's first elected head of state. The Soviet state was historically a land power, partly because of its physical characteristics and political culture, but also because of its historical experience of external threats from many points. Its modern military capability was shaped accordingly. This does not mean that the Soviet system did not develop air and sea capabilities. But because Soviet military thinking and doctrine were shaped primarily by land warfare, creating and maintaining large ground forces became the priority. Its conventional capability in Europe, for example, was concentrated on ground warfare. Although some Western analysts argued that Soviet power in Europe was not all that it seemed, Soviet strategy, doctrine, and mobilization capabilities were oriented toward the European battlefield. Similarly, Soviet ground forces had an extremely effective chemical and biological capability, much of it directed toward Europe.

The concentration on land warfare was also evident in nuclear weaponry. The bulk of Soviet capability was in nuclear-armed ballistic missiles deployed and launched from ground bases, both mobile and fixed. In contrast, the United States developed a great capability in air- and sea-delivered nuclear missiles, as well as land-based ones.

The Soviet Union increased its power projection by developing a blue water navy, allowing the Soviets to show the flag in various parts of the world. Furthermore, the Soviet navy concentrated on submarine forces as a counter to the U.S. surface navy. In addition, the Soviets demonstrated a degree of mobility and logistical capability in support of military involvement in various parts of the world (e.g., in Ethiopia).

Increasingly, the Soviet Union paid more attention to airpower.

Although much of this was air defense (fighter-interceptors), strategic air-power (long-range bombers) was also an important component. Combined with the expanding sea capability, strategic airpower gave the Soviets even greater global power projection.

Another factor in the Soviet geostrategic posture was its evolution from nuclear inferiority to parity with the United States. In the early 1960s, the Soviet Union faced a nuclear superior United States, which lead to the Soviets' withdrawal from Cuba after the missile crisis of 1962. According to several analysts, that led Soviet leaders to embark on a deliberate arms buildup, especially in nuclear capability. This would counter future U.S. nuclear threats and was viewed as a key element in developing and main-taining Soviet superpower status. Thus over a period of two decades the Soviet Union moved from nuclear inferiority to adequacy to parity with the United States. Indeed, some Western observers feared that the Soviets had moved close to nuclear superiority. Yet as the Soviets moved toward and then attained parity in strategic nuclear forces in the 1970s, they became more willing to conclude strategic (nuclear) arms limitation treaties (e.g., SALT I and SALT II). Thereafter, maintaining nuclear parity with the United States became a cornerstone of Soviet policy until the Cold War ended.

A large part of Soviet strategy was the result of cautious Soviet policy, U.S. and Western reluctance or hesitancy, and instability in the third world. The cautious Soviet approach was intended to avoid direct confrontation with the United States and avoid incidents that could have provoked Western involvement. When there were direct U.S. interests and involve-ment, the Soviets attempted to maintain a distance. When a power vacuum existed or was created, the Soviets usually became involved if there was an opportunity to gain a geostrategic advantage. All of this was tempered by Soviet reluctance to commit military forces outside contiguous areas. However, there was no reluctance to provide military assistance, leader-ship, and *spetsnaz* forces (Soviet special operations forces) into the indige-nous areas. This occurred in Angola, among other places.[7]

Another factor was the Soviets' use of surrogates and proxies to achieve geostrategic advantage. Surrogates were other Marxist-Leninist systems that acted on behalf of the Soviet system and for the direct imple-mentation of Soviet policy. (They may have acted in their own interests but also in the interest of and with the support of the Soviet state.) Proxies were states acting for the Soviet system while pursuing their own interests. The Cubans played a proxy role in Angola. In 1988 it was reported that the Cubans maintained more than 20,000 troops in Angola to protect the Marxist-Leninist regime there from the insurgent forces under Jonas Savimbi. The legacy of these activities remains today in Angola. Similarly, several Eastern bloc states and North Korea—in addition to the Soviet Union—provided assistance to Nicaragua in 1988.

The link between Marxist-Leninist parties and the Communist Party of the Soviet Union provided an important channel to carry out a variety of activities. At the same time, this link allowed the Soviet government to maintain relationships with other states, placing it in a position to decry U.S. government policies of intervention and interference into the internal affairs of others.

The broad issue of U.S.-Soviet relations during the Cold War has prompted some to downplay the dangers that were involved, arguing that the United States should have made greater efforts to get along with the Soviet Union. This has been criticized by John Lewis Gaddis:

> The United States and its allies, at the end of World War II, were not deal-ing with a normal, everyday, run-of-the-mill, statesmanlike head of gov-ernment. They confronted instead a psychologically disturbed but fully functional and highly intelligent dictator who had projected his own per-sonality not only onto those around him but onto an entire nation and thereby, with catastrophic results, remade it in his image.[8]

Put simply, fascism, but not authoritarianism, was defeated in World War II. Little could have been done to get along with the Soviet Union under Stalin given his despotic purposes and disturbed personality.

U.S.-Russia Security After the Cold War

The end of the Cold War and the dissolution of the Soviet Union do not diminish the significance of the relationship between the United States and Russia. To the contrary, Russia has become more important as a geostrate-gic centerpiece in U.S. and allied efforts to stabilize East-Central Europe and Central Eurasia. A nonhostile Russia also permits easier Western access to important natural resources and markets in the former Soviet Union; for example, U.S. and other Western oil companies want to drill for oil in the Caspian Sea Basin. A third factor is that a democratic and stable Russia is a more reliable security partner for the United States and NATO in control-ling the nuclear arms race.

The world breathed a sigh of relief when the nuclear weapons tem-porarily dispersed among Belarus, Kazakhstan, and Ukraine by the demise of the Soviet Union were relocated under Russian control. After the elec-tion of President Vladimir Putin to succeed Boris Yeltsin in 2001, the Russian Duma (parliament) ratified the START II agreement, reducing both sides' strategic nuclear forces to 3,000–3,500 warheads each. Although START II was never completed, many expected that the two states could proceed immediately toward a START III agreement, reducing their respec-tive arsenals even more. In May 2002, it was announced that U.S. president George W. Bush and Russian president Vladimir Putin had agreed to reduce the number of nuclear warheads in both countries.

The United States had an equal interest in the safety and security of Russia's nuclear weapons inventory and in the accurate accounting of Russia's fissile materials (enriched uranium and plutonium). The former Soviet system of accounting for warheads, and especially for fissile materials, left much to be desired. After the Soviet Union was dissolved in December 1991, U.S. experts feared that former Soviet weapons or their constituent elements would trickle outside Russia's borders and into the hands of state and nonstate purchasers. These buyers of ill-gotten former Soviet nukes might include terrorists with agendas hostile to the United States or frustrated state actors with equally malign intentions. Therefore, through a variety of programs under the so-called Nunn-Lugar legislation passed by Congress during President Clinton's first term, the United States provided Russia with military aid and technical expertise to improve materials and weapons accountability, to increase the safe and secure transport and storage of fissile materials, and to retrain Russian nuclear scientists for work on environmental or other nondefense projects.

Bowing to congressional pressure, President Clinton in 1999 signed legislation that could lead to the deployment of a limited National Missile Defense system (NMD, not to be confused with theater missile defenses of shorter range and coverage). Under the Yeltsin regime, the growing U.S. interest in homeland missile defense against rogue states and accidental launches impeded START negotiations. The successor Putin government first indicated a possible willingness to compromise on the issue of ballistic missile defense (BMD) in favor of progress on START, but Russia's foreign and defense ministries were suspicious of National Missile Defense—the label preferred by the Clinton and George W. Bush administrations.

NMD is a sensitive issue in U.S. domestic politics. Proponents of the Anti-Ballistic Missile Treaty, signed by the United States and Soviet Union in 1972, claimed that NMD would conflict with treaty restrictions or at least undermine the treaty-based assumption that such defenses were destabilizing, not stabilizing, of nuclear arms races. Russian military planners and political leaders feared that any U.S. BMD system could nullify Russia's second-strike capability, its claim to major-power status in the post–Cold War world. President Bush announced in December 2001 that the United States would withdraw from the ABM Treaty. Russia's official reaction was one of disappointment to the inevitable. Putin sought a better U.S.-Russia relationship after September 11 and thus swallowed NMD on missile defense and the ABM Treaty. U.S.-Russia cooperation against terrorism after September 11 was an important shift in perspective for both countries.

NATO's bombing of Yugoslavia in 1999 was a watershed for many Russians who were uncertain whether the United States could be a reliable security partner after the Cold War. Russia's political leadership, Duma, and public rejected NATO's rationale for the bombing as necessary to prevent ethnic cleansing in Serbia. Regarding the issues in Kosovo as a domestic conflict and judging U.S. and NATO actions as illegal and outside the United Nations Charter, Russia adopted a much harder line in foreign policy toward NATO and U.S. interests. This less pro-Western stance showed on the issue of Kosovo, in Russia's revised military doctrine of 1999–2000, and in its conduct of the war in Chechnya from August 1999 through February 2000.

With regard to Russia's military doctrine, it was revised in 1999 and 2000, in addition to a national security concept issued under Putin in 2000. The 1999 military doctrine reaffirmed Russia's declared willingness to use nuclear weapons first in a war under certain conditions, a notable departure from the Soviet precedent of no first use. The 2000 national security concept articulated Russia's concern that the United States and NATO were attempting to impose a unipolar world that posed potentially serious threats to Russian security. In Chechnya, Russia determined to make up for its frustration and stalemate in the war against Chechen Islamic freedom fighters (or rebels, from the Russian perspective) from 1994 through 1996. Russia's 1999 military campaign in Chechnya employed large-scale artillery barrages and air strikes to devastate and clear large areas, which were later occupied by Russian troops. Massive civilian casualties were simply accepted as part of the price of destroying rebel resistance. In January and February 2000, Russia captured and invested Grozny, the capital of Chechnya, after having largely demolished it. Chechen resistance fled to the southern mountains of this troubled territory to prepare for protracted insurgency against occupying Russian forces.

Russia's more assertive military doctrine and its war in Chechnya were loosely but unmistakably connected to the anti-Western drift in its security policies, given impetus by NATO's bombing of Yugoslavia. NATO attacks against Serbia over Russian objections advertised Russia's post–Cold War military weakness compared to the United States and belied Russia's claims to global political influence. Russia recognized its own deficiencies in the lack of combat readiness of its cash-starved conventional military forces, falling short of its own conscription and voluntary recruiting targets throughout the 1990s.[9] Russia also failed to stem the tacitly approved system of brutal hazing (*dedovshchina*, literally, "rule by grandfathers" or senior enlisted persons), a carryover from the former Soviet armed forces. In 2000 Putin faced the task of finding money to modernize Russia's military, which had declined from superpower status into a virtual third world force by 1996.

Russia's military performance in Chechnya in 1999 and early 2000 was somewhat more impressive than its sorry showing in 1994–1996. But the second Chechen War, as well as the first, strained Russian military capabilities and finances.[10] More important for U.S. security planners was the determination shown by the Putin administration, in contrast to Yeltsin, to prevail at any cost against efforts to disconnect any part of the Russian federation from Moscow's centralized political control. Putin also anticipated a lower profile of criticism from the Bush administration after September 11 on Russian policy in Chechnya. Putin combined this hard military line against outright secession with a lesser willingness, compared to Yeltsin, to indulge regional authorities with increased political autonomy in return for revenues for Russia's central treasury. Putin's KGB background (the former Soviet security services) caused observers to predict that his administration, compared to Yeltsin's, would be tougher on the corruption and lawlessness that had become standard operating procedure in Russia, including within the Kremlin. Putin was judged by U.S. Secretary of State Madeleine Albright as a man that the United States could do business with but not one to be taken lightly.

Others

Most of the states in the "other" category are non-European or fall outside the U.S.-Western cultural system. The tendency to place all states outside Europe and North America into the third world prevails in much of the literature. The categorization is useful in broad terms but is of little use in close examination of U.S. national security interests and in assessment of U.S. policy. To place India, Chad, and Taiwan, for example, in the same third world category ignores the cultural, political, and economic differences, as well as geographic distinctions, among those three states. The same reasoning applies to many other third world states.

Furthermore, several states in the third world are important to U.S. national security in terms of their geostrategic position and oil resources. Thus Kenya, on the eastern coast of Africa, may be of importance because of its location and potential as a naval base. Until recently, Clark Air Force Base and Subic Naval Base in the Philippines were of military importance, although the U.S. military withdrawal from the islands changed that. Still, the effectiveness and direction of the Philippine political system is important given past U.S.-Philippine relations and possible future cooperation in the war against international terrorism.

China, with its vast human resources and geostrategic position in Asia, is in a special category. Although it is a developing state, it has tremendous influence throughout Asia. China's potential as an aspiring regional hegemon and superpower is very real. Indeed, for many Western observers, little can be done in Asia and Southeast Asia without considering the role of China. The Chinese attempts at liberalization and modernization, including free-market areas, have yet to set a pattern for its political future. Like Russia, the new China will have an important impact on U.S. national security interests.

U.S. policy planners will have to deal with a twenty-first-century China that has escaped the confines of purely Maoist strategic military thinking built around people's war and national liberation.[11] China has modernized its armed forces and continues to improve its nuclear capabilities and ballistic missile forces.

China's theater ballistic missiles could serve as counterdeterrents to U.S. conventional military deployments in the Pacific supported by the implicit threat of U.S. nuclear arms (i.e., as antiaccess forces). The range of Chinese, Indian, and other Asian ballistic missiles and weapons of mass destruction (WMDs) has the potential to redefine the entire concept of geostrategic space in Asia. Asian countries armed with WMDs and medium- or long-range ballistic missiles might be transformed from "map takers" (states largely acted upon by others) to "map makers" (states that determine the geostrategic policy agenda in a region).[12]

It was evident to most observers that China would play more assertive political, economic, as well as military roles in the Pacific in the early twenty-first century. Compared to the Cold War geopolitical setting, China faced a more permissive environment expanding its influence, backed by a growing economy and increasing military power. The Clinton administration made favorable U.S. relations with China on trade and other issues a high priority, and to some extent it succeeded. But serious differences remain, including China's resentment over the inadvertent U.S. bombing of the Chinese embassy in Belgrade during NATO's air war against Serbia in 1999. Also, a scandal over alleged Chinese espionage against U.S. nuclear weapons laboratories clouded U.S. relations with Beijing during Clinton's second term. The uproar led to congressional Republican demands for investigation of alleged security lapses and resulted in some tweaking of Chinese diplomatic sensitivities. The U.S. and Chinese governments also disagreed on other issues, including Chinese export of ballistic missile technology to rogue states with anti-U.S. agendas and U.S. claims of Chinese human rights abuses.

China, in turn, faced the problem of maintaining perestroika without glasnost: continuing to restructure and modernize its economy along capitalist, free-market lines without releasing the control over political life held by the Chinese Communist Party and central government. Capitalism without democracy might work in the short run, but the long-term incompatibility of free markets with totalitarian politics has been well documented by historians and political scientists. Freed of the myths that propped up Soviet power and fed up with the lack of consumer goods easily available to other Europeans, Russians and other nationalities and republics revolted against the entire concept of the Soviet Union. The Chinese leadership wants to avoid Mikhail Gorbachev's fate at all costs, but it also wants to be a great power.

India is not a U.S. adversary, but it will play larger in the next century in U.S. security calculations. India is now an acknowledged nuclear power (it publicly tested a nuclear device in 1998, soon followed by Pakistan). India sees China and Pakistan as potential threats to its security, and nuclear weapons are now a part of their defense posture. Pakistan, in turn, sees India as the major military threat. China during the Cold War was mostly allied with Pakistan on security issues; the Soviet Union allied with India for the most part. Whether those patterns will persist into the twenty-first century is not clear, but China and Pakistan are thought to be cooperating on the transfer of nuclear and missile technology to Iran and other states with potentially anti-U.S. or anti-Western agendas.

The growing ballistic missile arsenals in the Middle East, South Asia, and North Asia, and the possibility of nuclear proliferation in those regions, change U.S. geopolitical calculations. U.S. regional conflict strategy is no longer as dependent on permanent forward basing, as at Subic and Clark in the Philippines. Instead, it now assumes that rapid deployment of forces from the homeland or other bases can meet a crisis, getting forces into the theater of operations in good time.

However, the potential spread of WMDs and ballistic missiles in Asia challenges the assumption of unopposed U.S. power projection along the Pacific Rim or into the Middle East and southwest Asia. If, for example, Saddam Hussein had been able to fire nuclear-capable ballistic missiles at Saudi Arabia in 1990, the deployment of massive U.S. forces in that country to expel Iraq from Kuwait may have been at risk.

The Middle East has its own set of political and geostrategic characteristics, many of which impact U.S. national security interests. The U.S. link to Israel, combined with the U.S. need to maintain reasonably friendly relationships with some Arab states, mean the Middle East is a fragile security area, more so after the Gulf War and the peace accords between Israel and Palestine. Islamic links among the Arab states and sensitivity to non-Arab involvement in the Middle East give the area a degree of cultural homogeneity and offer a bastion against Israeli and Western power projections and influence. Included in the Middle East imbroglio are the Persian Gulf and its oil reserves, the increasing political-military capability of Iran, and weapons proliferation. The importance of this region to U.S. national security has been well documented. The United States is a major actor in the area, whether it likes it or not.

In the summer of 2000, President Clinton and his foreign policy experts nearly brokered a peace agreement between Yasir Arafat's Palestinian Authority and the Israeli government to resolve the issues that divided the two sides. The status of Jerusalem was among the most difficult questions that kept the negotiators short of fulfillment. Nevertheless, the intensive involvement of the United States created a favorable climate for peace. But the second Palestinian uprising—the Intifada—began in September 2000 and was met by Israeli military escalation. The Ehud Barak government fell in 2001, replaced by the more hard-line administration of Prime Minister Ariel Sharon. The crisis came to a head in early 2001 as hundreds of casualties, from Palestinian suicide bombs and Israeli military attacks, fell to the decades-long conflict.

Meanwhile, the worst-ever terrorist attack on U.S. soil, on September 11, 2001, added fuel to the combustible mixture of politics, religion, and nationalism that kept the Middle East and Southwest Asia in turmoil. The suspects in the attacks included Osama bin Laden and his Al-Qaida terrorist network, with headquarters in Afghanistan and cells reportedly spread across thirty or more countries. Fighting this new, nonstate enemy without seeming to launch a holy war of Western Christendom against Islamic and Arab communities was the challenge facing President Bush and his experienced national security team. Military action in the war on terrorism, including special operations, airpower, carrier-based forces, and ground fighting, had to be contained within the larger policy framework of political de-escalation to avoid entrapping the United States in an open-ended series of unwinnable conflicts.

Summary and Conclusions

The United States is the world's only remaining superpower—a hyperpower of unprecedented military and economic strength. But not all situations are amenable to the use of U.S. power, especially military power, whether in support of diplomacy or actual war. Military power is an effective persuader under certain, and very selective, conditions. These conditions can include the willingness of allies to help carry the burden. NATO has been among the most successful military alliances in modern history. The peaceful dissolution of the Soviet Union in 1991 opened the door for NATO to transform itself from a defense guarantor against Soviet attack into a promoter of a pan-European security community. Toward that end, NATO has worked with the EU to develop options for contingency operations that might not necessarily involve the United States or formally commit NATO forces. Nevertheless, in 1999 only NATO had the military capability and political clout to intervene in Kosovo to stop Serbian ethnic cleansing.

History shows that the decision to label other states as U.S. allies, friends, enemies, or others is a matter of national interest, but it is also influenced by the cultural, social, and political characteristics of other regimes. Currently the United States has no official enemy comparable to the former Soviet Union. But the complexity of international politics in the twenty-first century argues against complacency. "Enemies" in the plural who are opposed to aspects of U.S. policy will certainly appear, and some may be willing to risk everything—including annihilation—for their cause. The September 11 suicide hijackers are testimony to that. But the United States can meet such challenges more effectively if it can call upon existing alliances like NATO, or if it can assemble purpose-built coalitions, as during the Gulf War. Relations with allies can also lead to strain (e.g., over burden-sharing in peacekeeping deployments). The George W. Bush administration indicated in 2001 that it would raise the issue of NATO burden-sharing in peace operations with respect to U.S. commitments in Bosnia and in Kosovo. And the war against terrorism meant that a new framework for cooperation had to be constructed. Nevertheless, the United States is apparently prepared to go forward by itself, if need be, to remove the tools of genocide from state and nonstate actors who may be willing to risk everything.

Notes

1. Susan L. Woodward, "Upside-Down Policy: The U.S. Debate on the Use of Force and the Case of Bosnia," in H. W. Brands, ed., *The Use of Force After the Cold War* (College Station: Texas A&M University Press, 2000), pp. 111–136.

2. See Samuel P. Huntington, "The Clash of Civilizations?" *Foreign Affairs* 72, no. 3 (Summer 1993): 22–49.

3. See, e.g., Daniel Burroughs, "Joining the Club: NATO Debates Terms for Welcoming Former Foes," *Armed Forces Journal International* (December 1993): 25. See also John G. Roos, "Partnership for Peace: Cautious Movement Toward the 'Best Possible Future,'" *Armed Forces Journal International* (March 1994): 17–20.

4. Earl H. Fry, Stan A. Taylor, and Robert S. Wood, *America the Vincible: U.S. Foreign Policy for the Twenty-First Century* (Englewood Cliffs, NJ: Prentice-Hall, 1994), p. 193.

5. Dr. Peter Schmidt, "ESDI: Separable but Not Separate?" *NATO Review* (Spring/Summer 2000): 12–15.

6. Dr. Elinor Sloan, "DCI: Responding to the U.S.-Led Revolution in Military Affairs," *NATO Review* (Spring/Summer 2000): 4–7.

7. See, e.g., Daniel S. Papp, *Soviet Policies Toward the Developing World During the 1980s* (Maxwell Air Force Base, AL: Air University Press, December 1986).

8. John Lewis Gaddis, "The Tragedy of Cold War History: Reflections on Revisionism," *Foreign Affairs* 73, no. 1 (January/February 1994): 164.

9. On the condition of the Russian military at the turn of the century, see Dale R. Herspring, "The Continuing Disintegration of the Russian Military," in Michael H. Crutcher, ed., *The Russian Armed Forces at the Dawn of the Millennium* (Carlisle Barracks, PA: Center for Strategic Leadership, U.S. Army War College, December 2000), pp. 135–148.

10. For an expert assessment, see Pavel K. Baev, "Russia in the Caucasus: Sovereignty, Intervention, and Retreat," in Michael H. Crutcher, ed., *The Russian Armed Forces at the Dawn of the Millennium* (Carlisle Barracks, PA: Center for Strategic Leadership, U.S. Army War College, December 2000), pp. 239–260.

11. Michael Pillsbury, "PLA Capabilities in the 21st Century: How Does China Assess Its Future Security Needs?" in Larry M. Wortzel, ed., *The Chinese Armed Forces in the 21st Century* (Carlisle Barracks, PA: Strategic Studies Institute, U.S. Army War College, December 1999), pp. 89–158, esp. pp. 111–127.

12. Paul Bracken, *Fire in the East: The Rise of Asian Military Power and the Second Nuclear Age* (New York: Harper Collins, 1999), passim.

PART 4

Conclusions

14

Long-Range Issues of National Security

THIS BOOK ANALYZES THE PROCESS OF MAKING U.S. NATIONAL security policy. Without understanding the process of policymaking, the results would make little sense. Yet a complete picture must also take into account the substantive issues of national security over which policymakers struggle. Such issues matter, for the process is not simply an end in itself.

The six major categories of issues are: national security as a concept; strategic cultures; geostrategy; homeland security; technology and economics; and the communications revolution. How such matters are viewed, interpreted, and implemented varies, but they need to be examined—not to determine the proper course for U.S. policy but to assess their scope, importance, and difficulty within the national security system and policy process.

These six categories raise long-range issues, not amenable to short-range perspectives and ad hoc responses. Each issue requires constant evaluation and analysis, followed by adjustments and refinements to national security policy and strategy. The interrelationships between the six categories compound the difficulty in designing policy: a response to one category of issues will affect issues within other categories.

National Security as a Concept

Our concept of national security is broad, based on concepts and organizational structure characteristic of the post–Cold War period. Recognizing the problems of defining and conceptualizing national security, we offered the following statement in Chapter 1: *"National security" is the confidence held by the great majority of the nation's people that it has the military capability and effective policy to prevent adversaries from using force to prevent the pursuit of U.S. national interests.* From this, the definition was expanded to include a variety of components ranging from economics and humanitarian concerns to refugee assistance and institution-building. In fact, many of these components are not pure national security issues but fall more into foreign policy and finances.

Taking a page from Sun-tzu, if national security includes virtually everything, then it includes nothing. Put simply, the scope of national security became so broad in the 1990s that it lost its meaning and conceptual credibility. In this context, the primary function of the Department of Defense and the military has become lost in a muddled maze of fragmented policy, clouded strategy, and questionable, politically driven issues that in the long term may erode U.S. capability. As a result the U.S. military—especially the U.S. Army—now faces an extremely difficult environment. The conceptual basis and meaning of national security in the current environment have gone beyond any meaningful notion, with dangerous implications.[1]

We need to reexamine our definition with a view toward focusing the conceptual basis and clarifying the strategic purpose. It might be useful to revise the definition to something more narrow, that is, the use of military force to protect vital national interests based on core (First Order) priorities. In this respect, it is useful to revisit the Weinberger Doctrine (see Chapter 7), for it outlines important criteria for using the military and directly links those criteria to notions of national security and national interests.

An important part of the concept of national security is *strategic vision*. The link between national security and national security strategy is vision—seeing how one proceeds from one to the other. This has yet to be fully developed by the United States in the new security landscape. For example, in the 1990s the Department of Defense and the military services outlined broad aspects of future warfare and how the United States should prepare to deal with twenty-first-century security challenges. Unfortunately, these studies (primarily *Joint Vision 2010* and *Joint Vision 2020*), placed little emphasis on asymmetrical warfare, the kind practiced by terrorists on September 11.

In sum, there is a compelling need to rethink the concept of national security to ensure its relevancy in the post–Cold War period and to design a strategic vision and operating principles for the U.S. military. At present, there is a serious gap between the political rhetoric of national security and the capability and effectiveness of the U.S. military—both as an institution and as a professional system.

Strategic Cultures and Philosophical-Ideological Confrontations

During the Cold War, it was often said that the real struggle—with a direct impact on U.S. national security—was between the tenets of Western democracy and those of Marxism-Leninism as practiced in the Soviet Union and Eastern Bloc. In the post–Cold War period, however, the tenets of democracy are confronting those of non-Western cultures such as Islam, Hinduism, Buddhism, and Confucianism. Religious fundamentalism, which can include anti-U.S. virulence, is especially important in this context.

Philosophy establishes the moral tenets of a system. *Ideology* provides the political rationale and basis of legitimacy of that system. The struggles over these issues reach into virtually all parts of the world. The critical dimension is not so much the imposition of one culture over the other but whether the legitimacy and credibility of one type of political system prevails in the long run. This is not meant to imply that we are undergoing a war between civilizations, where one culture tries to overcome another. And this is not meant to imply that such a struggle necessarily evolves into military conflict. On the contrary, such struggles are primarily political-psychological. This is also not meant to imply that other states need to adopt one cultural system as their own. But there is an inherent and universal struggle between the open systems of the West and the closed systems of other cultures. As Samuel Huntington has written: "Western ideas of individualism, liberalism, constitutionalism, human rights, equality, liberty, the rule of law, democracy, free markets, the separation of Church and state, often have little resonance in Islamic, Confucian, Japanese, Hindu, Buddhist or Orthodox cultures."[2]

Philosophy and ideology have much to do with the degree of cultural affinity and commonality of purpose between the United States and a state. Obviously, U.S. national security policy is best served by open political systems based on the Judeo-Christian heritage and democratic ideology. This is not to suggest, however, that commonality of purpose cannot be achieved with non–Judeo-Christian states such as India or those in the Middle East. If such states are striving for openness and a democratic ideology (not necessarily defined in Western terms), then it is important for U.S. national security interests to develop friendly relationships with them.

The broader notion of strategic cultures can be better understood by reviewing Marxist-Leninist ideology and its attempt to establish a communist cultural system. This background will help our understanding of what evolved from the Cold War and what remains in place in Russia, former Soviet republics, and elsewhere.

No single explanation does justice to the socio-ideological themes of Karl Marx and V. I. Lenin. The issue becomes even more difficult when the evolution of Marxist ideology is examined in the context of the Soviet state.[3] The change in tactics and the preoccupation with ideological relevancy make it difficult to get a clear picture of the strategy and tactical maneuvering inherent in the ideology. Mikhail Gorbachev's rise to power added another dimension, unclear despite glasnost and perestroika.

The Marxist-Leninist thrust was based on several important concepts: the view that the party was the primary organ of power; the goal of establishing socialist systems throughout the world; and the notion that there was a basic contradiction between capitalism and Soviet communism that could lead only to the demise of the capitalist state. As Mikhail Gorbachev, the last Soviet head of state, revealed in his address in Moscow on November 2, 1987, marking the seventieth anniversary of the Bolshevik Revolution,

> The world communist movement grows and develops upon the soil of each of the countries concerned. . . . Born of the October Revolution, the movement has turned into a school of internationalism and revolutionary brotherhood. And more—it has made internationalism an effective instrument furthering the interests of the working people and promoting the social progress of big and small nations.[4]

Gorbachev was a product of Soviet culture and the Marxist-Leninist legacy. This culture was nurtured over a period of seventy years and was rooted in central control and disciplined social behavior; control of the state by a small elite, perpetuating its own power and recruiting its own. The party remained the real power in a system in which the party established policy and supervised the instruments of the state in carrying out that policy.

There is a significant residue of Marxism-Leninism represented in the large number of Communist Party representatives in the Russian Duma today, in the resentment by many elderly and poor Russians at their decline in status since the Soviet Union disintegrated, and in the nostalgia held by some elites and others in Russia for the imperial trappings and international respect that were formerly accorded the Soviet Union. As an ideology capable of capturing the government and being reestablished as an official public doctrine or faith, however, Marxism-Leninism lacks some of the attributes that would be required for restoration. It cannot offer a blueprint for reforming the Russian economy or making it competitive in international trade and finance. To the contrary, Marxism-Leninism would be a retreat into history: in the actual (as opposed to the idealized) Soviet Union, a few party and government elites lived well while the masses lacked adequate consumer goods and any real political influence.

Other Ideologies and Philosophical Systems

The Chinese System

Variations on the Marxist-Leninist theme were the basis for the Chinese communist system under Mao Tse-tung. With about 1 billion Chinese on the mainland and a drive for modernity in the post-Mao period, the Chinese state has the potential to evolve into a superpower before too long. Yet serious questions remain regarding the future of China. Chinese influence throughout Asia and Southeast Asia has increased since the Maoist era, especially in economics, and increasingly as a result of attempts to modernize the military system.[5] To be sure, the Confucian cultural system is part of China's overall development. Additionally, the Chinese mainland shares a long border with the Soviet Union, India, and states in Southeast Asia. Indeed, China is even contiguous to Afghanistan. Since the early 1980s, China has been involved in shooting confrontations with India, the Soviet Union, and the former North Vietnam.

Confucianism, a somewhat pragmatic approach to external relationships, combined with an underpinning of historical power considerations of the Middle Kingdom and mandate of heaven, establish an amalgam of Chinese ideology and the substance of Chinese culture. Chinese culture dates back centuries before the time of Christ and remains deeply embedded in modern China, despite attacks by the ruling Chinese Communist Party. Yet it is clear that many changes are taking place that could transform the country into an economic giant with a modern version of Chinese culture; such changes could also lead to a Balkanization of China, a modern version of the warlord system that predominated during the 1920s and 1930s.

The long history of Chinese influence throughout Asia and its potential as a hegemon in the twenty-first century make the People's Republic of China an important regional player, a pivot for U.S. foreign policy in the region. The Clinton administration took advantage of China's economic modernization in the post-Mao era by aggressively promoting trade and cultural exchange with Beijing. China was also asked to play a part in supporting a U.S.-led solution to the problem of containing North Korea's nuclear ambitions (by giving Beijing's blessing to the so-called Framework Agreement of 1994). Still, the 1990s witnessed some major controversies in U.S.-China relations, including charges of Chinese espionage against U.S. nuclear weapons laboratories. At home, Republican opponents of President Clinton also claimed that his 1996 Democratic presidential campaign accepted laundered money from enterprises controlled by the Chinese military and intelligence services.

The United States and China also tangled over nonproliferation issues in the 1990s. The United States sought to persuade Beijing not to provide nuclear know-how and missile technology to states of concern in Asia and the Middle East, especially Iran, Pakistan, and North Korea. Issues of proliferation reminded U.S. officials that China's relationships with Russia, Japan, and the two Koreas were important variables affecting the U.S.-China dialogue on arms control.

Although U.S. pessimists argued in the 1990s that China sought super-power status, the Chinese political leadership expressed more moderate objectives. Much of China's economy remains underdeveloped by European, U.S., and Japanese standards. In addition, if China is to modern-ize its semimarketizing economy in order to compete with the leading financial powers, the degree of authoritarian political control over investors and entrepreneurs will have to loosen. For example, China still imposes controls over Internet access for political purposes. And even though China's attempts to modernize its armed forces (driven by advances in computers, communications, and electronics) were bearing some fruit, its overall defense budget, large by international standards, pales in compari-son to that of the United States.

The United States must pay special attention to China's relationships with Japan, Russia, and India. India officially joined the nuclear club in 1998 partly due to a perceived threat from China (which is also a nuclear power). Russia, still powerful in North Asia, seeks rapprochement with Japan, including the settlement of territorial disputes outstanding from World War II. Japan is concerned with China's waxing military capability, as well as any Chinese pretensions to superpower or hegemon status. Additional Japan-Russia cooperation on security matters, leaving China on the outside looking in, is something that China will likely work to forestall. Russia under President Vladimir Putin has taken steps to improve dialogue on security issues with China; for example, both states suspect that NMD will accelerate the nuclear arms race.

The Middle East

The terrorist suicide bombings of the World Trade Center and Pentagon on September 11, 2001, stunned many U.S. citizens and confounded many U.S. security experts. The sophisticated preparation required to carry out the attacks, combined with the high degree of fanaticism and self-sacrifice on the part of the perpetrators, offered a new variation on an old problem: terrorism and unconventional, or "asymmetrical," warfare. The terrorists cleverly exploited U.S. vulnerabilities (e.g., U.S. civil society and demo-cratic openness) in the classical manner of Sun-tzu. Many people asked whether religious hatred motivated the terrorist attacks; the problem was not religion per se but rather politics with a religious undercurrent.

In the 1990s the Islamic and Arab worlds collided with globalization, or the internationalization of finance, information, and technology. Traditional geographic borders and regional and local cultures were pene-trated by outside influences, with billions of investment dollars moving at the speed of light. Governments begin to feel a loss of control over their own destiny and citizens. This vulnerability to the forces of globalization divided those who were prepared to benefit ideologically or financially and those who are not. The nonbeneficiaries often included traditional religious leaders in villages and rural areas.

Traditional elites and politicians now feel that their values are under siege, and many blame the United States and the West. Symbols of Westernization often go hand in hand with globalization—the Golden Arches, Mickey Mouse, Madonna. For Muslims and Arabs with access to money and arms, their building resentment expressed itself in revolts against secular regimes in their own states (e.g., Algeria and Egypt in the 1990s) and sometimes through their support of global terrorism (e.g., Osama bin Laden's Al-Qaida, the leading suspects in the 2001 terrorist attacks).

In the immediate aftermath of September 11, some pundits foresaw a clash of civilizations between militant Islam and the West, between holy warriors and decadent capitalists. This pessimistic view mistakenly blames the entire Islamic culture for the actions of a few murderers using religion to justify terrorism. Islam, as in the case of Christianity, Judaism, Buddhism, and other belief systems, attracts followers with many different *political* agendas, and some of them use religious justifications for sacrilegious acts. For example, many Christians today would acknowledge with embarrassment the atrocities of the Crusades from the eleventh through the fourteenth centuries as well as the Spanish Inquisition. None of the world's great belief systems, properly understood, justifies mass murder; but many have called forth religious rationales for imperialism, persecution, and terror. We should expect this pattern to continue.

To his credit, President George W. Bush spoke forcefully in September 2001 about U.S. determination to bring the terrorists to justice while emphasizing U.S. unwillingness to wage a war against Islamic and Arab communities. Bush emphasized U.S. multiculturalism and inclusiveness and deplored the attacks by bigots against Arab and Islamic U.S. citizens. In addition, Bush sought to develop a broad-based coalition for the U.S. war against terrorism and states that support terrorism, including Arab and Islamic states. His success in lining up support from Saudi Arabia, Egypt, and other Islamic and Arab states was a message to U.S. citizens as well as to potential enemies of the United States.

Yet pummeling the Taliban and Al-Qaida into submission in Afghanistan did not end challenges to U.S. security, especially in the Middle East, from other sources. The Palestinian Intifada continued to reflect secular and religious hatreds, and U.S. support for Israel remained a sore spot throughout the Muslim and Arab communities. Absent a miraculous breakthrough, the United States had to strike a careful balance between its security commitments to Israel and its desire for better relations with Arab and Islamic communities.

Arab and Islamic sentiment toward Israel is also clouded by Israel's reputation for military effectiveness (earned through many Arab-Israeli wars) as well as U.S. military aid and diplomatic support since the founding of the state. Iraqi President Saddam Hussein and terrorist leader Osama bin Laden were the two leading examples of this continuing bitterness, but the fact is that the United States also supports conservative and moderate Islamic and Arab regimes. And despite some public chiding of Israeli military action by U.S. officials in 2002, the "special" U.S.-Israel relationship remained in place, a legacy of U.S. domestic politics and the Holocaust.

Other Systems

Other parts of the third world reflect socialism, democracy, communism, authoritarianism, military rule, and personalism, often influenced and shaped by Islam, Hinduism, Buddhism, Christianity, and animism. The point is that U.S. and Western forms of democracy and open systems compete with a variety of other philosophical and ideological systems.

Finally, South America and Central America are important in terms of ideology and philosophical principles. The historical involvement of the United States in Central America and, more recently, in South America has provided a notable element in the ideological and philosophical dimension of national security. To be sure, the Southern Hemisphere has a cultural dimension that includes a colonial legacy from the Old World, including Britain, France, Spain, and Portugal—all states with a Christian heritage. This legacy reflects a range of political orientations, from monarchical to authoritarian to democratic. But many states in the Southern Hemisphere developed political cultures with distinct interpretations of Christianity and social structure, in which the concepts of openness and democracy take on a different connotation. There is a distinct Hispanic culture with roots in the Old World intermixed with indigenous cultures. Additionally, the increasing Hispanic population in the United States adds a cultural as well as emotional link to the Southern Hemisphere. The U.S. census of 2000 revealed that the population of Hispanics grew by some 58 percent in the preceding decade.

Sub-Saharan Africa, although far from representing a coherent philosophical or ideological entity, presents a unique dimension nevertheless. Its colonial history and legacy of the slave trade have put sub-Saharan Africa in a special relationship with the United States. African Americans account for about 12 percent of the total U.S. population, in 1993 numbering about

30 million. Most Americans of African ancestry feel a link with the continent of Africa, no matter how inchoate, which is reinforced by the history of slavery in the United States and the civil rights movement. Although in the short term there may not be a compelling national security issue in sub-Saharan Africa, in the long term this link is sure to be influential in shaping U.S. national security interests. Although much political turbulence and regime change took place in sub-Saharan Africa in the 1990s, there were some developments favorable to the spread of open systems (e.g., in the government of South Africa).

In summary, U.S. security interests must deal with a variety of cultures and ideological and philosophical tenets that perceive the world in distinctly different terms. U.S. values, norms, and political systems may be seen as a threat by some states, as imperialistic by others, and as interventionist by still others. Thus U.S. security policy and strategy, although appearing reasonable, rational, and moral from the U.S. perspective, can be seen as arrogant and immoral by others.

The design of U.S. national security policy and strategy must therefore be based on intellectual and policy horizons that are not strictly bound by Western culture, ideologies, and philosophies. Thus, to design national security policy in the context of our home-grown democracy with the expectation that it will find favor elsewhere is naive and dangerous to U.S. interests. Yet for many states the concept of democracy is shaped by their distinct experience and cultures, which remain important avenues for the development and expansion of open systems. In dealing with the variety of cultures that exist in the world today, the United States must understand the substance of such cultures and pursue U.S. national security policy with prudence and patience. This does not require that the United States and Western cultures be compromised. But it does require an appreciation of the limits imposed by the external environment and a recognition that the pursuit of U.S. national security policy takes time.

Geostrategy

Major powers usually place themselves at center stage in world politics. They see the world from their own physical location and with their own worldview. In the early twentieth century, this tendency became systematic, elevating geopolitics to a major dimension of the strategic maneuvering of major powers. Geopolitics stressed the importance of geography as a factor in determining the power of a state. In more current versions, geopolitics has spawned a geostrategic component, combining geography and strategy into a national security perspective.

The location of states, their natural resources, and their power relative to other states are critical elements of geostrategy.[6] It is now common knowledge, for example, that energy resources (e.g., oil) make many states in the Middle East extremely important to the national security of Western states dependent on foreign oil. Sitting astride important sea lanes and trade routes (e.g., the Panama and Suez Canals, the Strait of Hormuz, the Caribbean passage) also enhances a state's geostrategic importance. The location and policy of a state with respect to major power strategies can also make it geostrategically important. Nicaragua, Cuba, and the eastern coast of Africa are but a few examples. Although minor states such as Nicaragua might not be geostrategically important in and of themselves, manipulation by other powers (i.e., as conduits for power projection and the pursuit of national security goals) carries national security implications for the United States.

Geostrategic components may well be the less difficult (but not necessarily the simplest) of any element of U.S. national security policy and strategy, but they cannot be considered in isolation. Cultural issues influence geostrategic considerations and, in some instances, reinforce geostrategic importance. For example, the geostrategic importance of Israel is reinforced by the fact that it is a relatively open system whose values are generally compatible with those of the United States. In other instances, ideological and philosophical issues can be temporarily subordinated to geostrategic considerations, creating a condition in which the United States has few options other than to deal with a nondemocratic state. U.S. support of the Pakistani government in 1987 and 1988 and again in 2001–2002 are specific examples.

In relating geostrategic elements to the specifics of national interests, the United States faces contradictory forces and contending ideologies. As a result, U.S. policy and strategy can appear vacillating and unclear. Geostrategic considerations must be included in formulating policy and designing strategy, but they cannot simply be quick fixes and short-term responses. Rather, geostrategy must be included as part of a broader concept, one that provides a systematic application based upon a geostrategic vision. For example, the containment policy adopted by the Harry Truman administration just after World War II was rooted in geostrategic concepts that implied a principle of selection. The United States would not attempt to defend everything everywhere: primary security interests lay in preventing any single power, especially the Soviet Union, from imposing hegemony over Western Europe and Japan. When the idea of containment was extended (through the domino theory) to include every trouble spot under threat of communist revolution, as in Vietnam, it became muddled and provided less compelling policy guidance.

As an integral part of national security policy and strategy, therefore, the United States must develop and articulate a broad geostrategic vision. This can be the guiding framework for those in the national security establishment to design strategy on a global scale. Equally important, we must evolve a sense of where the United States stands with respect to adversaries and potential adversaries, the international security environment, and its national security policy. It is in geostrategic terms that global vision, policy, and strategy are given specific meaning (i.e., commitment to a specific state or region in the context of U.S. national security).

The Contemporary Period

The modern age of weapons technology appeared to reduce the relevance of geopolitical and geostrategic approaches to national security issues. Advanced aircraft, surface vessels, and submarines, combined with space technology and high-tech weapons, have tended to replace the views of Halford Mackinder ("Heartland" and land power), Nicholas Spykman ("Rimland" and sea power), Alfred Thayer Mahan (seapower and bases), and the airpower theorists (albeit to a lesser degree) with more advanced strategies of forward presence and crisis response, as well as new concepts of land and sea warfare.[7] But the new approaches fail to grasp the fundamental global perspectives inherent in the earlier geopolitical-geostrategic views (although some elements have been borrowed and assimilated). New viewpoints focus more on war-fighting, operations other than war, and regional issues than on global visions of security relationships.

Critics of geopolitical models have long argued that geographical determinism is a dangerous concept because it assumes geography alone determines national power and policy. It is as great an error, according to critics, to translate geopolitical notions into geostrategic ones—that is, to make geopolitical factors into strategic ones by rationalizing their importance in national security. "Geopolitics is a pseudoscience erecting the factor of geography into an absolute that is supposed to determine the power, and hence the fate, of nations."[8] Nonetheless, geostrategic theory has taken on prominence in the contemporary period primarily because of global industrialization and economic interdependence. Ironically, the demise of the superpower era created situations in which some states adopted policies precipitating less than major wars and engaging in unconventional conflicts to achieve political goals. All of these issues include geostrategic elements and clusters that have important consequences for U.S. national security. "There are areas that are crucial to the functioning of the world economy and our interests."[9] Put simply, this means that some geostrategic and power clusters are critical to U.S. national security policy.

A Global View: Competing Power Clusters

The global view of U.S. national security, based on competing power clusters, recognizes that the world has moved away from the bipolarity of past decades. In addition, it acknowledges the emergence of a variety of states whose power and security postures preclude, or considerably reduce, the major powers' control and influence. With multipower centers forming power clusters, the focus of U.S. policy and strategy, in geostrategic terms, should be to stabilize balances or create equilibrium among competing ideologies and systems to establish a basis for resolving conflicts through alliances. An essential part of this approach is the assumption that conflict between major powers must be avoided, partly by recognizing legitimate interests, partly by removing conflicts from the battlefield, and finally by effectively resolving conflicts between competing power clusters. (This view incorporates elements of Spykman, Mackinder, and the balance-of-power theories but is not dominated by one or the other.) For U.S. national security, the global view of competing power clusters has some essential premises.

First, it does not reduce the U.S. need to maintain a deterrent capability in its nuclear strategy or the U.S. need to pursue arms reductions, arms control, and conflict limitation. But it does require a concentrated effort to develop realistic alliances and form mutually supporting power clusters within a modern vision of geopolitics and geostrategic perspectives. In such alliances, the United States does not always need to take a dominant role; indeed, a supportive role with very low visibility could better serve U.S. security interests. Second, the overarching purpose is to create a directed balance of power against the most likely aggressor in the area. The Gulf War Coalition is an excellent case in point. But this directed balance should not be so rigid as to limit U.S. flexibility in responding to unforeseen security issues. Moreover, it cannot preclude the United States from developing political-psychological and economic support networks of mutual benefit among a variety of states, even those that are not democratic.

Third, an important part of U.S. security policy and strategy is to ensure that centralized systems—totalitarian and authoritarian—with expansionist ideologies face a network of alliances shaped by geostrategic considerations. Alliances can serve as roadblocks, as well as containment, and deterrent, and defensive forces. These alliances, although primarily a security response to potential and real aggressive behavior and thus concentrating on security issues, also need to provide a framework for other policy issues. And finally, alliances can become part of an effective strategy only if states feel that entering such alliances will enhance their own national interests.

In summary, competing power clusters are an important characteristic of the world security setting. An effective response, as well as a security posture that can provide for policy initiatives, rest on the earlier global visions of Mackinder and Spykman, refined to accommodate characteristics of the contemporary period. These initiatives in turn are driven by the broader policy issues for a stable world order, peaceful conflict resolution, and democratic values. The global strategy evolving from the competing power-cluster view can serve as the context within which other supporting strategies are designed and implemented.

The Limits of Geostrategy

Political, psychological, and economic considerations are beyond geostrategic influences. For example, the effectiveness of governments, ideologies, and nationalistic movements are not bound or necessarily influenced by geostrategic considerations. Islamic fundamentalism, for example, cannot be explained by geostrategic factors.

Furthermore, technological breakthroughs can reduce the impact of geostrategic factors. Technological advances have always had an impact on geostrategic perspectives; for example, airpower reduced the effectiveness of the physical containment based on land power inherent in the Mackinder thesis. Similarly, space technology and improvements in weapons have reduced the importance of land bases and ground-based troops. In a work recognized as an important study of international relations, Quincy Wright examined political geography and concluded:

> It has been the hope of some geographers that because of the apparent permanence of geographic conditions, geography might become the master science of international relations. This hope seems vain. Geography is primarily a descriptive discipline . . . [and] does not determine international relations. . . . The apparent permanence of geographical conditions is illusory. Civilized man uses his environment to serve ends which come from other sources. . . . Geography cannot develop concepts and conceptual systems applicable beyond a limited time and area in which a given state of the arts, of population, and of society can be assumed.[10]

Geostrategy and National Security

A geostrategic vision is an important component in designing global strategy. The competing power-cluster approach to geostrategy, although shaped in somewhat new terms and requiring concentrated effort in developing alliances, is not so different from established U.S. policy and strategy as to cause massive restructuring. It does, however, require some strategic rethinking. The approach does not demand the presence of U.S. military forces in quantity to conduct effective military operations; rather it requires a specialization within alliances and various networks so that each state contributes its fair share (i.e., what it's good at and what it can afford). Conversely, the states within the alliance or network best equipped and positioned to implement a particular alliance strategy can be called on to do so. Finally, Wright's criticism of political geography is equally appropriate for geostrategy. Geostrategic determinism distorts the importance of the dynamics of the security environment and ignores the changing nature of the physical environment. Furthermore, geostrategic determinism cannot account for the nonphysical dimensions of security policy and strategy, such as national will, political resolve, and staying power, which in the long run are more important than geostrategic considerations. Yet geostrategic considerations have some influence on the posturing of forces and strategic alternatives; they must be included as part of the security equation.

Homeland Security

September 11, 2001, changed the U.S. national security agenda overnight. The terrorist attackers did not use weapons of mass destruction—nuclear, biological, or chemical weapons launched from offshore or released on U.S. soil. That phase came later, in October, when either domestic or foreign terrorists mailed anthrax spores to various U.S. government offices and prominent news media. The resulting publicity set off a national anthrax scare and numerous warnings from the U.S. government that more attacks might be in store. President George W. Bush established an Office of Homeland Security and a homeland security council to coordinate domestic policy efforts against terrorism. As noted previously, this will be replaced by the Department of Homeland Security if Congress enacts appropriate legislation called for by President Bush.

The phrase "weapons of mass destruction" conceals more than it reveals, however. Nuclear weapons remained the ultimate deterrent in the hands of five permanent members of the UN Security Council (the United States, Russia, China, Britain, and France). Other states aspired to acquire nuclear weapons as symbols of great power status, and India and Pakistan went publicly nuclear in 1998. The concomitant spread of nuclear weapons and long-range delivery systems (ballistic and cruise missiles and bombers) created the possibility of dangerous regional rivalries and attacks on the U.S. homeland by dissatisfied rogue states of concern such as North Korea, Iran, and Iraq (which Bush described as an "axis of evil").

Biological and chemical weapons can also be used in long-range missile attacks. But chemical strikes would be destructive on a scale well below even small nuclear attacks. And the weaponization of biological pathogens for long-range missile attacks is a tricky business; atmospheric conditions and other uncertainties make the impacts very unpredictable. Nuclear weapons, in contrast, were road-tested in actual detonations and in simulations throughout the Cold War. Societies struck by even limited nuclear wars of the kind imagined by Cold War planners would be returned to prehistory.

The U.S. national security and intelligence communities were unprepared for the October 2001 anthrax attacks, which used the U.S. mail system and hit various U.S. government offices. Some people suspected foreign terrorists, especially Al-Qaida. But U.S. law enforcement did not rule out the possibility of domestic terrorists seeking to disguise their activities under the cloak of suspicion about foreign adversaries.

Regardless of the identity of the perpetrators, the anthrax attacks led to demands for new powers of investigation for the Department of Justice against suspected terrorists, especially immigrants holding temporary visas that had expired. By the end of October 2001, about 1,000 persons were being held in U.S. detention facilities based on alleged ties to terrorist organizations, related charges, or immigration violations. Repeated warnings from U.S. Attorney General John Ashcroft and Homeland Security Director Tom Ridge, to the effect that more attacks at home or abroad could be expected, raised public and media awareness of the lethal potential of biological weapons. Despite the media frenzy and public anxiety, military professionals cautioned that biological weapons were probably not as useful in combat operations as in creating mass fear among civilians. Even the world's largest militaries had little experience in testing biological warfare under realistic conditions. Biological warheads and chemical munitions on ballistic missiles might be used for strikes deep into an enemy's rear to disrupt command and control and logistics. Such attacks could force the defenders to don protective suits and protect equipment and thereby inhibit personnel and vehicular movement, which might slow down forces at the front. Yet forward-deploying U.S. forces might adopt several responses, not excluding their own use of WMD, against enemy forces. This was borne out by a report in early 2002 on the U.S. Nuclear Posture Review that options for using nuclear weapons were expanding, not contracting.

Cruise missiles provide another weapon for attacking the U.S. homeland and U.S. forces with biological and chemical weapons. Cruise missiles are pilotless projectiles designed to exploit aerodynamic lift and precision guidance to attack surface targets on land or at sea. Widely available to some seventy countries by 2001, cruise missiles designed or modified for land attack can deliver biological and chemical munitions over distances up to 3,000 kilometers against shore-based targets, including cities and military installations. Cruise missiles can be launched from land installations, from vessels at sea, and from aircraft. Cruise missiles can be guided during flight to attain precision targeting; they can also fly at high and low altitudes to confuse air defenses.[11] It would be easier for third world countries and terrorists to acquire, conceal, and modify cruise missiles, as opposed to ballistic missiles, for land attacks.

Strategic realism suggests that enemy states might be cautious about attacking the U.S. homeland with long-range ballistic or cruise missiles and WMDs. States have geographical locations and vulnerable populations that would surely be subjected to U.S. retaliation in kind. Saddam Hussein arguably did not employ chemical or biological weapons against U.S. forces during Desert Storm because he feared possible U.S. nuclear retaliation. Undisguised attacks on U.S. soil that caused mass casualties would be suicide for heads of state and many of their citizens.

Terrorists are another matter, however. Terrorists have no permanent address and usually lack the assets, such as infrastructure, that can be threatened by retaliatory strikes. The best deterrent is preemptive—anticipating attacks and capturing or killing the planners and perpetrators. But preemption requires extensive human intelligence from inside the terrorist organization, something very difficult to acquire in a reliable and timely fashion. The effectiveness of deterrence through intelligence is still an open question, but if the absence of further attacks is the definition of success, then it has been successful, at least in the short term.

Terrorists' use of WMD and other mass-casualty weapons (like fuel-loaded airliners) are examples of *asymmetrical warfare*, something U.S. adversaries may use more of in the future. No state or nonstate actor (except perhaps Saddam Hussein) is likely to confront the U.S. military one-on-one. Its superiority in technology, conventional warfare, and innovation (e.g., in command, control, communications, computers, intelligence, surveillance, and reconnaissance) would make such a conflict suicidal. Future U.S. opponents will surely pursue the strategies established by Osama bin Laden and Al-Qaida. WMD in the hands of terrorists (even state actors) provide a potential force multiplier, an asymmetrical counterweight to U.S. superiority. To defeat WMD and asymmetrical strategies, the United States must emphasize brains instead of brawn. Improved intelligence overall, better exploitation of human and technical sources, and intelligence support for theater commanders are necessary parts of any U.S. response to asymmetrical threats.

WMD thus pose unique problems for U.S. policymakers today. During the Cold War, nuclear weapons were symbols of great power status, the objects of envy by dissatisfied nonnuclear states. Today, nuclear weapons and other WMD are potential instruments of the weaker against the stronger. U.S. and allied superiority in information, technology, and conventional warfare will be tested by asymmetrical strategies that include the use of WMD as threats or actual methods of attack. The U.S. homeland is no longer a sanctuary of safety, and homeland security is now a strategic mission of first importance. The use of WMD, including nuclear weapons, against U.S. citizens en masse became a frightening possibility.

Technology and Economics

The U.S. public has become accustomed to the daily conveniences of technology. Modern appliances, electronic gadgets at work, home, and school, and sophisticated medical treatments have become the rule rather than the exception. The enhanced quality of life has tended to personalize the impact of technology. As a result, the U.S. public too often overlooks the impact of technology on the power of the state and its effect on the economy. In addition, many have little appreciation for the relationship between technological advances and the course of human history.

Technology is the utilization of science and inventions to the benefit of society. It reaches virtually all levels of society and the economy. Furthermore, technological developments tend to precipitate other technologies, creating a technological impetus that in turn can drive technology for technology's sake.

Technology spawned the industrial revolution in the United States and Europe. Because industrial growth and technological change feed off one another, technology ultimately became part of the culture of industrial states. Indeed, it is now well recognized that competitiveness in the world economic system relies upon technology. In turn, technological capability depends upon a society that is postured to accept and demand technological change and growth. Similarly, this is dependent upon research and development within society and a commitment to scientific education. Put simply, continuing economic growth requires a society that is attuned to technology and can adapt to it while incorporating technology into the political-social culture of the system.

Two Dimensions of Technology

The two major national security dimensions of technology are: the power of a state, and its military capability. The initial period of the Industrial Revolution brought the rise of Great Britain as a world power and the era of Pax Britannica. Technological breakthroughs in steam power, metallurgy, and weapons development provided Great Britain a technological edge in developing its economy and military power, which led to the development of a superior navy and also protected British interests. Mechanization—the substitution of mechanical for human power—allowed the more efficient use of resources and nurtured the design of new industrial organizations to manage the production of goods. Improved means of communication brought societies closer together and allowed states to consolidate power and develop more effective control over the governing instruments.

The state possessing advanced technology could develop a dominant power position, allowing it to create conditions favorable to policy goals. Its quick reaction to events, its ability to gather information, its control over foreign policy, and its military were, to a large degree, dependent on technological developments in communications, transportation, economic capacity, and weapons development. The shift to mechanization, as well as efficient industrial organization, were the springboards to effectiveness in the international field.

The second national security dimension is military technology, which has shaped the conduct and characteristics of war. Thus the state possessing advanced military technology had a distinct advantage on the battlefield.

The invention of gunpowder and the refinement of rifling in guns changed battlefield tactics. The introduction of the Gatling gun, followed by the machine gun, had a dramatic impact on infantry tactics. More accurate and longer-range artillery engulfed civilians, threatening towns and cities well behind the defined battle area. The introduction of the battle tank in World War I opened the battlefield to further mechanization and tactics that stressed mobility and rapid movement. The rapid development of aircraft for military use changed the face of war. Similar advances in shipbuilding made naval warfare more destructive and far-reaching. These dramatic technological innovations of the nineteenth century and first part of the twentieth century have their contemporary counterparts: the nuclear era, the electronic revolution, and space-age capability have again altered the dynamics of the battlefield and pushed the qualitative as well as quantitative dimensions of war almost beyond comprehension. States possess a destructiveness well beyond anything envisioned in the past.

But technological advances do not guarantee a dominant power position. Historians are quick to point out that Great Britain lost its technological edge to Germany in the latter part of the nineteenth century, as German innovations in chemicals, electronics, and the steel industry gave rise to a powerful state. In the twentieth century the Industrial Revolution in the United States provided the economic base for it to develop into a superpower, militarily and economically. This technological advantage helped to vault the United States into the "postmodern" era of high-technology in computers, electronics, and communications ahead of other powers.

This brings us to an important phenomenon of the technological dimension: the diffusion of technology from one state to other states. According to one authority, "The diffusion of military and economic technology from more advanced societies to less advanced societies is a key element in the international redistribution of power. Although technology is expensive and not easily created, once it is created it usually diffuses relatively easily."[12] Diffusion of technology allows new powers to emerge while reducing the power of existing technologically advanced states. It is clear that industrialization and a variety of "economic factors in particular have become an important source of national power and advantage." This in turn is contingent upon technology. But "in time . . . this technological advantage disappears."[13]

The diffusion of technology, with the resulting decline of one state and the rise of others, has led many to develop a sense of historical determinism about technology. Once a state reaches the limits of its expansion, then it begins a period of decline; "it has great difficulty in maintaining its position and arresting its eventual decline."[14] If one accepts this view, then retrenchment and consolidation follow, and an increasingly inward-looking culture evolves. Some point to U.S. technological diffusion, a view reinforced by the limits of U.S. power. If this is true, it follows that the United States must substantively change its national security posture, reducing its commitments and developing a better match between capabilities and national security policy.

Although technology is not the sole determinant of national power, there is no question that it is a most important one. It has a direct impact on industrial and military capacity and has a pervasive effect on all aspects of life. The penetration of technological culture into society is a sure sign of its secular character. As one authority concluded, "Taking mankind as a whole, there has been an irreversible movement of technological progress. Techniques once invented have seldom been wholly lost although they may have been lost in local areas."[15]

Technological Aspects

No state can develop and maintain high-technology without a strong economic base. Furthermore, an industrialized society needs to develop and nurture a scientific commitment within its educational systems and research communities. With a broad-based scientific culture and an industrial base that can translate scientific advances into technological developments, society can improve quality of life.

Such advances are contingent upon an industrial economy that is stimulated by consumer buying as well as continuous and growing investments in new plants and products. Government fiscal and monetary policies are important factors in shaping economic growth, as are market forces and international markets and trade. Thus a strong industrial economy, scientific culture, and technological advances are inextricable and essential in maintaining a state's ability to pursue national security goals.

It this environment technology benefits military development, which in turn benefits the economy. But these mutual benefits are dependent upon the nature of the political system and its ideological orientation. The link between the economy, technology, and military development can be considerably distorted by government action and the ideological framework of the system—its cultural system.

In the United States, a key indicator of technological effort is the resources committed to defense and military research and development. Since Vietnam, there has been much debate (and disagreement) over the proper balance between guns and butter. Critics point out that the defense budget and its emphasis on research and development have had a negative impact on the economy—that military expenditures tended to rob the civilian economy of financial resources and scientific talent. Defense research and development rose 64 percent during the period 1981–1987; at the same time, "nondefense research and development fell 26 percent after inflation."[16] However, there are hidden benefits in defense spending on research and development. "Hundreds of U.S. companies that engage in defense work in one form or another compete vigorously for contracts. . . . Firms will spend significant sums of their private research and development funds to prepare for making a bid on a defense contract."[17]

In the contemporary period, however, new concerns have surfaced.

> As the twentieth century draws to an end, the United States finds itself faced with few significant military threats. Instead, it is confronted with a global economic competition for which it is by no means as well or as uniquely qualified as competitors.[18]

The issue is no longer military technology but civilian technology from which the military can benefit. Thus the issue of technology, military developments, a strong military establishment, and the need for a strong economic base are sure to be persistent political issues within the U.S. administration and political and military policymaking circles. To this date, there is little to suggest that anyone has designed a magic formula to balance these competing interests. There seems to be little question, however, that in the United States a strong industrial base, scientific culture, and technological commitment are essential in providing for an effective national security posture.

One fear is that technology, whether civilian or military, increasingly tends to drive technology, that is, there is the concern that a technological culture will develop to a point that technology will be seen as a good in its own right, with little reference to its impact on the quality of life, values, and morals of society. In its extreme form, the fear is that technology will advance without recourse to its social utility, and society will be compelled to adapt to it rather than technology adapting to society. Biotechnology is a good example; some scientists claim that human cloning is inevitable and will some day become routine.

Several important issues emerge from these observations on technology. Technological developments are critical in nurturing economic progress, and military modernization and capability are contingent upon military technology. The link between technological progress in the economy and military modernity seem fairly obvious, as both factors are extremely important for U.S. national security policy and capability. It is also clear that in an open system the strength of the economy is perhaps the first priority in sustaining an effective national security posture. Another dimension is related to the economy as a whole. In the 1980s and the 1990s, there was serious concern about the increasing involvement of foreign firms in the U.S. economy, even though most from friendly countries. British, West German, French, and Japanese enterprises gained control over several U.S. manufacturing firms—including defense-related industries—as well as supermarkets, banks, and other businesses. Large tracts of real estate in some major U.S. cities—Washington, New York, Chicago, and Honolulu—were bought by foreign companies, and brokerage houses on Wall Street acquired several foreign partners. As a result of foreign economic penetration, some feared economic control by foreign companies as well as political control evolving from economic leverage. These fears raised more questions about allowing transfer of technology and access to defense products, even among friendly states. Some of these fears were confirmed during the 1991 Gulf War when it was revealed that the Patriot missile used in defending against Iraqi SCUD missile attacks had important internal guidance parts produced primarily by Japan.

Thus the fundamental problem facing the president and those in the U.S. national security establishment is how to balance resources within the defense budget, ensure economic growth and technological advances on a broad scale, and minimize the unauthorized transfer of high-tech material and information to foreign states. At the same time, the U.S. public must share certain technologies with allies to strengthen alliances and provide important national security benefits to the United States.

The problem is compounded by the fact that the president and members of his national security staff do not have the power or authority to direct and shape all the instruments of national security; neither can they put into place policies without the cooperation of other political actors, especially Congress. Even when there is general agreement between the president and Congress about national security issues with respect to economics and technology, there is likely to be disagreement over military technology and the means to pursue national security goals—except in the most extreme cases when there is a direct threat to U.S. national security interests. Thus, except during crises, the U.S. economy is driven by market forces outside the purview of government that create a largely amorphous, free-market system that is not well suited to central direction and control.

During the Cold War a symbiotic relationship grew among the U.S. military establishment, defense contractors, and members of Congress seeking defense spending in their districts. This triangle of influence will not disappear entirely, but it will be subjected to considerable turbulence as technology from the civilian sector begins to drive military innovation toward a revolution in military affairs. The computer, communications, and electronics revolutions were not driven by government laboratories but by entrepreneurial spirit and inventiveness. The Internet and the globalization of information and finance now make it possible for medium and small powers to acquire advanced technology. A more diffuse international security power structure will almost certainly be one ramification of the information revolution. Hierarchies will be replaced by networks as the organizational frameworks of choice for much problem-solving in military and government circles. Traditional approaches to intelligence collection and analysis, including military intelligence, based on compartmentation and specialization may not work in this new era.[19]

The Communications Revolution

Given all the development surrounding the information superhighway, there is little question that the information age has arrived. A massive increase in news and entertainment sources is planned, much of it anchored in the hyperexpansion of available TV channels. In addition, microchip and laser technology, computer advances, and satellite networks have made access to information and entertainment global in scope. The ability of viewers to interact with TV messages (interactive television) will offer a variety of options for making political, commercial, and buying decisions through the TV set. Furthermore, numerous political, social, educational, and advocacy channels will be available to viewers. Add the ability of the print media as well as radio to extend their reach globally, and one can begin to appreciate the impact of the communications revolution.

The impact on national security will be no less dramatic. Continual monitoring of the conflict arena will provide commanders in the field with up-to-the-second and comprehensive visual scope of the battle arena. Penetration of the adversaries' military formations, political and social infrastructures, and target areas will be commonplace. Furthermore, access to the same information will be available to policymakers in Washington, as during the Gulf War, as well as global viewers and the media. It will be difficult to find any place to hide. And in the case of terrorist attacks intended to cause mass casualties for the purpose of visible defiance and exposing U.S. vulnerabilities, the media are the message. Vivid images of the destruction are instantly transmitted globally.

Moreover, the communications revolution will have a major impact on military command and control, and technology and communications will revolutionize weapons systems and the characteristics of conflicts—at least conventional conflicts. The electronic battlefield will be enhanced by sophisticated communications and stand-off conflicts (e.g., an exchange of missiles using highly sophisticated targeting).[20] Military training and education will need to incorporate the lessons of the communications revolution into the battle arena. In summary, it is conceivable that conflicts can be more closely controlled from the safety of the operations room in Washington, with civilian leaders being able to see and talk directly to commanders on the battlefield down the chain of command.

One danger is that perceptions of war can take on the feel of a video game, depersonalizing it to the point that only those in harm's way will really understand the personal nature of ground combat. Those outside the immediate combat area could well make decisions that have little to do with realities on the ground.

In the broader sense, it will be difficult to maintain secrecy in the national security policy process. The media will be able to gain access to or penetrate virtually any communications network used in the policy process. At the same time, there will be almost simultaneous global access to events and decisions in the national security area. The entire national security policy process will be under tremendous pressure for immediate response and rapid implementation. In an age when video-driven national security and foreign policy is becoming almost commonplace (e.g., Somalia in 1992–1993 and Bosnia-Herzegovina in 1995), the communications revolution carries serious implications for long-range national security planning, as well as short-range policy and strategy. How all of this will affect the national security establishment in the next decade is not clear. Although policymakers are quick to blame the media for exciting the public with vivid images of atrocities, some experts contend that the major impact of video is on political leaders themselves. President George Bush's insistence to send a U.S. peace mission to Somalia in December 1992 was partly motivated (by his own admission) by news footage of starving Somalis.[21]

Summary and Conclusions

This chapter is intended to provide a counterpoint to the process-oriented focus of earlier chapters. We suggest here that the international environment imposes fundamental constraints on security policymakers. Factors such as geography, economic power, and political viability of state actors, as well as those states' own definitions of allies and enemies, must be taken into account by U.S. defense and foreign policy planners and political leaders. Culture, which includes religious and regional factors, also influences whether states will be friendly or hostile toward the United States and its allies. For example, when the Soviet regime collapsed and democratic Russia succeeded it, the political character of the regime changed, as did the political and social culture pertinent to Russian foreign policy. This change, in turn, had consequences for the United States and NATO.

The information and communications revolutions illustrate the potential of technology to create a new context for military strategy. Persons tutored on so-called second-wave industrial military logic now find their engrained habits stressed by third-wave, or postindustrial, technologies that leap across state borders at the speed of light. The demassification of the military art, made possible by the new technologies of smart warfare, has profound implications for the character and size of armies. Smart and highly specialized soldiers, fighting in smaller units and with a greater degree of self-control, will pose challenges to enemies, as well as to their own superiors higher up the chain of command. And this sociological change to smaller, smarter armed forces in turn creates organizational and political issues within U.S. and other armed forces. With fewer grunts and greater numbers of special operations volunteers, the U.S. military may be better prepared for missions such as peace operations and low intensity conflicts. Yet a smarter and more autonomous military can pose other problems in civil-military relations, including a possible incongruity with the values of the society.[22]

Notes

1. Sam C. Sarkesian and Robert E. Connor Jr., *The U.S. Military Profession into the Twenty-first Century: War, Peace, and Politics* (London: Frank Cass, 1999), esp. pp. 67–69.

2. Samuel P. Huntington, "The Clash of Civilizations?" *Foreign Affairs* 72, no. 3 (Summer 1993): 40.

3. Dmitri Volkogonov, *Autopsy for an Empire: The Seven Leaders Who Built the Soviet Regime*, ed. and trans. Harold Shukman (New York: Free Press, 1998).

4. Mikhail S. Gorbachev, "Document: The Revolution and Perestroika," *Foreign Affairs* 66, no. 2 (Winter 1987/1988): 425 (excerpts from his speech; English translation distributed by the Soviet press agency TASS).

5. See Susan M. Puska, ed., *People's Liberation Army After Next* (Carlisle Barracks, PA: Strategic Studies Institute, U.S. Army War College, August 2000), for expert assessments of Chinese military modernization.

6. Colin S. Gray, *Modern Strategy* (Oxford, UK: Oxford University Press, 1999), pp. 165–166.

7. For a discussion of the various geopolitical theories, see Norman J. Padelford and George A. Lincoln, *The Dynamics of International Politics*, 2nd ed. (New York: Macmillan, 1967), pp. 106–112. See also Sir Harold J. Mackinder, *Democratic Ideals and Reality* (New York: Henry Holt, 1919), and Nicholas J. Spykman, *The Geography of Peace*, Helen R. Nickel, ed. (New York: Archon Books, 1969).

8. Hans J. Morgenthau, *Politics Among Nations: The Struggle for Power and Peace*, 6th ed. rev. Kenneth W. Thompson (New York: Alfred A. Knopf, 1985), p. 634.

9. Ibid.

10. Quincy Wright, *The Study of International Relations* (New York: Appleton-Century-Crofts, 1955), p. 348.

11. For the potential of cruise missiles in WMD attacks, see Lt. Col. Rex R. Kiziah, USAF, *Assessment of the Emerging Biocruise Threat* (Maxwell Air Force Base, AL: USAF Counterproliferation Center, Counterproliferation Papers, Future Warfare Series, No. 6, August 2000).

12. Robert Gilpin, *War and Change in World Politics* (Cambridge, MA: Cambridge University Press, 1983), p. 177. See also Paul Kennedy, *The Rise and Fall of the Great Powers: Economic Change and Military Conflict from 1500 to 2000* (New York: Random House, 1988).

13. Ibid., p. 173.

14. Ibid., p. 185.

15. Wright, *The Study of International Relations*, p. 385.

16. William R. Neikerk, "Civilian Research Can't Break Pentagon's Grip," *Chicago Tribune*, December 30, 1987, pp. 1, 10. See also *Report of the Secretary of Defense Frank C. Carlucci to the Congress on the FY1988/FY1989 Biennial Budget and FY 1988–92 Defense Programs* (Washington, DC: U.S. Government Printing Office, amended February 18, 1988), p. 297.

17. Neikirk, "Civilian Research," pp. 1, 10.

18. Leonard Sullivan Jr., "The Defense Budget in Transition," in Joseph Kruzel, ed., *American Defense Annual, 1993* (New York: Lexington Books, 1993), p. 51.

19. Bruce D. Berkowitz and Allan E. Goodman, *Best Truth: Intelligence in the Information Age* (New Haven: Yale University Press, 2000), esp. pp. 58–98.

20. Thomas A. Keaney and Eliot A. Cohen, *Revolution in Warfare? Air Power in the Persian Gulf* (Annapolis, MD: Naval Institute Press, 1995), pp. 188–226.

21. For perspective on this issue, see Christopher Jon Lamb, "The Impact of Information Age Technologies on Operations Other Than War," in Robert L. Pfaltzgraff and Richard H. Shultz Jr., eds., *War in the Information Age* (Washington, DC: Brassey's, 1997), pp. 247–278.

22. Sarkesian and Connor, *The U.S. Military Profession*, esp. pp. 50–62.

15

National Security and Nuclear Weapons

SINCE 1945 THE AVAILABILITY OF NUCLEAR WEAPONS HAS BEEN a critical issue in U.S. national security policy and strategy. For much of that time the primary concern was superpower relations. Later, the acquisition of nuclear weapons by other states complicated the balance of power between the United States and Soviet Union. With the collapse of the Soviet empire, some accommodation has been made between the United States and Russia over the size of their nuclear arsenals. Nonetheless, the issue remains contentious.

This is complicated by developments in the international landscape. This landscape is ill-defined and is also characterized by access to nuclear technology and weapons by international terrorist groups and rogue states. And the India-Pakistan dispute over Kashmir (both are nuclear powers) highlights problems that can evolve. Combined with U.S. involvement in the war on terrorism in the aftermath of September 11, it is no wonder that nuclear weapons remains a critical issue. In this chapter we review the evolution of nuclear weapons as a critical component of U.S. national security; it is likely to remain a longstanding national security issue. To understand the current policy and strategy, we must study the evolution of nuclear weapons policies and strategies emerging from the U.S.-Soviet rivalry to the current period.

During the Cold War the U.S. homeland faced the possibility of nuclear attack, which never materialized. But on September 11, 2001, the U.S. national security agenda changed overnight. We examine this new context for assessing threats to U.S. national security posed by weapons of mass destruction, whether in the hands of terrorists or states. Nuclear weapons will receive most attention because nuclear danger remains the most geopolitically critical. This claim is supported by the interest of the George W. Bush administration and many in the U.S. Congress in developing and deploying National Missile Defenses (NMD) as soon as technology makes it practicable to do so, possibly in the face of Russian and Chinese objections and some U.S. domestic opposition. Are missile defenses the answer to Americans' prayers to be able to sleep more securely at night or a false security blanket? The complex relationships among U.S.-Russian nuclear arms control, proliferation, missile defense, and homeland security provide a large challenge for U.S. policy planners.

Nuclear Weapons Strategies

From 1945 to the end of the Cold War (1989–1991), theorists and military officers asked whether nuclear weapons had forever changed the relationship between war and politics.[1] This question remained relevant in the twenty-first century. Indeed, the issue of nuclear weapons and their proliferation remains a complex and uncertain dimension of U.S. national security.

The end of the Cold War and the demise of the Soviet Union cast further doubt on the political utility of nuclear forces and, perhaps, the threat of nuclear force. Without a global opponent and favoring regionally oriented military strategies, U.S. military planners are uncertain as to the relevance of nuclear weapons except as a last resort.

Nuclear weapons also appeared to reverse the traditional relationship between offensive and defensive military strategies. In traditional strategy, offensive attacks were thought to be riskier than defensive stands. But the speed and lethality of nuclear weapons made offensive technology, but not necessarily an offensive *strategy*, look more imposing. Nuclear weapons that survived a first strike could be used to retaliate, and unless the attacker could protect itself against retaliation, the difference between the attacker's and the defender's postwar worlds might be politically and militarily insignificant.

The paradoxical implications of nuclear weapons for military strategy and U.S. national security led to an advocacy of nuclear strategic policies that followed one of two paths: Mutually Assured Destruction (MAD), or nuclear flexibility. Some U.S. officials and military thinkers favored a strategy of assured retaliation as the necessary and sufficient deterrent against any Soviet provocation, including Soviet attacks on U.S. allies with conventional weapons. Assured retaliation, or MAD, required that the United States be able to absorb a Soviet surprise first strike of any size and retaliate, destroying the Soviet Union as a viable society. Assured retaliation became official U.S. declaratory policy under Secretary of Defense Robert S. McNamara in the Kennedy and Johnson administrations.

MAD had many critics in and out of government. Some thought MAD required too much of the U.S. nuclear arsenal; others thought that MAD would not be enough to deter a Soviet attack under some circumstances. The view that MAD was an excessive burden for U.S. forces gained little ground among officials during the Cold War. But the opposite view gained some ground during the Nixon, Ford, Carter, and Reagan administrations.

As for nuclear flexibility, under Richard Nixon and Gerald Ford U.S. nuclear weapons policy was revised to emphasize options short of all-out war between the superpowers. Under Jimmy Carter, Presidential Directive 59 expanded the previous guidance and called for the creation of nuclear retaliatory forces sufficiently flexible and durable to fight a protracted, or a limited, nuclear war, as might be directed by the U.S. president in pressing circumstances. In addition, Carter policy called for the development of nuclear command-and-control systems that would permit the United States to fight an all-out nuclear war through various phases until victory was denied to the Soviet Union.

Critics of nuclear flexibility argued that its justifications were really disguised arguments for building up nuclear arsenals well beyond the requirements of deterrence. In addition, the Soviets showed little apparent interest in flexible nuclear response as a means of bargaining, especially in the case of strategic nuclear weapons exploded on Soviet territory. Nevertheless, the construction of a Soviet adversary determined to exploit any relative counterforce imbalance was all too often perceived by policymakers as a necessary part of the case for counterforce and nuclear flexibility. Although Soviet military doctrine in its political-military aspects (grand strategy) remained essentially defensive and potentially open to the concept of limited war, Soviet military doctrine offered little in the way of encouragement. The General Staff and Politburo showed little interest in the actual conduct of nuclear strikes once deterrence had failed according to agreed rules.[2]

Nuclear Weapons as a Deterrent

The effectiveness of nuclear weapons as a deterrent was accepted as fact by most policymakers and analysts. But carrying out war plans if deterrence failed would have been left to organizations that operated with rigid, preplanned, and detail-driven parameters, not subject to crisis control and wartime policymakers. Theorists and strategists conceived elegant ways to fight limited wars and to dominate the process of escalation, and Soviet–Warsaw Pact planners dreamed of blasting holes in NATO's forward defenses with tactical nuclear strikes during the initial phase of war. It was, for the most part, an effort to cover up mutual fears. The greatest was that there was no way to fight a nuclear war at an acceptable cost, making nuclear deterrence a potentially dangerous bluff.

Colin Gray is thus correct (up to a point) to insist that all nuclear deterrence strategies were tantamount to contingent nuclear war-fighting strategies.[3] Military chains of command were tasked to prepare plans for what to do if deterrence ever failed. As Cold War arsenals grew in size and complexity, some of these plans and the planning process itself took lives of their own. The U.S. Single Integrated Operational Plan for nuclear war was driven by calculations of "damage expectancy" against designated classes of targets, and damage expectancies had to be satisfied above and beyond other requirements of the war plan. U.S. war plans were often characterized by a lack of clear policy guidance beyond vague statements to win or prevail, as if the definition were self-evident. Target planners at Strategic Air Command in Omaha, Nebraska, were often forced to assign weapons to targets on the basis of hunches or rules of thumb. Few, if any, U.S. presidents ever familiarized themselves with the details of nuclear war plans.[4]

The nuclear policy of the Nixon, Ford, and Carter years called for improved U.S. counterforce capabilities: selective attacks on Soviet land-based missiles, missile submarines, and nuclear bombers, as well as their supporting military command-and-control systems. None of the U.S. nuclear policy guidance of the 1970s, however, offered any hope of protecting the U.S. homeland in the event that deterrence failed. The Nixon administration, in signing the 1972 Anti-Ballistic Missile (ABM) Treaty, made U.S. reliance on the threat of offensive retaliation for deterrence official. Defenses were marginalized by the ABM Treaty, which constrained the size of missile defenses as well as the kinds of defenses that could be built. Both constraints were intended to preclude any possibility that either side would later deploy an effective system for the defense of its national territory.

The Strategic Defense Initiative

In March 1983, President Ronald Reagan called for the U.S. research-and-development community to transcend deterrence based on offensive retaliation. Reagan's proposed Strategic Defense Initiative (known derisively to many as "Star Wars") caught his own defense bureaucrats by surprise and alarmed Moscow.[5] The technology was not available during Reagan's terms in office, or even a decade later, to provide reliable protection against a large-scale missile attack against U.S. territory. Continued deterrence through MAD remained the only plausible option when the Cold War expired, and it remained so into the twenty-first century.

Several other strategic doctrines were considered by policymakers, experts, and critics: assured retaliation, escalation dominance, victory denial, defense dominance, and minimum deterrence.[6] In November 2001, a Texas meeting between Russian president Vladimir Putin and U.S. president George W. Bush about nuclear weapons and the 1972 ABM Treaty changed the context for nuclear stability by opening the door to unprecedented offensive arms reductions. In December 2001, President Bush announced that the United States would no longer be bound by the 1972 ABM Treaty.

Nuclear Arms Control and U.S.-Soviet Policy

Following the October 1962 Cuban missile crisis, U.S. and Soviet leaders perceived a mutual interest in strategic arms limitation, in the avoidance of accidental and inadvertent nuclear war, and in preventing the spread of nuclear weapons. This led to the Nuclear Test Ban Treaty of 1963 and the Hot Line, a direct communications link for emergency discussions between the U.S. and Soviet heads of state. Discussions between Moscow and Washington about strategic arms limitation got under way during the latter years of the Johnson administration, continued under Nixon, and culminated in the Strategic Arms Limitation Talks Agreement of 1972 (SALT I). A year earlier, Washington and Moscow had concluded two agreements on the prevention of accidental and inadvertent war and the avoidance of unnecessary fears of surprise attack.[7]

The interim agreement on offensive arms limitation embodied in SALT I was superseded by SALT II, signed in 1979 and carried forward (although never formally ratified by the United States) until it was transformed into START (Strategic Arms Reduction Talks) during the Reagan administration. The ABM Treaty remained as the cornerstone of U.S-Soviet strategic arms limitation until the end of the Cold War. As amended by a 1974 protocol signed at Vladivostok, it limited both sides' national missile defense systems to one site of no more than 100 defensive interceptors. The United States chose to deploy its ABMs at Grand Forks, North Dakota, the Soviets around Moscow. (The U.S. system was closed down by Congress in the mid-1970s.)

The ABM Treaty became a powerful symbol of affinity for advocates of mutual deterrence based on offensive retaliation. When the Reagan administration proposed Star Wars in 1983, opponents argued that it would overturn the ABM Treaty and reopen the race in offensive weapons being capped by the SALT/START process.

Even more entrenched than the ABM Treaty was the Nuclear Non-Proliferation Treaty (NPT), ratified in 1970 and supported by both the United States and the Soviet Union. The agreement was intended to prevent the spread of nuclear weapons and weapons-related technology. The NPT outlasted the Cold War and has become even more relevant today. NPT was extended indefinitely in 1995 with near-unanimous approval, with the important exceptions of India, Pakistan, and Israel. The favorable climate established by the NPT extension carried forward into the 1996 multilateral agreement on a comprehensive test ban on nuclear weapons testing, extending and deepening the impact of the original test-ban treaty and the subsequent treaties on threshold test bans and peaceful nuclear explosions.

Weapons Reduction

The nuclear arms control dialogue between East and West during the Cold War contributed to the reduction of political tensions in various ways. First, continuing arms control negotiations educated both sides during the Cold War about one another's strategic and defense cultures. Second, the strategic arms limitation agreements of the 1970s and 1980s (SALT/START) provided a framework that allowed both sides to avoid expensive deployments of systems that would have been militarily unnecessary and eventually obsolete in the face of improved technology. Third, cooperation between Washington and Moscow to limit the spread of nuclear weapons technology helped limit the number of nuclear aspirants during the Cold War and set a useful precedent for multilateral cooperation against proliferation afterward. U.S.-Russia post–Cold War cooperation against the spread of nuclear weapons included the Cooperative Threat Reduction law, authorized by the U.S. Congress in 1991 to encourage denuclearization and demilitarization within states of the former Soviet Union, especially the four successor states that inherited the Soviet nuclear arsenal (Russia, Belarus, Kazakhstan, and Ukraine).[8]

Efforts to limit the significance of nuclear weapons during the Cold War were complicated by the role of nuclear weapons in U.S. and NATO strategy for the prevention of war in Europe and for the establishment of a credible defense plan if deterrence failed. Some U.S. and European analysts and policymakers doubted that conventional deterrence was feasible; others feared that it might be. Those who doubted that conventional deterrence was feasible tended to see a viable Soviet threat of invasion, absent strong NATO military preparedness. Those who feared that conventional defense was feasible noted that a conventional war in Europe would involve very different sacrifices for Americans and Europeans. A conventional deterrent for NATO might not be as convincing as a conventional defense backed by nuclear deterrence.

NATO's willingness to settle for active-duty deployment in Western Europe of some thirty ground divisions was not forced by the economics of defense, as some politicians contended. NATO could have created conventional forces capable of credible deterrence against Soviet attack precisely because nuclear weapons made success problematic, to say the least. Nuclear weapons added a component of uncertainty and risk to Soviet calculations. Yet nuclear weapons were also a curse for NATO strategy. As the numbers of tactical nuclear weapons deployed with air and ground forces multiplied, the problem of NATO command and control, including obtaining political approval for first use, became more complicated. Whether NATO's inefficient policymaking process could ever have authorized nuclear release in time was widely debated. Regardless, the deployment of U.S. nuclear weapons in Europe would link the defense of Europe and North America. In fact the United States, by spreading its nuclear deterrent outside of North America, risked an attack on the U.S. homeland in order to defend Europe from a Soviet offensive.

The End of the Superpower Standoff

Neither Mikhail Gorbachev's political career nor the Soviet Union survived the end of the Cold War—but nuclear weapons did. The Russian Federation assumed responsibility for former Soviet nuclear weapons and for continuing the process of nuclear arms control with the United States in the START negotiations. U.S. political relations with post-Soviet Russia were much improved. Under Nunn-Lugar and other projects, the United States provided funds to help Russia account for its fissile materials, transport and store its remaining nuclear weapons, dismantle obsolete or disarmed weapons and launchers, and employ displaced Russian nuclear scientists on other projects. The United States and Russia have both ratified (but not implemented) the START II agreement calling for reductions in both states' strategic nuclear warheads to a maximum of 3,000–3,500. In 1997, they discussed a possible START III agreement, with expected reductions to 2,000–2,500 warheads for each side. In May 2002, Bush and Putin signed the Moscow Treaty to reduce long-range nuclear weapons to a maximum of 2,200 deployed nuclear warheads for each state by the year 2012. This agreement, together with the creation of a new NATO-Russia Council for consultation on terrorism, nonproliferation, and other issues, signified for many the de facto end of the Cold War.

Russia prefers lower force ceilings than does the United States. Its economy will be hard-pressed to pay for the simultaneous modernization of its land-based, sea-based, and airborne launch platforms. Russia has proposed mutual reductions to a force of 1,500 maximum warheads on strategic launchers. Russia has various ways of mixing its forces at the 2,500- or 1,500-warhead level, as does the United States (see Table 15.1).[9]

Through the end of Boris Yeltsin's tenure as Russia's first democratically elected head of state, Russian military and political leaders remained hostile to the idea of amending the 1972 ABM Treaty to permit either the United States or both states to deploy national missile defenses. The Clinton administration announced in 1999 that the decision to commit to the eventu-

Table 15.1 Strategic Nuclear Warheads: United States and Russia/Former Soviet Union (as of January 1, 1999)

United States

Delivery System	Launchers	Warheads/ Launcher	Total Warheads
ICBM[a]			
Minuteman II	1	1	1
Minuteman III	650	3	1,950
MX	50	10	500
Total ICBM	701		2,451
SLBM[a]			
Poseidon	32	10	320
Trident I	192	8	1,536
Trident II	240	8	1,920
Total SLBM	464		3,776
Bombers			
B-1B	91	1	91
B-2	20	1	20
B-52	48	1	48
B-52 ALCM	156[b]	10	1,572
Total Bombers	315		1,731
Grand Total	1,480		7,958

Russian and Other Former Soviet Union States

Delivery System	Launchers	Warheads/ Launcher	Total Warheads
ICBM			
SS-18	180	10	1,800
SS-19	160	6	960
SS-24	90	10	900
SS-25	370	1	370
Total ICBM	800		4,030
SLBM			
SS-N-8	152	1	152
SS-N-18	208	3	624
SS-N-20	120	10	1,200
SS-N-23	112	4	448
Total SLBM	592		2,424
Bombers			
Blackjack/ALCM	24	8	192
Bear/ALCM	89	8	712
Bear	4	1	4
Total Bombers	117		908
Grand Total	1,509		7,362

Source: Adapted from David B. Thomson, *A Guide to the Nuclear Arms Control Treaties* (Los Alamos, N.M.: Los Alamos National Laboratory, LA-UR-99-31-73, July 1999), pp. 316–317.

Notes: a. ICBM = intercontinental ballistic missiles; SLBM = submarine-launched ballistic missiles.

b. Six are counted with twelve warheads each per START I accounting rules.

al deployment of a limited NMD system would be made by the summer of 2000; Clinton then deferred the deployment decision again, leaving it for the next administration. Newly elected President George W. Bush indicated in early 2001 that his administration was committed to deploying NMD as soon as technology made it feasible (see Table 15.2, which summarizes the evolution of NMD). Russian President Vladimir Putin initially opposed the U.S. system but in the fall of 2001 appeared ready to accept the inevitable U.S. decision to withdraw from the ABM Treaty and a limited U.S. NMD program. In return, Putin anticipated several quid pro quos, including Russian acceptance as a more explicit security partner with NATO in conflict prevention and management in Europe and Central Eurasia.

The purposes of a limited U.S. NMD system would be to deter, and to defeat, if necessary, attacks on U.S. territory by rogue states such as North Korea, to destroy any ballistic missiles accidentally launched at the U.S. homeland, and to deter the use of such weapons by international terrorists and other nonstate actors. However, testing of weapons technologies for hit-to-kill exoatmospheric nonnuclear interception, the most promising U.S. technology, produced inconsistent results. Although U.S. NMD technology remained well below the threshold of confident deployability, prominent Russian officials remained wary lest the United States create a first-strike capability against Russia's deterrent, backed by defenses good enough to absorb Russia's retaliatory strike.

The diminished quality of Russia's conventional military forces since the end of the Cold War pressured Moscow's military planners to increase their reliance on its remaining nuclear deterrent. Several versions of Russia's post-1991 military doctrine officially declared that Russia's

Table 15.2   Development of National Missile Defense

NMD Program	Mission	Defense
Phase I (1987–1989)	Enhance deterrence of Soviet first strike.	Thousands of interceptors, ground- and space-based.
Global Protection Against Limited Strikes (GPALS) (1989–1992)	Protect against accidental or unauthorized launch.	Hundreds of interceptors, ground- and space-based.
Technology Readiness (1993–1995)	Prepare technology to reduce deployment time.	Ground-based system— deployment not a consideration.
Deployment Readiness— "3 + 3" (1996–1999)	Integrate systems; prepare for deployment three years after a future decision.	Tens of interceptors, ground-based only.
NMD Acquisition (1999–2005)	Prepare for initial deployment in 2005.	Tens of interceptors, ground-based only.

Source: Ballistic Missile Defense Organization, *Fact Sheet,* No. Jn-00-04 (January 2000), p. 1.

nuclear forces might be used not only in response to a nuclear attack but also in variety of other contingencies, including a conventional attack on Russian territory. NATO enlargement in 1999 added three states (Poland, the Czech Republic, and Hungary) in East-Central Europe, and NATO's defense umbrella included nuclear protection. In addition to an expanded NATO and a cash-starved Russian military, Russian nervousness about the instability of its borders also gave nuclear weapons a higher priority among Russian military options. Although Russia reassured the United States and its NATO allies that every precaution had been taken against a failure of its nuclear command-and-control system, the United States offered its expertise to Russia in order to prevent computer failures and other disasters that might contribute to nuclear instability.

The Danger of Proliferation

The spread of nuclear weapons and WMD in the twenty-first century poses new challenges for U.S. and allied policymakers and their militaries. There is a justified concern on the part of U.S. and other policymakers about the potential spread of ballistic missiles and other long-range delivery systems. The 1998 entries of India and Pakistan into the nuclear club showed that some states value nuclear weapons as symbols of power and status, contrary to the assumptions underlying the NPT (reaffirmed by signatories in 1995) and other arms control efforts.

Two schools of thought characterize the U.S. approach to nuclear proliferation.[10] One school, continuous with the dominant tendency in Cold War thinking, holds that any spread of nuclear weapons is inherently bad. All states aspiring to obtain nuclear arsenals should be discouraged, and all states now possessing nuclear forces (with the exception of the five permanent members of the UN Security Council) should be urged to roll them back. The second school of thought sees the first approach as doomed to failure in the twenty-first century, regardless of its utility during the Cold War. This school favors selective U.S. opposition to nuclear/WMD proliferation, based on the willingness of the state to adhere to acceptable norms of international behavior.[11] Of course, the predominant norm is nonaggression. According to this approach, the United States and its allies would not necessarily attempt to dissuade or discourage nuclear proliferation in states satisfied with the international status quo. Only those states determined to disrupt the geopolitical status quo, such as Iraq, would be targeted for counterproliferation—active measures to prevent the state from obtaining nuclear weapons and to deny them the effective ability to use them once obtained (see Table 15.3, which summarizes nuclear weapons arsenals).[12]

Since the status quo works to the U.S. advantage in the current and

Table 15.3   Nuclear Proliferation: Status and Summary Indicators

Country	Delivery Systems	Warheads	Total Warheads
United States			
Deployed ICBMs and SLBMs[a]	1,165	6,227	
Bombers (START I counting rules)	315	1,731	
Other warheads estimated		4,112	
Total Warheads			12,070
Russia			
Deployed ICBMs and SLBMs	1,392	6,454	
Bombers (START I counting rules)	117	908	
Other warheads estimated		15,138	
Total Warheads			22,500
China			
ICBMs and SLBMs	~30	~30	
Other missiles	~80	~80	
Other warheads estimated			
Total Warheads			>400
France			
Total Warheads			>450
United Kingdom			
Total Warheads			260
India[b]			
Total Warheads			~70
Israel[c]			
Total Warheads			~100
Pakistan[b]			
Total Warheads			~15

Notes: North Korea's nuclear program is supposedly frozen under International Atomic Energy Agency safeguards. In 1994 North Korea signed the Agreed Framework with the United States, calling for it to freeze and subsequently give up all parts of its nuclear weapons program. In return, the United States promised to arrange for North Korea to receive two 1,000-megawatt light-water reactors (LWRs), plus annual allotments of 500,000 tons of heavy fuel oil until the first LWR is completed. Implementation of the Agreed Framework has been assigned to the Korean Peninsula Energy Development Organization, also including South Korea, Japan, and the European Union.

a. ICBM = intercontinental ballistic missiles; SLBM = submarine-launched ballistic missiles.

b. India and Pakistan declared themselves nuclear powers after each completed a series of tests in May 1998. India is estimated to have sixty to eighty weapons and Pakistan ten to fifteen. Neither state is a signatory to the Nuclear Non-Proliferation Treaty (NPT).

c. Israel is thought to have between seventy and 125 weapons. Israel is not a signatory to the NPT.

near-term international system, the selective approach to nonproliferation appears hypocritical to those on the receiving end. Why, for example, should India and Pakistan feel the sting of U.S. disapproval while Israel suffered nothing for its "bomb in the basement" nuclear status? In the case of U.S. NATO allies such as Britain and France, it could be argued that the

NATO defense pact gives U.S. officials continuing contact with allied counterparts and might act, in some circumstances, as a restraint on an otherwise unilateral decision for nuclear use.

But Israel is part of no such alliance, and its nuclear decisions are accountable only to its own state interests. Israel, given its perceived defense predicament and small territorial size, makes a strong case for its own nuclear capacity: to deter any nuclear/WMD attack, to deny the possibility of another Holocaust, and to thwart adversaries who might engage in nuclear coercion.[13] Despite this logic, third world and other states aspiring to nuclear status cannot help but notice the selective application of U.S. nonproliferation norms. This point, among others, has led some states to withhold their signatures from the Comprehensive Test Ban Treaty promoted by the Clinton administration and opened for signature in 1996.

Proponents of nuclear disarmament contend that selective nonproliferation shares the old fixation on partial instead of complete solutions to nuclear peril. The willingness to live with the existence of nuclear weapons, even in small quantities and in the hands of "reputable" states, runs the unacceptable risk of nuclear first use followed by a war of unprecedented destruction. Proponents of nuclear disarmament have a respectable intellectual and political tradition going back to the very beginning of the nuclear age.[14] But they are up against the practical objection that the level of international trust necessary for verified elimination of all nuclear forces does not yet exist. And even if states trusted one another to disarm completely, the knowledge of how to build nuclear weapons cannot be de-invented, and arsenals once destroyed can eventually be rebuilt. Thus some have proposed that states could disarm weapons already assembled and ready to fire, although arsenals could be reconstituted if necessary.

Conclusion

Nuclear weapons, acquisition, and proliferation remain critical to U.S. national security policy and strategy, as well as those of its allies and adversaries. At the same time, the availability of related technology—and perhaps actual weapons—to groups willing to use them has magnified the problem for the United States. This seems to be the basis for NMD, among other options.

If new technology makes antinuclear defenses viable in the coming years, how will that change the relationship between deterrence and proliferation? This depends on how good the defense technology is and who owns it. Various technologies for airborne or ground-based interception of ballistic missiles seemed more promising at the end of the 1990s than they did a decade earlier. However, technological innovation does not by itself constitute a strategic breakthrough. Strategy involves a reactive opponent. Offensive countermeasures exist for many of the kinds of defenses that have been proposed. The era of offense-dominant nuclear strategy will probably continue unless space-based defenses operating at the speed of light can be deployed and protected. Until then, we are talking not about a shift from offense dominance to defense dominance, as President Ronald Reagan hoped for, but from offense dominance to offense-defense competitiveness.[15]

If antimissile defenses become cost-effective compared to ballistic missile offenses, then the effect will almost certainly be to dissuade interest in ballistic missile strikes whether nuclear or not. There are other ways to deliver nuclear weapons, and one need not rely on missiles that lend themselves to interception and destruction. The terrorist attacks of September 11 were reminders that mass destruction can be accomplished in the U.S. homeland without missile attacks, nuclear weapons, or even regular armed forces. In addition, if antimissile defenses become good enough to make missile strikes obsolete, those defenses will have ominous offensive (i.e., first-strike) capabilities against a variety of target sets and raise the problem of preemption to another technological level. Defenses that can intercept incoming ballistic missiles may also be able to destroy satellites, thereby disrupting communications and command and control and deny the enemy a clear picture of the battlespace. Competent antimissile defenses or other space-based weapons may be the leading edge of an information warfare strategy for the twenty-first century.

Notes

1. On the development of nuclear strategy, see, e.g., Keith B. Payne, *Deterrence in the Second Nuclear Age* (Lexington: University Press of Kentucky, 1996); Colin S. Gray, *The Second Nuclear Age* (Boulder: Lynne Rienner Publishers, 1999); and Stephen J. Cimbala, *Nuclear Deterrence in the Twenty-First Century* (Westport, CT: Praeger, 2000). On the early years of U.S. strategic theorizing, see Marc Trachtenberg, *History and Strategy* (Princeton, NJ: Princeton University Press, 1991), pp. 3–46. The logic of deterrence and deterrence rationality receives especially insightful treatment in Phil Williams, "Nuclear Deterrence," in John Baylis, Ken Booth, John Garnett, and Phil Williams, *Contemporary Strategy: I: Theories and Concepts* (New York: Holmes and Meier, 1987), pp. 113–139. The nuclear revolution is put into historical context in Bernard Brodie, *War and Politics* (New York: Macmillan, 1973), pp. 375–496, and in Michael Mandelbaum, *The Nuclear Revolution: International Politics Before and After Hiroshima* (Cambridge, UK: Cambridge University Press, 1981).

2. For evidence of Soviet views on controlling and possibly terminating a major war, see Raymond L. Garthoff, *Deterrence and the Revolution in Soviet Military Doctrine* (Washington, DC: Brookings Institution, 1991), chap. 5, and Garthoff, "New Soviet Thinking on Conflict Initiation, Control and Termination,"

in Stephen J. Cimbala and Sidney R. Waldman, eds., *Controlling and Ending Conflict* (Westport, CT: Greenwood, 1992), pp. 65–94.

3. Colin S. Gray, *Modern Strategy* (Oxford, UK: Oxford University Press, 1999), pp. 309–318.

4. Desmond Ball, "The Development of the SIOP, 1960–1983," in Desmond Ball and Jeffrey Richelson, eds., *Strategic Nuclear Targeting* (Ithaca: Cornell University Press, 1986), pp. 57–83. See also Richard Ned Lebow, *Nuclear Crisis Management: A Dangerous Illusion* (Ithaca: Cornell University Press, 1987), pp. 118–122.

5. Frances Fitzgerald, *Way Out There in the Blue: Reagan, Star Wars, and the End of the Cold War* (New York: Simon and Schuster, 2000), p. 198.

6. For an alternate perspective, see Charles Glaser, "Why Do Strategists Disagree About the Requirements of Strategic Nuclear Deterrence," in Lynn Eden and Steven E. Miller, eds., *Nuclear Arguments: Understanding the Startegic Nuclear Arms and Arms Control Debates* (Ithaca: Cornell University Press, 1989), esp. pp. 113–117.

7. Nicolai N. Petro and Alvin Z. Rubinstein, *Russian Foreign Policy: From Empire to Nation-State* (New York: Addison-Wesley, 1997), pp. 135–136, 140–143.

8. William J. Perry, Secretary of Defense, *Annual Report to the President and the Congress* (Washington, DC: U.S. Government Printing Office, March, 1996), pp. 63–70.

9. Adapted from David B. Thomson, *A Guide to the Nuclear Arms Control Treaties* (Los Alamos, NM: Los Alamos National Laboratory, LA-UR-99-31-73, July 1999), pp. 316–317.

10. See Scott D. Sagan and Kenneth N. Waltz, eds., *The Spread of Nuclear Weapons: A Debate* (New York: W. W. Norton, 1995), for arguments and counterarguments with regard to nuclear proliferation.

11. See Stephen J. Cimbala, ed., *Deterrence and Proliferation in the Twenty-first Century* (Westport, CT: Praeger, 2001) for diverse perspectives on this topic by experts on arms control and military strategy. On the relationship between strategy and proliferation (or nonproliferation), see Colin S. Gray, *The Second Nuclear Age* (Boulder: Lynne Rienner Publishers, 1999), pp. 47–78.

12. Updated and adapted from David B. Thomson, *A Guide to the Nuclear Arms Control Treaties* (Los Alamos, NM: Los Alamos Naitonal Laborataory, LA-UR-99-31-73, July 1999), pp. 318–319; Arms Control Association, Fact Sheet, *The State of Nuclear Proliferation* (Washington, DC: May, 1998).

13. The case for an Israeli nuclear deterrent is summarized in Louis Rene Beres, *Security Threats and Effective Remedies: Israel's Strategic, Tactical, and Legal Options* (Shaarei Tikva, Israel: Ariel Center for Policy Research, April 2000), pp. 39–47.

14. Lawrence Freedman, "Eliminators, Marginalists, and the Politics of Disarmament," in John Baylis and Robert O'Neill, eds., *Alternative Nuclear Futures: The Role of Nuclear Weapons in the Post–Cold War World* (Oxford, UK: Oxford University Press, 2000), pp. 56–69.

15. For a summary of the evolution of the U.S. missile defense program, see Ballistic Missile Defense Organization, *Fact Sheet*, No. Jn-00-04, January 2000, p.1.

16

Making the System Work

GIVEN THE VARIETY OF AGENCIES AND INDIVIDUALS INVOLVED in U.S. national security, it is no wonder that many consider it to be a confusing system with a muddled process. Designing coherent policy and strategy in such a system is like trying to complete a complex jigsaw puzzle; to be assembled correctly, it takes time, and sometimes the actors merely "muddle through." This is a disturbing overall view. To complicate matters, national security issues lead to serious disagreements within Congress, and the U.S. public may be confused as to how the system actually works. Furthermore, bureaucratic turf battles and power struggles can lead to internecine warfare of a sort, causing serious problems in defining national interests and designing national security policy and strategy.

September 11 changed all this, at least in the short term. The U.S. war on terrorism may well provide the basis for a more focused and coordinated process. It has been declared that we're in this war for the long haul, at least several years and perhaps decades. The determined focus on countering international terrorism may lead to a reformation of the national security system. Such a reformation would be based on the assumption that the United States is committed to a long-term strategy to defeat international terrorists and hound states that support them.

Despite outward appearances, there is a well-established pattern and institutional system. The problem is that internal posturing and divergent political perceptions and mind-sets can often muddle the policy process. This was especially the case in the post–Cold War era and into the beginning of the twenty-first century. The passing of the Cold War swept away familiar and convenient frameworks of analysis and categories of thought about international politics. Scholars and policymakers alike have slipped their previous intellectual moorings, and certainties from the past have given way to ambiguities in the present.[1]

Coherence and effective functioning within the national security sys-

295

tem are not self-executing—they require hard work. The sense of directed purpose and implementation is established only as a result of effective leadership putting the major pieces together. Without such leadership, the system becomes a series of political-bureaucratic fiefdoms, with each trying to dominate the others.

In these last two chapters, we examine the problems facing presidents in bringing together the agencies and individuals in the national security establishment in order to design coherent policy and strategy. Regardless of how well that is done, there is always disagreement and bureaucratic infighting. The key is to allow disparate points of view, to identify a variety of options, and to maintain a reasonably good working relationship with Congress while ensuring that the president's worldview and strategic perspective prevail.

It should be stressed that the national security establishment and those in the policy process cannot be viewed simply in theoretical terms, as intellectual curiosities. People are the foundation of the national security system, whether bureaucrats, staff members, political appointees, or members of Congress. They all come with imperfections, previous social and political relationships, divergent goals, ambitions, and human frailties. To speak of "the establishment" and "the process" in clinical terms, isolated from the real world and human dynamics, is to neglect the most important dimension of national security: the human factor. Thus a realistic sense of the national security establishment and the effectiveness of the policy process must include how the human factor shapes and influences U.S. national security. This dimension is too often neglected by those studying U.S. national security.

We have examined the scope and complexity of national security, its institutional and political dimensions, and the variety of interests and forces involved in the policy process. That process has become even more complicated and broader in scope due to the U.S. determination to fight the war on terrorism. Thus there are many challenges to U.S. security interests that defy simple solution; many of these challenges are not amenable to U.S. policy initiatives. Also, U.S. national security has a great deal of continuity that reaches back more than five decades. And important elements shaping national security are part of the U.S. political culture and are embedded in U.S. history. What can be made of all of this? How can these be properly weighed and shaped to design the most effective U.S. national security policy?

The search for answers can begin by applying what has been studied and analyzed in this book, recognizing that there are no perfect or immutable solutions to U.S. national security. On the one hand, there are persistent U.S. national interests; on the other, those interests must come to grips with a changing international security environment. *The key to suc-*

cess is the leadership exercised by the president and his ability to pull together all the pieces of the system. The president must shape the boundaries, determine the directions, and establish the critical points to map out U.S. national interests, priorities, policy, and strategy.

The President and National Security: Retrospections

The scope of presidential power expanded over the course of the twentieth century, and the prerogatives of the presidency have been closely guarded by the executive, regardless of party affiliation and political orientation. Presidential power in national security, resting on such concepts as executive privilege and the interests of national security, was rarely challenged. In the post–World War II period (at least until Vietnam), roles and responsibilities as commander in chief, chief executive, and head of state gave the president control over policy and intelligence-gathering instruments, and he was seen by most U.S. citizens as the focal point for foreign and national security policies. But political and organizational developments since the end of World War II have constrained presidential power.

The International Arena: Into the Twenty-First Century

Compounding the problems of presidential leadership is the international security environment of the twenty-first century. It has become more difficult to define U.S. national interests, national security policy, and strategy in the domestic and international arenas. To be sure, combating international terrorism became the priority, yet past lessons from Vietnam and Watergate have increased concerns about the extent of executive power. On the heels of those controversial events, Congress reasserted itself in foreign and national security affairs—the period of the "imperial Congress." Although this abated during the Ronald Reagan presidency, the assertive role of Congress remains an important factor in limiting presidential power. And in the early part of the twenty-first century, as it did throughout the 1990s, the U.S. public in general reflected a healthy skepticism toward politics and politicians.

The Vietnam legacy underpinned much of the congressional opposition and public resistance to extending U.S. commitments beyond well-established treaty obligations. That legacy remains as an important conditioner of U.S. attitudes, even though the victory in the 1991 Gulf War helped to erode the so-called Vietnam syndrome. But the failed U.S. efforts in Somalia, with the humiliating deaths of Rangers in Mogadishu, as well as U.S. involvement in Bosnia and Kosovo, seemed to have rekindled the Vietnam syndrome, at least for some. Mind-sets also reflect a growing conviction that there are limits to U.S. ability to influence events around the world. Indeed, some even argue for a revived isolationism. But the United States remains the lone superpower, with responsibilities that extend beyond the U.S. homeland. This is underpinned by efforts to extend U.S. values into other parts of the world and to establish democratic systems. Combined with lessened fears of major wars and the increasingly accepted ideas that democracies do not fight one another, there is the notion that the United States should attempt to shape events around the world. But old demons have been replaced by new ones:

> It was May 1989. . . . "I'm running out of demons," complained Army General Colin Powell. However, on 1 September 1993 when he unveiled DoD's Bottom-Up review, he amended his original statement: "Fortunately, history and central casting have supplied me with new ones along the way."[2]

The new demons range from ethnic, religious, and nationalistic conflicts to international terrorism and drug cartels. Add to this the proliferation of nuclear weapons and increasing concerns about chemical and biological terrorism and information warfare, and the number of potential enemies is daunting.

The National Security System

Actors in the policy process have their own political constituencies and perspectives. They jealously guard their prerogatives, jockeying for power positions vis-à-vis Congress and the president.

The national security establishment, although directly under the control of the president, is not immune from congressional initiatives and oversight. Congressional initiatives, for example, have focused on intelligence activities and the defense budget process. Part of this effort reflects congressional reluctance to allow the establishment to operate outside congressional control. The legislation passed in 1996 requiring the secretary of defense to complete a Quadrennial Defense Review every four years is but one example (see Chapter 6). Combined with bureaucratic concerns about agency power and programs, interagency power struggles, and budget constraints, congressional criticism and domestic political considerations have solidified efforts to constrain the national security establishment. In the current period, presidential power in national security is being defined in more stringent terms, with greater limits.

All this changed in the aftermath of September 11. Furthermore, various components of national security policy, such as budget considerations, weapons acquisitions, and strategy, are not solely determined by military and national security issues. The defense budget, for example, reflects a series of political compromises, many shaped by domestic policy issues rather than political-military policy and strategy. Nonetheless, the president has been given a broad mandate to win the war on terrorism.

The complexity and potential volatility of national security issues make the problem of presidential control and guidance even more difficult. The technical aspects of strategic weapons, information-age technology, the complexities of logistics, and the evolution of the electronic battlefield, for example, require that the president rely heavily on military and civilian experts for interpretations of weapons requirements, as well as advice on their strategic implications. One consequence is that there is a built-in propensity for struggle among agencies to gain access to the president and to convince him of the wisdom of their view. The internal struggles are compounded by gatekeepers who can be primarily concerned about preserving existing power structures. All of this makes the president vulnerable to agency biases, in some instances making him a captive of technicians, strategists, and midlevel bureaucrats. As Henry Kissinger once argued, "Because of our cult of specialization, sovereign departments negotiate national policy among themselves with no single authority, except an overburdened President, able to take an over-all view or to apply decisions over a period of time."[3]

In summary, the power and posture of agencies within the national security establishment, the interplay of personalities within the executive, the power of Congress in the national security policy process, the tendency to politicize national security issues, and the demands of domestic politics and policy—all in a changing international security environment—have created a far more complicated situation compared to previous eras. Even in the post–Cold War era, the 1991 Gulf War reflected a conflict that evolved from a European scenario characteristic of the Cold War era. In the search for answers and a systematic approach to national security, we need to focus on two dimensions: the presidential power base and constituency, and the national security environment. Although fears have been raised about conflict on the Korean Peninsula and between India and Pakistan, conflicts like the Gulf War are not likely to characterize wars in the early twenty-first century.[4] The more likely scenarios are found in the NATO involvement in Bosnia (1995 and beyond) and later in Kosovo (1999 and beyond). The U.S. involvement in Somalia and Haiti in the 1990s are also characteristic of likely future conflicts. The past and ongoing conflicts in Africa reinforce this view. Countering international terrorism with a global strategy adds a complex and challenging dimension to the conflict environment.

The Presidential Power Base and Constituency

The presidential power base is shaped by four elements: the legal and political dimensions of the presidency in national security; democratic ideology and open systems; domestic political actors and the domestic political environment; and presidential character and accountability (see Chapter 5).

First, since the end of World War II presidents have generally assumed office with similar legal and political power to conduct national security policy—the War Powers Resolution notwithstanding. The president is the commander in chief, head of state, and chief executive. The legal and political powers derived from those roles have provided presidents the opportunity to engage in a range of initiatives in the conduct of national security. How such powers are used is a function of the president's personality and character, leadership style, and worldview. Thus each president places his own stamp on national security policy and the way that the national security establishment functions.

Second, the extent of presidential power in national security policy is limited and conditioned by the values and expectations of democratic ideology. The moral and ethical content of democracy and the public expectations that U.S. international behavior should reflect values such as individual freedom, justice, and dignity limit the options in national security strategy, temper the means used, and establish an overarching presence in the way the president conducts national security policy. All this creates an inherent moral and ethical dichotomy between the ends-means relationships in U.S. national security policy and strategy, that is, moral and ethical means to reach moral and ethical ends—a gap that presidents often find difficult to bridge. Furthermore, the president usually shares this commitment to democratic ideology and its moral and ethical imperatives, which shapes his mind-set and determines the boundaries within which he functions. In short, there is a self-imposed restraint and limitations on those reaching the Oval Office.

Third, there are several domestic political actors with power to affect national security policy, chief among them Congress. Vietnam, Watergate, and Iran-contra, among other events, galvanized Congress to assert itself in the national security policy process. This was shown by criticism of the Clinton administration's efforts in Somalia, Haiti, Bosnia, and Kosovo, among others. Before September 11, the George W. Bush administration came in for its own criticism on several issues, including the perception that it tended to ignore international opinion and to avoid commitments on issues ranging from global warming to control of small arms. This was reinforced by the power of congressional incumbency—one that often goes beyond presidential incumbency.

In addition, the mass media has a significant influence in the policy process. Investigative reporting, brought to its high point in the Watergate affair, has become an institutionalized method of analyzing and reporting the news as well as for setting the agenda. Combined with the traditional adversarial relationship between the media and the national security establishment, this makes it difficult for the president to remain unchallenged in many of his policy pronouncements and in shaping that establishment. Equally important, representatives of the media have their own informal networks of information that penetrate the core of the national security establishment, making it difficult to develop policy out of public view when necessary. Political predispositions of the media elite—perceived as left-leaning—add to the problem, with certain national security policy and strategy issues presented in highly critical terms.[5] Media critics argue, however, that much of the media subdued their criticism of the Clinton administration because of Clinton's domestic social agenda, which conformed to the media's view.[6] Some of this changed with the serious questions raised about Clinton's questionable use of the pardon just prior to his leaving office. The election of President George W. Bush in 2000 brought an experienced group into the national security establishment. Its ideology and strategic vision differ considerably from those of the previous administration.

Several groups and institutions in the public domain, including special interest groups and single issue groups, seek to influence national security policy and strategy. Their involvement has increasingly politicized and publicized nuclear, environmental, and human rights issues, linking them to national security. This was the case even in the new war on terrorism. This creates a greater awareness about national security issues and defense policy, and the public becomes more sensitive to presidential postures on such issues. For example, in 2000 some people in the Clinton administration suggested that AIDS be a national security issue.

Furthermore, power clusters within the administration can also act as rallying points for advocating one or the other direction in national security policy and strategy, leading to struggles between the president's inner circle and the rest of the administration.

Fourth, even though the president has a freer hand in national security policy, the nature of the office makes him accountable to the public. This is not limited to elections every four years but includes a variety of measures and instruments that counterbalance presidential actions and require explanation. There is a constant political and intellectual interplay that tests presidential accountability, ranging from opinion polls, interest group activity, party cohesion, congressional-executive relationships, and the president's own staff and bureaucracy. The power clusters and the policy and strategic options they represent force the president to develop some degree of consensus and political coherence in policy and strategy, regardless of his leadership style and decisionmaking preferences.

Although several conclusions can be drawn from these observations, one stands out: the importance of presidential leadership. The president's leadership style and how he shapes and directs the national security establishment are primary determinants of the effectiveness of U.S. national security policy and strategy. This shapes national will, political resolve, and staying power. The challenge of international terrorism will surely test the resolve of the U.S. public and the president's leadership.

Presidential Leadership and the National Security Establishment

The boundaries within which the president must operate and the latitude of his legal and political power to deal with the national security system and environment are a consequence of his power base and constituency. The president's leadership, personality, and character are critical in determining his effectiveness. In this respect, *system* is defined to include the variety of political actors, the national security establishment, the policy process, and all of the informal procedures that are important parts of national security policymaking. The *environment* refers to the characteristics of the international security dimension of world politics, the capabilities and policies of external political actors, and the dynamics created by their interactions.

Although model-building and theoretical frameworks for analyzing the presidency are a useful and necessary undertaking, they have limits. Presidential performance is not bound by any single model; neither does the president necessarily engage in a conscious effort to adopt a particular model and shape his performance accordingly. Furthermore, the rigid application of models and theories can fail to account for a president's ability to change his approach and adopt ad hoc decisionmaking to resolve problems and challenges. Finally, choosing a single model as the sole basis for examining the presidency tends to favor a managerial perspective, highlighting the mechanics rather than the political and social components of presidential performance.

The psychopolitical approach is a useful vantage point from which to address the political, social, and humanistic components of presidential performance. Given the dominance of the political component in virtually all national security considerations, the psychopolitical framework can provide a useful and pointed focus on the president and his role in shaping the national security environment. This is based on the premise that presidential leadership—fashioned by the president's personality and character—and keen political instincts and intuitiveness are key elements in presidential performance. These qualities must flow from a mind-set that projects a national security posture that is coherent, purposeful, and in accord with the norms of democracy.

This is not to suggest that national security policy needs to be a noncontentious process. It does mean that a reasonably effective national security policy requires presidential leadership at major points in the national security establishment and in the policy process. This is more important than mastery of organizational procedures, managerial techniques, and knowledge of the details and technical aspects of national security issues.

Presidents who expect to be successful should begin with a deep understanding of the organizational dynamics within the national security establishment. This must go hand in hand with political acumen in dealing with Congress and the public. Put simply, the president must be a creative political leader.

To ensure that the presidential presence permeates the national security establishment and that presidential views of national interests, policy, and strategy guide the system, the president must begin by placing his mark on three areas: the national security triad, the national security establishment, and the national security system. It must be remembered that none of this can be accomplished unless the president is able to first deal with his power base and constituency to create a domestic environment that is receptive and conducive to his leadership.

The president must appoint the triad—secretary of state, secretary of defense, and National Security Advisor—making sure that their worldviews are in general accord with his own. In the 2001 Bush administration, Secretary of State Colin Powell, Secretary of Defense Donald Rumsfeld, and National Security Advisor Condoleezza Rice fit the Bush worldview. This does not mean that members of the triad must be obsequious or without disagreement on some issues, for the entire system would suffer from lack of initiative and options. Each member of the triad must possess the personality, character, and leadership style that allow for effective engagement in the difficult interplay of designing national security policy and strategy. Each must be able to deal with the others in the triad in a firm but prudent way, with commitment to the most effective policy overriding any agency or department loyalty. Each member of the triad must combine political skills with national security expertise to ensure that the best posture will emerge as a result of the dynamics within the triad. Finally, members of the triad must not only be competent advisers to the president; they must be skilled managers and leaders to deal effectively with their own bureaucracies.

Although not part of the triad, the Director of Central Intelligence (DCI) and the chairman of the Joint Chiefs of Staff (JCS) are key players in shaping the national security system. In each case, the president must appoint individuals whose philosophical range and worldviews are compatible with his own. As is the case with the triad, the DCI and the JCS chairman must be skilled advisers, politically wise, and capable of effective control and direction of their own structures. This also applies to the director of the Office of Homeland Security.

The personal strength and power of the members of the triad, the DCI, and the JCS chairman do not guarantee smooth dynamics or relationships within the national security establishment and system. But the strength of character, political acumen, and leadership skills of these individuals, combined with their commitment to the president and effective national security, are essential ingredients for coherent policy, realistic strategy, and effective implementation. This is true even if the public and the media see discord within the establishment.

The president must also establish cooperative links with key members of the congressional establishment—members who have important roles in intelligence oversight, budget policies, and armed services matters. Cooperative links are established and reinforced by the president's sincere efforts to provide timely and relevant information on national security matters, articulating national interests and policy goals, and nurturing and expanding the president's power base and constituency support. The triad, DCI, and JCS chairman are important persons in these cooperative links; they are an extension of the president but are not presidential clones.

Finally, all of these matters must coalesce into workable ways to deal with the external security environment, in which sovereign states—many of which have differing ideologies and political systems contrary to U.S. values and norms—look to their own self-interests. Their policies and conceptions of national security can contradict the goals of U.S. security policy. The difficulties are magnified by the emergence of regional powers with their own policy agendas and relative immunity to pressure from external powers. With globalization complicating all of these developments, conflict in some form is inevitable. It remains to be seen how the threat of international terrorism will affect efforts to design an effective global security effort.

The complexities of the external security environment are compounded by the shifts in the locations of power (e.g., the power center emerging in Asia linking China and Japan). Europe has already established itself as a major power system, even though it faces bickering over sovereignty of individual members and the rights of the European Union. Russia's effort to regain its position of power within the international community is another complicating matter in world politics. It is conceivable that new power relationships will emerge. These might include, for example, U.S.-Europe (including Russia); U.S.-Canada-Mexico; China-Japan; Russia and the Commonwealth of Independent States (former Soviet states); and perhaps India and other Southeast Asian states. It is also conceivable that some Middle East states will form something more than the current oil cartel, focusing their attention even more on Israel. This may lead to Samuel Huntington's proposed "clash of civilizations."[7] Combined with existing competing power clusters, the security environment is undergoing major changes in the twenty-first century, requiring rethinking of the U.S. security position and its global strategy. In this respect, international terrorist organizations add an especially challenging dimension.

The interplay of innumerable factors makes the national security arena difficult to understand and respond to. The U.S. public tends to adopt simplistic perspectives and policy postures. This reflects frustration over the limited ability to achieve moralistic goals emerging from U.S. ideology; a response to the complexity of such issues as nuclear strategy and weapons proliferation; the complexities of information-age technology; as well as the public's lack of understanding and knowledge regarding the nature and character of modern warfare—especially unconventional conflicts and operations other than war.

To respond to the complex international security environment and its challenges, the United States must have an effective national security policymaking process. This requires a national security establishment staffed by skilled people who are properly organized and directed to respond and act effectively. But a perfectly skilled and bureaucratically efficient establishment and a Congress perfectly supportive of the president would be for naught if presidential leadership is found to be lacking. *Presidential leadership is the key to the effective functioning of the national security establishment.*

The Establishment and the Policy Process

Regardless of how well policy is articulated and world conditions are understood, the process by which policy is determined and strategies designed has an important impact on the end result. Furthermore, how well the national security establishment and the policymaking machinery function determines the relevance of policy and the effectiveness of strategy. If it is true that a flawed policy process is likely to lead to bad policy and strategy, how effective is the national security establishment and the policymaking process in coming to grips with the policy and strategic issues outlined here? How well can the establishment incorporate the necessary understanding and knowledge, balanced by keen intuitive insights, into the policymaking process? Is the current structure of the national security establishment relevant to the strategic landscape of the twenty-first century? These are the critical questions to which we now turn.

From the analyses of the national security policy process and the way the establishment functions, at least three conclusions are clear: (1) The national security process is cumbersome; (2) the diffusion of power makes it difficult to adopt innovative policies and strategies; and (3) the national security establishment as it existed in the Cold War is outmoded.

With respect to the way the U.S. political system operates, Roger Hilsman concludes: "Reflecting on the complexity and difficulty of these problems and the untidy, frequently stalemated American political system, one wonders how the system can cope."[8] He points out the fact that the policy process involves many power centers within the system. With respect to foreign and national security policy, "a long-run increase in the number of power centers, finally, seems inevitably to work to lessen the power of presidents in foreign affairs."[9] The same is true in national security policy. Hilsman goes on to say, "So many centers of power make building a consensus for positive action a formidable task. . . . What is discouraging is how difficult it will be to get such a disparate myriad of power centers to agree on policies for meeting these complex problems."[10] This comment remains valid today. The exception is when there is a clear and serious threat to U.S. national interests; this is reflected in national will, political resolve, and staying power.

Short of serious and recognized threats, much of the problem of myriad power centers stems from the emergence of Congress as a more powerful component in the national security policy process. This emergence has not necessarily concentrated more power in Congress as such but has shifted power away from the executive and into the hands of bureaucratic gatekeepers, midlevel managers, and other decisionmakers. Gatekeepers filter information and policy recommendations and determine what can flow upward, usually for the purpose of protecting bureaucratic power bases, maintaining the status quo, and gaining more power. Furthermore, a coalition of a few members of Congress can frustrate the design of national security policy, because the policy process is extremely susceptible to a veto by small groups. Their power is strengthened by the inevitable iron triangle (key members of Congress, small sections of the bureaucracy, and special interest groups).

The irony, according to Hilsman, is that on the one hand there must be a certain concentration of power to come to grips with problems of policy; on the other hand, there must also be a balance of power to limit and restrain adventurous policy and strategy in foreign and national security affairs. The result is a virtual stalemate. "But power diffused can lead to evil as surely as power concentrated. Here is the irony."[11] In short, there are structural problems as well as political and intellectual ones in the national security establishment as well as in the national security policy process.

Given the nature of the international security environment and the need to clarify national interests, policy choices, and strategic alternatives, what needs to be done to develop an effective structure for dealing with national security policy? The current establishment and policy process have evolved over five-plus decades, reflecting the lessons learned from the issues and crises during the Cold War, the politics of congressional-executive struggles, and entrenched habits.

Periodically, there have been calls to change the national security establishment and the way that policy is formulated. Many such calls have been initiated by scholars, think tanks, and government sources. Some of the recommendations came from the president's Special Review Board (the Tower Commission) in a 1987 report on the Iran-contra affair, and the 1986 report by the National Security Planning and Budgeting, "A Report to the President by the President's Blue Ribbon Commission on Defense Management" (the Packard Commission), whose suggestions focus on the national security establishment and its role in the national security policy process.[12] For example, the Packard Commission recommended structural and procedural changes to the National Security Council, the secretary of defense, the JCS, Congress, and the defense budget process.

> The Commission concluded that new procedures are required to help the Executive Branch and Congress do the long-range planning necessary to develop, fund, and implement a national military program to meet national security objectives. . . . Reforms must deal with three major problems in the current national security planning and budgeting process: the need to relate military plans more adequately to available resources; the instability of the defense budget process in both the Executive Branch and Congress; and the inefficient role of Congress in the review of the defense budget.[13]

This was followed in 1988 by the Commission on Integrated Long-Term Strategy, which focused on national security strategy in the context of a changing international security environment. This commission concluded, in part:

> Our strategy must be designed for the long term, to guide force development, weapons procurement, and arms negotiations. Armaments the Pentagon chooses today will serve our forces well into the next century. Arms agreements take years to negotiate and remain in force for decades.
> Our strategy must also be integrated. We should not decide in isolation questions about new technology, force structure, mobility and bases, conventional and nuclear arms, extreme threats and Third World conflicts. We need to fit together our plans and forces for a wide range of conflicts, from the lowest intensity and highest probability to the most apocalyptic and least likely.[14]

Although written years earlier, these reports tried to create a starting point for shaping the national security establishment into a more efficient structure and for providing a more effective and expeditious national security policy process. Little was done to implement their recommendations.

Other studies called for structural and organizational changes in the national security establishment and the policy process.[15] For example, Carnes Lord suggested two changes: "the establishment of a separate staff component charged with planning, and the breakdown of compartmentalization throughout the staff."[16] Put simply, the establishment must be more streamlined and responsive to the initiatives of the executive as well as more adept at anticipating potential problems and creating innovative national security policy and strategy formulations. These include new procedures to develop a more integrated and long-range defense budget that is realistic as to resources, requirements, and capabilities. Congress must streamline the committee system and the budget process, and new structures should be developed to provide closer executive-legislative coordination and cooperation. Furthermore, these reports stated that national interests and national security objectives need to be spelled out more clearly and that a U.S. strategy that can respond to conflicts across the spectrum on a long-term basis should be designed. These reports and studies are especially relevant in the new century. But there is little to indicate that these changes and procedures will be implemented.

Other recent reports also focus on transforming the national security system and national strategy. These include the 1997 report of the National Defense Panel, *Transforming Defense: National Security in the 21st Century*.[17] In 2000 and 2001, the United States Commission on National Security/21st Century created guidelines to restructure the national security establishment and national strategy (see Chapters 6 and 7).[18] For example, its report criticizes the functioning of the National Security Council (NSC).[19] "In many ways the NSC staff has become more like a government agency than a Presidential staff." Then it recommends the following:

> The National Security Council (NSC) should be responsible for advising the president and for coordinating the multiplicity of national security activities, broadly defined to include economic and domestic law enforcement activities as well as the traditional national security agenda. The NSC Advisor and staff should resist the temptation to assume a central policymaking and operational role.[20]

What seems most instructive in all of these analyses and recommendations is that the role of the president is central to the policy process. He is charged with taking the initiative and developing the mechanisms to make the national security policy process work effectively. To be sure, Congress has a major role, but a body of 500-plus members cannot establish the necessary consensus and direction to lead the nation in national security policy. The fact remains that national security policymaking and execution rest primarily with the president.

And thus we come back to the issue raised by Hilsman—the irony of the diffusion of power and the concentration of power. Where is the balance between enough power for effective national security yet not enough to override the will of the people?

Conclusion

Structural and procedural changes are not enough for successful national security policy. Also needed is a political-psychological direction that provides coherent visions of national interests, clarity of national security policy, and clear directions to the design of strategy. Equally important, there must be a new formulation and rethinking of the meaning of national interests and national security, including whether national security issues should include such issues as the environment, refugee assistance, economics, and peacekeeping. In addition, the many power centers and forces involved in the political-psychological dimensions of national security make it difficult to give the necessary coherency to national security policy as it responds to the changing international security environment. But by exercising effective leadership and by providing a sense of purpose and vision in articulating national interests, the president can shape the boundaries, determine the directions, and establish the critical points to map out U.S. national security policy and strategy.

Notes

1. Sean M. Lynn-Jones and Steven E. Miller, eds., *The Cold War and After: Prospects for Peace*, exp. ed. (Cambridge: MIT Press, 1993), p. xxi.

2. David Silverberg, "Old Demons, New Demons," *Armed Forces Journal International* (November 1993): 14.

3. Henry A. Kissinger, *Nuclear Weapons and Foreign Policy*, abridged ed. (Garden City, NY: Doubleday Anchor Books, 1958), p. 198.

4. See, e.g., Donald Snow, *Distant Thunder: Third World Conflicts and the New International Order* (New York: St. Martin's, 1993).

5. S. Robert Lichter, Stanley Rothman, Linda S. Lichter, *The Media Elite* (Bethesda, MD: Adler and Adler, 1986), pp. 20–21, 23, 294.

6. See ibid.

7. Samuel P. Huntington, "The Clash of Civilizations?" *Foreign Affairs* 72, no. 3 (Summer 1993): 22–49.

8. Roger Hilsman, *The Politics of Policymaking in Defense and Foreign Affairs: Conceptual Models and Bureaucratic Politics* (Englewood Cliffs, NJ: Prentice-Hall, 1987), p. 313.

9. Ibid., p. 316.

10. Ibid., p. 317.

11. Ibid., p. 318.

12. *Report of the President's Special Review Board* (Washington, DC: U.S.

Government Printing Office, February 26, 1987), and *National Security Planning and Budgeting: A Report to the President by the President's Blue Ribbon Commission on Defense Management* (Washington, DC: U.S. Government Printing Office, June 1986).

13. *National Security Planning and Budgeting*, p. 1.

14. *Discriminate Deterrence: Report of the Commission on Integrated Long-Term Strategy* (Washington, DC: U.S. Government Printing Office, January 1988).

15. See, e.g., James C. Gaston, ed., *Grand Strategy and the Decision-making Process* (Washington, DC: National Defense University Press, 1992).

16. Carnes Lord, "Strategy and Organization at the National Level," in Gaston, *Grand Strategy*, p. 156.

17. Report of the National Defense Panel, *Transforming Defense: National Security in the 21st Century* (Arlington, VA: n.p., December 1997).

18. United States Commission on National Security/21st Century, *Seeking a National Strategy: A Concert for Preserving Security and Promoting Freedom*, phase 2 report (April 15, 2000). Phase 1 of the commission's report was *New World Coming: American Security in the 21st Century* (September 15, 1999). The final draft report of phase 3, *Building for Peace*, was published in January 2001.

19. United States Commission on National Security/21st Century, *Road Map for National Security: Imperative for Change*, final draft report (January 31, 2001), p. 50.

20. Ibid.

17

The Study of National Security: The Presidential Mandate

IN THIS FINAL CHAPTER WE REFOCUS OUR ATTENTION ON THE role of the president in national security. Notwithstanding the variety of perspectives and approaches, our framework, offered here, is based on the themes presented in this book.

Without some direction and coherency in research focus, one is likely to be overwhelmed by the vast amount of published literature on U.S. national security. With this in mind, we offer a relatively simple study framework to help organize our thinking on this complex topic. The cornerstones of this framework are shown in Figure 17.1. The major components are: presidential character, personality, and leadership; the shape of the national security establishment; and the meaning of national interests and national security in the new era. How well the president deals with these major components has been the primary concern of this study.

Many components of the national security establishment are continuations from the Cold War era. Yet the meaning of national security, as well as its conceptual basis, have expanded to include several nonmilitary factors such as the environment, refugee control, economics, domestic assistance, humanitarian and peacekeeping operations, and a larger role for the United Nations. And September 11 demonstrated the primary role of the president in countering international terrorism and unifying the nation. This study considers national security in that context.

In the final analysis, the president is human; mistakes will be made, directions misinterpreted, and goals frustrated. The success of national security policy is, in no small way, a function of the president's ability to limit the damage of mistakes and bad judgments, reshape the directions of policy, and ensure proper functioning of the national security establishment while maintaining his presence and credibility throughout the establishment, with Congress, and with domestic and foreign constituencies. Although we cannot expect the president to be superhuman, we should

Figure 17.1   Framework for the Study of National Security

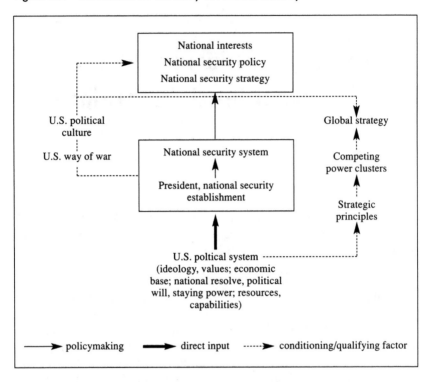

expect a creative political leader, one who can articulate national interests and shape policy to reflect them, one who can project his presence to guide the national security establishment in carrying out effective strategies.

At the same time, the U.S. public and the political actors involved in the national security policy process must be realistic about the presidency. There are limits to the office, even beyond those imposed by law. All things cannot be done all the time. This is especially true in the national security arena, where the United States must deal with sovereign states possessing ideologies and political systems that may not be compatible with ours. Moreover, the president can only rarely accomplish great things by himself; indeed, success generally begins with broad support from the public and a degree of consensus within the national security establishment. This brings us full circle: *developing and maintaining broad support and consensus are primarily contingent upon the leadership style and ability of the president to set and maintain the tone and style of his administration, which after all reflects his own personality and character.* Whatever the president's leadership style, it is secondary to the impact of his personality and character and the scope and substance of his mind-set. In turn, what emerges in national security is the composite impact of these qualities on the agencies and policy instruments in the national security establishment, the other branches of government, political circles in Washington, the media, and the domestic and international political environments.

We repeat here Roos's earlier comment regarding the George W. Bush administration on the importance of defining the national security system of the new administration and the role of the president:

> The first few weeks of President George W. Bush's tenure as Commander-in-Chief portend significant changes in the national security arena. Old hands in dealing with both domestic and international ramifications of defense affairs—Cheney, Rumsfeld, Rice, and Powell—are contributing their collective expertise in fashioning the national security construct that will frame the political boundaries during the next four years. Even at this early stage of the new Administration's tenure, there are strong indications that substance is replacing style as the primary catalyst in national security decision-making.[1]

Four additional conclusions are in order. First, presidential personality and character must be of a quality that promotes leadership in the broadest sense—the ability to lead in a manner consistent with democratic values and expectations so that a high degree of credibility is established within both domestic and foreign constituencies. Second, effective leadership depends on the president's ability to understand the capabilities of the national security establishment, its political tendencies, and its power; it depends as well on his political insights into the Washington political environment, congressional politics, the international arena, and the effective use of power to deal with that environment. Third, the president and the policy triad (secretary of state, secretary of defense, and National Security Advisor) must rethink U.S. policy and strategy in light of the new international dynamics and changing strategic landscape. The twenty-first century requires a new strategic vision and organizational reshaping. Fourth, the president cannot succeed without skilled and committed leaders in the national security establishment. There must also be a high degree of trust and confidence between the president and the Director of Central Intelligence and the chairman of the Joint Chiefs of Staff. In addition, there must be a special quality of trust and confidence between the president, the operational elements in the military, and the intelligence agencies.

But effectiveness and success in all of these areas will not necessarily lead to effective national security policy. Several important factors are beyond presidential power and control. Even the best intentions of personality and character give no assurance that the leadership style and exercise of presidential power will be effectively translated through the Oval Office to shape the national security establishment and the policy process accordingly.

Finally, national interests and policy coherence require a clear articulation of what the United States stands for and its role in the international arena. Furthermore, national will, political resolve, and staying power are needed to expend the resources and use the instruments necessary to achieve national security goals. Given the nature of the international security environment and the imperatives of U.S. national security policy, the president is placed in a position that requires a reconciliation of the ideals of democracy with the commitment necessary to further these goals—all in an environment that can resort to the military instrument and to the implementation of strategies that can stretch the notion of democracy.

It is fitting to conclude this discussion by reference to Clinton Rossiter's classic study of the presidency. Regarding the power of the president, he wrote,

> Our pluralistic system of restraints is designed to keep him from going out of bounds, not to paralyze him in the field that has been reserved for his use. He will feel few checks upon his power if he uses that power as he should. This may well be the final definition of the strong and successful President: the one who knows just how far he can go in the direction he wants to go. If he cannot judge the limits of his power, he cannot call upon its strength. If he cannot sense the possible, he will exhaust himself attempting the impossible. The power of the Presidency moves as a mighty host only *with* the grain of liberty and morality.[2]

None of this can be easily accomplished. Furthermore, the national security component of presidential responsibilities cannot easily be separated from all the other responsibilities of office. Regardless of the political actors involved in national security policy, the focal point is fixed on the presidency—the starting point for any analysis of U.S. national security. It is the quality and capability of the president that determines the success and failure of U.S. national security policy and strategy.

Notes

1. John G. Roos, "A New Beginning," *Armed Forces Journal International* (March 2001): 2.

2. Clinton Rossiter, *The American Presidency,* 2nd ed. (New York: Mentor Books, 1960), p. 69.

Reading List

The following reading list is intended to complement the themes and focus of this book. It is not comprehensive; the inclusion or exclusion of any particular work is not an indication of its importance. For additional references, see the notes in each chapter.

Allison, Graham, and Philip Zelikow. *Essence of Decision: Explaining the Cuban Missile Crisis.* 2nd ed. New York: Longman, 1999.

Arquilla, John, and David Ronfeldt, eds. *In Athena's Camp: Preparing for Conflict in the Information Age.* Santa Monica, CA: RAND, 1997.

Art, Robert J., and Kenneth N. Waltz, eds. *The Use of Force: Military Power and International Politics.* 5th ed. Lanham, MD: Rowman and Littlefield, 1999.

Barber, James David. *The Presidential Character: Predicting Performance in the White House.* 3rd ed. Englewood Cliffs, NJ: Prentice-Hall, 1985.

Barnes, Rudolph C. Jr. *Military Legitimacy: Might and Right in the New Millennium.* London: Frank Cass, 1996.

Bracken, Paul. *Fire in the East: The Rise of Asian Military Power and the Second Nuclear Age.* New York: HarperCollins, 1999.

Carnegie Commission on Preventing Deadly Conflict. *Preventing Deadly Conflict* (Final Report). Washington, DC: Carnegie Corporation of New York, December 1997.

Carter, Ashton B., and William J. Perry. *Preventive Defense: A New Security Strategy for America.* Washington, DC: Brookings Institution, 1999.

Cimbala, Stephen J. *Nuclear Strategy in the Twenty-first Century.* New York: Praeger, 2000.

Clark, General Wesley K., USA (ret.). *Waging Modern War: Bosnia, Kosovo, and the Future of Combat.* New York: PublicAffairs, 2001.

Crocker, Chester A., Fen Osler Hampson, and Pamela Aall, eds. *Turbulent Peace: The Challenge of Managing International Conflict.* Herndon, VA: United States Institute of Peace, 2001.

Davis, Richard. *Politics and the Media.* Englewood Cliffs, NJ: Prentice-Hall, 1994.

Dempsey, Gary T., with Roger W. Fontaine. *Fool's Errands: America's Recent Encounters with Nation Building.* Washington, DC: Cato Institute, 2001.

Desch, Michael C. *Civilian Control of the Military: The Changing Security Environment.* Baltimore: Johns Hopkins University Press, 1999.

Feaver, Peter D., and Richard H. Kohn, eds. *Soldiers and Civilians: The Civil-Military Gap and American National Security.* Cambridge: MIT Press, 2001.

Friedman, Thomas L. *The Lexus and the Olive Tree.* New York: Farrar, Straus, Giroux, 1999.

Gray, Colin S. *Modern Strategy.* Oxford, UK: Oxford University Press, 1999.

Hays, Peter L., Brenda J. Vallance, and Alan R. Van Tassel, eds. *American Defense Policy.* 7th ed. Baltimore: Johns Hopkins University Press, 1997.

Hilsman, Roger, with Laura Gaughran and Patricia A. Weitsman. *The Politics of Policy Making in Defense and Foreign Affairs: Conceptual Models and Bureaucratic Politics.* 3rd ed. Englewood Cliffs, NJ: Prentice-Hall, 1993.

Huntington, Samuel P. *The Soldier and the State: The Theory and Practice of Civil-Military Relations.* New York: Vintage Books, 1957.

Janowitz, Morris. *The Professional Soldier: A Social and Political Portrait.* New York: Free Press, 1971.

Joes, Anthony James. *America and Guerrilla Warfare.* Lexington: University of Kentucky Press, 2000.

Jordan, Amos A., William J. Taylor Jr., and Michael J. Mazarr. *American National Security.* 5th ed. Baltimore: Johns Hopkins University Press, 1999.

Kagan, Donald, and Frederick W. Kagan. *While America Sleeps: Self-Delusion, Military Weakness, and the Threat to Peace Today.* New York: St. Martin's, 2000.

Kegley, Charles W. Jr., and Gregory Raymond. *Exorcising the Ghost of Westphalia: Building World Order in the New Millennium.* Upper Saddle River, NJ: Prentice-Hall, 2002.

———. *How Nations Make Peace.* New York: St. Martin's/Worth, 1999.

Klare, Michael T., and Yogesh Chandrani. *World Security: Challenges for a New Century.* 3rd ed. New York: St. Martin's, 1998.

McCormick, James M. *American Foreign Policy and Process.* 3rd ed. Itasca, IL: F. E. Peacock, 1998.

Metz, Steven. *Armed Conflict in the 21st Century: The Information Revolution and Post-Modern Warfare.* Carlisle, PA: Strategic Studies Institute, U.S. Army War College, April 2000.

Millett, Allan R., and Peter Maslowski. *For the Common Defense: A Military History of the United States of America.* New York: Free Press, 1994.

Morrow, William L. *A Republic, If You Can Keep It: Constitutional Politics and Public Policy.* Upper Saddle River, NJ: Prentice-Hall, 2000.

Moskos, Charles C., with John Sibley Butler. *All That We Can Be: Black Leadership and Racial Integration the Army Way.* New York: Basic Books, 1996.

Moskos, Charles C., John Allen Williams, and David R. Segal, eds. *The Postmodern Military: Armed Forces After the Cold War.* New York: Oxford University Press, 2000.

Nye, Joseph S. Jr. *Understanding International Conflicts: An Introduction to Theory and History.* 3rd ed. New York: Longman, 2000.

O'Hanlon, Michael. *Technological Change and the Future of Warfare.* Washington, DC: Brookings Institution, 2000.

Peters, Ralph. *Fighting for the Future: Will America Triumph?* Mechanicsburg, PA: Stackpole Books, 1999.

Prados, John. *Keepers of the Keys: A History of the National Security Council from Truman to Bush.* New York: William Morrow, 1991.

Revel, Jean-Francois. *How Democracies Perish.* New York: Harper and Row, 1984.

Richelson, Jeffrey T. *The U.S. Intelligence Community.* 4th ed. Boulder: Westview, 1999.

Ricks, Thomas E. *Making the Corps.* New York: Touchstone, 1998.

Sagan, Scott D., and Kenneth N. Waltz. *The Spread of Nuclear Weapons: A Debate.* New York: W. W. Norton, 1995.

Sarkesian, Sam C., and Robert E. Connor Jr. *The U.S. Military Profession into the Twenty-First Century.* London: Frank Cass, 1999.

Sarkesian, Sam C., John Allen Williams, and Fred B. Bryant. *Soldiers, Society, and National Security.* Boulder: Lynne Rienner Publishers, 1995.

Sarkesian, Sam C., and John Mead Flanagin, eds. *U.S. Domestic and National Security Agendas: Into the Twenty-First Century.* Westport, CT: Greenwood, 1994.

Sarkesian, Sam C., and John Allen Williams, eds. *The U.S. Army in a New Security Era.* Boulder: Lynne Rienner Publishers, 1990.

Snider, Don M., and Miranda A. Carlton-Carew. *U.S. Civil-Military Relations in Crisis or Transition?* Washington, DC: Center for Strategic and International Studies, 1995.

Snow, Donald M. *National Security: Defense Policy in a Changed International Order.* 4th ed. New York: St. Martin's, 1998.

Snow, Donald M., and Eugene Brown. *Puzzle Palace and Foggy Bottom: U.S. Foreign and Defense Policy-Making in the 1990s.* New York: St. Martin's, 1994.

Stoessinger, John G. *Why Nations Go to War.* 8th ed. Boston: Bedford/St. Martin's, 2001.

Toffler, Alvin, and Heide Toffler. *War and Anti-War.* New York: Little, Brown, 1993.

Van Creveld, Martin. *The Transformation of War.* New York: Free Press, 1991.

Viotti, Paul R., and Mark V. Kauppi. *International Relations and World Politics: Security, Economy, Identity.* 2nd ed. Upper Saddle River, NJ: Prentice-Hall, 2001.

Weigley, Russell F. *The American Way of War: A History of United States Military Strategy and Policy.* Bloomington: Indiana University Press, 1973.

Zeigler, David W. *War, Peace, and International Politics.* 8th ed. New York: Longman, 2000.

Index

About the Book

THIS THOROUGHLY REVISED EDITION OF *U.S. NATIONAL SECURITY* reflects the most recent changes in the U.S. and global political arenas, in the concept of national security, in the national security establishment, and in national security issues in the aftermath of the September 11 terrorist attacks. It also includes entirely new chapters on civil-military relations and weapons of mass destruction. Unchanged, however, is the book's lucid presentation of the actors, institutions, and processes involved in U.S. national security.

Sam C. Sarkesian is professor emeritus of political science at Loyola University Chicago. He is the author of numerous books and articles on national security, unconventional conflicts, civil-military relations, and military professionalism; his most recent book is *The U.S. Military Profession into the Twenty-First Century* (with Robert Connor Jr.). He has served as president and chair of the Inter-University Seminar on Armed Forces and Society and chair of the Academic Advisory Council of the National Strategy Forum. He is a retired lieutenant colonel of the U.S. Army. **John Allen Williams,** professor of political science at Loyola University Chicago, is also executive director of the Inter-University Seminar on Armed Forces and Society and chair of the Academic Advisory Council of the National Strategy Forum. His many publications on national security, civil-military relations, and military professionalism include, most recently, *The Post-Modern Military: Armed Forces After the Cold War* (coedited with Charles Moskos and David Segal). He is a retired captain in the U.S. Naval reserve. **Stephen J. Cimbala** is professor of political science at Pennsylvania State University (Delaware County) and a faculty associate of the university's Institute of Nonlethal Defense Technologies. Among his many books and articles in the fields of international security, defense studies, arms control, and U.S.-Russian military policy, his recent publications are *The Past and Present of Nuclear Deterrence* and *Coercive Military Strategy.* Professor Cimbala is a winner of Penn State's Eisenhower Award for exceptional teaching.

de la compagnie; qu'il n'avait pas même salué monsieur l'évêque avec ce respect mêlé de cordialité qu'il avait témoigné à cette belle demoiselle. Elle prit le parti de s'adresser à elle dans ce grand embarras; elle la pria d'interposer son crédit pour engager le Huron à se faire baptiser de la même manière que les Bretons, ne croyant pas que son neveu pût jamais être chrétien s'il persistait à vouloir être baptisé dans l'eau courante.

Mlle de Saint-Yves rougit du plaisir secret qu'elle sentait d'être chargée d'une si importante commission : elle s'approcha modestement de l'Ingénu et, lui serrant la main, d'une manière tout à fait noble : « Est-ce que vous ne ferez rien pour moi? » lui dit-elle; et, en prononçant ces mots, elle baissait les yeux et les relevait avec une grâce attendrissante. « Ah! tout ce que vous voudrez, mademoiselle, tout ce que vous me commanderez : baptême d'eau, baptême de feu, baptême de sang, il n'y a rien que je vous refuse[1]. » Mlle de Saint-Yves eut la gloire de faire, en deux paroles, ce que ni les empressements du prieur, ni les interrogations réitérées du bailli, ni les raisonnements même de monsieur l'évêque n'avaient pu faire. Elle sentit son triomphe, mais elle n'en sentait pas encore toute l'étendue.

Le baptême fut administré et reçu avec toute la décence, la magnificence, tout l'agrément possibles. L'oncle et la tante cédèrent à M. l'abbé de Saint-Yves et à sa sœur l'honneur de tenir l'Ingénu sur les fonts. Mlle de Saint-Yves rayonnait de joie de se voir marraine. Elle ne savait pas à quoi ce grand titre l'asservissait; elle accepta cet honneur sans en connaître les fatales conséquences. (2)

Comme il n'y a jamais eu de cérémonie qui ne fût suivie d'un grand dîner, on se mit à table au sortir du baptême. Les goguenards de Basse-Bretagne dirent qu'il ne fallait pas baptiser son vin. M. le prieur disait que le vin, selon

---

1. Dans l'article « Baptême » du *Dictionnaire philosophique*, Voltaire note : « Plusieurs autres sociétés chrétiennes appliquèrent un cautère au baptisé avec un fer rouge, déterminées à cette étonnante opération par ces paroles de saint Jean Baptiste, rapportées par saint Luc : *Je baptise par l'eau, mais celui qui vient après moi baptisera par le feu* (saint Luc, III, 16). »

■ QUESTIONS ■

2. Montrez que l'intervention de Mlle de Saint-Yves est amenée par la logique des caractères et des sentiments. Que révèlent les courtes répliques, les jeux de physionomie, les attitudes de Mlle de Saint-Yves? Comment faut-il entendre l'expression *fatales conséquences*?

Une image que les « Bas Bretons » de Voltaire
Gravure de Grégoire Huret représentant le

Salomon, réjouit le cœur de l'homme[1]. M. l'évêque ajoutait que le patriarche Juda devait lier son ânon à la vigne et tremper son manteau dans le sang du raisin[2], et qu'il était bien triste qu'on n'en pût faire autant en Basse-Bretagne, à laquelle Dieu avait dénié les vignes. Chacun tâchait de dire un bon mot sur le baptême de l'Ingénu, et des galanteries à la marraine. Le bailli, toujours interrogant, demandait au Huron s'il serait fidèle à ses promesses. « Comment voulez-vous que je manque à mes promesses, répondit le Huron, puisque je les ai faites entre les mains de Mlle de Saint-Yves? »

Le Huron s'échauffa : il but beaucoup à la santé de sa marraine. « Si j'avais été baptisé de votre main, dit-il, je sens que l'eau froide qu'on m'a versée sur le chignon m'aurait brûlé. » Le bailli trouva cela trop poétique, ne sachant pas combien l'allégorie est familière au Canada. Mais la marraine en fut extrêmement contente.

On avait donné le nom d'Hercule au baptisé. L'évêque de Saint-Malo demandait toujours quel était ce patron dont il n'avait jamais entendu parler. Le jésuite, qui était fort savant, lui dit que c'était un saint qui avait fait douze miracles. Il y en avait un treizième qui valait les douze autres, mais dont il ne convenait pas à un jésuite de parler : c'était celui d'avoir changé cinquante filles en femmes en une seule nuit. Un plaisant qui se trouvait là releva ce miracle avec énergie. Toutes les dames baissèrent les yeux, et jugèrent à la physionomie de l'Ingénu qu'il était digne du saint dont il portait le nom. (3) (4)

---

1. Ecclésiaste, XL, 20 : « Le vin et la musique réjouissent le cœur », phrase reprise de l'Ecclésiaste de Salomon; 2. Dans la Genèse (IL, 11), Jacob s'adresse ainsi à Juda et lui annonce le Messie « qui doit être envoyé » : « Il liera son ânon à la vigne, il liera, ô mon fils, son ânesse à la vigne. Il lavera sa robe dans le vin, et son manteau dans le sang des raisins. »

— QUESTIONS —

3. Depuis le début du chapitre, les sentiments de Mlle de Saint-Yves et de l'Ingénu se précisent : étudiez, de ce point de vue, la progression logique du récit. — A l'ignorance des ecclésiastiques, Voltaire oppose la science du jésuite : pourquoi? — Chaque fois que les propos deviennent scabreux, les deux *dames* prennent exactement la même attitude : relevez quelques-unes de ces répétitions; quel effet produisent-elles?

4. SUR L'ENSEMBLE DU CHAPITRE IV. — L'attitude de l'Ingénu : caractérisez-la; d'où vient son comique?

— La critique religieuse dans ce chapitre : ses thèmes; la méthode de Voltaire. Quel rôle jouent à ce propos les diverses polissonneries qui émaillent le texte? — Relevez les emprunts à la Bible que contiennent les chapitres III et IV. Signalez ceux qui se retrouvent dans la *Bible expliquée*, ouvrage que médite déjà Voltaire.

pouvaient avoir de la vie en « Huronie ».

martyre de missionnaires jésuites au Canada.

CHAPITRE V

L'Ingénu amoureux.

Il faut avouer que depuis ce baptême et ce dîner, Mlle de Saint-Yves souhaita passionnément que monsieur l'évêque la fît encore participante de quelque beau sacrement avec M. Hercule l'Ingénu. Cependant, comme elle était bien élevée et fort modeste, elle n'osait convenir tout à fait avec elle-même de ses tendres sentiments; mais, s'il lui échappait un regard, un mot, un geste, une pensée, elle enveloppait tout cela d'un voile de pudeur infiniment aimable. Elle était tendre, vive, et sage.

Dès que monsieur l'évêque fut parti, l'Ingénu et Mlle de Saint-Yves se rencontrèrent sans avoir fait réflexion qu'ils se cherchaient. Ils se parlèrent sans avoir imaginé ce qu'ils se diraient. L'Ingénu lui dit d'abord qu'il l'aimait de tout son cœur, et que la belle Abacaba, dont il avait été fou dans son pays, n'approchait pas d'elle. Mademoiselle lui répondit, avec sa modestie ordinaire, qu'il fallait en parler au plus vite à monsieur le prieur son oncle et à mademoiselle sa tante, et que de son côté elle en dirait deux mots à son frère l'abbé de Saint-Yves, et qu'elle se flattait d'un consentement commun.

L'Ingénu lui répond qu'il n'avait besoin du consentement de personne, qu'il lui paraissait extrêmement ridicule d'aller demander à d'autres ce qu'on devait faire; que quand deux parties sont d'accord, on n'a pas besoin d'un tiers pour les accommoder. « Je ne consulte personne, dit-il, quand j'ai envie de déjeuner ou de chasser ou de dormir : je sais bien qu'en amour il n'est pas mal d'avoir le consentement de la personne à qui on en veut; mais comme ce n'est ni de mon oncle ni de ma tante que je suis amoureux, ce n'est pas à eux que je dois m'adresser dans cette affaire, et, si vous m'en croyez, vous vous passerez aussi de monsieur l'abbé de Saint-Yves. »

On peut juger que la belle Bretonne employa toute la délicatesse de son esprit à réduire son Huron aux termes de la bienséance. Elle se fâcha même, et bientôt se radoucit. Enfin on ne sait comment aurait fini cette conversation, si le jour baissant, M. l'abbé n'avait ramené sa sœur à son abbaye. L'Ingénu laissa coucher son oncle et sa tante, qui étaient un peu fatigués de la cérémonie et de leur long dîner. Il passa une partie de la nuit à faire des vers en langue huronne pour sa bien-aimée : car il faut savoir qu'il n'y a aucun pays de la terre où l'amour n'ait rendu les amants poètes. **(1)**

Le lendemain, son oncle lui parla ainsi après le déjeuner, en présence de Mlle de Kerkabon, qui était tout attendrie : « Le ciel soit loué de ce que vous avez l'honneur, mon cher neveu, d'être chrétien et Bas-Breton! Mais cela ne suffit pas; je suis un peu sur l'âge; mon frère n'a laissé qu'un petit coin de terre qui est très peu de chose; j'ai un bon prieuré : si vous voulez seulement vous faire sous-diacre[1], comme je l'espère, je vous résignerai[2] mon prieuré, et vous vivrez fort à votre aise, après avoir été la consolation de ma vieillesse. »

L'Ingénu répondit : « Mon oncle, grand bien vous fasse! Vivez tant que vous pourrez. Je ne sais pas ce que c'est que d'être sous-diacre ni que de résigner; mais tout me sera bon pourvu que j'aie Mlle de Saint-Yves à ma disposition. — Eh! Mon Dieu! Mon neveu, que me dites-vous là? Vous aimez donc cette belle demoiselle à la folie? — Oui, mon oncle. — Hélas! Mon neveu, il est impossible que vous l'épousiez. — Cela est très possible, mon oncle; car non seulement elle m'a serré la main en me quittant, mais elle m'a promis qu'elle me demanderait en mariage; et assurément je l'épouserai. — Cela est impossible, vous dis-je; elle est votre marraine : c'est un péché épouvantable à une marraine de serrer la main de son filleul; il n'est pas permis d'épouser sa marraine; les lois divines et humaines s'y opposent[3]. — Morbleu! Mon oncle, vous vous moquez de moi; pourquoi serait-il défendu d'épouser sa marraine, quand elle est jeune et jolie? Je n'ai point vu dans le livre que vous m'avez donné qu'il fût mal d'épouser les filles qui ont aidé les gens à être baptisés. Je m'aperçois tous les jours qu'on fait ici une infinité de choses qui ne sont point dans votre livre, et qu'on n'y fait rien de tout ce qu'il dit : je vous avoue que cela m'étonne et me fâche. Si on me

---

1. Le *diacre* est un ecclésiastique qui a reçu un ordre immédiatement inférieur à la prêtrise; le *sous-diacre* est son subordonné immédiat; 2. *Résigner :* se démettre d'un bénéfice en faveur de quelqu'un; 3. C'était vrai alors, le mariage civil n'existant pas. Voltaire fait souvent allusion à cette interdiction.

──────── **QUESTIONS** ────────

1. Il y a dans cette page un emploi exceptionnel chez Voltaire du style indirect; seule la réplique catégorique de l'Ingénu est en style direct : quel effet est ainsi obtenu? Pourquoi Voltaire glisse-t-il sur une suite d'événements où se complaisaient les auteurs de romans au XVIIIe siècle? Analysez le comique de cette page : qualité, formes, effet produit.

prive de la belle Saint-Yves, sous prétexte de mon baptême, je vous avertis que je l'enlève, et que je me débaptise. »

Le prieur fut confondu; sa sœur pleura. « Mon cher frère, dit-elle, il ne faut pas que notre neveu se damne; notre Saint Père le Pape peut lui donner dispense, et alors il pourra être chrétiennement heureux avec ce[1] qu'il aime. » L'Ingénu embrassa sa tante. « Quel est donc, dit-il, cet homme charmant qui favorise avec tant de bonté les garçons et les filles dans leurs amours? Je veux lui aller parler tout à l'heure[2]. »

On lui expliqua ce que c'était que le pape; et l'Ingénu fut encore plus étonné qu'auparavant. « Il n'y a pas un mot de tout cela dans votre livre, mon cher oncle; j'ai voyagé, je connais la mer; nous sommes ici sur la côte de l'océan; et je quitterais Mlle de Saint-Yves pour aller demander la permission de l'aimer à un homme qui demeure vers la Méditerranée, à quatre cents lieues d'ici, et dont je n'entends point la langue! Cela est d'un ridicule incompréhensible. Je vais sur-le-champ chez M. l'abbé de Saint-Yves, qui ne demeure qu'à une lieue de vous, et je vous réponds que j'épouserai ma maîtresse[3] dans la journée. » **(2)**

Comme il parlait encore, entra le bailli, qui, selon sa coutume, lui demanda où il allait. « Je vais me marier », dit l'Ingénu en courant; et au bout d'un quart d'heure il était déjà chez sa belle et chère Basse-Brette, qui dormait encore. « Ah! Mon frère! disait Mlle de Kerkabon au prieur, jamais vous ne ferez un sous-diacre de notre neveu. »

Le bailli fut très mécontent de ce voyage : car il prétendait que son fils épousât la Saint-Yves : et ce fils était encore plus sot et plus insupportable que son père. **(3)**

---

1. Cet emploi du neutre pour désigner l'objet aimé est un peu archaïque : il faisait partie de la langue de la galanterie au XVIIe siècle; 2. *Tout à l'heure :* aussitôt, immédiatement; 3. *Maîtresse :* femme que l'on aime et dont on est aimé. Au sens XVIIe siècle du mot : « On le dit particulièrement d'une fille qu'on recherche en mariage » (Dictionnaire de Furetière, 1690).

--- **QUESTIONS** ---

2. Thème de ce passage; comment est-il amené? Que veut démontrer Voltaire? Les différentes étapes du développement : soulignez-en la progression. A quoi aboutit-on? — En utilisant les renseignements donnés en note, montrez que ce passage contient des idées auxquelles le conteur est attaché. Pourquoi?

3. SUR L'ENSEMBLE DU CHAPITRE V. — La satire : son objet; ses moyens d'expression; sa portée.
— Le comique : au détriment de qui et de quoi s'exerce-t-il? L'Ingénu est-il comique de la même façon que ses antagonistes?

CHAPITRE VI

L'Ingénu court chez sa maîtresse et devient furieux.

A peine l'Ingénu était arrivé, qu'ayant demandé à une vieille servante où était la chambre de sa maîtresse, il avait poussé fortement la porte mal fermée, et s'était élancé vers le lit. Mlle de Saint-Yves, se réveillant en sursaut, s'était écriée : « Quoi! C'est vous! Ah! C'est vous! Arrêtez-vous, que faites-vous? » Il avait répondu : « Je vous épouse », et en effet il l'épousait, si elle ne s'était pas débattue avec toute l'honnêteté d'une personne qui a de l'éducation.

L'Ingénu n'entendait pas raillerie; il trouvait toutes ces façons-là extrêmement impertinentes. « Ce n'était pas ainsi qu'en usait Mlle Abacaba, ma première maîtresse; vous n'avez point de probité; vous m'avez promis mariage, et vous ne voulez point faire mariage : c'est manquer aux premières lois de l'honneur; je vous apprendrai à tenir votre parole, et je vous remettrai dans le chemin de la vertu. »

L'Ingénu possédait une vertu mâle et intrépide, digne de son patron Hercule, dont on lui avait donné le nom à son baptême; il allait l'exercer dans toute son étendue, lorsqu'aux cris perçants de la demoiselle plus discrètement vertueuse accourut le sage abbé de Saint-Yves, avec sa gouvernante, un vieux domestique dévot, et un prêtre de la paroisse. Cette vue modéra le courage de l'assaillant. « Eh, mon Dieu! Mon cher voisin, lui dit l'abbé, que faites-vous là? — Mon devoir, répliqua le jeune homme; je remplis mes promesses, qui sont sacrées. »

Mlle de Saint-Yves se rajusta en rougissant. On emmena l'Ingénu dans un autre appartement. L'abbé lui remontra l'énormité du procédé. L'Ingénu se défendit sur les privilèges de la loi naturelle[1], qu'il connaissait parfaitement. L'abbé voulut prouver que la loi positive devait avoir tout l'avantage, et que, sans les conventions faites entre les hommes, la loi de nature ne serait presque jamais qu'un brigandage naturel. « Il faut, lui disait-il, des notaires, des prêtres, des témoins,

---

1. Selon Voltaire, *loi de nature*, d'ailleurs synonyme de *droit naturel*, signifie tout ce qui est possible à un être selon les forces que lui donne la nature, sans aucune idée de bien ou de mal, puisqu'il n'existe pas encore de loi positive. C'est le sens où l'entend Spinoza, qu'il ne faut pas confondre avec celui que lui donne J.-J. Rousseau.

des contrats, des dispenses. » L'Ingénu lui répondit par la réflexion que les sauvages ont toujours faite : « Vous êtes donc de bien malhonnêtes gens, puisqu'il faut entre vous tant de précautions. »

L'abbé eut de la peine à résoudre cette difficulté. « Il y a, dit-il, je l'avoue, beaucoup d'inconstants et de fripons parmi nous; et il y en aurait autant chez les Hurons s'ils étaient rassemblés dans une grande ville; mais aussi il y a des âmes sages, honnêtes, éclairées, et ce sont ces hommes-là qui ont fait les lois. Plus on est homme de bien, plus on doit s'y soumettre : on donne l'exemple aux vicieux, qui respectent un frein que la vertu s'est donné elle-même[1]. »

Cette réponse frappa l'Ingénu. On a déjà remarqué qu'il avait l'esprit juste. On l'adoucit par des paroles flatteuses; on lui donna des espérances : ce sont les deux pièges où les hommes des deux hémisphères se prennent; on lui présenta même Mlle de Saint-Yves quand elle eut fait sa toilette. Tout se passa avec la plus grande bienséance; mais, malgré cette décence, les yeux étincelants de l'Ingénu Hercule firent toujours baisser ceux de sa maîtresse, et trembler la compagnie.

On eut une peine extrême à le renvoyer chez ses parents. Il fallut encore employer le crédit de la belle Saint-Yves; plus elle sentait son pouvoir sur lui, et plus elle l'aimait. Elle le fit partir, et en fut très affligée; enfin, quand il fut parti, l'abbé, qui non seulement était le frère très aîné de Mlle de Saint-Yves, mais qui était aussi son tuteur, prit le parti de soustraire sa pupille aux empressements de cet amant terrible. Il alla consulter le bailli, qui destinant toujours son fils à la sœur de l'abbé, lui conseilla de mettre la pauvre fille dans une communauté. Ce fut un coup terrible : une indifférente qu'on mettrait en couvent jetterait les hauts cris; mais une amante, et une amante aussi sage que tendre, c'était de quoi la mettre au désespoir.

L'Ingénu, de retour chez le prieur, raconta tout avec sa naïveté ordinaire. Il essuya les mêmes remontrances, qui firent quelque effet sur son esprit, et aucun sur ses sens; mais le

---

1. « Une société ne peut subsister sans lois » est une idée sur laquelle Voltaire n'a cessé d'insister. Ainsi dans les *Lettres philosophiques* (1728) [éd. Lanson, t. II, page 22] : « Nulle société d'hommes ne peut subsister un seul jour sans règles »; dans le *Traité de métaphysique* (1734) : « Pour qu'une société subsistât, il fallait des lois, comme il faut des règles à chaque jeu » (éd. Moland, t. XXII, page 224).

lendemain, quand il voulut retourner chez sa belle maîtresse pour raisonner avec elle sur la loi naturelle et sur la loi de convention, M. le bailli lui apprit avec une joie insultante qu'elle était dans un couvent. « Eh bien! dit-il, j'irai raisonner dans ce couvent. — Cela ne se peut », dit le bailli. Il lui expliqua fort au long ce que c'était qu'un couvent ou un convent; que ce mot venait du latin *conventus*, qui signifie assemblée; et le Huron ne pouvait comprendre pourquoi il ne pouvait pas être admis dans l'assemblée. Sitôt qu'il fut instruit que cette assemblée était une espèce de prison où l'on tenait les filles renfermées, chose horrible, inconnue chez les Hurons et chez les Anglais[1], il devint aussi furieux que le fut son patron Hercule lorsque Euryte, roi d'Œchalie, non moins cruel que l'abbé de Saint-Yves, lui refusa la belle Iole sa fille, non moins belle que la sœur de l'abbé. Il voulait aller mettre le feu au couvent, enlever sa maîtresse, ou se brûler avec elle. Mlle de Kerkabon, épouvantée, renonçait plus que jamais à toutes les espérances de voir son neveu sous-diacre, et disait en pleurant qu'il avait le diable au corps depuis qu'il était baptisé. **(1)**

CHAPITRE VII

L'Ingénu repousse les Anglais.

L'Ingénu, plongé dans une sombre et profonde mélancolie, se promena vers le bord de la mer, son fusil à deux coups sur

---

1. A rapprocher d'un fragment de lettre à Frédéric II (5 avril 1767) : « Votre idée de l'attaquer [la superstition] par les moines est d'un grand capitaine. Les moines une fois abolis, l'erreur est exposée au mépris universel. » Dans *l'Observateur hollandais*, t. I, page 219, on lit : « La philosophie qui pénètre insensiblement dans toutes les classes des citoyens a de beaucoup tari les monastères, asiles de la bigoterie et du fanatisme. » En 1775, Diderot fera paraître *la Religieuse*, roman dirigé contre les vocations contraintes.

■ **QUESTIONS**

1. SUR LE CHAPITRE VI. — Justifiez le titre donné par Voltaire à ce chapitre. Enferme-t-il toute la substance de ce passage? Pourquoi?

— Soulignez la progression dramatique et pathétique. Quel rôle joue la comparaison faite, à des moments déterminés, entre l'Ingénu et son patron Hercule?

— L'Ingénu et la société : Voltaire donne-t-il toujours raison à son héros? Effet produit par le fait que Mlle de Saint-Yves convainc l'Ingénu quand les raisonnements n'y parviennent pas.

— Les formes du comique dans ce chapitre.

DIALOGUES
Ou Entretiens entre un Sauvage,

Et le

BARON de LAHONTAN.

LAHONTAN.

'Est avec beaucoup de plaisir, mon cher Adario, que je veux raisonner avec toy de la plus importante affaire qui soit au Monde; puisqu'il s'agit de te découvrir les grandes veritez du Christianisme.

ADARIO.

Je suis prêt à t'écouter, mon cher Frére, afin de m'éclaircir de tant de choses que les Jésuites nous prêchent depuis long temps, & je veux que nous parlions ensemble avec autant de liberté que faire se pourra. Si ta Créance est semblable à celle que les Jésuites nous prêchent, il est inutile que nous entrions en Conversation, Car ils m'ont débité tant de fables, que tout ce que j'en puis croire, c'est qu'ils ont trop d'esprit pour les croire eux-mêmes.

LAHONTAN.

Je ne sçai pas ce qu'ils t'ont dit, mais je crois que leurs paroles & les miennes se rapor-

Une des sources de Voltaire, pour l'*Ingénu*, les *Dialogues ou Entretiens entre un sauvage et le baron de La Hontan,* publiés à Amsterdam en 1704.

l'épaule, son grand coutelas au côté, tirant de temps en temps sur quelques oiseaux, et souvent tenté de tirer sur lui-même; mais il aimait encore la vie, à cause de Mlle de Saint-Yves. Tantôt il maudissait son oncle, sa tante, et toute la Basse-Bretagne, et son baptême; tantôt il les bénissait, puisqu'ils lui avaient fait connaître celle qu'il aimait. Il prenait sa résolution d'aller brûler le couvent[1], et il s'arrêtait tout court, de peur de brûler sa maîtresse. Les flots de la Manche ne sont pas plus agités par les vents d'est et d'ouest que son cœur l'était par tant de mouvements contraires.

Il marchait à grands pas, sans savoir où, lorsqu'il entendit le son du tambour. Il vit de loin tout un peuple dont une moitié courait au rivage, et l'autre s'enfuyait. (1)

Mille cris s'élèvent de tous côtés; la curiosité et le courage le précipitent à l'instant vers l'endroit d'où partaient ces clameurs : il y vole en quatre bonds. Le commandant de la milice, qui avait soupé avec lui chez le prieur, le reconnut aussitôt; il court à lui, les bras ouverts : « Ah! c'est l'Ingénu, il combattra pour nous. » Et les milices, qui mouraient de peur, se rassurèrent et crièrent aussi : « C'est l'Ingénu! C'est l'Ingénu! »

« Messieurs, dit-il, de quoi s'agit-il? Pourquoi êtes-vous si effarés? A-t-on mis vos maîtresses dans des couvents? » Alors, cent voix confuses s'écrient : « Ne voyez-vous pas les Anglais qui abordent[2]? — Eh bien! répliqua le Huron, ce sont de braves gens; ils ne m'ont jamais proposé de me faire sous-diacre; ils ne m'ont point enlevé ma maîtresse. »

Le commandant lui fit entendre que les Anglais venaient piller l'abbaye de la Montagne, boire le vin de son oncle, et peut-être enlever Mlle de Saint-Yves; que le petit vaisseau sur lequel il avait abordé en Bretagne n'était venu que pour reconnaître la côte; qu'ils faisaient des actes d'hostilité sans

1. Le mot, qui s'écrivait tantôt *convent*, tantôt *couvent*, prend, depuis Richelet (1680), sa forme actuelle. L'étymologie que donne Voltaire au chapitre précédent est exacte (*conventus*, réunion); 2. Le récit est censé se dérouler en 1689. De fait, il y eut des débarquements anglais à cette époque : c'était durant les tentatives de Jacques II en vue de récupérer son royaume d'Irlande. Mais il y avait des souvenirs plus récents : en 1758, à Saint-Cast, avait eu lieu un débarquement anglais.

QUESTIONS

1. Les imprécations de l'Ingénu : montrez qu'elles constituent un lien avec la réflexion de Mlle de Kerkabon qui clôt le chapitre VI. Soulignez le comique d'expression ici et dans la fin du chapitre précédent.

avoir déclaré la guerre au roi de France, et que la province était exposée. « Ah! si cela est, ils violent la loi naturelle[1]; laissez-moi faire; j'ai demeuré longtemps parmi eux, je sais leur langue, je leur parlerai; je ne crois pas qu'ils puissent avoir un si méchant dessein. »

Pendant cette conversation, l'escadre anglaise approchait; voilà le Huron qui court vers elle, se jette dans un petit bateau, arrive, monte au vaisseau amiral, et demande s'il est vrai qu'ils viennent ravager le pays sans avoir déclaré la guerre honnêtement[2]. L'amiral et tout son bord firent de grands éclats de rire, lui firent boire du punch[3], et le renvoyèrent.

L'Ingénu, piqué, ne songea plus qu'à se bien battre contre ses anciens amis, pour ses compatriotes et pour M. le prieur. Les gentilshommes du voisinage accouraient de toutes parts; il se joint à eux : on avait quelques canons; il les charge, il les pointe, il les tire l'un après l'autre. Les Anglais débarquent; il court à eux, il en tue trois de sa main, il blesse même l'amiral, qui s'était moqué de lui. Sa valeur anime le courage de toute la milice; les Anglais se rembarquent, et toute la côte retentissait des cris de victoire : vive le roi, vive l'Ingénu! Chacun l'embrassait, chacun s'empressait d'étancher le sang de quelques blessures légères qu'il avait reçues. « Ah! disait-il, si Mlle de Saint-Yves était là, elle me mettrait une compresse. » (2)

Le bailli, qui s'était caché dans sa cave pendant le combat[4],

---

1. En 1751, Voltaire, retiré chez la margrave de Bayreuth, avait médité un *Poème sur la loi naturelle*; il y développait les thèmes essentiels d'un ouvrage de Diderot, composé en 1747, mais publié seulement en 1770 et intitulé *Suffisance de la religion naturelle* : il existe une morale universelle, indépendante de tout système philosophique ou religieux. C'est à cette loi naturelle, à cette religion naturelle, donc au déisme, que croit l'Ingénu. En somme, il obéit au sentiment de la justice que lui a donné Dieu; 2. Peut-être une réminiscence de *la Guerre picrocholine* : la correspondance de Voltaire avec Mme du Deffand révèle qu'au moment où il composait *l'Ingénu*, Voltaire, d'abord rebuté, revient à Rabelais; 3. Voltaire ne dédaigne pas toujours les images d'Épinal : l'Anglais, amateur de punch, en est une; 4. Il y a là probablement une transposition : le duc d'Aiguillon, en 1758, gouverneur de la province, s'était lui aussi caché, non dans une cave, mais dans un moulin : sur les instances du duc de Richelieu, Voltaire avait renoncé à monter en épingle, comme il en avait l'intention, cette attitude ridicule et lâche lorsqu'il rédigea le *Précis du siècle de Louis XV*; mais il ne résista pas à transposer l'aventure dans *l'Ingénu*.

QUESTIONS

2. Un débarquement repoussé : lieu commun de la littérature dramatique; citez-en quelques exemples; en quoi le thème est-il renouvelé ici par Voltaire? — De nouveau, l'Ingénu est le personnage central. Rappelez toutes les scènes dont il a été le héros jusqu'à maintenant. Le procédé varie-t-il cette fois? — Quel effet produit la dernière réplique de l'Ingénu?

vint lui faire compliment comme les autres. Mais il fut bien surpris quand il entendit Hercule l'Ingénu dire à une douzaine de jeunes gens de bonne volonté, dont il était entouré : « Mes amis, ce n'est rien d'avoir délivré l'abbaye de la Montagne; il faut délivrer une fille. » Toute cette bouillante jeunesse prit feu à ces seules paroles. On le suivait déjà en foule, on courait au couvent. Si le bailli n'avait pas sur-le-champ averti le commandant, si on n'avait pas couru après la troupe joyeuse, c'en était fait. On ramena l'Ingénu chez son oncle et sa tante, qui le baignèrent de larmes de tendresse.

« Je vois bien que vous ne serez jamais ni diacre ni sous-diacre, lui dit l'oncle; vous serez un officier encore plus brave que mon frère le capitaine, et probablement aussi gueux. » Et Mlle de Kerkabon pleurait toujours en l'embrassant, et en disant : « Il se fera tuer comme mon frère; il vaudrait bien mieux qu'il fût sous-diacre. »

L'Ingénu, dans le combat, avait ramassé une grosse bourse remplie de guinées[1], que probablement l'amiral avait laissé tomber. Il ne douta pas qu'avec cette bourse il ne pût acheter toute la Basse-Bretagne, et surtout faire Mlle de Saint-Yves grande dame. Chacun l'exhorta de faire le voyage de Versailles pour y recevoir le prix de ses services. Le commandant, les principaux officiers, le comblèrent de certificats. L'oncle et la tante approuvèrent le voyage du neveu. Il devait être, sans difficulté, présenté au roi : cela seul lui donnerait un prodigieux relief dans la province. Ces deux bonnes gens ajoutèrent à la bourse anglaise un présent considérable de leurs épargnes[2]. L'Ingénu disait en lui-même : « Quand je verrai le roi, je lui demanderai Mlle de Saint-Yves en mariage, et certainement il ne me la refusera pas. » Il partit donc aux acclamations de tout le canton, étouffé d'embrassements, baigné des larmes de sa tante, béni par son oncle, et se recommandant à la belle Saint-Yves. (3) (4)

---

1. Pièce de monnaie équivalant à l'actuel *souverain*; 2. Constitué au moyen de leurs économies.

─────── **QUESTIONS** ───────

3. Les « excentricités » de l'Ingénu; rappelez comment chacune d'elles provoque une intervention du bailli; quel effet résulte du retour de la même situation? — Montrez la constance de l'attitude de Mlle de Kerkabon depuis le début du roman.

Question 4, voir page 95.

CHAPITRE VIII

L'Ingénu va en cour. Il soupe en chemin avec des huguenots.

L'Ingénu prit le chemin de Saumur[1] par le coche, parce qu'il n'y avait point alors d'autre commodité. Quand il fut à Saumur, il s'étonna de trouver la ville presque déserte, et de voir plusieurs familles qui déménageaient. On lui dit que, six ans auparavant, Saumur contenait plus de quinze mille âmes, et qu'à présent il n'y en avait pas six mille. Il ne manqua pas d'en parler à souper dans son hôtellerie. Plusieurs protestants étaient à table : les uns se plaignaient amèrement, d'autres frémissaient de colère, d'autres disaient en pleurant :

> ... Nos dulcia linquimus arva,
> Nos patriam fugimus[2].

L'Ingénu, qui ne savait pas le latin, se fit expliquer ces paroles, qui signifient : Nous abandonnons nos douces campagnes, nous fuyons notre patrie.

« Et pourquoi fuyez-vous votre patrie, messieurs? — C'est qu'on veut que nous reconnaissions le pape — Et pourquoi ne le reconnaîtriez-vous pas? Vous n'avez donc point de marraines que vous vouliez épouser? Car on m'a dit que c'était lui qui en donnait la permission. — Ah! Monsieur, ce pape dit qu'il est le maître du domaine des rois. — Mais, messieurs, de quelle profession êtes-vous? — Monsieur, nous sommes pour la plupart des drapiers et des fabricants. — Si votre pape

---

1. A comparer avec l'article « Saumur » de l'*Encyclopédie*. Henri IV avait nommé un gouverneur qui « fit fleurir le calvinisme à Saumur, et y forma une académie de toutes les sciences. Cette ville n'est plus que l'ombre de ce qu'elle était alors; il y reste à peine cinq mille âmes; cette grande diminution vient de la suppression des temples, du collège, et de l'académie, qui y attiraient beaucoup de religionnaires étrangers »; 2. Virgile, *Eglogues*, I.

QUESTIONS

4. Sur l'ensemble du chapitre VII. — Relevez les passages qui s'apparentent au roman larmoyant.

— Qu'y a-t-il de comique dans l'opposition entre les sentiments de toutes les personnes présentes et le projet que médite secrètement l'Ingénu?

— Les derniers mots : en quel sens résument-ils et préparent-ils tous les états d'âme par lesquels passe l'Ingénu?

— Montrez comment, dans l'ensemble du chapitre VII, interfèrent les thèmes philosophiques chers à Voltaire, les réminiscences littéraires, les allusions historiques.

dit qu'il est le maître de vos draps et de vos fabriques, vous faites très bien de ne pas le reconnaître; mais pour les rois, c'est leur affaire; de quoi vous mêlez-vous? » Alors un petit homme noir prit la parole, et exposa très savamment les griefs de la compagnie. Il parla de la révocation de l'édit de Nantes avec tant d'énergie, il déplora d'une manière si pathétique le sort de cinquante mille familles fugitives[1] et de cinquante mille autres converties par les dragons, que l'Ingénu à son tour versa des larmes. « D'où vient donc, disait-il, qu'un si grand roi, dont la gloire s'étend jusque chez les Hurons, se prive ainsi de tant de cœurs qui l'auraient aimé, et de tant de bras qui l'auraient servi?

— C'est qu'on l'a trompé comme les autres grands rois, répondit l'homme noir[2]. On lui a fait croire que, dès qu'il aurait dit un mot, tous les hommes penseraient comme lui; et qu'il nous ferait changer de religion comme son musicien Lulli[3] fait changer en un moment les décorations de ses opéras. Non seulement il perd déjà cinq à six cent mille sujets très utiles, mais il s'en fait des ennemis; et le roi Guillaume, qui est actuellement maître de l'Angleterre, a composé plusieurs régiments de ces mêmes Français qui auraient combattu pour leur monarque.

« Un tel désastre est d'autant plus étonnant que le pape régnant, à qui Louis XIV sacrifie une partie de son peuple, est son ennemi déclaré[4]. Ils ont encore tous deux, depuis neuf ans, une querelle violente. Elle a été poussée si loin que la France a espéré enfin de voir briser le joug qui la soumet depuis tant de siècles à cet étranger et surtout de ne lui plus donner d'argent, ce qui est le premier mobile des affaires de ce monde. Il paraît donc évident qu'on a trompé ce grand roi sur ses intérêts comme sur l'étendue de son pouvoir, et que l'on a donné atteinte à la magnanimité de son cœur. »

---

1. Voir *le Siècle de Louis XIV*, chap. XXXVI, « Classiques Larousse », p. 114; 2. Il s'agit d'un pasteur protestant. Dans *Candide*, la même expression sert à désigner un prêtre catholique : « Un petit homme noir familier de l'Inquisition... » (*Candide*, chap. V, « Classiques Larousse »; *Contes*, II, page 26). Le « De quoi vous mêlez-vous? » qui précède immédiatement est la transposition d'une réponse de Fontenelle à un commerçant rouennais janséniste; 3. Depuis 1673, *Lulli* fut titulaire du privilège de l'Opéra, pendant exact du privilège des Comédiens du roi. A la mort de Molière, Lulli s'installa au Palais-Royal; 4. Allusion à la querelle dite « de la Régale ». Comparez avec Voltaire, *Histoire du parlement de Paris*, chap. LVIII.

L'Ingénu, attendri de plus en plus, demanda quels étaient les Français qui trompaient ainsi un monarque si cher aux Hurons. « Ce sont les jésuites[1], lui répondit-on; c'est surtout le père de La Chaise[2], confesseur de Sa Majesté. Il faut espérer que Dieu les en punira un jour, et qu'ils seront chassés comme ils nous chassent[3]. Y a-t-il un malheur égal aux nôtres? M. de Louvois nous envoie de tous côtés des jésuites et des dragons. — Oh bien, messieurs, répliqua l'Ingénu, qui ne pouvait plus se contenir, je vais à Versailles recevoir la récompense due à mes services; je parlerai à ce M. de Louvois : on m'a dit que c'est lui qui fait la guerre, de son cabinet. Je verrai le roi, je lui ferai connaître la vérité; il est impossible qu'on ne se rende pas à cette vérité quand on la sent. Je reviendrai bientôt pour épouser Mlle de Saint-Yves, et je vous prie à la noce. » Ces bonnes gens le prirent alors pour un grand seigneur qui voyageait *incognito* par le coche. Quelques-uns le prirent pour le fou du roi.

Il y avait à table un jésuite déguisé qui servait d'espion au révérend père de La Chaise. Il lui rendait compte de tout, et le père de La Chaise en instruisait M. de Louvois. L'espion écrivit. L'Ingénu et la lettre arrivèrent presque en même temps à Versailles. **(1)**

---

1. Ce passage est à rapprocher d'un ouvrage de d'Alembert, *Sur la destruction des jésuites en France,* que Voltaire fait rééditer à Genève en même temps qu'il compose *l'Ingénu;* **2.** L'influence du père de La Chaise, confesseur du roi depuis 1675, et qui le resta jusqu'en 1709, reste à prouver. Ne pas oublier que *l'Ingénu* a été publié trois ans après l'expulsion des jésuites; **3.** En 1767, les persécutions contre les protestants se poursuivaient. Et Voltaire s'occupait d'eux, comme le prouve entre autres une lettre à M. Vernes (septembre 1766).

═══ QUESTIONS ═══

1. SUR LE CHAPITRE VIII. — Le ton est-il le même que dans les chapitres précédents? Pourquoi? Quelle est l'importance du rôle de l'Ingénu ici? Montrez que le thème développé explique ce relatif effacement.

— Quel effet produit l'attitude toujours identique de l'Ingénu chaque fois qu'il fait une découverte? Rapprochez du chapitre précédent (épisode de l'amiral anglais).

— Relevez dans ce chapitre les éléments historiques authentiques. Relevez les transpositions historiques.

— En quoi, allusions et transpositions correspondent-elles aux préoccupations de Voltaire en 1767? Utilisez les documents donnés en note. Relevez les thèmes qui tiennent au cœur de l'auteur d'une manière permanente.

CHAPITRE IX

Arrivée de l'Ingénu à Versailles.
Sa réception à la cour.

L'Ingénu débarque en pot de chambre[1] dans la cour des cuisines. Il demande aux porteurs de chaise à quelle heure on peut voir le roi. Les porteurs lui rient au nez, tout comme avait fait l'amiral anglais. Il les traita de même, il les battit; ils voulurent le lui rendre, et la scène allait être sanglante s'il n'eût passé un garde du corps, gentilhomme breton, qui écarta la canaille[2]. « Monsieur, lui dit le voyageur, vous me paraissez un brave homme; je suis le neveu de monsieur le prieur de Notre-Dame de la Montagne; j'ai tué des Anglais, je viens parler au roi; je vous prie de me mener dans sa chambre. » Le garde, ravi de trouver un brave de sa province, qui ne paraissait pas au fait des usages de la cour, lui apprit qu'on ne parlait pas ainsi au roi, et qu'il fallait être présenté par Mgr de Louvois. « Eh bien! menez-moi donc chez ce Mgr de Louvois, qui sans doute me conduira chez Sa Majesté. — Il est encore plus difficile, répliqua le garde, de parler à Mgr de Louvois qu'à Sa Majesté; mais je vais vous conduire chez M. Alexandre, le premier commis[3] de la guerre : c'est comme si vous parliez au ministre. » Ils vont donc chez M. Alexandre, premier commis, et ils ne purent être introduits; il était en affaire avec une dame de la cour, et il y avait ordre de ne laisser entrer personne. « Eh bien! dit le garde, il n'y a rien de perdu; allons chez le premier commis de M. Alexandre : c'est comme si vous parliez à M. Alexandre lui-même. »

Le Huron, tout étonné, le suit; ils restent ensemble une demi-heure dans une petite antichambre. « Qu'est-ce donc que tout ceci? dit l'Ingénu; est-ce que tout le monde est invisible dans ce pays-ci? Il est bien plus aisé de se battre en Basse-Bretagne contre des Anglais que de rencontrer à Versailles les gens à qui on a affaire. » Il se désennuya en racontant ses amours à son compatriote. Mais l'heure en sonnant rappela

---

1. C'est une voiture de Paris à Versailles, laquelle ressemble à un petit tombereau couvert (note de Voltaire); 2. *La canaille* : les gens de la plus basse condition d'un lieu. « Petites gens » (Dictionnaire de Richelet, 1680); 3. Un *commis* est « celui qui est commis par un autre à quelque emploi dont il doit lui rendre compte » (Dictionnaire de l'Académie, 1694). Un *premier commis* est donc un directeur de service, qui vient immédiatement au-dessous du ministre. M. Alexandre avait effectivement tenu cet emploi auprès de Louvois.

le garde du corps à son poste. Ils se promirent de se revoir le lendemain, et l'Ingénu resta encore une autre demi-heure dans l'antichambre, en rêvant à Mlle de Saint-Yves, et à la difficulté de parler aux rois et aux premiers commis. (1)

Enfin le patron parut. « Monsieur, lui dit l'Ingénu, si j'avais attendu pour repousser les Anglais aussi longtemps que vous m'avez fait attendre mon audience, ils ravageraient actuellement la Basse-Bretagne tout à leur aise. » Ces paroles frappèrent le commis. Il dit enfin au Breton : « Que demandez-vous? — Récompense, dit l'autre; voici mes titres. » Il lui étala tous ses certificats. Le commis lut, et lui dit que probablement on lui accorderait la permission d'acheter une lieutenance¹. « Moi! que je donne de l'argent pour avoir repoussé les Anglais? Que je paye le droit de me faire tuer pour vous, pendant que vous donnez ici vos audiences tranquillement? Je crois que vous voulez rire. Je veux une compagnie de cavalerie pour rien; je veux que le roi fasse sortir Mlle de Saint-Yves du couvent, et qu'il me la donne par mariage; je veux parler au roi en faveur de cinquante mille familles que je prétends lui rendre. En un mot, je veux être utile; qu'on m'emploie, et qu'on m'avance.

— Comment vous nommez-vous, monsieur, qui parlez si haut? — Oh! Oh! reprit l'Ingénu, vous n'avez donc pas lu mes certificats? C'est donc ainsi qu'on en use? Je m'appelle Hercule de Kerkabon; je suis baptisé, je loge au *Cadran bleu*, et je me plaindrai de vous au roi. » Le commis conclut comme les gens de Saumur, qu'il n'avait pas la tête bien saine, et n'y fit pas grande attention.

Ce même jour, le révérend père de La Chaise, confesseur de Louis XIV, avait reçu la lettre de son espion, qui accusait le Breton Kerkabon de favoriser dans son cœur les huguenots, et de condamner la conduite des jésuites. M. de Louvois, de

---

1. Voltaire revient sans cesse sur la vénalité des charges. Ainsi dans *le Monde comme il va* (conte publié en 1748), il représente un chef militaire comparant sa charge avec celle d'un magistrat : « Pourquoi ne voulez-vous pas qu'on achète les emplois de la robe? J'ai bien acheté, moi, le droit d'affronter la mort à la tête de deux mille hommes, que je commande. »

--- **QUESTIONS** ---

1. Relevez les traits satiriques dirigés contre l'administration royale. En utilisant vos souvenirs de La Bruyère, de Saint-Simon et de Voltaire lui-même, montrez que ces allusions n'ont en soi rien de nouveau. En quoi le conte de Voltaire demeure-t-il pourtant original?

son côté, avait reçu une lettre de l'interrogant bailli, qui dépeignait l'Ingénu comme un garnement qui voulait brûler les couvents et enlever les filles. (2)

L'Ingénu, après s'être promené dans les jardins de Versailles[1], où il s'ennuya, après avoir soupé en Huron et en Bas-Breton, s'était couché dans la douce espérance de voir le roi le lendemain, d'obtenir Mlle de Saint-Yves en mariage, d'avoir au moins une compagnie de cavalerie, et de faire cesser la persécution contre les huguenots. Il se berçait de ces flatteuses idées, quand la maréchaussée entre dans sa chambre. Elle se saisit d'abord de son fusil à deux coups et de son grand sabre.

On fit un inventaire de son argent comptant, et on le mena dans le château que fit construire le roi Charles V, fils de Jean II, auprès de la rue Saint-Antoine, à la porte des Tournelles[2].

Quel était en chemin l'étonnement de l'Ingénu, je vous le laisse à penser. Il crut d'abord que c'était un rêve. Il resta dans l'engourdissement; puis tout à coup transporté d'une fureur qui redoublait ses forces, il prend à la gorge deux de ses conducteurs qui étaient avec lui dans le carrosse, les jette par la portière, se jette après eux, et entraîne le troisième qui voulait le retenir. Il tombe de l'effort, on le lie, on le remonte dans la voiture. « Voilà donc, disait-il, ce que l'on gagne à chasser les Anglais de la Basse-Bretagne! Que dirais-tu, belle Saint-Yves, si tu me voyais dans cet état? »

On arrive enfin au gîte qui lui était destiné. On le porte dans la chambre où il devait être enfermé, comme un mort qu'on porte dans un cimetière. Cette chambre était déjà occupée par un vieux solitaire de Port-Royal nommé Gordon, qui y languissait depuis deux ans. « Tenez, lui dit le chef des sbires, voilà de la compagnie que je vous amène. » Et sur-le-champ

---

1. Voltaire se promenait volontiers dans les jardins de Versailles : un rapport d'un commissaire de police, daté de 1745, signale cette habitude et précise qu'il prenait place « dans une des calèches à bras du roi traînée par des Suisses »; 2. Périphrase analogue dans le poème que consacra Voltaire à sa propre arrestation (*la Bastille*, 1717) : « Royal réduit que près Saint-Paul ont vu bâtir nos pères par Charles V. »

━━━━━ QUESTIONS ━━━━━

2. Le récit est solidement charpenté : montrez le parallélisme entre la scène de Saumur et celle de Versailles; entre les faits et la double dénonciation. — Quel effet produit l'interférence de l'aventure sentimentale du Huron et des hautes considérations dont il fait état à tout moment?

on referma les énormes verroux de la porte épaisse, revêtue de larges barres. Les deux captifs restèrent séparés de l'Univers entier. (3) (4)

CHAPITRE X

L'Ingénu enfermé¹ à la Bastille avec un janséniste.

M. Gordon était un vieillard frais et serein, qui savait deux grandes choses : supporter l'adversité, et consoler les malheureux. Il s'avança d'un air ouvert et compatissant vers son compagnon, et lui dit en l'embrassant : « Qui que vous soyez qui venez partager mon tombeau, soyez sûr que je m'oublierai toujours moi-même pour adoucir vos tourments dans l'abîme infernal où nous sommes plongés. Adorons la Providence qui nous y a conduits, souffrons en paix, et espérons². » Ces paroles firent sur l'âme de l'Ingénu l'effet des gouttes d'Angleterre³, qui rappellent un mourant à la vie, et lui font entr'ouvrir des yeux étonnés.

Après les premiers compliments, Gordon, sans le presser de lui apprendre la cause de son malheur, lui inspira, par la douceur de son entretien, et par cet intérêt que prennent deux malheureux l'un à l'autre⁴, le désir d'ouvrir son cœur et de

---

1. La situation permet sans invraisemblance de longues discussions philosophiques. Comparez avec *Candide* (chap. XX); 2. Voltaire a étudié de près les œuvres des solitaires de Port-Royal. Voir *le Siècle de Louis XIV*, chap. XXXVII; 3. *Gouttes d'Angleterre :* cordial qui aurait été inventé sous Cromwell par Jonathan Goddard (1617-1674); 4. Idée chère à Voltaire et qui jalonne toute son œuvre.

--- QUESTIONS ---

3. Rappelez comment, depuis Marot *(l'Enfer)*, le thème de la prison (arrestations, captivités, évasions, etc.) a connu en France une fortune toujours plus grande; au XVIIIᵉ siècle, Voltaire, Diderot, Beaumarchais n'ont cessé de l'enrichir.

4. SUR L'ENSEMBLE DU CHAPITRE IX. — Comment nous est présentée l'administration de Louis XIV ? Montrez que le comique accentue l'impression produite. La situation de l'Ingénu ne devient-elle pas ainsi paradoxale ?
— Le caractère du Huron : en quoi se révèle-t-il ici fidèle à sa manière générale d'agir ? Valeur dramatique et comique de sa confrontation avec l'administration de Versailles.
— Portée de la critique voltairienne dans ce chapitre.
— Originalité de ce chapitre IX.

déposer le fardeau qui l'accablait; mais il ne pouvait deviner le sujet de son malheur : cela lui paraissait un effet sans cause; et le bonhomme Gordon était aussi étonné que lui-même.

« Il faut, dit le janséniste au Huron, que Dieu ait de grands desseins sur vous, puisqu'il vous a conduit du lac Ontario en Angleterre et en France, qu'il vous a fait baptiser en Basse-Bretagne, et qu'il vous a mis ici pour votre salut[1]. — Ma foi, répondit l'Ingénu, je crois que le diable s'est mêlé seul de ma destinée. Mes compatriotes d'Amérique ne m'auraient jamais traité avec la barbarie que j'éprouve : ils n'en ont pas d'idée. On les appelle *sauvages;* ce sont des gens de bien grossiers, et les hommes de ce pays-ci sont des coquins raffinés. Je suis, à la vérité, bien surpris d'être venu d'un autre monde pour être enfermé dans celui-ci sous quatre verrous avec un prêtre; mais je fais réflexion au nombre prodigieux d'hommes qui partent d'un hémisphère pour aller se faire tuer dans l'autre, ou qui font naufrage en chemin, et qui sont mangés des poissons : je ne vois pas les gracieux desseins de Dieu sur tous ces gens-là. »

On leur apporta à dîner par un guichet. La conversation roula sur la Providence, sur les lettres de cachet, et sur l'art de ne pas succomber aux disgrâces auxquelles tout homme est exposé dans ce monde. « Il y a deux ans que je suis ici, dit le vieillard, sans autre consolation que moi-même et des livres; je n'ai pas eu un moment de mauvaise humeur.

— Ah! Monsieur Gordon, s'écria l'Ingénu, vous n'aimez donc pas votre marraine? Si vous connaissiez comme moi Mlle de Saint-Yves, vous seriez au désespoir. » A ces mots il ne put retenir ses larmes, et il se sentit alors un peu moins oppressé. « Mais, dit-il, pourquoi donc les larmes soulagent-elles? Il me semble qu'elles devraient faire un effet contraire.

— Mon fils, tout est physique en nous, dit le bon veillard; toute sécrétion fait du bien au corps; et tout ce qui le soulage soulage l'âme : nous sommes les machines de la Providence[2]. »

L'Ingénu qui, comme nous l'avons dit plusieurs fois, avait un grand fonds d'esprit, fit de profondes réflexions sur cette idée, dont il semblait qu'il avait la semence en lui-même.

---

1. La Providence divine, au sens janséniste du mot, fait de l'Ingénu un élu; 2. Dans les *Lettres philosophiques*, Voltaire avait déjà écrit : « ... nous sommes machines... nos âmes dépendent de l'action des corps. »

Après quoi il demanda à son compagnon pourquoi sa machine était depuis deux ans sous quatre verrous. « Par la grâce efficace[1], répondit Gordon ; je passe pour janséniste : j'ai connu Arnauld et Nicole ; les jésuites nous ont persécutés. Nous croyons que le pape n'est qu'un évêque comme un autre ; et c'est pour cela que le père de La Chaise a obtenu du roi, son pénitent, un ordre de me ravir, sans aucune formalité de justice, le bien le plus précieux des hommes, la liberté.

— Voilà qui est bien étrange, dit l'Ingénu ; tous les malheureux que j'ai rencontrés ne le sont qu'à cause du pape. A l'égard de votre grâce efficace, je vous avoue que je n'y entends rien ; mais je regarde comme une grande grâce que Dieu m'ait fait trouver dans mon malheur un homme comme vous, qui verse dans mon cœur des consolations dont je me croyais incapable. »

Chaque jour la conversation devenait plus intéressante et plus instructive. Les âmes des deux captifs s'attachaient l'une à l'autre. Le vieillard savait beaucoup, et le jeune homme voulait beaucoup apprendre. Au bout d'un mois il étudia la géométrie ; il la dévorait. Gordon lui fit lire la *Physique* de Rohault[2], qui était encore à la mode, et il eut le bon esprit de n'y trouver que des incertitudes.

Ensuite il lut le premier volume de la *Recherche de la vérité*[3]. Cette nouvelle lumière l'éclaira. « Quoi ! dit-il, notre imagination et nos sens nous trompent à ce point ! Quoi ! les objets ne forment point nos idées, et nous ne pouvons nous les donner nous-mêmes. » Quand il eut lu le second volume, il ne fut plus si content, et il conclut qu'il est plus aisé de détruire que de bâtir.

Son confrère, étonné qu'un jeune ignorant fît cette réflexion, qui n'appartient qu'aux âmes exercées, conçut une grande idée de son esprit, et s'attacha à lui davantage.

« Votre Malebranche, lui dit un jour l'Ingénu, me paraît

---

1. Ici apparaît la terminologie janséniste, qui émaillait par exemple les *Provinciales*. L'expulsion des jésuites n'a pas suffi à apaiser les philosophes, qui s'attaquent aussi aux jansénistes ; 2. « *Rohault* (Jacques), né à Amiens en 1620. Il abrégea et il exposa avec clarté et méthode la philosophie de Descartes ; mais aujourd'hui cette philosophie, erronée presque en tout, n'a d'autre mérite que celui d'avoir été opposée aux erreurs anciennes. Mort en 1675 » (Voltaire, *Catalogue des grands écrivains du siècle de Louis XIV*) ; 3. « *Malebranche* (Nicolas), né à Paris en 1638, de l'Oratoire, l'un des plus profonds méditatifs qui aient jamais écrit... Il a montré admirablement les erreurs des sens et de l'imagination, et, quand il a voulu sonder la nature de l'âme, il s'est perdu dans cet abîme comme les autres » (Voltaire, *Ibid.*).

avoir écrit la moitié de son livre avec sa raison, et l'autre avec son imagination et ses préjugés[1]. »

Quelques jours après, Gordon lui demanda : « Que pensez-vous donc de l'âme, de la manière dont nous recevons nos idées, de notre volonté, de la grâce, du libre arbitre? — Rien, lui repartit l'Ingénu; si je pensais quelque chose, c'est que nous sommes sous la puissance de l'Etre éternel comme les astres et les éléments; qu'il fait tout en nous[2], que nous sommes de petites roues de la machine immense dont il est l'âme; qu'il agit par des lois générales, et non par des vues particulières : cela seul me paraît intelligible; tout le reste est pour moi un abîme de ténèbres[3].

— Mais, mon fils, ce serait faire Dieu auteur du péché.

— Mais, mon père, votre grâce efficace ferait Dieu auteur du péché aussi : car il est certain que tous ceux à qui cette grâce serait refusée pécheraient; et qui nous livre au mal n'est-il pas l'auteur du mal[4]? »

Cette naïveté embarrassait fort le bonhomme; il sentait qu'il faisait de vains efforts pour se tirer de ce bourbier; et il entassait tant de paroles qui paraissaient avoir du sens et qui n'en avaient point (dans le goût de la prémotion physique[5]), que l'Ingénu en avait pitié. Cette question tenait évidemment à l'origine du bien et du mal; et alors il fallait que le pauvre Gordon passât en revue la boîte de Pandore, l'œuf d'Orosmade percé par Arimane, l'inimitié entre Typhon et Osiris, et enfin le péché originel; et ils couraient l'un et l'autre dans cette nuit profonde, sans jamais se rencontrer. Mais enfin ce roman de l'âme détournait leur vue de la contemplation de leur propre misère, et par un charme étrange, la foule des calamités répan-

---

1. Astucieux jeu de mots : d'une part, Malebranche met en garde contre les séductions de l'imagination; d'autre part, il donne libre cours à celle-ci lorsqu'il traite de l'âme; 2. Élève des jésuites, Voltaire se souvient des Actes des Apôtres : *In Deo vivimus, movemus, et sumus* (XVII, 28); 3. Thème maintes fois développé par Voltaire : voir *les Oreilles du comte de Chesterfield* (éd. Garnier, p. 556-557); 4. Rapprocher de *Tout en Dieu : commentaire sur Malebranche*, de Voltaire : « Pour le mal physique, il n'y a pas un seul système, pas une seule religion qui n'en fasse Dieu auteur... Mais le mal moral, les crimes!... Tout le monde dit : comment sous un Dieu bon y a-t-il tant de souffrances? Et là-dessus chacun bâtit un roman métaphysique : mais aucun de ces romans ne peut nous éclairer sur l'origine des maux, et aucun ne peut ébranler cette grande vérité que tout émane d'un principe universel »; 5. Laurent François Boursier (1679-1749) était l'auteur d'un traité intitulé *l'Action de Dieu sur les créatures, ou la Prémotion physique*, à propos duquel Voltaire écrivit : « Il n'y a que deux manières philosophiques d'expliquer la machine du monde : ou Dieu a ordonné une fois et la nature obéit toujours; ou Dieu ordonne continuellement à tout l'être.... un troisième parti est inexplicable. »

dues sur l'univers diminuait la sensation de leurs peines : ils n'osaient se plaindre quand tout souffrait.

Mais, dans le repos de la nuit, l'image de la belle Saint-Yves effaçait dans l'esprit de son amant toutes les idées de métaphysique et de morale. Il se réveillait les yeux mouillés de larmes; et le vieux janséniste oubliait sa grâce efficace, et l'abbé de Saint-Cyran[1], et Jansénius, pour consoler un jeune homme qu'il croyait en péché mortel.

Après leurs lectures, après leurs raisonnements, ils parlaient encore de leurs aventures; et, après en avoir inutilement parlé, ils lisaient ensemble ou séparément. L'esprit du jeune homme se fortifiait de plus en plus. Il serait surtout allé très loin en mathématiques sans les distractions que lui donnait Mlle de Saint-Yves.

Il lut des histoires, elles l'attristèrent. Le monde lui parut trop méchant et trop misérable. En effet, l'histoire n'est que le tableau des crimes et des malheurs. La foule des hommes innocents et paisibles disparaît toujours sur ces vastes théâtres. Les personnages ne sont que des ambitieux pervers. Il semble que l'histoire ne plaise que comme la tragédie, qui languit si elle n'est animée par les passions, les forfaits, et les grandes infortunes. Il faut armer Clio du poignard, comme Melpomène[2].

Quoique l'histoire de France soit remplie d'horreurs, ainsi que toutes les autres, cependant elle lui parut si dégoûtante dans ses commencements, si sèche dans son milieu, si petite enfin, même du temps de Henri IV, toujours si dépourvue de grands monuments, si étrangère à ces belles découvertes qui ont illustré d'autres nations, qu'il était obligé de lutter contre l'ennui pour lire tous ces détails de calamités obscures resserrées dans un coin du monde[3].

---

1. *Saint-Cyran* est le « *directeur chrétien* par excellence, dans toute sa rigueur, dans toute sa véracité et sa certitude, un rigide et sûr médecin des âmes... croyant... au mal et à la nécessité du remède, croyant à la Grâce... » (Sainte-Beuve, *Port-Royal*). Le père Gordon est un peu une caricature de Saint-Cyran; 2. A rapprocher de ce fragment d'une lettre au marquis d'Argenson (26 janvier 1740) : « ... il n'y a que des gens qui ont fait des tragédies qui puissent jeter quelque intérêt dans notre histoire sèche et barbare »; 3. A rapprocher de ce que Voltaire écrivait à son ami Thiériot lorsqu'il préparait son *Siècle de Louis XIV* (lettre du 15 juillet 1735) : « Quand je vous ai demandé des anecdotes sur le siècle de Louis XIV, c'est moins sur sa personne que sur les arts qui ont fleuri de son temps. J'aimerais mieux des détails sur Racine et Despréaux, sur Quinault, Lulli, Molière, Lebrun, Bossuet, Poussin, Descartes, etc., que sur la bataille de Steinkerque... il ne revient rien au genre humain de cent batailles données; mais les grands hommes dont je vous parle ont préparé des plaisirs purs et durables aux hommes qui ne sont point encore nés... »

La Bastille
au XVIIIe siècle,
où l'Ingénu apprit
tant de choses
sur les affaires
de ce monde
et de l'autre.

Gordon pensait comme lui. Tous deux riaient de pitié quand il était question des souverains de Fezensac[1], de Fesansaguet[2] et d'Astarac[3]. Cette étude en effet ne serait bonne que pour leurs héritiers, s'ils en avaient. Les beaux siècles de la république romaine le rendirent quelque temps indifférent pour le reste de la terre. Le spectacle de Rome victorieuse et législatrice des nations occupait son âme entière. Il s'échauffait en contemplant ce peuple qui fut gouverné sept cents ans par l'enthousiasme de la liberté et de la gloire.

Ainsi se passaient les jours, les semaines, les mois; et il se serait cru heureux dans le séjour du désespoir, s'il n'avait point aimé.

Son bon naturel s'attendrissait encore sur le prieur de Notre-Dame de la Montagne, et sur la sensible Kerkabon.

« Que penseront-ils, répétait-il souvent, quand ils n'auront point de mes nouvelles? Ils me croiront un ingrat. » Cette idée le tourmentait; il plaignait ceux qui l'aimaient, beaucoup plus qu'il ne se plaignait lui-même. (1)

---

1. *Fezensac* : petit bourg réuni au comté d'Armagnac en 1140; 2. *Fezensaguet* eut le même sort en 1418; 3. Le comté d'*Astarac* fut annexé en 1661 au duché de Roquelaure.

--- **QUESTIONS** ---

1. SUR LE CHAPITRE X. — Les thèmes successifs évoqués ici; les liens qui les unissent.

— Montrez comment Voltaire ne fait dans ce chapitre que développer d'une manière plaisante une vue maintes fois exprimée, et notamment dans l'*Essai sur les mœurs* : « La doctrine des deux principes est de Zoroastre. Orosmade ou Oromaze, le dieu des Jours, et Arimane, le génie des Ténèbres, sont l'origine du manichéisme. C'est l'Osiris et le Typhon des Égyptiens, c'est la Pandore des Grecs; c'est le vain effort de tous les sages pour expliquer l'origine du bien et du mal. »

— La Chalotais, en prison, victime des jésuites comme l'Ingénu, auteur de quatre mémoires, dont trois parurent en 1766 et 1767, se dresse contre les fanatiques qui s'opposent au progrès de la vérité dans les esprits. En quel sens l'Ingénu soutient-il la même cause que La Chalotais?

— « Je charge mon fusil de sel avec les uns, de grosses balles avec les autres », écrivait Voltaire à d'Alembert le 10 août 1767. Montrez comment, depuis le début du roman, le sel alterne avec les grosses balles.

— Le prisonnier partagé entre les préoccupations philosophiques et les tourments de la séparation : n'y a-t-il pas là une transposition de ce que fut la vie de Voltaire à la Bastille?

CHAPITRE XI

Comment l'Ingénu développe son génie.

La lecture agrandit l'âme, et un ami éclairé la console. Notre captif jouissait de ces deux avantages, qu'il n'avait pas soupçonnés auparavant. « Je serais tenté, dit-il, de croire aux métamorphoses, car j'ai été changé de brute en homme.[1] » Il se forma une bibliothèque choisie d'une partie de son argent dont on lui permettait de disposer. Son ami l'encouragea à mettre par écrit ses réflexions. Voici ce qu'il écrivit sur l'histoire ancienne :

« Je m'imagine que les nations ont été longtemps comme moi, qu'elles ne se sont instruites que fort tard, qu'elles n'ont été occupées pendant des siècles que du moment présent qui coulait, très peu du passé, et jamais de l'avenir. J'ai parcouru cinq ou six cents lieues du Canada[2], je n'y ai pas trouvé un seul monument; personne n'y sait rien de ce qu'a fait son bisaïeul. Ne serait-ce pas là l'état naturel de l'homme? L'espèce de ce continent-ci me paraît supérieure à celle de l'autre. Elle a augmenté son être depuis plusieurs siècles par les arts et par les connaissances. Est-ce parce qu'elle a de la barbe au menton, et que Dieu a refusé la barbe aux Américains? Je ne le crois pas : car je vois que les Chinois n'ont presque point de barbe, et qu'ils cultivent les arts depuis plus de cinq mille années. En effet, s'ils ont plus de quatre mille ans d'annales, il faut bien que la nation ait été rassemblée et florissante depuis plus de cinquante siècles[3].

« Une chose me frappe surtout dans cette ancienne histoire de la Chine, c'est que presque tout y est vraisemblable et naturel. Je l'admire en ce qu'il n'y a rien de merveilleux.

« Pourquoi toutes les autres nations se sont-elles donné des origines fabuleuses? Les anciens chroniqueurs de l'histoire de France, qui ne sont pas fort anciens, font venir les Français d'un Francus[4], fils d'Hector; les Romains se disaient issus d'un Phrygien, quoiqu'il n'y eût pas dans leur langue un seul

---

1. Idée longuement développée par Voltaire à l'article « Homme » du *Dictionnaire philosophique* et que l'on retrouve dans le *Contrat social* de J.-J. Rousseau (liv. I, chap. VIII); **2.** Voltaire faisait peu de cas des colonies françaises du Canada; **3.** *L'Essai sur les mœurs* est plus précis : « Ces annales se suivent sans interruption. Presque toutes circonstanciées, toutes sages, sans aucun mélange de merveilleux, toutes appuyées sur des observations astronomiques depuis quatre mille cent cinquante-deux ans »; **4.** Allusion à *la Franciade* de Ronsard.

mot qui eût le moindre rapport à la langue de Phrygie; les dieux avaient habité dix mille ans en Égypte, et les diables, en Scythie, où ils avaient engendré les Huns. Je ne vois avant Thucydide que des romans semblables aux Amadis, et beaucoup moins amusants[1]. Ce sont partout des apparitions, des oracles, des prodiges, des sortilèges, des métamorphoses, des songes expliqués, et qui font la destinée des plus grands empires et des plus petits États : ici des bêtes qui parlent, là des bêtes qu'on adore, des dieux transformés en hommes, et des hommes transformés en dieux. Ah! s'il nous faut des fables, que ces fables soient du moins l'emblème de la vérité! J'aime les fables des philosophes, je ris de celles des enfants, et je hais celles des imposteurs. »

Il tomba un jour sur une histoire de l'empereur Justinien[2]. On y lisait que des apédeutes[3] de Constantinople avaient donné, en très mauvais grec, un édit contre le plus grand capitaine du siècle, parce que ce héros avait prononcé ces paroles dans la chaleur de la conversation : « La vérité luit de sa propre lumière, et on n'éclaire pas les esprits avec les flammes des bûchers. » Les apédeutes assurèrent que cette proposition était hérétique, sentant l'hérésie, et que l'axiome contraire était catholique, universel, et grec : « On n'éclaire les esprits qu'avec la flamme des bûchers, et la vérité ne saurait luire de sa propre lumière. » Ces linostoles[4] condamnèrent ainsi plusieurs discours du capitaine, et donnèrent un édit.

« Quoi! s'écria l'Ingénu, des édits rendus par ces gens-là!

— Ce ne sont point des édits, répliqua Gordon, ce sont des contr'édits dont tout le monde se moquait à Constantinople, et l'empereur tout le premier : c'était un sage prince, qui avait su réduire les apédeutes linostoles à ne pouvoir faire que du bien. Il savait que ces messieurs-là et plusieurs autres pastophores[5] avaient lassé de contr'édits la patience des empereurs ses prédécesseurs en matière plus grave.

— Il fit fort bien, dit l'Ingénu; on doit soutenir les pastophores et les contenir. »

---

1. Voltaire connaît mal nos premières œuvres lyriques. L'expression *les Amadis* désigne les chansons de chevalerie, la plupart d'auteurs anonymes, que se transmettaient oralement troubadours et trouvères; 2. Bélisaire, le héros du roman de Marmontel censuré en 1767 par la Sorbonne, était un général de l'empereur Justinien Ier (527-565); celui-ci, chassé par l'empereur, devenu aveugle, vit misérablement, lorsque l'empereur, sans se faire reconnaître, entreprend avec son ancien serviteur une longue discussion sur la tolérance; 3. *Apédeute* : ignorant; 4. *Linostole* (= habillé de lin) : docteur de Sorbonne; 5. *Pastophore* : prêtre.

Il mit par écrit beaucoup d'autres réflexions qui épouvantèrent le vieux Gordon. « Quoi! dit-il en lui-même, j'ai consumé cinquante ans à m'instruire, et je crains de ne pouvoir atteindre au bon sens naturel de cet enfant presque sauvage! je tremble d'avoir laborieusement fortifié des préjugés; il n'écoute que la simple nature. »

Le bonhomme avait quelques-uns de ces petits livres de critique, de ces brochures périodiques où des hommes incapables de rien produire dénigrent les productions des autres, où les Visé[1] insultent aux Racine, et les Faydit[2] aux Fénelon. L'Ingénu en parcourut quelques-uns. « Je les compare, disait-il, à certains moucherons qui vont déposer leurs œufs dans le derrière des plus beaux chevaux : cela ne les empêche pas de courir. » A peine les deux philosophes daignèrent-ils jeter les yeux sur ces excréments de la littérature.

Ils lurent bientôt ensemble les éléments de l'astronomie; l'Ingénu fit venir des sphères : ce grand spectacle le ravissait. « Qu'il est dur, disait-il, de ne commencer à connaître le ciel que lorsqu'on me ravit le droit de le contempler! Jupiter et Saturne roulent dans ces espaces immenses; des millions de soleils éclairent les milliards de mondes; et dans le coin de terre où je suis jeté, il se trouve des êtres qui me privent, moi être voyant et pensant, de tous ces mondes où ma vue pourrait atteindre, et de celui où Dieu m'a fait naître! La lumière faite pour tout l'univers est perdue pour moi. On ne me la cachait pas dans l'horizon septentrional où j'ai passé mon enfance et ma jeunesse. Sans vous, mon cher Gordon, je serais ici dans le néant. » **(1)**

---

1. Donneau de Visé, fondateur du *Mercure galant* (1672), qui devait devenir *le Mercure de France*. Il combattit sans succès Racine, Molière et Boileau; 2. *Faydit* : auteur de la *Télémachomanie*, où il attaquait Fénelon; il fut expulsé de la congrégation des Oratoriens pour avoir défendu le cartésianisme. Ces lignes sont à rapprocher de l'article « Critique » du *Dictionnaire philosophique*. Voltaire y écrit notamment ceci : « Il y a d'autres critiques qui attendent qu'un bon ouvrage paraisse pour faire vite un livre contre lui. Plus le libelliste attaque un homme accrédité, plus il est sûr de gagner quelque argent; il vit quelques mois de la réputation de son adversaire. Tel était un nommé Faydit, qui tantôt écrivait contre Bossuet, tantôt contre Tillemont, tantôt contre Fénelon... »

QUESTIONS

1. SUR LE CHAPITRE XI. — Thème général du chapitre. Composition. Comment Voltaire parvient-il à donner quelque variété à cet ensemble? — Révélez l'intention de l'auteur : pourquoi nous entretenir des réflexions et des idées de l'Ingénu? Que symbolise ce dernier? (Suite page 111.)

CHAPITRE XII

Ce que l'Ingénu pense des pièces de théâtre.

Le jeune Ingénu ressemblait à un de ces arbres vigoureux qui, nés dans un sol ingrat, étendent en peu de temps leurs racines et leurs branches quand ils sont transplantés dans un terrain favorable; et il était bien extraordinaire qu'une prison fût ce terrain.

Parmi les livres qui occupaient le loisir des deux captifs, il se trouva des poésies, des traductions de tragédies grecques, quelques pièces du théâtre français. Les vers qui parlaient d'amour portèrent à la fois dans l'âme de l'Ingénu le plaisir et la douleur. Ils lui parlaient tous de sa chère Saint-Yves. La fable des *Deux Pigeons* lui perça le cœur; il était bien loin de pouvoir revenir à son colombier[1].

Molière l'enchanta[2]. Il lui faisait connaître les mœurs de Paris et du genre humain. « A laquelle de ses comédies donnez-vous la préférence? — Au *Tartuffe*, sans difficulté. — Je pense comme vous, dit Gordon; c'est un tartuffe qui m'a plongé dans ce cachot, et peut-être ce sont des tartuffes qui ont fait votre malheur. Comment trouvez-vous ces tragédies grecques?

— Bonnes pour des Grecs[3] », dit l'Ingénu. Mais quand il

---

1. La Fontaine, « unique dans sa naïveté et dans les grâces qui lui sont propres, se mit, par les choses les plus simples, presque à côté de ces hommes sublimes [il s'agit des grands dramaturges du XVIIe siècle] ... Il était, malgré son génie, presque aussi simple que les héros de ses fables » (*le Siècle de Louis XIV*, chap. XXXII, « Des beaux-arts »); 2. Dans *le Temple du goût*, Molière est ainsi apostrophé :

Tu fus le peintre de la France,
Nos bourgeois à sots préjugés,
Nos petits marquis rengorgés,
Nos robins toujours arrangés,
Chez toi venaient se reconnaître;
Et tu les aurais corrigés,
Si l'esprit humain pouvait l'être;

3. « Nous devons nous-mêmes, en blâmant les tragédies des Grecs, respecter le génie de leurs auteurs; leurs fautes sont sur le compte de leur siècle, leurs beautés n'appartiennent qu'à eux; et il est à croire que, s'ils étaient nés de nos jours, ils auraient perfectionné l'art qu'ils ont presque inventé de leur temps. » (*Lettre III, sur l'Œdipe de Sophocle.*)

QUESTIONS

— Analysez les idées émises ici. Les éléments polémiques. Les faits positifs.
— N'y a-t-il pas un reproche possible contre un tel chapitre, actuellement? Le roman ne paraît-il pas arrêté, sinon oublié?

lut l'*Iphigénie* moderne, *Phèdre*, *Andromaque*, *Athalie*, il fut en extase, il soupira, il versa des larmes, il les sut par cœur sans avoir envie de les apprendre.

« Lisez *Rodogune*, lui dit Gordon; on dit que c'est le chef-d'œuvre du théâtre; les autres pièces qui vous ont fait tant de plaisir sont peu de chose en comparaison. » Le jeune homme, dès la première page, lui dit : « Cela n'est pas du même auteur. — A quoi le voyez-vous? — Je n'en sais rien encore; mais ces vers-là ne vont ni à mon oreille ni à mon cœur. — Oh! ce n'est rien que les vers », répliqua Gordon. L'Ingénu répondit : « Pourquoi donc en faire? »

Après avoir lu très attentivement la pièce, sans autre dessein que celui d'avoir du plaisir, il regardait son ami avec des yeux secs et étonnés, et ne savait que dire. Enfin, pressé de rendre compte de ce qu'il avait senti, voici ce qu'il répondit : « Je n'ai guère entendu le commencement[1]; j'ai été révolté[2] du milieu; la dernière scène m'a beaucoup ému, quoiqu'elle me paraisse peu vraisemblable[3] : je ne me suis intéressé pour personne, et je n'ai pas retenu vingt vers, moi qui les retiens tous quand ils me plaisent.

— Cette pièce passe pourtant pour la meilleure que nous ayons. — Si cela est, répliqua-t-il, elle est peut-être comme bien des gens qui ne méritent pas leurs places. Après tout, c'est ici une affaire de goût; le mien ne doit pas encore être formé : je peux me tromper; mais vous savez que je suis assez accoutumé à dire ce que je pense, ou plutôt ce que je sens. Je soupçonne qu'il y a souvent de l'illusion, de la mode, du caprice, dans les jugements des hommes[4]. J'ai parlé d'après la nature; il se peut que chez moi la nature soit très imparfaite; mais il se peut aussi qu'elle soit quelquefois peu consultée par la plupart des hommes. » Alors il récita des vers d'*Iphigénie*, dont

---

1. La scène d'exposition amène dans le *Théâtre de Pierre Corneille* (Cramer, 1764) les critiques suivantes : « Les défauts de cette exposition sont : 1º qu'on ne sait point qui parle; 2º qu'on ne sait point de qui l'on parle; 3º qu'on ne sait point où l'on parle »; 2. C'est exactement le mot de Voltaire dans les *Commentaires*; 3. Sans approuver le dénouement, Voltaire reconnaît le « succès prodigieux » de la dernière scène, « grande réponse à tous les critiques ». Et il ajoute : « L'action qui termine cette scène fait frémir; c'est le tragique porté au comble » (*Ibid.*). En somme, dans l'*Ingénu*, Voltaire répète sous une forme plus plaisante ce qu'il écrivait à Mᵐᵉ du Deffand le 1ᵉʳ juillet 1764 : « Corneille a des éclairs dans une nuit profonde... Racine m'enchante et Corneille m'ennuie... » 4. A rapprocher de l'article « Goût » du *Dictionnaire philosophique*, où il y a une analyse de la formation du goût qui commente exactement ce qu'éprouve l'Ingénu.

il était plein; et quoiqu'il ne déclamât pas bien, il y mit tant
de vérité et d'onction qu'il fit pleurer le vieux janséniste[1].
Il lut ensuite *Cinna;* il ne pleura point, mais il admira[2]. (1)

CHAPITRE XIII

La belle Saint-Yves va à Versailles.

Pendant que notre infortuné s'éclairait plus qu'il ne se
consolait; pendant que son génie, étouffé depuis si longtemps,
se déployait avec tant de rapidité et de force; pendant que la
nature, qui se perfectionnait en lui, le vengeait des outrages
de la fortune, que devinrent monsieur le prieur et sa bonne
sœur, et la belle recluse Saint-Yves? Le premier mois, on fut
inquiet, et au troisième on fut plongé dans la douleur : les
fausses conjectures, les bruits mal fondés, alarmèrent; au bout
de six mois, on le crut mort. Enfin M. et Mlle de Kerkabon
apprirent, par une ancienne lettre qu'un garde du roi avait
écrite en Bretagne, qu'un jeune homme semblable à l'Ingénu
était arrivé un soir à Versailles, mais qu'il avait été enlevé
pendant la nuit, et que depuis ce temps personne n'en avait
entendu parler.

« Hélas! dit Mlle de Kerkabon, notre neveu aura fait quelque

---

1. On trouve aussi, dans les *Commentaires sur Corneille :* « J'avoue que je regarde
Iphigénie comme le chef-d'œuvre de la scène »; 2. « *Cinna*... était unique. J'ai connu
un ancien domestique de la maison de Condé, qui disait que le grand Condé, à
l'âge de vingt ans, étant à la première représentation de *Cinna*, versa des larmes à
ces paroles d'Auguste : « Je suis maître de moi comme de l'univers... », et c'étaient
là des larmes de héros. Le grand Corneille faisant pleurer le grand Condé d'admiration est une époque bien célèbre dans l'histoire de l'esprit humain » (*Siècle de
Louis XIV*, chap. XXXII, « Des beaux-arts »).

--- **QUESTIONS** ---

1. SUR LE CHAPITRE XII. — Le premier paragraphe répète une idée
exprimée déjà plusieurs fois : situez ces rappels; justifiez-les; en quoi
celui-ci est-il original?
— Voltaire transpose chez les deux prisonniers son admiration pour
Tartuffe : en quoi est-elle liée à l'action?
— Justifiez par le goût de l'époque et celui de Voltaire la présence
et la teneur de ce chapitre. Pourquoi tout ce développement sur le
théâtre plutôt que sur un autre aspect de la littérature? Y a-t-il ici une
part de polémique?
— Comparez, en vous aidant des notes, les goûts de l'Ingénu et celui
de Voltaire. Le rapprochement prête-t-il à sourire?

sottise, et se sera attiré de fâcheuses affaires. Il est jeune, il est Bas-Breton, il ne peut savoir comme on doit se comporter à la cour. Mon cher frère, je n'ai jamais vu Versailles ni Paris; voici une belle occasion, nous retrouverons peut-être notre pauvre neveu : c'est le fils de notre frère; notre devoir est de le secourir. Qui sait si nous ne pourrons point parvenir enfin à le faire sous-diacre, quand la fougue de la jeunesse sera amortie? Il avait beaucoup de dispositions pour les sciences. Vous souvenez-vous comme il raisonnait sur l'Ancien et sur le Nouveau Testament? Nous sommes responsables de son âme; c'est nous qui l'avons fait baptiser; sa chère maîtresse Saint-Yves passe les journées à pleurer. En vérité il faut aller à Paris. S'il est caché dans quelqu'une de ces vilaines maisons de joie dont on m'a fait tant de récits, nous l'en tirerons. » Le prieur fut touché des discours de sa sœur. Il alla trouver l'évêque de Saint-Malo, qui avait baptisé le Huron, et lui demanda sa protection et ses conseils. Le prélat approuva le voyage. Il donna au prieur des lettres de recommandation pour le père de La Chaise, confesseur du roi, qui avait la première dignité du royaume, pour l'archevêque de Paris Harlay[1], et pour l'évêque de Meaux Bossuet. (1)

Enfin le frère et la sœur partirent; mais, quand ils furent arrivés à Paris, ils se trouvèrent égarés comme dans un vaste labyrinthe, sans fil et sans issue. Leur fortune était médiocre, il leur fallait tous les jours des voitures pour aller à la découverte, et ils ne découvraient rien.

Le prieur se présenta chez le révérend père de La Chaise[2] : il était avec Mlle du Tron, et ne pouvait donner audience à des prieurs. Il alla à la porte de l'archevêque : le prélat était enfermé avec la belle Mme de Lesdiguières pour les affaires de l'Église. Il courut à la maison de campagne de l'évêque de

---

1. Ce prélat, de vie privée scandaleuse, avait refusé la sépulture à Molière; 2. Le père de La Chaise, confesseur du roi; voir plus haut, p. 97, note 2; Mlle du Tron était la nièce de Bontemps, premier valet de chambre de Louis XIV.

QUESTIONS

1. Le thème de la métamorphose de l'Ingénu est repris trois fois de suite (débuts des chap. XI, XII, XIII) : quel est le sens philosophique de ce rappel? — La prière de Mlle de Kerkabon : montrez son allure dramatique (constance du caractère du personnage; rappel de l'impression profonde qu'avait produite sur elle l'Ingénu; style de la comédie larmoyante, etc.). — Est-ce la première fois que Voltaire fait un retour dans le passé? Relevez les rappels précédents. Quels effets produisent-ils?

Meaux[1] : celui-ci examinait, avec Mlle de Mauléon, l'amour mystique de Mme Guyon[2]. Cependant il parvint à se faire entendre de ces deux prélats; tous deux lui déclarèrent qu'ils ne pouvaient se mêler de son neveu, attendu qu'il n'était pas sous-diacre. (2)

Enfin il vit le jésuite[3]; celui-ci le reçut à bras ouverts, lui protesta qu'il avait toujours eu pour lui une estime particulière, ne l'ayant jamais connu. Il jura que la Société avait toujours été attachée aux Bas-Bretons. « Mais, dit-il, votre neveu n'aurait-il pas le malheur d'être huguenot? — Non, assurément, mon révérend père. — Serait-il point janséniste? — Je puis assurer à Votre Révérence qu'à peine est-il chrétien : il y a environ onze mois que nous l'avons baptisé. — Voilà qui est bien, voilà qui est bien; nous aurons soin de lui. Votre bénéfice est-il considérable? — Oh! fort peu de chose, et mon neveu nous coûte beaucoup. — Y a-t-il quelques jansénistes dans le voisinage? Prenez bien garde, mon cher monsieur le prieur, ils sont plus dangereux que les huguenots et les athées. — Mon révérend père, nous n'en avons point; on ne sait ce que c'est que le jansénisme à Notre-Dame de la Montagne. — Tant mieux; allez, il n'y a rien que je ne fasse pour vous. » Il congédia affectueusement le prieur, et n'y pensa plus.

Le temps s'écoulait, le prieur et la bonne sœur se désespéraient.

Cependant le maudit bailli pressait le mariage de son grand benêt de fils avec la belle Saint-Yves, qu'on avait fait sortir

---

1. La liaison de Bossuet avec Mlle Desvieux fait l'objet de plusieurs allusions. Voltaire s'appuie sur les relations de Jurieu et de Jean-Baptiste Denis; 2. Le « quiétisme » de Mme Guyon fut condamné en 1696 par une commission que présidait Bossuet. Cette doctrine déclarait inutiles les sacrements et exhortait les adeptes à rechercher par une attitude mystique un anéantissement complet de l'âme en Dieu; 3. Pascal, celui des *Provinciales*, que Voltaire admirait, avait mis en scène des jésuites : se souvenir des premières lignes de la IVe *Provinciale* : « Il n'est rien tel que les jésuites... J'ai donc vu un des plus habiles... « Très volontiers, me dit-il; « car j'aime les gens curieux... Vous avez raison...; il n'en faut pas railler; il n'y a « point ici d'équivoque... » Or, le jésuite par lequel l'abbé de Kerkabon parvient à se faire recevoir est lui aussi d'une extrême complaisance et de manières fort douces; cette première figure de jésuite oriente le conte.

---

2. D'où vient le comique du récit? — Comment le lecteur est-il tenu en haleine? — Quel effet produit la proposition *attendu qu'il n'était pas sous-diacre?*

exprès du couvent. Elle aimait toujours son cher filleul autant qu'elle détestait le mari qu'on lui présentait. L'affront d'avoir été mise dans un couvent augmentait sa passion; l'ordre d'épouser le fils du bailli y mettait le comble. Les regrets, la tendresse, et l'horreur bouleversaient son âme. L'amour, comme on sait, est bien plus ingénieux et plus hardi dans une jeune fille que l'amitié ne l'est dans un vieux prieur et dans une tante de quarante-cinq ans passés. De plus, elle s'était bien formée dans son couvent par les romans qu'elle avait lus à la dérobée. (3)

La belle Saint-Yves se souvenait de la lettre qu'un garde du corps avait écrite en Basse-Bretagne, et dont on avait parlé dans la province. Elle résolut d'aller elle-même prendre des informations à Versailles; de se jeter aux pieds des ministres si son mari était en prison, comme on le disait, et d'obtenir justice pour lui. Je ne sais quoi l'avertissait secrètement qu'à la cour on ne refuse rien à une jolie fille; mais elle ne savait pas ce qu'il en coûtait.

Sa résolution prise, elle est consolée, elle est tranquille, elle ne rebute plus son sot prétendu; elle accueille le détestable beau-père, caresse son frère, répand l'allégresse dans la maison; puis, le jour destiné à la cérémonie, elle part secrètement à quatre heures du matin avec ses petits présents de noce, et tout ce qu'elle a pu rassembler. Ses mesures étaient si bien prises qu'elle était déjà à plus de dix lieues lorsqu'on entra dans sa chambre, vers le midi. La surprise et la consternation furent grandes. L'interrogant bailli fit ce jour là plus de questions qu'il n'en avait fait dans toute la semaine; le mari resta plus sot qu'il ne l'avait jamais été. L'abbé de Saint-Yves, en colère, prit le parti de courir après sa sœur. Le bailli et son fils voulurent l'accompagner. Ainsi la destinée conduisait à Paris presque tout ce canton de la Basse-Bretagne.

La belle Saint-Yves se doutait bien qu'on la suivrait. Elle était à cheval; elle s'informait adroitement des courriers s'ils n'avaient point rencontré un gros abbé, un énorme bailli, et

─────────── **QUESTIONS** ───────────

3. Les questions que pose le jésuite : que révèlent-elles sur ses préoccupations? A propos des jansénistes, le jésuite réitère sa question sous une forme à peine différente : pourquoi? Que pensez-vous de la phrase qui clôt le dialogue entre le prieur et le jésuite? Comparez les manières de ce personnage avec celles des jésuites de Pascal (IVe *Provinciale* en particulier). — Le bailli et son fils : par quel procédé purement littéraire l'auteur rappelle-t-il leur caractère odieux?

un jeune benêt, qui couraient sur le chemin de Paris. Ayant appris au troisième jour qu'ils n'étaient pas loin, elle prit une route différente, et eut assez d'habileté et de bonheur pour arriver à Versailles tandis qu'on la cherchait inutilement dans Paris. **(4)**

Mais comment se conduire à Versailles? Jeune, belle, sans conseil, sans appui, inconnue, exposée à tout, comment oser chercher un garde du roi? Elle imagina de s'adresser à un jésuite du bas étage; il y en avait pour toutes les conditions de la vie, comme Dieu, disaient-ils, a donné différentes nourritures aux diverses espèces d'animaux. Il avait donné au roi son confesseur, que tous les solliciteurs de bénéfices appelaient *le chef de l'Église gallicane;* ensuite venaient les confesseurs des princesses; les ministres n'en avaient point : ils n'étaient pas si sots. Il y avait les jésuites du grand commun, et surtout les jésuites des femmes de chambre par lesquelles on savait les secrets des maîtresses; et ce n'était pas un petit emploi. La belle Saint-Yves s'adressa à un de ces derniers, qui s'appelait le père Tout-à-tous[1]. Elle se confessa à lui, lui exposa ses aventures, son état, son danger, et le conjura de la loger chez quelque bonne dévote qui la mît à l'abri des tentations.

Le père Tout-à-tous l'introduisit chez la femme d'un officier du gobelet[2], l'une de ses plus affidées pénitentes. Dès qu'elle y fut, elle s'empressa de gagner la confiance et l'amitié de cette femme; elle s'informa du garde breton, et le fit prier de venir chez elle. Ayant su de lui que son amant avait été enlevé après avoir parlé à un premier commis, elle court chez ce commis : la vue d'une belle femme l'adoucit, car il faut convenir que Dieu n'a créé les femmes que pour apprivoiser les hommes.

---

1. Au passage, Voltaire stigmatise la politique de « présence universelle », secret de l'ordre des Jésuites. Le nom du personnage est emprunté à un ouvrage de d'Alembert, *Sur la destruction des jésuites en France.* L'auteur y affirme qu'un jésuite doit savoir se faire « pour ainsi dire *tout à tous*, suivant une expression de l'Écriture » : le choix de ce nom intègre *l'Ingénu* dans la polémique que les encyclopédistes mènent contre les jésuites; 2. Officier de la maison du roi, chargé du vin, du pain, du fruit et du linge.

──────── **QUESTIONS** ────────

4. L'amour ingénieux : jusqu'à quel point la biographie de Voltaire a-t-elle illustré ce thème? A quelles sources puise Mlle de Saint-Yves? La part d'habileté naïve dans son comportement? Montrez que la comparaison implicite avec le bailli et ses amis rehausse le portrait de la jeune fille. Sort-on néanmoins d'un certain schématisme?

Le plumitif[1] attendri lui avoua tout. « Votre amant est à la Bastille depuis près d'un an, et sans vous il y serait peut-être toute sa vie. » La tendre Saint-Yves s'évanouit. Quand elle eut repris ses sens, le plumitif lui dit : « Je suis sans crédit pour faire du bien ; tout mon pouvoir se borne à faire du mal quelquefois. Croyez-moi, allez chez M. de Saint-Pouange[2], qui fait le bien et le mal, cousin et favori de Mgr de Louvois. Ce ministre a deux âmes : M. de Saint-Pouange en est une ; Mme du Belloy[3], l'autre ; mais elle n'est pas à présent à Versailles ; il ne vous reste que de fléchir le protecteur que je vous indique. »

La belle Saint-Yves, partagée entre un peu de joie et d'extrêmes douleurs, entre quelque espérance et de tristes craintes, poursuivie par son frère, adorant son amant, essuyant ses larmes et en versant encore, tremblante, affaiblie, et reprenant courage, courut vite chez M. de Saint-Pouange. (5) (6)

CHAPITRE XIV

Progrès de l'esprit de l'Ingénu.

L'Ingénu faisait des progrès rapides dans les sciences, et surtout dans la science de l'homme. La cause du développement rapide de son esprit était due à son éducation sauvage presque autant qu'à la trempe de son âme : car, n'ayant rien appris dans son enfance, il n'avait point appris de préjugés. Son entendement, n'ayant point été courbé par l'erreur, était demeuré dans toute sa rectitude. Il voyait les choses comme elles sont, au lieu que les idées qu'on nous donne dans l'enfance nous les font voir toute notre vie comme elles ne sont point.

---

1. *Plumitif* : familièrement et par plaisanterie, homme de plume ; commis de bureau ; 2. Il s'agit du comte de Saint-Florentin ; 3. Il s'agit de Mme Dufresnoi.

---

5. Relevez les éléments symétriques, les divergences et les similitudes dans l'expérience de Versailles que font l'Ingénu et Mlle de Saint-Yves. Comment le rythme de ce passage traduit-il l'évolution de l'aventure ? — Que prépare le dernier paragraphe ?

6. SUR L'ENSEMBLE DU CHAPITRE XIII. — Le chapitre est construit comme un petit drame : indiquez-en tous les éléments dramatiques (dialogues, coups de théâtre, personnages principaux, personnages secondaires, maintien du spectateur en haleine, passages larmoyants).

« Vos persécuteurs sont abominables, disait-il à son ami Gordon. Je vous plains d'être opprimé, mais je vous plains d'être janséniste. Toute secte me paraît le ralliement de l'erreur. Dites-moi s'il y a des sectes en géométrie? — Non, mon cher enfant, lui dit en soupirant le bon Gordon; tous les hommes sont d'accord sur la vérité quand elle est démontrée, mais ils sont trop partagés sur les vérités obscures. — Dites sur les faussetés obscures. S'il y avait eu une seule vérité cachée dans vos amas d'arguments qu'on ressasse depuis tant de siècles, on l'aurait découverte sans doute; et l'univers aurait été d'accord au moins sur ce point-là. Si cette vérité était nécessaire comme le soleil l'est à la terre, elle serait brillante comme lui. C'est une absurdité, c'est un outrage au genre humain, c'est un attentat contre l'Etre infini et suprême de dire : Il y a une vérité essentielle à l'homme, et Dieu l'a cachée. »

Tout ce que disait ce jeune ignorant, instruit par la nature, faisait une impression profonde sur l'esprit du vieux savant infortuné. « Serait-il bien vrai, s'écria-t-il, que je me fusse rendu malheureux pour des chimères? Je suis bien plus sûr de mon malheur que de la grâce efficace. J'ai consumé mes jours à raisonner sur la liberté de Dieu et du genre humain; mais j'ai perdu la mienne; ni saint Augustin ni saint Prosper[1] ne me tireront de l'abîme où je suis. »

L'Ingénu, livré à son caractère, dit enfin : « Voulez-vous que je vous parle avec une confiance hardie? Ceux qui se font persécuter pour ces vaines disputes de l'école me semblent peu sages; ceux qui persécutent me paraissent des monstres. »

Les deux captifs étaient fort d'accord sur l'injustice de leur captivité. « Je suis cent fois plus à plaindre que vous, disait l'Ingénu; je suis né libre comme l'air; j'avais deux vies, la liberté et l'objet de mon amour : on me les ôte. Nous voici tous deux dans les fers, sans en savoir la raison et sans pouvoir la demander. J'ai vécu Huron vingt ans; on dit que ce sont des barbares, parce qu'ils se vengent de leurs ennemis; mais ils n'ont jamais opprimé leurs amis. A peine ai-je mis le pied en France, que j'ai versé mon sang pour elle; j'ai peut-être sauvé une province, et pour récompense je suis englouti dans ce tombeau des vivants, où je serais mort de rage sans vous. Il n'y a donc point de lois dans ce pays? On condamne

---

1. Saint Prosper d'Aquitaine vécut au ve siècle; disciple de saint Augustin, il combattit les semi-pélagiens, puis vint à Rome, où il devint le familier de saint Léon.

les hommes sans les entendre! Il n'en est pas ainsi en Angleterre[1]. Ah! ce n'était pas contre les Anglais que je devais me battre. » Ainsi sa philosophie naissante ne pouvait dompter la nature outragée dans le premier de ses droits, et laissait un libre cours à sa juste colère. (1)

Son compagnon ne le contredit point. L'absence augmente toujours l'amour qui n'est pas satisfait, et la philosophie ne le diminue pas. Il parlait aussi souvent de sa chère Saint-Yves que de morale et de métaphysique. Plus ses sentiments s'épuraient, et plus il aimait. Il lut quelques romans nouveaux; il en trouva peu qui lui peignissent la situation de son âme. Il sentait que son cœur allait toujours au-delà de ce qu'il lisait. « Ah! disait-il, presque tous ces auteurs-là n'ont que de l'esprit et de l'art. » Enfin le bon prêtre janséniste devenait insensiblement le confident de sa tendresse. Il ne connaissait l'amour auparavant que comme un péché dont on s'accuse en confession. Il apprit à le connaître comme un sentiment aussi noble que tendre, qui peut élever l'âme autant que l'amollir, et produire même quelquefois des vertus. Enfin, pour dernier prodige, un Huron convertissait un janséniste. (2) (3)

---

1. Sur ce point Voltaire n'a pas varié depuis les *Lettres philosophiques*. Comparez aussi avec l'article « Gouvernement » du *Dictionnaire philosophique*.

■ **QUESTIONS** ■
---

1. Encore la métamorphose de l'Ingénu : comment, cette fois, le thème est-il amplifié et précisé? — Une situation paradoxale : le père Gordon converti par l'Ingénu; précisez de quelle façon nous y sommes amenés logiquement; comment, de cette situation, Voltaire tire-t-il une teinte humoristique? — Il est bien exact que, dans *l'Ingénu*, Voltaire attaque toutes les sectes. En quoi cette attaque est-elle cependant nuancée?

2. De quelle manière est amenée une nouvelle discussion littéraire? Comparez-la aux précédentes : longueur, précision, lien avec l'intrigue. *Presque tous ces auteurs-là n'ont que de l'esprit et de l'art* : montrez la justesse de cette critique, et qu'elle rejoint ce que Voltaire écrivait de Marivaux : « ... je lui reprocherais... de trop détailler les passions, et de manquer quelquefois le chemin du cœur, en prenant des routes un peu détournées. J'aime d'autant plus son esprit que je le prierais de le moins prodiguer. » (*Lettre à M. Berger*, à Cirey, février 1736.)

3. SUR L'ENSEMBLE DU CHAPITRE XIV. — Pourquoi est-on revenu à l'Ingénu dans sa prison? Comparez ce chapitre à ceux qui précèdent le chapitre XIII : ressemblances, différences.
— Les aspects polémiques de ce texte : qui est attaqué cette fois? Montrez la progression accomplie. Soulignez la fusion entre discussion générale et problèmes propres à l'Ingénu et à sa situation.
— Quelle semble être finalement la position de Voltaire à l'égard de toute secte religieuse?

CHAPITRE XV

La belle Saint-Yves résiste à des propositions délicates.

La belle Saint-Yves, plus tendre encore que son amant, alla donc chez M. de Saint-Pouange, accompagnée de l'amie chez qui elle logeait, toutes deux cachées dans leurs coiffes[1]. La première chose qu'elle vit à la porte ce fut l'abbé de Saint-Yves, son frère, qui en sortait. Elle fut intimidée; mais la dévote amie la rassura. « C'est précisément parce qu'on a parlé contre vous qu'il faut que vous parliez. Soyez sûre que dans ce pays les accusateurs ont toujours raison si on ne se hâte de les confondre. Votre présence d'ailleurs, ou je me trompe fort, fera plus d'effet que les paroles de votre frère. »

Pour peu qu'on encourage une amante passionnée, elle est intrépide. La Saint-Yves se présente à l'audience. Sa jeunesse, ses charmes, ses yeux tendres, mouillés de quelques pleurs, attirèrent tous les regards. Chaque courtisan du sous-ministre oublia un moment l'idole du pouvoir pour contempler celle de la beauté. Le[2] Saint-Pouange la fit entrer dans un cabinet; elle parla avec attendrissement et avec grâce. Saint-Pouange se sentit touché. Elle tremblait, il la rassura. « Revenez ce soir, lui dit-il; vos affaires méritent qu'on y pense et qu'on en parle à loisir; il y a ici trop de monde; on expédie les audiences trop rapidement : il faut que je vous entretienne à fond de tout ce qui vous regarde. » Ensuite, ayant fait l'éloge de sa beauté et de ses sentiments, il lui recommanda de venir à sept heures du soir.

Elle n'y manqua pas; la dévote amie l'accompagna encore, mais elle se tint dans le salon, et lut le *Pédagogue chrétien*[3], pendant que le Saint-Pouange et la belle Saint-Yves étaient dans l'arrière-cabinet. « Croiriez-vous bien, mademoiselle, lui dit-il d'abord, que votre frère est venu me demander une lettre de cachet contre vous? En vérité j'en expédierais plutôt

---

1. *Coiffe :* « morceaux de taffetas rond, plissés par derrière et ourlés tout autour, dont les dames et les bourgeoises se couvraient la tête, qu'elles tournaient autour de leurs visages et nouaient un peu au-dessous du menton » (Dictionnaire de Richelet, 1680); 2. L'article défini devant un nom propre *peut* avoir un sens péjoratif : c'est le cas ici; 3. Traité de formation religieuse, qui devait comporter quatre tomes. L'auteur, un certain Outreman ou Oultreman, mourut le 16 mai 1652, et les deux derniers tomes ne virent jamais le jour. Composé en latin, l'ouvrage fut traduit en français.

une pour le renvoyer en basse-Bretagne. — Hélas! monsieur, on est donc bien libéral de lettres de cachet dans vos bureaux, puisqu'on en vient solliciter du fond du royaume, comme dans des pensions. Je suis bien loin d'en demander une contre mon frère. J'ai beaucoup à me plaindre de lui, mais je respecte la liberté des hommes; je demande celle d'un homme que je veux épouser, d'un homme à qui le roi doit la conservation d'une province, qui peut le servir utilement, et qui est fils d'un officier tué à son service. De quoi est-il accusé? Comment a-t-on pu le traiter si cruellement sans l'entendre? »

Alors le sous-ministre lui montra la lettre du jésuite espion et celle du perfide bailli. « Quoi! il y a de pareils monstres sur la terre! et on veut me forcer ainsi à épouser le fils ridicule d'un homme ridicule et méchant! et c'est sur de pareils avis qu'on décide ici de la destinée des citoyens! » Elle se jeta à genoux, elle demanda avec des sanglots la liberté du brave homme qui l'adorait. Ses charmes dans cet état parurent dans leur plus grand avantage. Elle était si belle que le Saint-Pouange, perdant toute honte, lui insinua qu'elle réussirait si elle commençait par lui donner les prémices de ce qu'elle réservait à son amant. La Saint-Yves, épouvantée et confuse, feignit longtemps de ne le pas entendre; il fallut s'expliquer plus clairement. Un mot lâché d'abord avec retenue en produisait un plus fort, suivi d'un autre plus expressif. On offrit non seulement la révocation de la lettre de cachet, mais des récompenses, de l'argent, des honneurs, des établissements; et plus on promettait, plus le désir de n'être pas refusé augmentait.

La Saint-Yves pleurait, elle était suffoquée, à demi renversée sur un sofa, croyant à peine ce qu'elle voyait, ce qu'elle entendait. Le Saint-Pouange, à son tour, se jeta à ses genoux. Il n'était pas sans agréments, et aurait pu ne pas effaroucher un cœur moins prévenu; mais Saint-Yves adorait son amant, et croyait que c'était un crime horrible de le trahir pour le servir. Saint-Pouange redoublait les prières et les promesses : enfin la tête lui tourna au point qu'il lui déclara que c'était le seul moyen de tirer de sa prison l'homme auquel elle prenait un intérêt si violent et si tendre. Cet étrange entretien se prolongeait. La dévote de l'antichambre, en lisant son *Pédagogue chrétien*, disait : « Mon Dieu! que peuvent-ils faire là depuis deux heures? Jamais monseigneur de Saint-Pouange n'a donné une si longue audience; peut-être qu'il a tout refusé à cette pauvre fille, puisqu'elle le prie encore. »

Enfin sa compagne sortit de l'arrière-cabinet, tout éperdue, sans pouvoir parler, réfléchissant profondément sur le caractère des grands et des demi-grands, qui sacrifient si légèrement la liberté des hommes et l'honneur des femmes.

Elle ne dit pas un mot pendant tout le chemin. Arrivée chez l'amie, elle éclata, elle lui conta tout. La dévote fit de grands signes de croix. « Ma chère amie, il faut consulter dès demain le père Tout-à-tous, notre directeur; il a beaucoup de crédit auprès de M. de Saint-Pouange; il confesse plusieurs servantes de sa maison; c'est un homme pieux et accommodant, qui dirige aussi des femmes de qualité : abandonnez-vous à lui, c'est ainsi que j'en use, je m'en suis toujours bien trouvée. Nous autres, pauvres femmes, nous avons besoin d'être conduites par un homme. — Eh bien donc! ma chère amie, j'irai trouver demain le père Tout-à-tous. » (1)

CHAPITRE XVI

Elle consulte un jésuite.

Dès que la belle et désolée[1] Saint-Yves fut avec son bon confesseur, elle lui confia qu'un homme puissant et voluptueux lui proposait de faire sortir de prison celui qu'elle devait

---

1. *Désolé :* laissé seul, délaissé (ex. « une épouse désolée », Bossuet). Ce sens très fort est dû au verbe latin *desolare*, qui signifie « rendre absolument seul, isoler ».

QUESTIONS

1. SUR LE CHAPITRE XV. — Étudiez dans l'ensemble du chapitre les nuances de sens introduites par l'article défini *le* ou *la* placé devant un nom propre.

— Montrez que l'audience de Saint-Pouange est construite comme une scène de théâtre : le style direct; les exclamations de Mlle de Saint-Yves s'opposent aux propos ignobles du sous-ministre, que l'auteur laisse seulement imaginer; — les gestes de Mlle de Saint-Yves, auxquels s'oppose l'attitude implacable de Saint-Pouange; — le sous-ministre de plus en plus pressant (soulignez la progression dramatique); — en contraste avec l'ensemble, l'inquiétude comique de la vieille dévote cherchant à tromper son attente et son inquiétude avec le *Pédagogue chrétien*. En quoi tout cela correspond-il à la conception voltairienne du théâtre?

— Les propos de la vieille dévote et ses conseils : pourquoi font-ils rire le lecteur?

— Élément satirique et élément humoristique dans le portrait du père Tout-à-tous vu par la vieille dévote.

épouser légitimement, et qu'il demandait un grand prix de son service; qu'elle avait une répugnance horrible pour une telle infidélité, et que, s'il ne s'agissait que de sa propre vie, elle la sacrifierait plutôt que de succomber.

« Voilà un abominable pécheur! lui dit le père Tout-à-tous. Vous devriez bien me dire le nom de ce vilain homme : c'est à coup sûr quelque janséniste; je le dénoncerai à sa révérence le père de La Chaise, qui le fera mettre dans le gîte où est à présent la chère personne que vous devez épouser. »

La pauvre fille, après un long embarras et de grandes irrésolutions, lui nomma enfin Saint-Pouange.

« Monseigneur de Saint-Pouange! s'écria le jésuite; ah! ma fille, c'est tout autre chose; il est cousin du plus grand ministre que nous ayons jamais eu, homme de bien, protecteur de la bonne cause, bon chrétien; il ne peut avoir eu une telle pensée; il faut que vous ayez mal entendu. — Ah! mon père, je n'ai entendu que trop bien; je suis perdue, quoi que je fasse; je n'ai que le choix du malheur et de la honte : il faut que mon amant[1] reste enseveli tout vivant, ou que je me rende indigne de vivre. Je ne puis le laisser périr, et je ne puis le sauver. » **(1)**

Le père Tout-à-tous tâcha de la calmer par ces douces paroles :

« Premièrement, ma fille, ne dites jamais ce mot *mon amant;* il y a quelque chose de mondain qui pourrait offenser Dieu. Dites *mon mari;* car, bien qu'il ne le soit pas encore, vous le regardez comme tel; et rien n'est plus honnête.

« Secondement, bien qu'il soit votre époux en idée, en espérance, il ne l'est pas en effet[2] : ainsi vous ne commettriez pas un adultère, péché énorme qu'il faut toujours éviter autant qu'il est possible.

---

1. *Amant :* celui « qui aime et qui est aimé » (Dictionnaire de Richelet, 1680). Prétendant agréé par la jeune fille; fiancé. Ce sens diffère de celui de « amoureux » (qui aime sans être aimé); 2. *En effet :* en réalité.

━━━━━ QUESTIONS ━━━━━

1. Jusqu'à maintenant Voltaire écrivait *la belle Saint-Yves.* Il écrit maintenant *la belle et désolée Saint-Yves :* quel effet produit ce changement dans le jeu des épithètes? — *Un homme puissant et voluptueux :* la première épithète est attendue; que prépare la seconde? — *Grand prix; répugnance horrible; infidélité; succomber.* Montrez ce qu'il y a de précieux dans l'aveu de la belle Saint-Yves. — Qu'y a-t-il de comique dans les deux répliques du jésuite? — Le caractère dramatique de la réponse de la belle Saint-Yves à l'ultime exclamation de son confesseur.

Un « sauvage » frotté de « civilisation » :
portrait de l'artiste Zacharie Vincent et de son fils Cyprien.
Musée de la province du Québec.

« Troisièmement, les actions ne sont pas d'une malice de coulpe quand l'intention est pure[1], et rien n'est plus pur que de délivrer votre mari.

« Quatrièmement, vous avez des exemples dans la sainte antiquité, qui peuvent merveilleusement servir à votre conduite. Saint Augustin rapporte que sous le proconsulat de Septimius Acyndinus, en l'an 340 de notre salut, un pauvre homme, ne pouvant payer à César ce qui appartenait à César, fut condamné à la mort, comme il est juste, malgré la maxime : *Où il n'y a rien le roi perd ses droits.* Il s'agissait d'une livre d'or; le condamné avait une femme en qui Dieu avait mis la beauté et la prudence. Un vieux richard promit de donner une livre d'or, et même plus, à la dame, à condition qu'il commettrait avec elle le péché immonde[2]. La dame ne crut point mal faire en sauvant la vie à son mari. Saint Augustin approuve fort sa généreuse résignation. Il est vrai que le vieux richard la trompa, et peut-être même son mari n'en fut pas moins pendu; mais elle avait fait tout ce qui était en elle pour sauver sa vie.

« Soyez sûre, ma fille, que quand un jésuite vous cite saint Augustin, il faut que ce saint ait pleinement raison. Je ne vous conseille rien, vous êtes sage; il est à présumer que vous serez utile à votre mari. Monseigneur de Saint-Pouange est un honnête homme, il ne vous trompera pas : c'est tout ce que je puis vous dire; je prierai Dieu pour vous, et j'espère que tout se passera à sa plus grande gloire. »

La belle Saint-Yves, non moins effrayée des discours du jésuite que des propositions du sous-ministre, s'en retourna éperdue chez son amie. Elle était tentée de se délivrer, par la mort, de l'horreur de laisser dans une captivité affreuse l'amant qu'elle adorait, et de la honte de le délivrer au prix de ce qu'elle avait de plus cher, et qui ne devait appartenir qu'à cet amant infortuné. **(2) (3)**

---

1. Rapprochez de Pascal, VIIᵉ *Provinciale ;* **2.** Le récit remonte à saint Augustin. Il est rapporté par Bayle à l'article « Acyndinus » de son Dictionnaire. En 1746, Voltaire en a fait un conte, *Cosi sancta* (illustration d'une prédiction faite par un ecclésiastique à une jeune janséniste : « Ma fille, ta vertu causera bien des malheurs; mais tu seras un jour canonisée pour avoir fait trois infidélités à ton mari »).

QUESTIONS
---

2. Le discours du père Tout-à-tous : citez d'autres discours analogues dans les contes de Voltaire : qu'y a-t-il d'inattendu dans celui-ci? — (Suite page 127.)

CHAPITRE XVII

Elle succombe par vertu.

Elle priait son amie de la tuer; mais cette femme, non moins indulgente que le jésuite, lui parla plus clairement encore. « Hélas! dit-elle, les affaires ne se font guère autrement dans cette cour si aimable, si galante, et si renommée. Les places les plus médiocres et les plus considérables n'ont souvent été données qu'au prix qu'on exige de vous. Écoutez, vous m'avez inspiré de l'amitié et de la confiance; je vous avouerai que si j'avais été aussi difficile que vous l'êtes, mon mari ne jouirait pas du petit poste qui le fait vivre; il le sait, et loin d'en être fâché, il voit en moi sa bienfaitrice, et il se regarde comme ma créature. Pensez-vous que tous ceux qui ont été à la tête des provinces, ou même des armées, aient dû leurs honneurs et leur fortune à leurs seuls services? Il en est qui en sont redevables à mesdames leurs femmes. Les dignités de la guerre ont été sollicitées par l'amour, et la place a été donnée au mari de la plus belle.

« Vous êtes dans une situation bien plus intéressante : il s'agit de rendre votre amant au jour et de l'épouser; c'est un devoir sacré qu'il vous faut remplir. On n'a point blâmé les belles et grandes dames dont je vous parle; on vous applaudira, on dira que vous ne vous êtes permis une faiblesse que par un excès de vertu.

— Ah! quelle vertu! s'écria la belle Saint-Yves; quel labyrinthe d'iniquités! quel pays! et que j'apprends à connaître les hommes! Un père de La Chaise et un bailli ridicule font

──────── QUESTIONS ────────

Qu'est-ce qui permet d'affirmer que Voltaire était exactement documenté sur les querelles entre jésuites et jansénistes? L'art de la palinodie : les propos du jésuite avant la révélation du nom du coupable contredisent heureusement ce qu'il dit immédiatement après : montrez comment les expressions elles-mêmes soulignent le comique des situations. Qu'y a-t-il de comique dans l'expression *Je ne vous conseille rien*?

3. Sur l'ensemble du chapitre XVI. — Composition de ce chapitre : montrez que les deux moments successifs s'opposent et qu'ainsi jaillit le comique. De quelle nature est celui-ci?

— Rapprochez l'attitude du jésuite de la VIIᵉ *Provinciale* de Pascal : identité de thème; discussion spéculative d'un côté, application concrète de l'autre.

— Y a-t-il coup de théâtre pour le lecteur dans le résultat de cette consultation? Pourquoi?

mettre mon amant en prison, ma famille me persécute, on ne
me tend la main dans mon désastre que pour me déshonorer.
Un jésuite a perdu un brave homme, un autre jésuite veut me
perdre; je ne suis entourée que de pièges, et je touche au
moment de tomber dans la misère[1]. Il faut que je me tue, ou
que je parle au roi; je me jetterai à ses pieds sur son passage,
quand il ira à la messe ou à la comédie.

— On ne vous laissera pas approcher, lui dit sa bonne amie;
et si vous aviez le malheur de parler, Mons. de Louvois et le
révérend père de La Chaise pourraient vous enterrer dans le
fond d'un couvent pour le reste de vos jours. » (1)

Tandis que cette brave personne augmentait ainsi les per-
plexités de cette âme désespérée, et enfonçait le poignard dans
son cœur, arrive un exprès de M. de Saint-Pouange avec une
lettre et deux beaux pendants d'oreille. Saint-Yves rejeta le
tout en pleurant; mais l'amie s'en chargea.

Dès que le messager fut parti, notre confidente lit la lettre
dans laquelle on propose un petit souper aux deux amies pour
le soir. Saint-Yves jure qu'elle n'ira point. La dévote veut lui
essayer les deux boucles de diamants. Saint-Yves ne le put
souffrir. Elle combattit la journée entière. Enfin, n'ayant en
vue que son amant, vaincue, entraînée, ne sachant où on la
mène, elle se laisse conduire au souper fatal. Rien n'avait pu
la déterminer à se parer de ses pendants d'oreilles; la confidente les apporta, elle les lui ajusta malgré elle avant qu'on
se mît à table. Saint-Yves était si confuse, si troublée, qu'elle
se laissait tourmenter; et le patron en tirait un augure très
favorable. Vers la fin du repas, la confidente se retira discrètement. Le patron montra alors la révocation de la lettre de
cachet, le brevet d'une gratification considérable, celui d'une
compagnie, et n'épargna pas les promesses. « Ah! lui dit Saint-
Yves, que je vous aimerais si vous ne vouliez pas être tant aimé! »

---

1. *Misère* : détresse morale.

QUESTIONS

1. Un personnage traditionnel de la comédie depuis Molière : la
conseillère satanique; montrez comment ici la femme *non moins indulgente que le jésuite* renouvelle le poncif! — Encore la caricature de
l'esprit « jésuite » : les énormités tournées en actes héroïques; d'où vient
le comique de la réplique *vous ne vous êtes permis une faiblesse que
par un excès de vertu ?* — Du point de vue du style, quelle différence
discernez-vous entre le discours de la *femme indulgente* et la réponse
de la belle Saint-Yves?

Enfin, après une longue résistance, après des sanglots, des cris, des larmes, affaiblie du combat, éperdue, languissante, il fallut se rendre. Elle n'eut d'autre ressource que de se promettre de ne penser qu'à l'Ingénu, tandis que le cruel jouirait impitoyablement de la nécessité où elle était réduite. (2) (3)

CHAPITRE XVIII

Elle délivre son amant et un janséniste.

Au point du jour elle vole à Paris, munie de l'ordre du ministre. Il est difficile de peindre ce qui se passait dans son cœur pendant ce voyage. Qu'on imagine une âme vertueuse et noble, humiliée de son opprobre, enivrée de tendresse, déchirée des remords d'avoir trahi son amant, pénétrée du plaisir de délivrer ce qu'elle adore! Ses amertumes, ses combats, son succès, partageaient toutes ses réflexions. Ce n'était plus cette fille simple dont une éducation provinciale avait rétréci les idées. L'amour et le malheur l'avaient formée. Le sentiment avait fait autant de progrès en elle que la raison en avait fait dans l'esprit de son amant infortuné. Les filles apprennent à sentir plus aisément que les hommes n'apprennent à penser. Son aventure était plus instructive que quatre ans de couvent.

Son habit était d'une simplicité extrême. Elle voyait avec horreur les ajustements sous lesquels elle avait paru devant son funeste bienfaiteur; elle avait laissé ses boucles de diamants à sa compagne sans même les regarder. Confuse et

―――――――― **QUESTIONS** ――――――――

2. La fin du chapitre est une scène de comédie : deux démarches astucieusement espacées de Saint-Pouange : précisez-les; montrez que chacune d'elles vient en temps opportun; le désespoir de la belle Saint-Yves et les propos de la femme indulgente; les protestations de la belle Saint-Yves et les silences de la femme; la parure finalement acceptée; la belle Saint-Yves et Saint-Pouange face à face : montrez comment la trame du conte n'est plus qu'une action dramatique conduite avec une logique toute classique.

3. SUR L'ENSEMBLE DU CHAPITRE XVII. — Le rythme de ce passage : sa rapidité; effet produit par référence aux deux chapitres précédents. Quelle est l'intention de Voltaire?

— Comment Voltaire parvient-il à maintenir la belle Saint-Yves dans l'estime générale malgré la chute?

— Énumérez les attaques contre la vénalité des offices. Ce sujet est-il neuf? Montrez qu'ici il n'est qu'un rappel secondaire dans la trame du chapitre.

charmée, idolâtre de l'Ingénu, et se haïssant elle-même, elle arrive enfin à la porte

> De cet affreux château, palais de la vengeance,
> Qui renferma souvent le crime et l'innocence[1].

Quand il fallut descendre du carrosse, les forces lui manquèrent; on l'aida; elle entra, le cœur palpitant, les yeux humides, le front consterné. On la présente au gouverneur; elle veut lui parler, sa voix expire; elle montre son ordre en articulant à peine quelques paroles. Le gouverneur aimait son prisonnier; il fut très aise de sa délivrance. Son cœur n'était pas endurci comme celui de quelques honorables geôliers ses confrères, qui, ne pensant qu'à la rétribution attachée à la garde de leurs captifs, fondant leurs revenus sur leurs victimes, et vivant du malheur d'autrui, se faisaient en secret une joie affreuse des larmes des infortunés.

Il fait venir le prisonnier dans son appartement. Les deux amants se voient, et tous deux s'évanouissent. La belle Saint-Yves resta longtemps sans mouvement et sans vie : l'autre rappela bientôt son courage. « C'est apparemment là madame votre femme, lui dit le gouverneur; vous ne m'aviez point dit que vous fussiez marié. On me mande que c'est à ses soins généreux que vous devez votre délivrance. — Ah! je ne suis pas digne d'être sa femme », dit la belle Saint-Yves d'une voix tremblante; et elle retomba encore en faiblesse.

Quand elle eut repris ses sens, elle présenta, toujours tremblante, le brevet[2] de la gratification, et la promesse par écrit d'une compagnie. L'Ingénu, aussi étonné qu'attendri, s'éveillait d'un songe pour retomber dans un autre. « Pourquoi ai-je été enfermé ici? comment avez-vous pu m'en tirer? où sont les monstres qui m'y ont plongé? Vous êtes une divinité qui descendez du ciel à mon secours. »

La belle Saint-Yves baissait la vue, regardait son amant, rougissait et détournait, le moment d'après, ses yeux mouillés de pleurs. Elle lui apprit enfin tout ce qu'elle savait, et tout ce qu'elle avait éprouvé, excepté ce qu'elle aurait voulu se cacher pour jamais, et ce qu'un autre que l'Ingénu, plus accoutumé au monde et plus instruit des usages de la cour, aurait deviné facilement.

---

1. *La Henriade*, IV, v. 456-457 (édition de 1723). Une partie de ce poème épique fut composée par Voltaire à la Bastille; 2. *Brevet :* lettre courte en parchemin contenant quelque grâce, quelque privilège accordé par le roi. (Dictionnaire de l'Académie, 1694.)

« Est-il possible qu'un misérable comme ce bailli ait eu le pouvoir de me ravir ma liberté? Ah! je vois bien qu'il en est des hommes comme des plus vils animaux; tous peuvent nuire. Mais est-il possible qu'un moine, un jésuite confesseur du roi, ait contribué à mon infortune autant que ce bailli, sans que je puisse imaginer sous quel prétexte ce détestable fripon m'a persécuté? M'a-t-il fait passer pour un janséniste? Enfin, comment vous êtes-vous souvenue de moi? je ne le méritais pas, je n'étais alors qu'un sauvage. Quoi? vous avez pu, sans conseil, sans secours, entreprendre le voyage de Versailles! Vous y avez paru, et on a brisé mes fers! Il est donc dans la beauté et dans la vertu un charme invincible qui fait tomber les portes de fer, et qui amollit les cœurs de bronze! »

A ce mot de *vertu*, des sanglots échappèrent à la belle Saint-Yves. Elle ne savait pas combien elle était vertueuse dans le crime qu'elle se reprochait.

Son amant continua ainsi : « Ange, qui avez rompu mes liens, si vous avez eu (ce que je ne comprends pas encore) assez de crédit pour me faire rendre justice, faites-la donc rendre aussi à un vieillard qui m'a le premier appris à penser, comme vous m'avez appris à aimer. La calamité nous a unis; je l'aime comme un père, je ne peux vivre ni sans vous ni sans lui.

— Moi! que je sollicite le même homme qui... — Oui, je veux tout vous devoir, et je ne veux devoir jamais rien qu'à vous : écrivez à cet homme puissant; comblez-moi de vos bienfaits, achevez ce que vous avez commencé, achevez vos prodiges. » Elle sentait qu'elle devait faire tout ce que son amant exigeait : elle voulut écrire, sa main ne pouvait obéir. Elle recommença trois fois sa lettre, la déchira trois fois; elle écrivit enfin, et les deux amants sortirent après avoir embrassé le vieux martyr de la grâce efficace.

L'heureuse et désolée Saint-Yves savait dans quelle maison logeait son frère; elle y alla; son amant prit un appartement dans la même maison.

A peine y furent-ils arrivés que son protecteur lui envoya l'ordre de l'élargissement du bonhomme Gordon, et lui demanda un rendez-vous pour le lendemain. Ainsi, à chaque action honnête et généreuse qu'elle faisait, son déshonneur en était le prix. Elle regardait avec exécration cet usage de vendre le malheur et le bonheur des hommes. Elle donna l'ordre de l'élargissement à son amant, et refusa le rendez-vous d'un bienfaiteur qu'elle ne pouvait plus voir sans expirer de douleur et de honte. L'Ingénu ne pouvait se séparer d'elle que pour aller délivrer un ami : il y vola. Il remplit ce devoir en réfléchissant sur les étranges événements de ce monde, et en admirant la vertu courageuse d'une jeune fille à qui deux infortunés devaient plus que la vie. (1)

CHAPITRE XIX

L'Ingénu, la belle Saint-Yves, et leurs parents sont rassemblés.

La généreuse et respectable infidèle était avec son frère l'abbé de Saint-Yves, le bon prieur de la Montagne, et la dame de Kerkabon. Tous étaient également étonnés; mais leur situation et leurs sentiments étaient bien différents. L'abbé de Saint-Yves pleurait ses torts aux pieds de sa sœur, qui lui pardonnait. Le prieur et sa tendre sœur pleuraient aussi, mais de joie; le vilain bailli et son insupportable fils ne troublaient point cette scène touchante. Ils étaient partis au premier bruit de l'élargissement de leur ennemi; ils couraient ensevelir dans leur province leur sottise et leur crainte.

Les quatre personnages, agités de cent mouvements divers, attendaient que le jeune homme revînt avec l'ami qu'il devait délivrer. L'abbé de Saint-Yves n'osait lever les yeux devant sa sœur; la bonne Kerkabon disait : « Je reverrai donc mon cher neveu! — Vous le reverrez, dit la charmante Saint-Yves, mais ce n'est plus le même homme; son maintien, son ton, ses idées, son esprit, tout est changé. Il est devenu aussi respectable qu'il était naïf et étranger à tout. Il sera l'honneur et la consolation de votre famille; que ne puis-je être aussi l'honneur de la mienne! — Vous n'êtes point non plus la même, dit le prieur; que vous est-il donc arrivé qui ait fait en vous un si grand changement? »

Au milieu de cette conversation l'Ingénu arrive, tenant par la main son janséniste. La scène alors devint plus neuve et

─────────── **QUESTIONS** ───────────

1. SUR LE CHAPITRE XVIII. — Analysez la progression dramatique, parallèle à la puissance pathétique. A quoi tiennent-elles?

— La psychologie des deux personnages : étudiez leurs réactions, leurs paroles. Quelle est l'importance des silences et des réticences dans ce « langage ». Les jeux de scène de la belle Saint-Yves et leur effet dramatique.

— En quel sens la situation de l'Ingénu est-elle comique?

plus intéressante. Elle commença par les tendres embrassements de l'oncle et de la tante. L'abbé de Saint-Yves se mettait presque aux genoux de l'Ingénu, qui n'était plus l'*Ingénu*. Les deux amants se parlaient par des regards qui exprimaient tous les sentiments dont ils étaient pénétrés. On voyait éclater la satisfaction, la reconnaissance, sur le front de l'un; l'embarras était peint dans les yeux tendres et un peu égarés de l'autre. On était étonné qu'elle mêlât de la douleur à tant de joie. **(1)**

Le vieux Gordon devint en peu de moments cher à toute la famille. Il avait été malheureux avec le jeune prisonnier, et c'était un grand titre. Il devait sa délivrance aux deux amants, cela seul le réconciliait avec l'amour; l'âpreté de ses anciennes opinions sortait de son cœur : il était changé en homme, ainsi que le Huron. Chacun raconta ses aventures avant le souper. Les deux abbés, la tante, écoutaient comme des enfants qui entendent des histoires de revenants, et comme des hommes qui s'intéressaient tous à tant de désastres. « Hélas! dit Gordon, il y a peut-être plus de cinq cents personnes vertueuses qui sont à présent dans les mêmes fers que Mlle de Saint-Yves a brisés : leurs malheurs sont inconnus. On trouve assez de mains qui frappent sur la foule des malheureux, et rarement une secourable. » Cette réflexion si vraie augmentait sa sensibilité et sa reconnaissance : tout redoublait le triomphe de la belle Saint-Yves; on admirait la grandeur et la fermeté de son âme. L'admiration était mêlée de ce respect qu'on sent malgré

QUESTIONS
---

1. Le sens du drame; le mouvement d'abord : les quatre personnages entre eux; puis les quatre personnages et l'Ingénu; enfin, intervention du père Gordon, mais après une longue présence « muette ». Montrez comment Voltaire ménage les effets exactement comme si ses personnages se mouvaient sur scène. — Les sentiments des personnages se marquent durant le premier paragraphe uniquement par des gestes et des jeux de physionomie : quel effet produit cette scène de pantomime? — Pourquoi Voltaire souligne-t-il l'absence du bailli et de son fils? Leur fuite confirme-t-elle ce que nous savions déjà de leurs caractères? — La préparation de l'entrée en scène de l'Ingénu par une longue réplique de Mlle de Saint-Yves sur le thème de la modification est-elle conforme à la technique dramatique de Voltaire? Rapprochez cette scène de tel ou tel fragment de l'œuvre dramatique de Voltaire. — Immédiatement avant l'arrivée de l'Ingénu, le prieur reprend le thème de la modification, lancé par Mlle de Saint-Yves, mais en le retournant contre elle : quel effet cette réplique produit-elle? — En quel sens la dernière phrase maintient-elle l'intérêt de curiosité? Quel événement Voltaire fait-il ainsi pressentir?

soi pour une personne qu'on croit avoir du crédit à la cour.
Mais l'abbé de Saint-Yves disait quelquefois : « Comment ma
sœur a-t-elle pu faire pour obtenir sitôt ce crédit? » (2)

On allait se mettre à table de très bonne heure. Voilà que
la bonne amie de Versailles arrive, sans rien savoir de tout
ce qui s'était passé; elle était en carrosse à six chevaux, et on
voit bien à qui appartenait l'équipage. Elle entre avec l'air
imposant d'une personne de cour qui a de grandes affaires,
salue très légèrement la compagnie, et tirant la belle Saint-
Yves à l'écart : « Pourquoi vous faire tant attendre? Suivez-
moi; voilà vos diamants que vous aviez oubliés. » Elle ne put
dire ces paroles si bas que l'Ingénu ne les entendît : il vit les
diamants; le frère fut interdit; l'oncle et la tante n'éprouvèrent
qu'une surprise de bonnes gens qui n'avaient jamais vu une
telle magnificence. Le jeune homme, qui s'était formé par un
an de réflexions, en fit malgré lui, et parut troublé un moment.
Son amante s'en aperçut; une pâleur mortelle se répandit sur
son beau visage, un frisson la, saisit, elle se soutenait à peine.
« Ah! madame, dit-elle à la fatale amie, vous m'avez perdue!
vous me donnez la mort! » Ces paroles percèrent le cœur de
l'Ingénu; mais il avait déjà appris à se posséder; il ne les releva
point, de peur d'inquiéter sa maîtresse devant son frère; mais
il pâlit comme elle. (3)

Saint-Yves, éperdue de l'altération qu'elle apercevait sur le
visage de son amant, entraîne cette femme hors de la chambre
dans un petit passage, jette les diamants à terre devant elle.
« Ah! ce ne sont pas eux qui m'ont séduite, vous le savez;
mais celui qui les a donnés ne me reverra jamais. » L'amie
les ramassait, et Saint-Yves ajoutait : « Qu'il les reprenne ou
qu'il vous les donne; allez, ne me rendez plus honteuse de

——————— **QUESTIONS** ———————

2. Qu'y a-t-il de comique dans la phrase *il était changé en homme,
ainsi que le Huron?* Montrez comment Voltaire rappelle ainsi avec discrétion le comique de situation déjà institué lors de la dernière scène
entre l'Ingénu et le père Gordon dans leur cachot. — La mise en scène :
les deux abbés; la tante écoutant les deux récitants; gestes, attitudes;
de plus en plus, la belle Saint-Yves triomphe; à la fin de la scène elle
est tout à fait le personnage central. Montrez que tout cela n'est plus
un conte, mais du théâtre.

3. Le coup de théâtre : le maintien de l'intruse est soigneusement
précisé; ses gestes; les sentiments de chaque personnage, et aussi ses
réflexes mondains, absolument naturels et émouvants; montrez que
c'est là non seulement l'œuvre d'un homme de théâtre, mais aussi de
quelqu'un qui a l'expérience des salons.

moi-même. » L'ambassadrice enfin s'en retourna, ne pouvant comprendre les remords dont elle était témoin.

La belle Saint-Yves, oppressée, éprouvant dans son corps une révolution qui la suffoquait, fut obligée de se mettre au lit; mais pour n'alarmer personne elle ne parla point de ce qu'elle souffrait, et, ne prétextant que sa lassitude, elle demanda la permission de prendre du repos; mais ce fut après avoir rassuré la compagnie par des paroles consolantes et flatteuses, et jeté sur son amant des regards qui portaient le feu dans son âme.

Le souper, qu'elle n'animait pas, fut triste dans le commencement, mais de cette tristesse intéressante qui fournit des conversations attachantes et utiles, si supérieures à la frivole joie qu'on recherche, et qui n'est d'ordinaire qu'un bruit importun.

Gordon fit en peu de mots l'histoire du jansénisme et du molinisme[1], des persécutions dont un parti accablait l'autre, et de l'opiniâtreté de tous les deux. L'Ingénu en fit la critique, et plaignit les hommes qui, non contents de tant de discordes que leurs intérêts allument, se font de nouveaux maux pour des intérêts chimériques, et pour des absurdités inintelligibles. Gordon racontait, l'autre jugeait; les convives écoutaient avec émotion, et s'éclairaient d'une lumière nouvelle. On parla de la longueur de nos infortunes et de la brièveté de la vie. On remarqua que chaque profession a un vice et un danger qui lui sont attachés, et que, depuis le prince jusqu'au dernier des mendiants, tout semble accuser la nature. Comment se trouve-t-il tant d'hommes qui, pour si peu d'argent, se font les persécuteurs, les satellites, les bourreaux des autres hommes? Avec quelle indifférence inhumaine un homme en place signe la destruction d'une famille, et avec quelle joie plus barbare des mercenaires l'exécutent!

« J'ai vu dans ma jeunesse, dit le bonhomme Gordon, un parent du maréchal de Marillac[2], qui, étant poursuivi dans

---

1. Le jésuite espagnol *Molina* publia à Lisbonne en 1588 un traité de théologie intitulé *De liberi arbitrii cum gratiae donis concordia* : il y était soutenu que la grâce divine est inefficace quand la volonté humaine lui résiste; efficace quand l'homme coopère. Cette doctrine, différente du jansénisme, déchaîna une querelle que le pape Paul V s'efforça en vain d'apaiser; 2. Voltaire vise évidemment Saint-Florentin et la profusion de lettres de cachet qu'il fit délivrer. Il écrit dans le feu des affaires Calas, Sirven, de La Barre; en juillet 1767, il réussit à faire reconnaître l'innocence d'un paysan nommé Martin, exécuté à tort. Le maréchal de Marillac (1573-1632), adversaire de Richelieu, fut décapité peu après la disgrâce de son frère, conseiller d'État.

sa province pour la cause de cet illustre malheureux, se cachait dans Paris sous un nom supposé. C'était un vieillard de soixante et douze ans. Sa femme, qui l'accompagnait, était à peu près de son âge. Ils avaient eu un fils libertin qui, à l'âge de quatorze ans, s'était enfui de la maison paternelle : devenu soldat, puis déserteur, il avait passé par tous les degrés de la débauche et de la misère; enfin, ayant pris un nom de terre, il était dans les gardes du cardinal de Richelieu (car ce prêtre, ainsi que le Mazarin, avait des gardes); il avait obtenu un bâton d'exempt dans cette compagnie de satellites. Cet aventurier fut chargé d'arrêter le vieillard et son épouse, et s'en acquitta avec toute la dureté d'un homme qui voulait plaire à son maître. Comme il les conduisait, il entendit ces deux victimes déplorer la longue suite des malheurs qu'elles avaient éprouvés depuis leur berceau. Le père et la mère comptaient parmi leurs plus grandes infortunes les égarements et la perte de leur fils. Il les reconnut; il ne les conduisit pas moins en prison, en les assurant que Son Éminence devait être servie de préférence à tout. Son Éminence récompensa son zèle.

« J'ai vu un espion du père de La Chaise trahir son propre frère, dans l'espérance d'un petit bénéfice qu'il n'eut point; et je l'ai vu mourir, non de remords, mais de douleur d'avoir été trompé par le jésuite.

« L'emploi de confesseur, que j'ai longtemps exercé, m'a fait connaître l'intérieur des familles; je n'en ai guère vu qui ne fussent plongées dans l'amertume, tandis qu'au dehors, couvertes du masque du bonheur, elles paraissaient nager dans la joie; et j'ai toujours remarqué que les grands chagrins étaient le fruit de notre cupidité effrénée.

— Pour moi, dit l'Ingénu, je pense qu'une âme noble, reconnaissante et sensible, peut vivre heureuse; et je compte bien jouir d'une félicité sans mélange avec la belle et généreuse Saint-Yves : car je me flatte, ajouta-t-il, en s'adressant à son frère avec le sourire de l'amitié, que vous ne me refuserez pas, comme l'année passée, et que je m'y prendrai d'une manière plus décente. »

L'abbé se confondit en excuses du passé et en protestations d'un attachement éternel.

L'oncle Kerkabon dit que ce serait le plus beau jour de sa vie. La bonne tante, en s'extasiant et en pleurant de joie, s'écriait : « Je vous l'avais bien dit que vous ne seriez jamais sous-diacre! ce sacrement-ci vaut mieux que l'autre; plût à

Dieu que j'en eusse été honorée! mais je vous servirai de mère. » Alors ce fut à qui renchérirait sur les louanges de la tendre Saint-Yves. (4)

Son amant avait le cœur trop plein de ce qu'elle avait fait pour lui, il l'aimait trop pour que l'aventure des diamants eût fait sur son cœur une impression dominante. Mais ces mots qu'il avait trop entendus, *vous me donnez la mort*, l'effrayaient encore en secret, et corrompaient toute sa joie, tandis que les éloges de sa belle maîtresse augmentaient encore son amour. Enfin on n'était plus occupé que d'elle; on ne parlait que du bonheur que ces deux amants méritaient; on s'arrangeait pour vivre tous ensemble dans Paris; on faisait des projets de fortune et d'agrandissement; on se livrait à toutes ces espérances que la moindre lueur de félicité fait naître si aisément. Mais l'Ingénu, dans le fond de son cœur, éprouvait un sentiment secret qui repoussait cette illusion. Il relisait ces promesses signées Saint-Pouange, et les brevets signés Louvois; on lui dépeignit ces deux hommes tels qu'ils étaient, ou qu'on les croyait être. Chacun parla des ministres et du ministère avec cette liberté de table, regardée en France comme la plus précieuse liberté qu'on puisse goûter sur la terre.

« Si j'étais roi de France, dit l'Ingénu, voici le ministre de la guerre que je choisirais[1] : je voudrais un homme de la plus haute naissance, par la raison qu'il donne des ordres à la noblesse. J'exigerais qu'il eût été lui-même officier, qu'il eût passé par tous les grades, qu'il fût au moins lieutenant général des armées, et digne d'être maréchal de France : car n'est-il pas nécessaire qu'il ait servi lui-même, pour mieux connaître

---

1. Voltaire glisse ici un éloge du duc de Choiseul. Il intéressa ce puissant ministre à la prospérité de son domaine de Ferney et aussi à la lutte philosophique. Voici un jugement d'un contemporain, le baron de Gleichen, sur Choiseul : « Bon, noble, franc, généreux, galant, magnifique, libéral, fier, audacieux, bouillant et emporté même, le duc de Choiseul rappelait... l'idée des anciens chevaliers français. » En 1774, Choiseul quitta le pouvoir; à partir de cette date les lettres de Voltaire s'espacent, et notre philosophe se met à cultiver Maupeou, le nouveau ministre.

——————— QUESTIONS ———————

4. En quel sens le comportement de la belle Saint-Yves fait-il pressentir le dénouement? — Un souper non frivole, mais philosophique : l'aspect autobiographique de l'ensemble du chapitre. — L'abbé de Saint-Yves réitère sous une forme chaque fois différente la même question : quel effet produit cette répétition? — Que vous rappelle l'exclamation finale de Mlle de Kerkabon? Rapprochez-la de son attitude au début du conte.

les détails du service? et les officiers n'obéiront-ils pas avec cent fois plus d'allégresse à un homme de guerre, qui aura comme eux signalé son courage, qu'à un homme de cabinet qui ne peut que deviner tout au plus les opérations d'une campagne, quelque esprit qu'il puisse avoir? Je ne serais pas fâché que mon ministre fût généreux, quoique mon garde du trésor royal en fût quelquefois un peu embarrassé. J'aimerais qu'il eût un travail facile, et que même il se distinguât par cette gaieté d'esprit, partage d'un homme supérieur aux affaires qui plaît tant à la nation, et qui rend tous les devoirs moins pénibles. » Il désirait qu'un ministre eût ce caractère, parce qu'il avait toujours remarqué que cette belle humeur est incompatible avec la cruauté. (5)

Mons. de Louvois n'aurait peut-être pas été satisfait des souhaits de l'Ingénu; il avait une autre sorte de mérite[1].

Mais pendant qu'on était à table, la maladie de cette fille malheureuse prenait un caractère funeste; son sang s'était allumé, une fièvre dévorante s'était déclarée, elle souffrait et ne se plaignait point, attentive à ne pas troubler la joie des convives.

Son frère, sachant qu'elle ne dormait pas, alla au chevet de son lit; il fut surpris de l'état où elle était. Tout le monde accourut; l'amant se présentait à la suite du frère. Il était, sans doute, le plus alarmé et le plus attendri de tous; mais il avait appris à joindre la discrétion à tous les dons heureux que la nature lui avait prodigués, et le sentiment prompt des bienséances commençait à dominer dans lui.

On fit venir aussitôt un médecin du voisinage. C'était un de ceux qui visitent leurs malades en courant, qui confondent la maladie qu'ils viennent de voir avec celle qu'ils voient, qui mettent une pratique aveugle dans une science à laquelle toute la maturité d'un discernement sain et réfléchi ne peut ôter son

---

1. Voltaire n'aimait pas Louvois. *Le Siècle de Louis XIV* monte en épingle les traits défavorables du personnage.

▬ QUESTIONS ▬

5. A la joie générale, Voltaire oppose les sombres pressentiments de l'Ingénu : comment ceux-ci sont-ils indiqués? Quel effet produisent ces contrastes? Contradictions aussi dans l'âme de l'Ingénu : en quel sens? — L'éloge du duc de Choiseul : montrez comment l'ensemble du paragraphe qui lui est consacré cadre avec la biographie du personnage. N'y a-t-il pas dans cet éloge une part d'apologie personnelle?

incertitude et ses dangers. Il redoubla le mal par sa précipitation à prescrire un remède alors à la mode. De la mode jusque dans la médecine! Cette manie était trop commune dans Paris.

La triste Saint-Yves contribuait encore plus que son médecin à rendre sa maladie dangereuse. Son âme tuait son corps. La foule des pensées qui l'agitaient portait dans ses veines un poison plus dangereux que celui de la fièvre la plus brûlante. (6) (7)

CHAPITRE XX

La belle Saint-Yves meurt[1], et ce qui en arrive.

On appela un autre médecin : celui-ci, au lieu d'aider la nature et de la laisser agir dans une jeune personne dans qui tous les organes rappelaient la vie, ne fut occupé que de contrecarrer son confrère. La maladie devint mortelle en deux jours. Le cerveau, qu'on croit le siège de l'entendement, fut attaqué aussi violemment que le cœur, qui est, dit-on, le siège des passions.

Quelle mécanique incompréhensible a soumis les organes au sentiment et à la pensée[2]? Comment une seule idée douloureuse dérange-t-elle le cours du sang? Et comment le sang à son tour porte-t-il ses irrégularités dans l'entendement humain? Quel est ce fluide inconnu et dont l'existence est certaine, qui, plus prompt, plus actif que la lumière, vole, en moins d'un

---

1. Le dénouement du conte de Voltaire est semblable à celui d'un roman de Duclos, *Histoire de Mᵐᵉ de Luz.* L'héroïne de Duclos meurt, elle aussi, d'une fièvre provoquée par le remords; 2. Voltaire a longuement médité Descartes, et surtout Malebranche : le problème de l'existence de l'âme et celui des rapports de l'âme et du corps le hantent (exemple *Cosi sancta*, 1787).

QUESTIONS

6. L'état de santé de Mˡˡᵉ de Saint-Yves : cette aggravation était-elle prévisible? Comment l'atmosphère ainsi créée tourne-t-elle à la tragédie? Relevez la satire traditionnelle des médecins : sur quel ton est-elle faite ici? Peut-on prévoir le dénouement?

7. Sur l'ensemble du chapitre XIX. — Montrez comment l'Ingénu est présenté sous un jour de plus en plus favorable. A quoi est due cette évolution?
— Évolution de l'atmosphère : tension et pathétique croissants. Relevez-en les étapes.
— La discussion, dans ce chapitre, est-elle exclusivement destructrice? Est-ce le cas le plus répandu dans *l'Ingénu?*

clin d'œil, dans tous les canaux de la vie, produit les sensations, la mémoire, la tristesse ou la joie, la raison ou le vertige, rappelle avec horreur ce qu'on voudrait oublier, et fait d'un animal pensant ou un objet d'admiration, ou un sujet de pitié et de larmes[1] ?

C'était là ce que disait le bon Gordon ; et cette réflexion si naturelle, que rarement font les hommes, ne dérobait rien à son attendrissement ; car il n'était pas de ces malheureux philosophes qui s'efforcent d'être insensibles. Il était touché du sort de cette jeune fille, comme un père qui voit mourir lentement son enfant chéri. L'abbé de Saint-Yves était désespéré, le prieur et sa sœur répandaient des ruisseaux de larmes. Mais qui pourrait peindre l'état de son amant ? Nulle langue n'a des expressions qui répondent à ce comble des douleurs ; les langues sont trop imparfaites[2]. (1)

La tante, presque sans vie, tenait la tête de la mourante dans ses faibles bras ; son frère était à genoux au pied du lit ; son amant pressait sa main, qu'il baignait de pleurs, et éclatait en sanglots : il la nommait sa bienfaitrice, son espérance, sa vie, la moitié de lui-même, sa maîtresse, son épouse. A ce mot d'épouse elle soupira, le regarda avec une tendresse inexprimable, et soudain jeta un cri d'horreur ; puis, dans un de ces intervalles où l'accablement, et l'oppression des sens, et les souffrances suspendues, laissent à l'âme sa liberté et sa force, elle s'écria : « Moi, votre épouse ! Ah ! cher amant, ce nom, ce bonheur, ce prix, n'étaient plus faits pour moi ; je meurs, et je le mérite. O dieu de mon cœur ! ô vous que j'ai sacrifié à des démons infernaux, c'en est fait, je suis punie, vivez heureux. » Ces paroles tendres et terribles ne pouvaient être comprises ; mais elles portaient dans tous les cœurs l'effroi et l'attendrissement ; elle eut le courage de s'expliquer. Chaque mot fit frémir d'étonnement, de douleur et de pitié, tous les assistants. Tous se réunissaient à détester l'homme puissant

---

1. Allusion évidente à Malebranche ; 2. Voltaire sacrifie ici à la mode du roman sentimental : l'attendrissement général est un lieu commun de ce genre littéraire.

─────── **QUESTIONS** ───────

1. *Aider la nature* : en quoi cette expression rappelle-t-elle Molière ? Relevez dans le premier paragraphe les termes appartenant à la terminologie cartésienne. Le second paragraphe est une méditation philosophique : à quels philosophes Voltaire songe-t-il ? — Comment Voltaire met-il en vedette la douleur de l'Ingénu ?

qui n'avait réparé une horrible injustice que par un crime, et qui avait forcé la plus respectable innocence à être sa complice.

« Qui? vous coupable! lui dit son amant; non, vous ne l'êtes pas; le crime ne peut être que dans le cœur, le vôtre est à la vertu et à moi. »

Il confirmait ce sentiment par des paroles qui semblaient remener à la vie la belle Saint-Yves. Elle se sentit consolée, et s'étonnait d'être aimée encore. Le vieux Gordon l'aurait condamnée dans le temps qu'il n'était que janséniste; mais, étant devenu sage, il l'estimait, et il pleurait. (2)

Au milieu de tant de larmes et de craintes, pendant que le danger de cette fille si chère remplissait tous les cœurs, que tout était consterné, on annonce un courrier de la cour. Un courrier! et de qui? et pourquoi? C'était de la part du confesseur du roi pour le prieur de la Montagne; ce n'était pas le père de La Chaise qui écrivait, c'était le frère Vadbled, son valet de chambre, homme très important dans ce temps-là, lui qui mandait aux archevêques les volontés du révérend père, lui qui donnait audience, lui qui promettait des bénéfices, lui qui faisait quelquefois expédier des lettres de cachet. Il écrivait à l'abbé de la Montagne que « Sa Révérence était informée des aventures de son neveu, que sa prison n'était qu'une méprise, que ces petites disgrâces arrivaient fréquemment, qu'il ne fallait pas y faire attention, et qu'enfin il convenait que lui prieur vînt lui présenter son neveu le lendemain, qu'il devait amener avec lui le bonhomme Gordon, que lui frère Vadbled les introduirait chez Sa Révérence et chez Mons. de Louvois, lequel leur dirait un mot dans son antichambre. »

Il ajoutait que l'histoire de l'Ingénu et son combat contre les Anglais avaient été contés au roi, que sûrement le roi daignerait le remarquer quand il passerait dans la galerie, et peut-être même lui ferait un signe de tête. La lettre finissait par l'espérance dont on le flattait, que toutes les dames de la cour s'empresseraient de faire venir son neveu à leur toilette, que plusieurs d'entre elles lui diraient : « Bonjour, monsieur l'Ingénu »; et qu'assurément il serait question de lui au souper

──────── QUESTIONS ────────

2. Un tableau dramatique comme les aimait Diderot : montrez comment la scène de désespoir autour de la belle Saint-Yves correspond au goût de l'époque. — Une situation hardie : les aveux de la belle Saint-Yves; citez un passage analogue dans *la Princesse de Clèves*; profitez de cette comparaison pour rappeler que l'œuvre romanesque du XVIIe siècle a préparé la comédie larmoyante et le roman par lettres.

du roi. La lettre était signée : « Votre affectionné Vadbled, frère jésuite. » **(3)**

Le prieur ayant lu la lettre tout haut, son neveu furieux, et commandant un moment à sa colère, ne dit rien au porteur; mais se tournant vers le compagnon de ses infortunes, il lui demanda ce qu'il pensait de ce style. Gordon lui répondit : « C'est donc ainsi qu'on traite les hommes comme des singes! On les bat et on les fait danser. » L'Ingénu, reprenant son caractère, qui revient toujours dans les grands mouvements de l'âme, déchira la lettre par morceaux, et les jeta au nez du courrier : « Voilà ma réponse. » Son oncle, épouvanté, crut voir le tonnerre et vingt lettres de cachet tomber sur lui. Il alla vite écrire et s'excuser, comme il put, ce qu'il prenait pour l'emportement d'un jeune homme, et qui était la saillie[1] d'une grande âme.

Mais des soins[2] plus douloureux s'emparaient de tous les cœurs. La belle et infortunée Saint-Yves sentait déjà sa fin approcher; elle était dans le calme, mais dans ce calme affreux de la nature affaissée qui n'a plus la force de combattre. « O mon cher amant! dit-elle d'une voix tombante, la mort me punit de ma faiblesse; mais j'expire avec la consolation de vous savoir libre. Je vous ai adoré en vous trahissant, et je vous adore en vous disant un éternel adieu. »

Elle ne se parait pas d'une vaine fermeté; elle ne concevait pas cette misérable gloire de faire dire à quelques voisins : « Elle est morte avec courage. » Qui peut perdre à vingt ans son amant, sa vie, et ce qu'on appelle l'*honneur*, sans regrets et sans déchirements? Elle sentait toute l'horreur[3] de son état[4], et le faisait sentir par ces mots et par ces regards mourants qui parlent avec tant d'empire. Enfin elle pleurait comme les autres dans les moments où elle eut la force de pleurer.

Que d'autres cherchent à louer les morts fastueuses[5] de ceux qui entrent dans la destruction avec insensibilité : c'est le sort

---

1. *Saillie* : emportement (léger archaïsme); 2. *Soins* : préoccupations; le mot se dit « des soucis, des inquiétudes qui émeuvent, qui troublent l'âme » (Dictionnaire de Furetière, 1690); 3. *Horreur* : saisissement que cause la pensée d'une chose affreuse : ce sens est très fort; il est dû au latin *horror*, « hérissement, frémissement qui fait dresser les cheveux et donne la chair de poule » (Dictionnaire de l'Académie, 1694); 4. *État* : situation d'une personne à un moment donné; conjoncture, circonstance; 5. *Fastueux* : adjectif dérivé de *faste*, qui signifie « vaine ostentation, affectation de paraître avec éclat » (Dictionnaire de l'Académie, 1694). L'adjectif *fastueux* s'emploie « toujours en mauvaise part » (Dictionnaire de Furetière).

—— **QUESTIONS** ——

3. L'intermède de frère Vadbled : quelle est son utilité?

de tous les animaux. Nous ne mourons comme eux avec indifférence que quand l'âge ou la maladie nous rend semblables
à eux par la stupidité[1] de nos organes. Quiconque fait une
grande perte a de grands regrets; s'il les étouffe, c'est qu'il
porte la vanité jusque dans les bras de la mort. **(4)**

Lorsque le moment fatal fut arrivé, tous les assistants jetèrent
des larmes et des cris. L'Ingénu perdit l'usage de ses sens.
Les âmes fortes ont des sentiments bien plus violents que les
autres quand elles sont tendres. Le bon Gordon le connaissait
assez pour craindre qu'étant revenu à lui il ne se donnât la
mort[2]. On écarta toutes les armes; le malheureux jeune homme
s'en aperçut; il dit à ses parents et à Gordon, sans pleurer,
sans gémir, sans s'émouvoir : « Pensez-vous donc qu'il y ait
quelqu'un sur la terre qui ait le droit et le pouvoir de m'empêcher de finir ma vie? » Gordon se garda bien de lui étaler ces
lieux communs fastidieux par lesquels on essaye de prouver
qu'il n'est pas permis d'user de sa liberté pour cesser d'être
quand on est horriblement mal, qu'il ne faut pas sortir de sa
maison quand on ne peut plus y demeurer, que l'homme est
sur la terre comme un soldat à son poste : comme s'il importait
à l'Être des êtres que l'assemblage de quelques parties de
matière fût dans un lieu ou dans un autre; raisons impuis-
santes qu'un désespoir ferme et réfléchi dédaigne d'écouter,
et auxquelles Caton ne répondit que par un coup de poignard.

Le morne et terrible silence de l'Ingénu, ses yeux sombres,
ses lèvres tremblantes, les frémissements de son corps, portaient dans l'âme de tous ceux qui le regardaient ce mélange

---

1. *Stupidité* : sorte de paralysie, d'engourdissement; 2. Voltaire n'approuve pas
le suicide; il n'en admire pas moins le courage de ceux qui se donnent la mort :
« Il faut une âme forte pour surmonter ainsi l'instinct le plus puissant de la nature. »
Il s'incline devant la force d'âme de « quelques anciens », dont Caton, qui se donnèrent
la mort. Et, à l'article « Suicide » du *Dictionnaire philosophique*, Voltaire écrivit
ceci : « Caton d'Utique, s'étant allié à Pompée, et se voyant après sa défaite en
46 avant Jésus-Christ poursuivi par César, préféra la mort à l'ignominie ou à la
clémence du vainqueur. Il se mit au lit, lut le *Phédon*, dialogue de Platon sur l'immortalité de l'âme, et puis se donna un coup de poignard. »

QUESTIONS
---

4. Précisez le sens des expressions suivantes : *il lui demanda ce qu'il
pensait « de ce style »; les grands « mouvements » de l'âme; cette misérable « gloire »; ce qu'on appelle l'« honneur »; c'est qu'il porte la
« vanité »...* — Pathétique et réflexion dans ce passage; montrez comment
la mort est douloureusement ressentie en même temps qu'analysée. A
quoi voit-on un frémissement de l'auteur derrière ses personnages et
leur aventure?

de compassion et d'effroi qui enchaîne toutes les puissances de l'âme, qui exclut tout discours, et qui ne se manifeste que par des mots entrecoupés. L'hôtesse et sa famille étaient accourues; on tremblait de son désespoir, on le gardait à vue, on observait tous ses mouvements. Déjà le corps glacé de la belle Saint-Yves avait été porté dans une salle basse, loin des yeux de son amant, qui semblait la chercher encore, quoiqu'il ne fût plus en état de rien voir. (5)

Au milieu de ce spectacle de la mort, tandis que le corps est exposé à la porte de la maison, que deux prêtres à côté d'un bénitier récitent des prières d'un air distrait, que des passants jettent quelques gouttes d'eau bénite sur la bière par oisiveté, que d'autres poursuivent leur chemin avec indifférence, que les parents pleurent, et qu'un amant est prêt de s'arracher la vie, le Saint-Pouange arrive avec l'amie de Versailles.

Son goût[1] passager, n'ayant été satisfait qu'une fois, était devenu de l'amour. Le refus de ses bienfaits l'avait piqué. Le père de La Chaise n'aurait jamais pensé à venir dans cette maison; mais Saint-Pouange ayant tous les jours devant les yeux l'image de la belle Saint-Yves, brûlant d'assouvir une passion qui par une seule jouissance avait enfoncé dans son cœur l'aiguillon des désirs, ne balança[2] pas à venir lui-même chercher celle qu'il n'aurait pas peut-être voulu revoir trois fois si elle était venue d'elle-même.

Il descend de carrosse; le premier objet qui se présente à lui est une bière; il détourne les yeux avec ce simple dégoût d'un homme nourri dans les plaisirs, qui pense qu'on doit

---

1. *Goût* : sympathie profonde; 2. *Balancer* : hésiter.

QUESTIONS
---

5. Comment Voltaire transforme un lieu commun romanesque : comparez la mort de la belle Saint-Yves avec, par exemple, la mort de Manon (la *Manon Lescaut* de l'abbé Prévost date de 1731; réédition en 1753) : « ... j'invoquai le secours du Ciel et j'attendis la mort avec impatience... il ne sortit point une larme de mes yeux ni un soupir de ma bouche. La consternation profonde où j'étais, et le dessein déterminé de mourir, avaient coupé le cours à toutes les expressions du désespoir et de la douleur... » — Le sens dramatique : quel effet Voltaire tire-t-il du contraste entre l'agitation de tous les personnages et le silence effrayant de l'Ingénu? Les jeux de physionomie : montrez comment l'attitude désespérée de l'Ingénu est une scène de mime.

lui épargner tout spectacle qui pourrait le ramener à la contemplation de la misère humaine. Il veut monter. La femme de
Versailles demande par curiosité qui on va enterrer; on pro-
nonce le nom de Mlle de Saint-Yves. A ce nom, elle pâlit et
poussa un cri affreux; Saint-Pouange se retourne; la surprise
et la douleur remplissent son âme. Le bon Gordon était là,
les yeux remplis de larmes. Il interrompt ses tristes prières
pour apprendre à l'homme de cour toute cette horrible
catastrophe. Il lui parle avec cet empire que donnent la douleur
et la vertu. Saint-Pouange n'était point né méchant; le torrent
des affaires et des amusements avait emporté son âme, qui
ne se connaissait pas encore. Il ne touchait point à la vieillesse,
qui endurcit d'ordinaire le cœur des ministres; il écoutait
Gordon, les yeux baissés, et il en essuyait quelques pleurs
qu'il était étonné de répandre : il connut le repentir. **(6)**

« Je veux voir absolument, dit-il, cet homme extraordinaire
dont vous m'avez parlé; il m'attendrit presque autant que
cette innocente victime dont j'ai causé la mort. » Gordon le
suit jusqu'à la chambre où le prieur, la Kerkabon, l'abbé de
Saint-Yves, et quelques voisins, rappelaient à la vie le jeune
homme retombé en défaillance.

« J'ai fait votre malheur, lui dit le sous-ministre, j'emploierai
ma vie à le réparer. » La première idée qui vint à l'Ingénu
fut de le tuer, et de se tuer lui-même après. Rien n'était plus
à sa place; mais il était sans armes et veillé de près. Saint-
Pouange ne se rebuta point des refus accompagnés du reproche,
du mépris, et de l'horreur qu'il avait mérités, et qu'on lui
prodigua. Le temps adoucit tout. Mgr de Louvois vint enfin
à bout de faire un excellent officier de l'Ingénu, qui a paru
sous un autre nom à Paris et dans les armées, avec l'approba-
tion de tous les honnêtes gens, et qui a été à la fois un guerrier
et un philosophe intrépide.

─────── ■ QUESTIONS ■ ───────

6. Le corps exposé à la porte de la maison : en quoi y a-t-il dans cette
scène un trait de mœurs de l'époque? Montrez que chaque personnage
a une attitude personnelle, qui révèle son état d'esprit. En quel sens la
scène est-elle satirique? — Étudiez l'attitude de Saint-Pouange dans ce
chapitre; ensuite, suivez-le depuis son entrée en scène : de cette étude,
déduisez la modification qui s'est opérée en lui. Même analyse en ce qui
concerne le père Gordon. — Comment ces « conversions » aboutissent-
elles à un puissant comique de situation? — Situez le coup de théâtre
qui change brusquement le mouvement de la scène. Montrez comment,
tout originale qu'elle est, celle-ci n'en subit pas moins l'influence de la
comédie larmoyante.

Il ne parlait jamais de cette aventure sans gémir; et cependant sa consolation était d'en parler. Il chérit la mémoire de la tendre Saint-Yves jusqu'au dernier moment de sa vie. L'abbé de Saint-Yves et le prieur eurent chacun un bon bénéfice; la bonne Kerkabon aima mieux voir son neveu dans les honneurs militaires que dans le sous-diaconat. La dévote de Versailles garda les boucles de diamants, et reçut encore un beau présent. Le père Tout-à-tous eut des boîtes de chocolat, de café, de sucre candi, de citrons confits, avec les *Méditations du révérend père Croiset*[1] et *la Fleur des saints*[2], reliées en maroquin. Le bon Gordon vécut avec l'Ingénu jusqu'à sa mort dans la plus intime amitié; il eut un bénéfice aussi, et oublia pour jamais la grâce efficace et le concours concomitant. Il prit pour sa devise : *malheur est bon à quelque chose*. Combien d'honnêtes gens dans le monde ont pu dire : *malheur n'est bon à rien!* **(7) (8)**

---

1. Jésuite marseillais, le père Croiset, recteur du noviciat d'Avignon, publia, à partir de 1694, de nombreuses *Méditations*; en 1710, l'œuvre fit l'objet d'une publication globale en 4 volumes in-12; la *Retraite spirituelle pour un jour de chaque mois*, en particulier, avait connu un vif succès; 2. Le jésuite espagnol Pedro Ribadeneira publia, en 1699, une *Flos sanctorum, o Libro de las vidas de los santos*. Ce travail est en réalité un extrait de la *Légende dorée*. Il a été souvent traduit en français.

──────── **QUESTIONS** ────────

7. La conversion de M. de Saint-Pouange : est-elle sincère? Montrez-le par des citations précises. Comment le sort de l'Ingénu lui est-il lié?
— La conclusion du conte : énoncez-la; est-elle entièrement satisfaisante pour l'esprit? Soulignez la note d'amertume. En quoi la revue des personnages et l'aperçu de ce qui leur arrive au-delà du conte ne font-ils que la mettre en relief dans certains cas (la dévote, le père Tout-à-tous)?

8. SUR L'ENSEMBLE DU CHAPITRE XX. — Montrez que la fin du conte est assez conforme au pessimisme raisonné de Voltaire. Démêlez les éléments positifs des éléments négatifs.

— Le dénouement; montrez comment : 1º l'Ingénu mis à part, chaque personnage a finalement un sort qui convient à ses désirs; 2º la moralité qui se dégage est que le régime est et pourri.

— Quelle moralité peut-on dégager du conte? Que voulait montrer Voltaire? Précisez les thèmes accessoires en indiquant comment ils se rattachent à l'idée principale.

DOCUMENTATION THÉMATIQUE

réunie par la rédaction des « Nouveaux Classiques Larousse ».

1. *Micromégas* ou le voyage philosophique.
2. Le « Bon Sauvage » et la littérature.
3. Voltaire et la littérature.

1. *MICROMÉGAS*
ou LE VOYAGE PHILOSOPHIQUE

Dans son étude sur *Voltaire dans ses contes* (Colin, 1966), M. Jacques Van Den Heuvel écrit en parlant de *Micromégas* :

> « [...] dans l'état où ce conte fut publié en 1752, il renvoie par toute une série d'allusions éparses aux préoccupations qui furent celles de Voltaire [...] vers 1738-1739. Il porte la marque de ses recherches philosophiques pendant cette même période » (page 109).

Ces préoccupations sont, selon le critique, de trois ordres qui se résument dans trois noms : Locke, Newton et Pope. Sans doute les rapports peuvent-ils paraître parfois fort lointains; ils n'en demeurent pas moins essentiels à la compréhension profonde de l'idée qui sous-tend le conte.

Nous ne nous arrêterons pas sur l'apport de Newton à l'œuvre de Voltaire : on se reportera aux pages 34-36 et 40-42 des *Œuvres philosophiques* de Voltaire en « Classiques Larousse ».

1. 1. VOLTAIRE ET LOCKE : LA MÉTHODE EXPÉRIMENTALE

Venus d'une autre planète, les deux voyageurs vont se trouver confrontés à un monde inconnu, dont il leur faudra, dans un délai aussi bref que possible, dresser un bilan complet — ou presque. Or, ce bilan, Micromégas va le faire *graduellement*, selon une démarche proche de celle de Locke, qui osait

> « modestement avancer que nous ne serons peut-être jamais capables de connaître si un être purement matériel pense ou non » (XIIIe *Lettre philosophique*).

L'ensemble de cette méthode sera défini de façon fort claire dans une longue note de la IIIe partie du poème sur la Loi naturelle :

> Le modeste et sage Locke est connu pour avoir développé toute la marche de l'entendement humain, et pour avoir montré les limites de son pouvoir. Convaincu de la faiblesse humaine, et pénétré de la puissance infinie du Créateur, il dit que nous ne connaissons la nature de notre âme que par la foi; il dit que l'homme n'a point par lui-même assez de lumières pour assurer que Dieu ne peut pas communiquer la pensée à tout être auquel il daignera faire ce présent, à la matière elle-même.
>
> Ceux qui étaient encore dans l'ignorance s'élevèrent contre lui. Entêtés d'un cartésianisme aussi faux en tout que le péripatétisme, ils croyaient que la matière n'est autre chose que l'étendue en longueur, largeur et profondeur : ils ne savaient pas qu'elle a la gravitation vers un centre, la force d'inertie, et d'autres propriétés; que ses éléments sont indivisibles, tandis que ses composés se divisent sans cesse. Ils bornaient la puissance de l'Etre tout-puissant; ils ne faisaient pas réflexion

qu'après toutes les découvertes sur la matière, nous ne connaissons point le fond de cet être. Ils devaient songer que l'on a longtemps agité si l'entendement humain est une faculté ou une substance; ils devaient s'interroger eux-mêmes, et sentir que nos connaissances sont trop bornées pour sonder cet abîme.

La faculté que les animaux ont de se mouvoir n'est point une substance, un être à part; il paraît que c'est un don du Créateur. Locke dit que ce même Créateur peut faire ainsi un don de la pensée à tel être qu'il daignera choisir. Dans cette hypothèse, qui nous soumet plus que toute autre à l'Être suprême, la pensée accordée à un élément de matière n'en est pas moins pure, moins immortelle que dans toute autre hypothèse. Cet élément indivisible est impérissable : la pensée peut assurément subsister à jamais avec lui, quand le corps est dissous. Voilà ce que Locke propose sans rien affirmer. Il dit ce que Dieu eût pu faire et non ce que Dieu a fait. Il ne connaît point ce que c'est que la matière; il avoue qu'entre elle et Dieu il peut y avoir une infinité de substances créées absolument différentes les unes des autres. La lumière, le feu élémentaire, paraît en effet, comme on l'a dit dans les *Eléments* de Newton, une substance mitoyenne entre cet être inconnu, nommé matière, et d'autres êtres encore plus inconnus. La lumière ne tend point vers un centre comme la matière, elle ne paraît pas impénétrable; aussi Newton dit souvent dans son *Optique* : « Je n'examine pas si les rayons de la lumière sont des corps ou non. »

Locke dit donc qu'il peut y avoir un nombre innombrable de substances, et que Dieu est le maître d'accorder des idées à ces substances. Nous ne pouvons deviner par quel art divin un être, quel qu'il soit, a des idées, nous en sommes bien loin : nous ne saurons jamais comment un ver de terre a le pouvoir de se remuer. Il faut dans toutes ces recherches s'en remettre à Dieu, et sentir son néant. Telle est la philosophie de cet homme, d'autant plus grand qu'il est plus simple : et c'est cette soumission à Dieu qu'on a osé appeler impiété; et ce sont les sectateurs, convaincus de l'immortalité de l'âme, qu'on a nommés matérialistes; et c'est un homme tel que Locke à qui un compilateur de quelque physique* a donné le nom d'ennuyeux.

Quand même Locke se serait trompé sur ce point (si l'on peut pourtant se tromper en n'affirmant rien), cela n'empêche pas qu'il ne mérite la louange qu'on lui donne ici : il est le premier, ce me semble, qui ait montré qu'on ne connaît aucun axiome avant d'avoir connu les vérités particulières; il est le premier qui ait fait voir ce que c'est que l'identité, et ce que c'est que d'être la même personne, le même *soi ;* il est le premier qui ait prouvé la fausseté du système des idées innées. Sur quoi je remarquerai qu'il y a des écoles qui anathématisèrent les idées innées quand Descartes les établit, et qui anathématisèrent ensuite les adversaires des idées innées, quand Locke les eut détruites. C'est ainsi que jugent les hommes qui ne sont pas philosophes.

Montrez comment Voltaire insère cette attitude philosophique dans son récit :

— sur le plan des idées;
— dans la structure même de l'œuvre.

Relevez les passages où Micromégas se fait le disciple et le porte-parole direct de Voltaire-Locke.

1. 2. VOLTAIRE ET POPE : L'HOMME DANS L'UNIVERS

Conte philosophique, *Micromégas* est en réalité un « essai de situation de l'homme par rapport au cosmos et une sagesse qui en découle : *Micromégas* s'inspire sans aucun doute de l'optimisme de Pope » (Van Den Heuvel, *op. cit.*, p. 106). Or, le Saturnien a un frère, aîné de quatorze ans, en la personne d'un sage lettré chinois curieux de la nature des choses. Ce personnage, héros du *Sixième Discours en vers sur l'Homme*, est l'héritier de Pope, dont Voltaire vante l'*Essay on Man*,

« le plus beau poème didactique, le plus sublime et le plus utile qu'on ait fait dans aucune langue ».

Ce sont les réflexions de ce lettré chinois que nous donnons ci-dessous :

Écoutez seulement un récit véritable,
Que peut-être Fourmont prendra pour une fable,
Et que je lus hier dans un livre chinois
Qu'un jésuite à Pékin traduisit autrefois.
    Un jour quelques souris se disaient l'une à l'autre :
« Que ce monde est charmant! quel empire est le nôtre!
Ce palais si superbe est élevé pour nous;
De toute éternité Dieu nous fit ces grands trous.
Vois-tu ces gras jambons sous cette voûte obscure?
Ils y furent créés des mains de la Nature;
Ces montagnes de lard, éternels aliments,
Sont pour nous en ces lieux jusqu'à la fin des temps.
Oui, nous sommes, grand Dieu, si l'on en croit nos sages,
Le chef-d'œuvre, la fin, le but de tes ouvrages.
Les chats sont dangereux et prompts à nous manger;
Mais c'est pour nous instruire et pour nous corriger. »
    Plus loin, sur le duvet d'une herbe renaissante,
Près des bois, près des eaux, une troupe innocente
De canards nasillants, de dindons rengorgés,
De gros moutons bêlants, que leur laine a chargés,
Disait : « Tout est à nous, bois, prés, étangs, montagnes;
Le ciel pour nos besoins fait verdir les campagnes. »
L'âne passait auprès, et, se mirant dans l'eau,

Il rendait grâce au ciel en se trouvant si beau :
« Pour les ânes, dit-il, le ciel a fait la terre;
L'homme est né mon esclave, il me panse, il me ferre,
Il m'étrille, il me lave, il prévient mes désirs,
Il bâtit mon sérail, il conduit mes plaisirs;
Respectueux témoin de ma noble tendresse,
Ministre de ma joie, il m'amène une ânesse;
Et je ris quand je vois cet esclave orgueilleux
Envier l'heureux don que j'ai reçu des cieux. »
    L'homme vint, et cria : « Je suis puissant et sage;
Cieux, terres, éléments, tout est pour mon usage :
L'océan fut formé pour porter mes vaisseaux;
Les vents sont mes courriers, les astres mes flambeaux.
Ce globe qui des nuits blanchit les sombres voiles
Croît, décroît, fuit, revient, et préside aux étoiles.
Moi, je préside à tout; mon esprit éclairé
Dans les bornes du monde eût été trop serré;
Mais enfin, de ce monde et l'oracle et le maître,
Je ne suis point encor ce que je devrais être. »
Quelques anges alors, qui là-haut dans les cieux
Règlent ces mouvements imparfaits à nos yeux,
En faisant tournoyer ces immenses planètes,
Disaient : « Pour nos plaisirs sans doute elles sont faites. »
Puis de là sur la terre ils jetaient un coup d'œil :
Ils se moquaient de l'homme et de son sot orgueil.
Le Tien[1] les entendit; il voulut que sur l'heure
On les fît assembler dans sa haute demeure,
Ange, homme, quadrupède, et ces êtres divers
Dont chacun forme un monde en ce vaste univers.
« Ouvrages de mes mains, enfants du même père,
Qui portez, leur dit-il, mon divin caractère,
Vous êtes nés pour moi, rien ne fut fait pour vous :
Je suis le centre unique où vous répondez tous.
Des destins et des temps connaissez le seul maître.
Rien n'est grand ni petit; tout est ce qu'il doit être.
D'un parfait assemblage instruments imparfaits,
Dans votre rang placés demeurez satisfaits. »
L'homme ne le fut point. Cette indocile espèce
Sera-t-elle occupée à murmurer sans cesse?
Un vieux lettré chinois, qui toujours sur les bancs
Combattit la raison par de beaux arguments,
Plein de Confucius, et sa logique en tête,
Distinguant, concluant, présenta sa requête.
    « Pourquoi suis-je en un point resserré par le temps?
Mes jours devraient aller par delà vingt mille ans;
Ma taille pour le moins dût avoir cent coudées;
D'où vient que je ne puis, plus prompt que mes idées,

Voyager dans la lune, et réformer son cours?
Pourquoi faut-il dormir un grand tiers de mes jours?
Pourquoi ne puis-je, au gré de ma pudique flamme,
Faire au moins en trois mois cent enfants à ma femme?
Pourquoi fus-je en un jour si las de ses attraits?
  — Tes pourquoi, dit le dieu, ne finiraient jamais.
Bientôt tes questions vont être décidées;
Va chercher ta réponse au pays des idées :
Pars. » Un ange aussitôt l'emporte dans les airs,
Au sein du vide immense où se meut l'univers,
A travers cent soleils entourés de planètes,
De lunes et d'anneaux, et de longues comètes.
Il entre dans un globe où s'immortelles mains
Du roi de la nature ont tracé les desseins,
Où l'œil peut contempler les images visibles
Et des mondes réels et des mondes possibles.
  Mon vieux lettré chercha, d'espérance animé,
Un monde fait pour lui, tel qu'il l'aurait formé.
Il cherchait vainement : l'ange lui fait connaître
Que rien de ce qu'il veut en effet ne peut être;
Que si l'homme eût été tel qu'on feint les géants,
Faisant la guerre au ciel, ou plutôt au bon sens,
S'il eût à vingt mille ans étendu sa carrière,
Ce petit amas d'eau, de sable, et de poussière,
N'eût jamais pu suffire à nourrir dans son sein
Ces énormes enfants d'un autre genre humain.
Le Chinois argumente : on le force à conclure
Que dans tout l'univers chaque être a sa mesure;
Que l'homme n'est point fait pour ces vastes désirs;
Que sa vie est bornée ainsi que ses plaisirs;
Que le travail, les maux, la mort sont nécessaires;
Et que, sans fatiguer par de lâches prières
La volonté d'un Dieu qui ne saurait changer,
On doit subir la loi qu'on ne peut corriger,
Voir la mort d'un œil ferme et d'une âme soumise.
Le lettré convaincu, non sans quelque surprise,
S'en retourne ici-bas ayant tout approuvé;
Mais il y murmura quand il fut arrivé :
« Convertir un docteur est une œuvre impossible. »
  Matthieu Garo chez nous eut l'esprit plus flexible;
Il loua Dieu de tout! Peut-être qu'autrefois
De longs ruisseaux de lait serpentaient dans nos bois;
La lune était plus grande, et la nuit moins obscure;
L'hiver se couronnait de fleurs et de verdure;
L'homme, ce roi du monde, et roi très fainéant,
Se contemplait à l'aise, admirait son néant,
Et, formé pour agir, se plaisait à rien faire.

Mais pour nous, fléchissons sous un sort tout contraire.
Contentons-nous des biens qui nous sont destinés,
Passagers comme nous, et comme nous bornés.
Sans rechercher en vain ce que peut notre maître,
Ce que fut notre monde, et ce qu'il devrait être,
Observons ce qu'il est, et recueillons le fruit
Des trésors qu'il renferme et des biens qu'il produit.
Si du Dieu qui nous fit l'éternelle puissance
Eût à deux jours au plus borné notre existence,
Il nous aurait fait grâce ; il faudrait consumer
Ces deux jours de la vie à lui plaire, à l'aimer.
Le temps est assez long pour quiconque en profite ;
Qui travaille et qui pense en étend la limite.
On peut vivre beaucoup sans végéter longtemps ;
Et je vais te prouver par mes raisonnements...
Mais malheur à l'auteur qui veut toujours instruire !
Le secret d'ennuyer est celui de tout dire.

    C'est ainsi que ma muse avec simplicité
Sur des tons différents chantait la vérité,
Lorsque, de la nature éclaircissant les voiles,
Nos Français à Quito cherchaient d'autres étoiles ;
Que Clairaut, Maupertuis, entourés de glaçons,
D'un secteur à lunette étonnaient les Lapons,
Tandis que, d'une main stérilement vantée,
Le hardi Vaucanson, rival de Prométhée,
Semblait, de la nature imitant les ressorts,
Prendre le feu des cieux pour animer les corps.

    Pour moi, loin des cités, sur les bords du Permesse
Je suivais la nature, et cherchais la sagesse ;
Et des bords de la sphère où s'emporta Milton,
Et de ceux de l'abîme où pénétra Newton,
Je les voyais franchir leur carrière infinie ;
Amant de tous les arts et de tout grand génie,
Implacable ennemi du calomniateur,
Du fanatique absurde, et du vil délateur ;
Ami sans artifice, auteur sans jalousie ;
Adorateur d'un Dieu, mais sans hypocrisie ;
Dans un corps languissant, de cent maux attaqué,
Gardant un esprit libre, à l'étude appliqué,
Et sachant qu'ici-bas la félicité pure
Ne fut jamais permise à l'humaine nature.

    Montrez comment Voltaire a donné corps aux paradoxes optimistes dans *Micromégas*. Comparez l'atmosphère de ce premier conte avec celles de *Candide* et de *l'Ingénu :* qu'en conclure si l'on se reporte aux réflexions et à la vie de l'écrivain à chacun des trois moments ?

2. LE « BON SAUVAGE » ET LA LITTÉRATURE

On a coutume de parler de cette vision de l'homme idéal comme d'un thème propre au XVIIIᵉ siècle : c'est oublier que depuis l'Antiquité bien des écrivains ont éprouvé le besoin de confronter leur société avec une vie idéale, dégagée des contraintes sociales.

2. 1. MARC-AURÈLE ET LA SAGESSE ANTIQUE

Dans ses *Pensées pour moi-même*, l'empereur des Romains a confié toutes ses convictions de sagesse intime : abordant les problèmes aussi bien politiques que familiaux, il s'essaie à une morale de la simplicité conduisant au bonheur. Les quelques lignes que nous donnons ci-dessous donneront un exemple de la vision idéale de l'homme dans les premiers siècles de l'ère chrétienne.

« Tout porte son fruit, l'homme, Dieu et le monde, et chacun le porte en sa saison propre. Quoique l'usage n'applique couramment ce mot qu'à la vigne et aux autres végétaux analogues, cela n'importe pas. La raison a un fruit à la fois collectif et particulier; de ce fruit en naissent d'autres semblables et de même nature que la raison même. » (Livre X, chapitre x.)

Retrouvez dans *l'Ingénu* des comparaisons empruntées au langage arboricole : que traduisent dans la conception foncière de l'homme naturel ces similitudes de vocabulaire?

« Le bonheur, c'est de posséder un bon génie, ou une bonne raison. Que fais-tu donc ici, imagination? Va-t-en, par les Dieux comme tu es venue! Je n'ai pas besoin de toi. Tu es venue selon ta vieille habitude; je ne t'en veux pas, seulement retire-toi! » (Livre VII, chapitre XVII.)

« Bonheur de l'homme : faire ce qui est le propre de l'homme. Et ce qui est le propre de l'homme, c'est d'être bienveillant envers ses pareils, de mépriser les mouvements des sens, de discerner les idées qui méritent créance, de contempler la nature universelle et tout ce qui arrive conformément à la loi. » (Livre VIII, chapitre XXVI.)

En quoi ces principes stoïciens sont-ils différents de ceux du Huron de Voltaire? Pouvons-nous les justifier?

2. 2. LE MYTHE DU « BON SAUVAGE »

Ce mythe continue de se développer dans la littérature : rappelons ici quelques pages célèbres. Montaigne, dans ses *Essais* (I, 31), nous parle des cannibales, chez lesquels il ne « trouve rien de barbare et de sauvage », mais au contraire un bon sens et une nature dignes d'admiration. Plus loin, à propos de la découverte du Nouveau Monde (III, 6), il nous offre un tableau de l'homme naturel très proche de celui que nous peindra le Siècle des lumières.

Au siècle suivant, peu d'écrivains s'intéresseront à l'homme sauvage : le classicisme et ses règles sociales semblant faire obstacle à la réflexion sur le bonheur personnel : on peut toutefois trouver quelques ébauches de ce thème chez La Fontaine, dans certaines *Satires* de Boileau et surtout chez La Bruyère, qui voit dans les paysans (XI, 128) le bonheur simple et naturel de l'homme proche de la terre (XI, 128).

Mais, incontestablement, c'est au XVIIIe siècle que revient le mérite d'avoir pour ainsi dire vulgarisé le thème au point d'en faire un élément omniprésent dans la création littéraire : le personnage du Bon Sauvage se retrouve aussi bien dans le roman ou le conte que dans le théâtre (Sébastien Mercier) ou dans l'essai philosophique (Rousseau). Pour l'importance de l'idée de l'homme naturel, on se reportera à *la Philosophie des lumières* (N. C. L., tome II, pp. 50-59). De même, on consultera les extraits cités plus haut dans les N. C. L. correspondants.

2. 3. L'HOMME CIVILISÉ ET L'HOMME NATUREL

Dans la longue dissertation placée en tête de son *Essai sur les mœurs*, Voltaire tente de définir selon son expression une « philosophie de l'Histoire » : cela nous vaut de pertinentes remarques sur la religion, les miracles, le fanatisme, la superstition et l'homme en général. Il développe ainsi une idée qui lui tient à cœur, celle selon laquelle tous les hommes sont semblables. Il trace ensuite l'évolution de l'humanité et distingue le primitif du sauvage et de l'homme naturel.

Nous allons donner le premier des deux *Entretiens d'un sauvage et d'un bachelier*, parce qu'il nous paraît apporter un éclairage intéressant à la lecture de *l'Ingénu*.

Un gouverneur de la Cayenne amena un jour un sauvage de la Guyane qui était né avec beaucoup de bon sens, et qui parlait assez bien le français. Un bachelier de Paris eut l'honneur d'avoir avec lui cette conversation.

LE BACHELIER. — Monsieur le sauvage, vous avez vu sans doute beaucoup de vos camarades qui passent leur vie tout seuls : car on dit que c'est là la véritable vie de l'homme, et que la société n'est qu'une dépravation artificielle?

LE SAUVAGE. — Jamais je n'ai vu de ces gens-là : l'homme me paraît né pour la société, comme plusieurs espèces d'animaux; chaque espèce suit son instinct; nous vivons tous en société chez nous.

LE BACHELIER. — Comment! en société! vous avez donc de belles villes murées, des rois qui tiennent une cour, des spectacles, des couvents, des universités, des bibliothèques, et des cabarets?

LE SAUVAGE. — Non; est-ce que je n'ai pas ouï dire que dans votre continent vous avez des Arabes, des Scythes, qui n'ont jamais rien eu de tout cela, et qui forment cependant des nations considérables? nous vivons comme ces gens-là. Les familles voisines se prêtent du secours. Nous habitons un pays chaud, où nous avons peu de besoins; nous nous procurons aisément la nourriture; nous nous marions, nous faisons des enfants, nous les élevons, nous mourons. C'est tout comme chez vous, à quelques cérémonies près.

LE BACHELIER. — Mais, Monsieur, vous n'êtes donc pas sauvage?

LE SAUVAGE. — Je ne sais pas ce que vous entendez par ce mot.

LE BACHELIER. — En vérité, ni moi non plus; il faut que j'y rêve. Nous appelons sauvage un homme de mauvaise humeur, qui fuit la compagnie.

LE SAUVAGE. — Je vous ai déjà dit que nous vivons ensemble dans nos familles.

LE BACHELIER. — Nous appelons encore sauvage les bêtes qui ne sont pas apprivoisées, et qui s'enfoncent dans les forêts; et de là nous avons donné le nom de sauvage à l'homme qui vit dans les bois.

LE SAUVAGE. — Je vais dans les bois, comme vous autres, quand vous chassez.

LE BACHELIER. — Pensez-vous quelquefois?

LE SAUVAGE. — On ne laisse pas d'avoir quelques idées.

LE BACHELIER. — Je serais curieux de savoir quelles sont vos idées; que pensez-vous de l'homme?

LE SAUVAGE. — Je pense que c'est un animal à deux pieds, qui a la faculté de raisonner, de parler et de rire, et qui se sert de ses mains beaucoup plus adroitement que le singe. J'en ai vu de plusieurs espèces, des blancs comme vous, des rouges comme moi, des noirs comme ceux qui sont chez monsieur le gouverneur de la Cayenne. Vous avez de la barbe, nous n'en avons point : les nègres ont de la laine, et vous et moi portons des cheveux. On dit que dans votre Nord tous les cheveux sont blonds; ils sont tout noirs dans notre Amérique; je n'en sais guère davantage.

LE BACHELIER. — Mais votre âme, Monsieur, votre âme? quelle notion en avez-vous? d'où vient-elle? qu'est-elle? que fait-elle? comment agit-elle? où va-t-elle?

LE SAUVAGE. — Je n'en sais rien; je ne l'ai jamais vue.

LE BACHELIER. — A propos, croyez-vous que les bêtes soient des machines?

LE SAUVAGE. — Elles me paraissent des machines organisées, qui ont du sentiment et de la mémoire.

LE BACHELIER. — Et vous, et vous, monsieur le sauvage, qu'ima-ginez-vous avoir par-dessus les bêtes?

LE SAUVAGE. — Une mémoire infiniment supérieure, beaucoup plus d'idées, et, comme je vous l'ai déjà dit, une langue qui forme incomparablement plus de sons que la langue des bêtes, et des mains plus adroites, avec la faculté de rire qu'un grand raisonneur me fait exercer.

LE BACHELIER. — Et s'il vous plaît, comment avez-vous tout cela? et de quelle nature est votre esprit? comment votre âme anime-t-elle votre corps? pensez-vous toujours? votre volonté est-elle libre?

LE SAUVAGE. — Voilà bien des questions. Vous me demandez comment je possède ce que Dieu a daigné donner à l'homme : c'est comme si vous me demandiez comment je suis né. Il faut bien, puisque je suis né homme, que j'aie les choses qui constituent l'homme, comme un arbre a de l'écorce, des racines et des feuilles. Vous voulez que je sache de quelle nature est mon esprit : je ne me le suis pas donné, je ne peux le savoir; comment mon âme anime mon corps : je n'en suis pas mieux instruit. Il me semble qu'il faut avoir vu le premier ressort de votre montre pour juger comment elle marque l'heure. Vous me demandez si je pense toujours. Non; j'ai quelquefois des demi-idées, comme quand je vois des objets de loin confusément; quelquefois j'ai des idées plus fortes, comme lorsque je vois un objet de plus près je le distingue mieux; quelquefois je n'ai point d'idées du tout, comme lorsque je ferme les yeux, je ne vois rien. Vous me demandez après cela si ma volonté est libre. Je ne vous entends point; ce sont des choses que vous savez, sans doute; vous me ferez plaisir de me les expliquer.

LE BACHELIER. — Oh! vraiment, oui, j'ai étudié toutes ces matières; je pourrais vous en parler un mois de suite sans discontinuer que vous n'y entendriez rien. Dites-moi un peu, connaissez-vous le bon et le mauvais, le juste et l'injuste? Savez-vous quel est le meilleur des gouvernements, le meilleur culte, le droit des gens, le droit public, le droit civil, le droit canon? comme se nommaient le premier homme et la première femme qui ont peuplé l'Amérique? Savez-vous à quel dessein il pleut dans la mer, et pourquoi vous n'avez point de barbe?

LE SAUVAGE. — En vérité, Monsieur, vous abusez un peu de l'aveu que j'ai fait d'avoir plus de mémoire que les animaux; j'ai peine à retrouver les questions que vous me faites. Vous parlez du bon et du mauvais, du juste et de l'injuste : il me paraît que tout ce qui nous fait plaisir sans faire tort à personne est très bon et très juste; que ce qui fait tort aux hommes sans nous faire de plaisir est abominable; et que ce qui nous fait plaisir en faisant du tort aux autres est bon pour nous dans le moment, très dangereux pour nous-mêmes, et très mauvais pour autrui.

LE BACHELIER. — Et avec ces maximes-là vous vivez en société?

LE SAUVAGE. — Oui, avec nos parents et nos voisins. Sans beaucoup de peines et de chagrins, nous attrapons doucement notre centaine d'années; plusieurs même vont à cent vingt : après quoi notre corps fertilise la terre dont il a été nourri.

LE BACHELIER. — Vous me paraissez avoir une bonne tête; je veux vous la renverser. Dînons ensemble : après quoi nous continuerons à philosopher avec méthode.

En recourant à une analyse comparative de ce dialogue et de *l'Ingénu*, vous montrerez la permanence des idées de Voltaire et l'agencement différent du récit dans les deux textes. Qu'est-ce qui vous paraît faire la supériorité littéraire du conte sur l'essai philosophique? Donnez des exemples précis.

2. 4. LA MORALE DU « BON SAUVAGE »

Bougainville avait fait le tour du monde de 1766 à 1769 : il en avait rapporté un livre auquel Diderot imagina de donner une suite sous le titre de *Supplément au Voyage de Bougainville*. Le passage que nous donnons est extrait de l'« entretien de l'aumônier et d'Orou ». L'aumônier du bord vient d'exposer au Tahitien Orou les préceptes de la religion chrétienne; voici ce que lui répond le Tahitien :

OROU. — Ces préceptes singuliers, je les trouve opposés à la nature, et contraires à la raison; faits pour multiplier les crimes, et fâcher à tout moment le vieil ouvrier, qui a tout fait sans mains, sans tête et sans outils; qui est partout, et qu'on ne voit nulle part; qui dure aujourd'hui et demain, et qui n'a pas un jour de plus; qui commande et qui n'est pas obéi; qui peut empêcher, et qui n'empêche pas. Contraires à la nature, parce qu'ils supposent qu'un être pensant, sentant et libre, peut être la propriété d'un être semblable à lui. Sur quoi ce droit serait-il fondé? Ne vois-tu pas qu'on a confondu, dans ton pays, la chose qui n'a ni sensibilité, ni pensée, ni désir, ni volonté; qu'on quitte, qu'on prend, qu'on garde, qu'on échange sans qu'elle souffre et sans qu'elle se plaigne, avec la chose qui ne s'échange point, ne s'acquiert point; qui a liberté, volonté, désir; qui peut se donner ou se refuser pour un moment; se donner ou se refuser pour toujours; qui se plaint et qui souffre; et qui ne saurait devenir un effet de commerce, sans qu'on oublie son caractère, et qu'on fasse violence à la nature? Contraires à la loi générale des êtres. Rien, en effet, te paraît-il plus insensé qu'un précepte qui proscrit le changement qui est en nous; qui commande une constance qui n'y peut être, et qui viole la liberté du mâle et de la femelle, en les enchaînant pour jamais l'un à l'autre; qu'une fidélité qui borne la plus capricieuse des jouissances à un même individu : qu'un serment d'immutabilité de deux êtres de chair, à la face d'un ciel qui n'est pas un instant le même, sous des antres qui menacent ruine; au bas d'une roche qui tombe en poudre; au pied d'un arbre qui se gerce; sur une pierre qui s'ébranle? Crois-moi, vous avez rendu la condition de l'homme pire que celle de l'animal. Je ne sais ce que c'est que ton grand ouvrier : mais je me réjouis qu'il n'ait point parlé à nos pères, et je souhaite qu'il ne parle point à nos enfants; car il pourrait par hasard leur dire les mêmes sottises, et ils feraient peut-être celle de le croire. Hier, en soupant, tu nous a entretenus de magistrats et de prêtres; je ne sais quels sont ces personnages que tu appelles *magistrats* et *prêtres*, dont l'autorité règle votre conduite; mais, dis-moi, sont-ils maîtres du bien et du mal? Peuvent-ils faire que ce qui est juste soit injuste, et que ce qui est injuste soit juste? dépend-il d'eux d'attacher le bien à des actions nuisibles, et le mal à des actions innocentes ou utiles? Tu ne saurais le penser, car, à ce compte, il n'y aurait ni vrai ni faux, ni bon ni mauvais, ni beau ni laid; du moins, que ce qu'il plairait à ton grand ouvrier, à tes magistrats, à tes prêtres, de prononcer tel; et, d'un moment à l'autre, tu serais obligé de changer d'idées et de conduite. Un jour l'on te dirait, de la part de l'un de tes trois maîtres : *tue*, et tu serais obligé, en conscience, de tuer; un autre jour : *vole*, et tu serais tenu de voler; ou : *ne mange pas de ce fruit*, et tu n'oserais en manger; *je te défends ce légume ou cet animal*, et tu te garderais d'y toucher. Il n'y a point de bonté qu'on ne pût t'interdire; point de méchanceté qu'on ne pût t'ordonner. Et où en serais-tu réduit, si tes trois maîtres, peu d'accord entre eux, s'avisaient de te permettre, de t'enjoindre et de te défendre la même chose, comme je pense qu'il arrive souvent? Alors, pour plaire au prêtre, il faudra que tu te brouilles avec le magistrat; pour satisfaire le magistrat, il faudra que tu mécontentes le grand ouvrier; et pour te rendre agréable au grand ouvrier, il faudra que tu renonces à la nature. Et sais-tu ce qui en arrivera? c'est que tu les mépriseras tous trois, et que tu ne seras ni homme, ni citoyen, ni pieux; que tu ne seras rien; que tu seras mal avec toutes les sortes d'autorités; mal avec toi-même; méchant, tourmenté par ton cœur, persécuté par tes maîtres insensés; et malheureux, comme je te vis hier au soir, lorsque je te présentai mes filles et ma femme et que tu t'écriais : Mais ma religion! mais mon état! Veux-tu savoir, en tous temps et en tous lieux, ce qui est bon et mauvais? Attache-toi à la nature des choses et des actions; à tes rapports avec ton semblable; à l'influence de ta conduite sur ton utilité particulière et le bien général. Tu es en délire, si tu crois qu'il y ait rien, soit en haut, soit en bas, dans l'univers, qui puisse ajouter ou retrancher aux lois de la nature. Sa volonté éternelle est que le bien soit préféré au mal, et le bien général au bien particulier. Tu ordonneras le contraire; mais tu ne seras pas obéi. Tu multiplieras les malfaiteurs et les malheureux par la crainte, par les châtiments et par les remords; tu dépraveras les consciences; tu corrompras les esprits; ils ne sauront plus ce qu'ils ont à faire ou à éviter. Troublés dans l'état d'innocence, tranquilles dans le forfait, ils auront perdu l'étoile polaire dans leur chemin. [...]

Quels sont les trois codes de morale que distingue Orou? Comment se définit pour Diderot la morale de son héros? Comparez-là à celle du Huron voltairien.

Orou et Hercule sont deux sauvages : quels sont leurs points communs et leurs différences? Leur langage et leur intelligence paraissent fonctionner à merveille : cherchez-en l'explication dans le texte de Voltaire.

2. 5. CONTRE LE « BON SAUVAGE »

Nous comprenons maintenant quelle est la vision idéale de l'humanité voltairienne : loin de vanter comme Rousseau les mérites de l'état sauvage et de nier les progrès de la civilisation, Voltaire entend réaliser un mélange harmonieux de bon sens naturel et de progrès social. C'est la même idée que défend le baron d'Holbach dans son *Système social*. (Livre I, chapitre XVI.)

On prétend que le sauvage est un être plus heureux que l'homme civilisé. Mais en quoi consiste son bonheur et qu'est-ce qu'un Sauvage? c'est un enfant vigoureux, privé de ressources, d'expériences, de raison, d'industrie, qui souffre continuellement la faim et la misère, qui se voit à chaque instant forcé de lutter contre les bêtes, qui d'ailleurs ne connaît d'autre loi que son caprice, d'autre règle que ses passions du moment, d'autre droit que la force, d'autre vertu que la témérité. C'est un être fougueux, inconsidéré, cruel, vindicatif, injuste, qui ne veut point de frein, qui ne prévoit pas le lendemain, qui est à tout moment exposé à devenir la victime, ou de sa propre folie, ou de la férocité des stupides qui lui ressemblent.

La Vie Sauvage ou l'*Etat de Nature*, auquel des spéculateurs chagrins ont voulu ramener les hommes, l'*âge d'or* si vanté par les poètes, ne sont dans le vrai que des états de misère, d'imbécillité, de déraison. Nous inviter d'y rentrer, c'est nous dire de rentrer dans l'enfance, d'oublier toutes nos connaissances, de renoncer aux lumières que notre esprit a pu acquérir; tandis que, pour notre malheur, notre raison n'est encore que fort peu développée, même dans les nations les plus civilisées.

[...] Les Partisans de la Vie Sauvage nous vantent la liberté dont elle met à portée de jouir, tandis que la plupart des nations civilisées sont dans les fers. Mais des Sauvages peuvent-ils jouir d'une vraie liberté? Des êtres privés d'expériences et de raison, qui ne connaissent aucun motif pour contenir leurs passions, qui n'ont aucun but utile, peuvent-ils être regardés comme des êtres vraiment libres? Un Sauvage n'exerce qu'une affreuse licence, aussi funeste pour lui-même, que nuisible pour les malheureux qui tombent en son pouvoir. La liberté entre les mains d'un être sans culture et sans vertu, est une arme tranchante entre les mains d'un enfant.

> Quelles sont les raisons qui poussent d'Holbach à condamner l'utopie du Bon Sauvage? Comparez ce texte à Rousseau (*Discours*, dans les N. C. L.) : d'où vient selon vous l'opposition des deux philosophes? Lequel vous paraît être en accord avec le mouvement général des idées de son siècle?

Poussant sa critique encore plus loin, d'Holbach en vient à défendre la ville contre la campagne : on cherchera les raisons profondes de cette attitude et on la comparera à celle de Voltaire, de Diderot ou de Rousseau.

> Se plaindre ou s'irriter des malheurs attachés à la vie sociale c'est se révolter contre la nécessité des choses. La corruption des peuples est l'effet nécessaire des causes puissantes qui conspirent à les aveugler et à les tenir dans une enfance éternelle. Etre surpris de voir tant de vices inonder la Société et de s'en trouver incommodé, c'est être émerveillé de marcher moins à l'aise dans une rue fréquentée, que lorsqu'on se promène dans les champs. Plus une société est nombreuse, plus les passions discordantes et multipliées produisent de fermentations. Si les grandes villes sont les plus corrompues, ce sont aussi celles où l'on trouve le plus de talents, de ressources et de vertus. Plus une machine est compliquée, plus ses mouvements sont faciles à déranger. Le frottement multiplié rend son jeu plus pénible, que celui d'une machine simple. Quelque force qu'on ait, il est difficile de ne pas être entraîné ou froissé, quand on se place dans la foule.

2. 6. CHATEAUBRIAND ET L'EXOTISME ROMANTIQUE

Toute la fin du siècle philosophique sera remplie de publications de voyages. Peu à peu, le thème philosophique est remplacé par un motif purement littéraire qui correspond au besoin d'évasion du préromantisme (voir *Paul et Virginie*). Ce mouvement aboutit à l'*Atala* de Chateaubriand, dont la Préface de 1801 est en certains endroits une critique de *l'Ingénu*. Après avoir décrit les circonstances de son voyage en Amérique, l'auteur en arrive à exposer la structure et le but de son récit :

> [...] De tous mes manuscrits sur l'Amérique, je n'ai sauvé que quelques fragments, en particulier *Atala*, qui n'était qu'un épisode des *Natchez*. *Atala* a été écrit dans le désert et sous les huttes des Sauvages. Je ne sais si le public goûtera cette histoire qui sort de toutes les routes connues, et qui présente une nature et des mœurs tout à fait étrangères à l'Europe. Il n'y a point d'aventures dans *Atala*. C'est une sorte de poème, moitié descriptif, moitié dramatique : tout consiste dans la peinture de deux amants qui marchent et causent dans la solitude; tout gît dans le tableau des troubles de l'amour, au milieu

du calme des déserts et du calme de la religion. J'ai donné à ce petit ouvrage les formes les plus antiques; il est divisé en *prologue, récit* et *épilogue.* Les principales parties du récit prennent une dénomination, comme les *chasseurs,* les *laboureurs,* etc.; et c'était ainsi que dans les premiers siècles de la Grèce, les Rhapsodes chantaient, sous divers titres, les fragments de *l'Iliade* et de *l'Odyssée.* Je ne dissimule point que j'ai cherché l'extrême simplicité de fond et de style, la partie descriptive exceptée; encore est-il vrai que, dans la description même, il est une manière d'être à la fois pompeux et simple. Dire ce que j'ai tenté, n'est pas dire ce que j'ai fait. Depuis longtemps je ne lis plus qu'Homère et la Bible; heureux si l'on s'en aperçoit, et si j'ai fondu dans les teintes du désert et dans les sentiments particuliers à mon cœur, les couleurs de ces deux grands et éternels modèles du beau et du vrai.

Je dirai encore que mon but n'a pas été d'arracher beaucoup de larmes; il me semble que c'est une dangereuse erreur, avancée, comme tant d'autres, par M. de Voltaire, *que les bons ouvrages sont ceux qui font le plus pleurer.* Il y a tel drame dont personne ne voudrait être l'auteur, et qui déchire le cœur bien autrement que *l'Enéide.* On n'est point un grand écrivain parce qu'on met l'âme à la torture. Les vraies larmes sont celles que fait couler une belle poésie; il faut qu'il s'y mêle autant d'admiration que de douleur. [...]

Voilà les seules larmes qui doivent mouiller les cordes de la lyre, et en attendrir les sons. Les muses sont des femmes célestes qui ne défigurent point leurs traits par des grimaces; quand elles pleurent, c'est avec un secret dessein de s'embellir.

Au reste, je ne suis point comme M. Rousseau, un enthousiaste des Sauvages; et quoique j'aie peut-être autant à me plaindre de la société que ce philosophe avait à s'en louer, je ne crois point que la *pure nature* soit la plus belle chose du monde. Je l'ai toujours trouvée fort laide, partout où j'ai eu l'occasion de la voir. Bien loin d'être d'opinion que l'homme qui pense soit un *animal dépravé,* je crois que c'est la pensée qui fait l'homme. Avec ce mot de *nature,* on a tout perdu. De là les détails fastidieux de mille romans où l'on décrit jusqu'au bonnet de nuit, et à la robe de chambre; de là ces drames infâmes, qui ont succédé aux chefs-d'œuvre des Racine. Peignons la nature, mais la belle nature : l'art ne doit pas s'occuper de l'imitation des monstres.

En quoi la pensée de Chateaubriand se trouve-t-elle ici en accord avec celle de Voltaire? Relevez la critique littéraire et comparez là :
— aux idées des classiques;
— aux sentiments de l'Ingénu;
— aux grands manifestes romantiques.

Poursuivant l'analyse de son ouvrage, l'auteur de *René* s'arrête sur ses personnages :

> [...] On trouvera peut-être dans la femme que j'ai cherché à peindre, un caractère assez nouveau. C'est une chose qu'on n'a pas assez développée, que les contrariétés du cœur humain : elles mériteraient d'autant plus de l'être, qu'elles tiennent à l'antique tradition d'une dégradation originelle, et que conséquemment elles ouvrent des vues profondes sur tout ce qu'il y a de grand et de mystérieux dans l'homme et son histoire.
>
> *Chactas*, l'amant d'*Atala*, est un Sauvage, qu'on suppose né avec du génie, et qui est plus qu'à moitié civilisé, puisque non seulement il sait les langues vivantes, mais encore les langues mortes de l'Europe. Il doit donc s'exprimer dans un style mêlé, convenable à la ligne sur laquelle il marche, entre la société et la nature. Cela m'a donné de grands avantages, en le faisant parler en Sauvage dans la peinture des mœurs, et en Européen dans le drame et la narration. Sans cela il eût fallu renoncer à l'ouvrage : si je m'étais toujours servi du style indien, *Atala* eût été de l'hébreu pour le lecteur.
>
> Quant au missionnaire, j'ai cru remarquer que ceux qui jusqu'à présent ont mis le prêtre en action, en ont fait ou un scélérat fanatique, ou une espèce de philosophe. Le *P. Aubry* n'est rien de tout cela. C'est un simple chrétien qui parle sans rougir *de la croix*, *du sang de son divin maître*, *de la chair corrompue*, etc., en un mot, c'est le prêtre tel qu'il est. Je sais qu'il est difficile de peindre un pareil caractère aux yeux de certaines gens, sans toucher au ridicule. Si je n'attendris pas, je ferai rire : on en jugera.

Quelles sont les critiques qui s'attachent directement à l'œuvre de Voltaire : pouvez-vous les expliquer? Le personnage du Huron ne vous paraît-il pas plus naturel que les héros de Chateaubriand? Trouvez-en les raisons dans l'utilisation même de l'homme naturel chez les deux écrivains.

3. VOLTAIRE ET LA LITTÉRATURE

La captivité de l'Ingénu, c'est aussi son éducation. En compagnie du bonhomme Gordon, il fait son apprentissage littéraire. En réalité, si ce chapitre nous paraît être une péripétie annexe, sans rapport profond avec l'action centrale, il convient d'y voir l'un des paradoxes essentiels de la pensée de Voltaire : « éclairée » socialement et politiquement, le patriarche de Ferney a de tout temps fait preuve de classicisme dans son goût artistique (on peut même dire qu'il est rétrograde par rapport à certains esprits de la fin du siècle de Louis XIV).

Or, ce paradoxe, Voltaire l'a développé en maintes pages de son œuvre. Dès les *Lettres philosophiques*, il affirmait la supériorité des tragiques français sur Shakespeare, qu'il accuse de « transformer la scène en un lieu de carnage ». Son *Dictionnaire philosophique* reviendra sur le sujet; il consacrera un ouvrage entier à ce parallèle en publiant le *Discours sur la tragédie*. En même temps, il opposera Corneille à Racine, ainsi qu'il le fait dans *l'Ingénu*.

Tout un chapitre du *Siècle de Louis XIV* est consacré à la littérature française du siècle classique : nous en extrayons les lignes suivantes consacrées à Corneille, Racine et Molière. Tout d'abord, Voltaire nous propose Corneille, sans qui « le génie des prosateurs ne se serait pas développé » :

> Cet homme est d'autant plus admirable qu'il n'était environné que de très mauvais modèles quand il commença à donner des tragédies. Ce qui devait encore lui fermer le bon chemin, c'est que ces mauvais modèles étaient estimés; et, pour comble de découragement, ils étaient favorisés par le cardinal de Richelieu, le protecteur des gens de lettres et non pas du bon goût. Il récompensait de méprisables écrivains, qui d'ordinaire sont rampants; et, par une hauteur d'esprit si bien placée ailleurs, il voulait abaisser ceux en qui il sentait avec quelque dépit un vrai génie, qui rarement se plie à la dépendance. Il est bien rare qu'un homme puissant, quand il est lui-même artiste, protège sincèrement les bons artistes.
>
> Corneille eut à combattre son siècle, ses rivaux, et le cardinal de Richelieu. Je ne répéterai point ici ce qui a été écrit sur *le Cid*. Je remarquerai seulement que l'Académie, dans ses judicieuses décisions entre Corneille et Scudéri, eut trop de complaisance pour le cardinal de Richelieu en condamnant l'amour de Chimène. Aimer le meurtrier de son père, et poursuivre la vengeance de ce meurtre, était une chose admirable. Vaincre son amour eût été un défaut capital dans l'art tragique, qui consiste principalement dans les combats du cœur. Mais l'art était inconnu alors à tout le monde, hors à l'auteur.

Puis citant des vers de *Cinna*, il en vient à conclure sur l'auteur du *Cid* :

> C'étaient là des larmes de héros. Le grand Corneille faisant pleurer le grand Condé d'admiration est une époque bien célèbre dans l'histoire de l'esprit humain.
>
> La quantité de pièces indignes de lui qu'il fit plusieurs années après n'empêcha pas la nation de le regarder comme un grand homme, ainsi que les fautes considérables d'Homère n'ont jamais empêché qu'il ne fût sublime. C'est le privilège du vrai génie, et surtout du génie qui ouvre une carrière, de faire impunément de grandes fautes.

Ensuite, l'auteur nous présente Racine, type de l'écrivain qui émane de son siècle : c'est là une manière d'analyser la littérature toute moderne en tenant compte des circonstances extérieures au métier d'écrivain. Certes, Voltaire ne pousse pas son analyse, mais on peut y remarquer néanmoins un refus de l'étude globale et systématique du siècle précédent :

> Corneille s'était formé tout seul; mais Louis XIV, Colbert, Sophocle et Euripide contribuèrent tous à former Racine. Une ode qu'il composa à l'âge de dix-huit ans, pour le mariage du roi, lui attira un présent qu'il n'attendait pas et le détermina à la poésie. Sa réputation s'est accrue de jour en jour, et celle des ouvrages de Corneille a un peu diminué. La raison en est que Racine, dans tous ses ouvrages, depuis son *Alexandre*, est toujours élégant, toujours correct, toujours vrai; qu'il parle au cœur; et que l'autre manque trop souvent à tous ces devoirs. Racine passa de bien loin les Grecs et Corneille dans l'intelligence des passions, et porta la douce harmonie de la poésie, ainsi que les grâces de la parole, au plus haut point où elles puissent parvenir. Ces hommes enseignèrent à la nation à penser, à sentir, et à s'exprimer. Leurs auditeurs, instruits par eux seuls, devinrent enfin des juges sévères pour ceux mêmes qui les avaient éclairés.
>
> Il y avait très peu de personnes en France, du temps du cardinal de Richelieu, capables de discerner les défauts du *Cid*; et en 1702, quand *Athalie*, le chef-d'œuvre de la scène, fut représentée chez Madame la duchesse de Bourgogne, les courtisans se crurent assez habiles pour la condamner. Le temps a vengé l'auteur; mais ce grand homme est mort sans jouir du succès de son plus admirable ouvrage. Un nombreux parti se piqua toujours de ne pas rendre justice à Racine. Mme de Sévigné, la première personne de son siècle pour le style épistolaire, et surtout pour conter des bagatelles avec grâce, croit toujours que Racine *n'ira pas loin*. Elle en jugeait comme du café, dont elle dit *qu'on se désabusera bientôt*. Il faut du temps pour que les réputations mûrissent.

Enfin, Voltaire en arrive à Molière, dont il loue la puissance satirique :

> La singulière destinée de ce siècle rendit Molière contemporain de Corneille et de Racine. Il n'est pas vrai que Molière, quand il parut, eût trouvé le théâtre absolument dénué de bonnes comédies. Corneille lui-même avait donné *le Menteur*, pièce de caractère et d'intrigue, prise du théâtre espagnol comme *le Cid*; et Molière n'avait encore fait paraître que deux de ses chefs-d'œuvre lorsque le public avait *la Mère coquette* de Quinault, pièce à la fois de caractère et d'intrigue, et même modèle d'intrigue. Elle est de 1664; c'est la première comédie où l'on ait peint ceux que l'on a appelés depuis les *marquis*. La plupart des grands seigneurs de la cour de Louis XIV voulaient imiter cet air de grandeur, d'éclat et de dignité qu'avait leur

maître. Ceux d'un ordre inférieur copiaient la hauteur des premiers; et il y en avait enfin, et même en grand nombre, qui poussaient cet air avantageux et cette envie dominante de se faire valoir jusqu'au plus grand ridicule.

Ce défaut dura longtemps. Molière l'attaqua souvent, et il contribua à défaire le public de ces importants subalternes, ainsi que de l'affectation des *précieuses*, du pédantisme des *femmes savantes*, de la robe et du latin des médecins. Molière fut, si on ose le dire, un législateur des bienséances du monde. Je ne parle ici que de ce service rendu à son siècle : on sait assez ses autres mérites.

Et, pour conclure, Voltaire rassemble en quelques lignes la substance merveilleuse des lettres classiques : c'est par cette admiration qu'il se montre le plus stagnant dans son goût; on peut aimer ce qui a été, mais il faut croire en son époque et en son art :

C'était un temps digne de l'attention des temps à venir que celui où les héros de Corneille et de Racine, les personnages de Molière, les symphonies de Lulli, toutes nouvelles pour la nation, et (puisqu'il ne s'agit ici que des arts) les voix des Bossuet et des Bourdaloue, se faisaient entendre à Louis XIV, à Madame, si célèbre par son goût, à un Condé, à un Turenne, à un Colbert, et à cette foule d'hommes supérieurs qui parurent en tout genre. Ce temps ne se retrouvera plus où un duc de La Rochefoucauld, l'auteur des *Maximes*, au sortir de la conversation d'un Pascal et d'un Arnauld, allait au théâtre de Corneille.

JUGEMENTS SUR « L'INGÉNU »
ET SUR LES CONTES DE VOLTAIRE EN GÉNÉRAL

On se tromperait en croyant donner plus de piquant aux variétés philosophiques par le mélange des personnages et des aventures qui servent de prétexte aux raisonnements. On ôte à l'analyse sa profondeur, au roman son intérêt, en les réunissant ensemble. Pour que les événements inventés vous captivent, il faut qu'ils se succèdent avec une rapidité dramatique; pour que les raisonnements amènent la conviction, il faut qu'ils soient suivis et conséquents; et quand vous coupez l'intérêt par la discussion, et la discussion par l'intérêt, loin de reposer les bons esprits, vous fatiguez leur attention [...]. Les succès de Voltaire ont inspiré le désir de faire, à son exemple, des contes philosophiques; mais il n'y a point d'imitation possible pour ce qui caractérise cette sorte d'écrits de Voltaire, la gaieté piquante et la grâce toujours variée. Il se trouve sans doute un résultat philosophique à la fin de ses contes; mais l'agrément et la tournure du récit sont tels, que vous ne vous apercevez du but que lorsqu'il est atteint.

Mme de Staël,
De la littérature, Ire partie, chap. XVII (1800).

Un roman de Voltaire est une idée de Voltaire se promenant à travers des aventures divertissantes destinées à lui servir et d'illustrations et de preuves. C'est un article du *Dictionnaire philosophique* conté, au lieu d'être déduit, par Voltaire. — Et c'est pour cela qu'il est exquis; c'est Voltaire lui-même, mais moins âpre et moins irascible, au moins dans la forme, qui s'arrange et s'attife, et se compose une physionomie et un sourire, et glisse ses épigrammes, au lieu d'assener ses violences, avec un joli geste, adroitement nonchalant, de la main. Quand on ferme un de ces petits livres, on n'a vécu ni avec Zadig ni avec Candide; mais avec Voltaire, dans une demi-intimité très piquante, qui a quelque chose d'accueillant, de gracieux et d'inquiétant.

E. Faguet,
XVIIIe Siècle, p. 270 (1890).

C'est un lieu commun de dire qu'il n'y a pas de psychologie dans Voltaire. On a raison si, par psychologie, on entend l'invention de Racine ou de Marivaux. Voltaire, comme Lesage, est moraliste plus que psychologue. Il utilise la psychologie faite pour construire les bonshommes composés de sentiments moyens ou possédés de manies intenses dont ses thèses ont besoin.

Il est artiste plus que psychologue, et c'est par là justement qu'il enrichit la psychologie. Il n'analyse pas des caractères, il dessine des silhouettes. Chacun des fantoches qui vont à la chasse au bonheur est saisi en son attitude expressive, qui révèle le ressort dont il est mû. Chacun a le pli, l'accent de son état ou de sa nation. Leurs noms révèlent leurs races : la marquise de Parolignac, Vanderdendur, le baron de Thunder-ten-tronckh, don Fernando d'Ibaraa y Figueroa y Mascarenes y Lampourdo y Souza, etc. Toutes les idées que Voltaire se fait de la société et des parties qui la composent, des gouvernements, de la religion et des mœurs des divers pays, s'inscrivent dans les croquis dont il remplit ses contes, déterminent le choix des actes et des propos qui expriment ses personnages. Il distingue l'Anglais, l'Italien, l'Allemand, le Français, le Turc, comme l'anabaptiste et le calviniste, le jésuite et le capucin, l'officier et le négociant. La psychologie des professions et la psychologie ethnique sont très observées et précises chez lui [...]. Mais le réalisme pittoresque de Voltaire n'est que la transposition du sensualisme dans l'art; sa fin est de procurer des idées justes. Il est soumis à la pensée philosophique qui crée l'œuvre, et demeure ainsi profondément symbolique. Tous ces petits traits, ces circonstances dessinent la chose, et, avec la chose, le jugement de la « raison » sur la chose. Ils la déforment pour mettre dans son image la réaction de l'esprit de l'auteur ou le rapport à la thèse. Ces légers croquis sont des charges. La pitié même et l'indignation se traduisent en sarcasmes, en bouffonneries. L'art mondain de donner des ridicules est mis au service de la philosophie. Toutes les misères de l'homme et du monde sont traduites devant l'intelligence et apparaissent en sottises : sûre tactique pour révolter des esprits clairs contre les causes de la souffrance sociale. Les romans de Voltaire sont des démonstrations du progrès par l'absurde.

G. Lanson,
Voltaire, p. 152-154 (1906).

Parmi toutes les qualités intellectuelles que ce genre réclame, je n'en vois pas une qui manque à Voltaire. Sa fantaisie, lestée de bon sens, est à la fois mesurée dans son vol et audacieuse dans son parcours. Je ne connais pas de conteur qui se faufile avec plus d'agilité au milieu des événements, ni qui soit plus habile à se débarrasser de l'accessoire et à ne retenir que l'indispensable. Il n'a pas l'imagination forte : il n'est point de ceux qui créent des Panurge et des Tartuffe. Il ne va jamais jusqu'à la grande peinture; il s'arrête à la silhouette, au croquis, à la fine caricature, à la pochade. Mais il y est inimitable. La vie qui sort de lui est une vie menue et grêle; mais c'est de la vie. Ses personnages ne sont pas à la taille humaine; mais comme les Lilliputiens de Swift, ils font les gestes et nourrissent les passions des hommes. Ils sont nés au fond de son encrier : il les a vus en soulever le couvercle, se culbuter sur sa table, grimper sur son lit et sur ses fauteuils, courir dans les rayons de sa bibliothèque, se poursuivre par toute sa chambre. Il s'est amusé de leurs ébats, les a costumés, leur a forgé de petites armes méchantes; puis il a ouvert sa fenêtre et les a lâchés sur la rose des vents. Et tous ces gnomes, tous ces lutins, tous ces djinns se sont répandus dans le monde, s'accrochant aux clochers des églises, pénétrant dans les salons, s'insinuant dans les cours et dans les parlements, entrant partout « un arc et une flèche dans les mains et un carquois sur le dos », comme les guerriers de Lilliput, et capables, comme eux, de vous ligoter un géant des pieds à la tête.

[...] Quant à la conclusion « Cultivons notre jardin », tant de fois citée et que Voltaire se plaisait à répéter dans ses lettres, elle convient assurément à la plupart des hommes; mais elle laisse leurs coudées beaucoup trop franches à tous les tripoteurs, les politiqueurs et les réformateurs pour être le dernier mot de la sagesse. Si l'on entend par là qu'il faut travailler, et travailler dans sa compétence, au lieu de courir les aventures, on a mille fois raison. Si c'est un conseil de désintéressement des choses publiques et du gouvernement de la cité, on a mille fois tort. Avant tout, il serait bon de définir notre jardin. Le jardin de Voltaire ressemblait à celui d'Armide qui n'avait point de frontières.

A. Bellessort,
Essai sur Voltaire, chap. VII (1926).

L'Ingénu est le meilleur roman de Voltaire parce qu'il est le seul, au moins parmi les plus importants, où les personnages et leur sort s'adressent réellement à nos sentiments d'humanité, où surtout ils soient véritablement hommes.

Strauss,
Voltaire, six conférences, p. 163 (Leipzig, 1924).

Il nous faut avouer ou proclamer — selon les goûts — que Voltaire est spécifiquement français... que son nom excite encore chez nous, après deux cent cinquante ans, des réactions très sensibles et fortement opposées. [...] Qu'on le maudisse ou qu'on l'exalte [...] Voltaire vit, Voltaire dure; il est indéfiniment actuel.

Paul Valéry,
Voltaire (discours prononcé en Sorbonne
le 10 décembre 1944).

[...] la pureté antique et la sensibilité moderne... cette transparence, cette ironie, cette simplicité, cette générosité, cette chaleur que les cœurs secs ont qualifiée de sécheresse, tout m'enivra, m'enchanta.

Roger Peyrefitte,
Préface à une édition des romans de Voltaire
(Livre de poche, 1965).

SUJETS DE DEVOIRS ET D'EXPOSÉS

● Dans quelle mesure ce jugement de Maupertuis sur les *Lettres persanes* peut-il s'appliquer aux contes de Voltaire, en particulier à *Micromégas* et à *l'Ingénu* : « Jamais on ne vit tant de sagesse avec tant d'agrément, tant de sens condensé en si peu de mots. Ce n'est pas ici un bel esprit qui, après les plus grands efforts, n'a été qu'un philosophe superficiel; c'est un philosophe profond qui s'est trouvé un bel esprit » ?

● Expliquez et discutez, en les appliquant à *Micromégas* et à *l'Ingénu*, ces réflexions de Germaine de Staël : « Dans le siècle de Louis XIV, la perfection même de l'art d'écrire était le principal objet des écrivains, mais dans le XVIII⁰ siècle on voit la littérature prendre un caractère différent. Ce n'est plus un art seulement, c'est un moyen; elle devient une arme pour l'esprit humain, qu'elle s'était contentée jusque-là d'instruire et d'amuser. »

● Un critique contemporain déclare que la pensée au XVIII⁰ siècle « ne cesse jamais de poursuivre deux quêtes : l'une vers le bonheur; l'autre, qui lui est plus indispensable encore, et plus chère, vers la vérité ». Ces deux préoccupations apparaissent-elles dans *Micromégas* et dans *l'Ingénu* ?

● Peut-on appliquer à l'auteur de *Micromégas* et de *l'Ingénu* ce jugement de Maine de Biran : « Les philosophes du XVIII⁰ siècle n'ont pas connu l'homme » ?

● « Il ne faut pas mettre du vinaigre dans ses écrits; il faut y mettre du sel », ainsi s'exprimait Pascal (*Pensées*, III, 312) : Voltaire vous paraît-il avoir suivi ce précepte ?

● A propos des *Lettres persanes*, Pierre Salomon a écrit (*Précis d'histoire de la littérature française*, p. 216) : « La sévérité de cette critique souvent audacieuse, qui n'épargne ni l'Église ni le roi, se tempère d'humour et de gaieté. Imitateur de La Bruyère, Montesquieu est plus désinvolte. » Ce jugement pourrait-il s'appliquer à *Micromégas* et à *l'Ingénu* ?

● Commentez, en empruntant vos exemples à *Micromégas* et à *l'Ingénu*, ce jugement de Daniel Mornet (*la Pensée française au XVIII⁰ siècle*, Paris, 1926) : « Les contes de Voltaire sont les rencontres de la raison et des déraisons de la fortune ou des hommes. »

● Commentez ce jugement de William R. Jones (Introduction à une édition critique de *l'Ingénu*, Paris, 1957) : « *Micromégas*, ce conte fantastique genre Swift, démasque sans pitié l'espèce humaine et son orgueil ridicule, s'éloignant singulièrement de l'optimisme de *Zadig*. »

● Vous vous efforcerez d'appliquer à *Micromégas* et à *l'Ingénu* cet éloge prononcé en Sorbonne par Paul Valéry le 10 décembre 1944 : « Notre homme d'esprit par excellence, tout à coup, et comme il entre au dernier tiers de sa vie, et comme si tout cet esprit ne lui eût été donné, et qu'il ne l'eût exercé, informé, aiguisé, et envenimé, pendant quarante ans, que pour s'en faire une arme destinée aux plus nobles combats, se trouve une vocation et une ardeur toutes nouvelles. Sec et superficiel, le dit-on, soit! mais combien de gens profonds, combien d'hommes sensibles n'ont pas fait pour les hommes en général ce que fit alors ce sceptique, ce versatile Voltaire? Il faut bien reconnaître que son « sourire hideux » éclaira, esquissa la ruine de mainte chose hideuse. »

● Montrez comment Voltaire a su appliquer aux formes traditionnelles du conte ou du roman sa conception particulière. Peut-être serez-vous aidé par ce fragment de lettre de Voltaire à Marmontel (28 janvier 1764) : « Vous devriez bien nous faire des contes philosophiques, où vous rendriez ridicules certains sots et certaines sottises, certaines méchancetés et certains méchants; le tout avec discrétion; en prenant bien votre temps et en rognant les griffes de la bête quand vous la trouverez un peu endormie. »

● Commentez cette appréciation de William R. Jones (Introduction à une édition critique de *l'Ingénu*, Paris, 1957) : « Tout Voltaire y [dans *l'Ingénu*] est : tout son talent, sa diversité, sa philosophie. »

● Commentez ce jugement de D. Mornet : « *L'Ingénu* est la satire de toute la machine administrative de l'ancien régime, des abus, des crimes d'un ordre social où l'on pouvait embastiller sans jugement un honnête homme, dont le seul crime était d'avoir sur Dieu des idées à lui; où rien ne s'obtenait que par la brigue... sans compter, chemin faisant, les ironies coutumières sur la religion et ses ministres... bien des choses étaient pourries... »

● Dans quelle mesure peut-on appliquer à *Micromégas* et à *l'Ingénu* cette pensée de Voltaire lui-même : « Presque tout est imitation. Les esprits les plus originaux empruntent les uns des autres. Il en est des livres comme du feu dans nos foyers; on va prendre du feu chez le voisin, on l'allume chez soi, et il appartient à tous » (*Lettres philosophiques*, n° XXII (addition de 1756)?

● Appliquez à *Micromégas* et à *l'Ingénu* ce jugement de William R. Jones (Préface de l'édition critique de *l'Ingénu*, Paris, Droz, 1957, pages 7 et 8) : « Nulle part... Voltaire ne s'est révélé aussi complètement que dans ses romans et ses contes. Ce sont de petits chefs-d'œuvre spirituels, impertinents, délicieux, extravagants peut-être, mais par ailleurs parfaitement sérieux et remplis d'idées. De tous les genres littéraires que Voltaire a cultivés, le conte philosophique est celui qui lui a le mieux réussi. »

● Commentez ce jugement de William R. Jones : « Le récit grave de la mort de la belle Saint-Yves a déplu aux uns, suscité l'admiration des autres, mais tout le monde est d'accord pour y voir quelque chose de bien original chez Voltaire : une belle page de roman, calculée pour provoquer notre émotion. »

● Bengesco, dans sa Préface aux *Romans de Voltaire* (Jouaust, Paris, 1888), s'exprime ainsi à propos du personnage de Mlle de Saint-Yves : « charme ingénu », « grâce pudique », « fraîcheur de sentiments », « délicatesse de conscience », « sympathique », « digne de pitié » : l'auteur donne-t-il ainsi une idée exacte du personnage?

● En utilisant ce que vous savez des « sources » ou prétendues « sources » de *Micromégas* et de *l'Ingénu*, vous discuterez ce jugement de William R. Jones : « Il [Voltaire] se plagie lui-même volontiers; c'était son droit; aux autres il se contente d'emprunter un cadre pour ses tableaux, une petite étincelle pour allumer son grand feu, ou un renseignement pour compléter ce qu'il sait déjà. » De votre analyse, vous dégagerez une appréciation de l'originalité de Voltaire.

● Dans *l'Ingénu*, William R. Jones discerne « une fraîcheur de style, une force d'imagination et un fond d'originalité qui ne viennent point du dehors ». En faisant la part des « sources » de Voltaire que vous connaissez, vous vous efforcerez de montrer la justesse de cette observation.

● « Ces ouvrages d'ordinaire ne réussissent qu'à la faveur de l'air étranger; on met avec succès dans la bouche d'un Asiatique la satire de notre pays, qui serait bien moins accueillie dans la bouche d'un compatriote; ce qui est commun par soi-même devient alors singulier. » Ainsi s'exprimait Voltaire à propos des *Lettres persanes*. Et Montesquieu lui-même avait goûté *l'Espion du grand seigneur* de J.-B. Marana. Mais *l'Ingénu* est français. Ce seul fait renouvelle une situation devenue « lieu commun ». De cet ensemble de faits déduisez l'originalité de Voltaire dans *l'Ingénu*.

● « ... la justesse, la facilité, la clarté et la chaleur, voilà les quatre qualités qui font le bon style », écrit Mme du Deffand en parlant du style de Voltaire, qu'elle « estime » et « aime » (Lettre de Mme du Deffand à Mme la duchesse de Choiseul, 29 juillet 1766). Vérifiez la justesse de ce jugement en utilisant les deux contes qui font l'objet de la présente édition.

● Gustave Lanson conclut ainsi une étude sur Voltaire (1906) : « Il me paraît hors de doute que, si Voltaire a encore quelque action à exercer dans notre France, ce doit être surtout une action littéraire et intellectuelle de pure forme. Les définitions et les servitudes du goût de Voltaire ne reprendront jamais autorité; mais à mesure que se dissipera et s'éloignera le romantisme, il se pourra que l'on reprenne le désir des idées claires et bien filtrées, l'amour de l'expression simple et fine, et qu'on demande quelques leçons d'analyse et de style aux parties de l'œuvre voltairienne les plus dégagées des règles et des ornements classiques, aux mélanges, aux romans et à la correspondance. Il semble que, depuis la chute du naturalisme et la crise symboliste, l'évolution de la prose se fasse vers l'aisance et la lumière, c'est-à-dire vers le XVIIIᵉ siècle et Voltaire. » A la lumière de ce que vous savez de l'histoire des lettres françaises depuis Voltaire, vous montrerez la justesse de cette appréciation.

● « Un grand esprit si français par les qualités et les défauts. » C'est ainsi que Sainte-Beuve conclut une étude sur Voltaire (*Causeries du lundi*, 20 octobre 1856). En utilisant ces deux contes, vous apprécierez le jugement de Sainte-Beuve.

● Commentez ce portrait de Voltaire par Sainte-Beuve : « Il était de ceux à qui le plaisir de penser et d'écrire en liberté tient lieu de tout, et un moment il songea à se livrer sans réserve à cette passion dans un pays libre et en renonçant au sien... Il avait besoin aussi de l'amitié, des arts, des excitations sympathiques de chaque jour. »

● Frédéric II, irrité par les « principes » sans cesse affirmés par le philosophe, écrivit à sa sœur la margrave de Baireuth : « ... le poète dogmatise toujours. » Jusqu'à quel point cette remarque est-elle justifiée ?

● Dans une causerie (*Causeries du lundi*, 4 novembre 1850), Sainte-Beuve note : « Vous trouvez, écrivait Voltaire, que je m'explique assez « clairement : je suis comme les petits ruisseaux, ils sont transparents « parce qu'ils sont peu profonds. » Il disait cela en riant; on se dit ainsi à soi-même bien des demi-vérités. » Vous préciserez la pensée de Sainte-Beuve et, à la lumière des textes inclus dans ce recueil, vous en vérifierez la finesse.

● « Mon devoir de professeur est très distinct du rôle de critique : le critique s'inquiète avant tout... de chercher le nouveau et de découvrir le talent, le professeur de maintenir la tradition et de conserver le goût. » Ainsi s'exprime Sainte-Beuve dans sa leçon d'ouverture à l'École normale le 12 avril 1858. Montrez que Voltaire a été un professeur et un critique.

● Que pensez-vous de ce portrait de Saint-Simon (1750) : « Arouet, fils d'un notaire qui l'a été de mon père et de moi jusqu'à sa mort, fut exilé et envoyé à Tulle pour des vers fort satiriques et fort impudents. Je ne m'amuserais pas à marquer une si petite bagatelle si ce même Arouet, devenu grand poète et académicien, sous le nom de Voltaire, n'était devenu, à travers force aventures tragiques, une manière de personnage dans la République des Lettres, et même une manière d'important parmi un certain monde » ?

● Montrez la justesse de ce jugement de Gustave Lanson : « Nature complexe, riche de bien et de mal, mêlée de tous les contraires, dispersée en tous les sens, mais tendant avec une énergie inépuisable au vrai et au bien, du moins à ce qu'il croit être le vrai et le bien, active surtout et aspirant à exercer tous les modes possibles de l'activité humaine. »

● D'Angleviel, protestant du Languedoc, dit La Beaumelle, a écrit de Voltaire : « Un bouffon et un nain. » Discutez ce propos de l'adversaire du philosophe.

● Appréciez ce jugement de Frédéric II sur Voltaire : « Vous seriez parfait si vous n'étiez pas homme. »

● A la lumière de *Micromégas* et de *l'Ingénu*, appréciez ce jugement de Jacques Bainville *(Lectures)* : Voltaire « pense surtout par réaction, par contradiction, et même par simple agacement ».

TABLE DES MATIÈRES

Mame Imprimeurs - 37000 Tours
Dépôt légal Novembre 1970. - N° 23770. - N° de série Éditeur 15483
IMPRIMÉ EN FRANCE. *(Printed in France)*. - 870 187 I. Avril 1990.